Lethal State

## Justice, Power, and Politics

The Justice, Power, and Politics series publishes new works in history that explore the myriad struggles for justice, battles for power, and shifts in politics that have shaped the United States over time. Through the lenses of justice, power, and politics, the series seeks to broaden scholarly debates about America's past as well as to inform public discussions about its future.

More information on the series, including a complete list of books published, is available at http://justicepowerandpolitics.com/.

# Lethal State

## A History of the Death Penalty in North Carolina

· · · · · · · · · · · · · · · · · · · · · · · · · · · · · · · · · · · · · · · · · · · · · · · · · · · · · ·

SETH KOTCH

The University of North Carolina Press   Chapel Hill

*This book was published with the assistance of the H. Eugene and Lillian Youngs Lehman Fund of the University of North Carolina Press. A complete list of books published in the Lehman Series appears at the end of the book.*

Set in Charis by Westchester Publishing Services
Manufactured in the United States of America

The University of North Carolina Press has been a member of the Green Press Initiative since 2003.

Library of Congress Cataloging-in-Publication Data
Names: Kotch, Seth, author.
Title: Lethal state : a history of the death penalty in North Carolina / Seth Kotch.
Other titles: Justice, power, and politics.
Description: Chapel Hill : University of North Carolina Press, [2019] | Series: Justice, Power, and Politics | Includes bibliographical references and index.
Identifiers: LCCN 2018021265| ISBN 9781469649863 (cloth : alk. paper) | ISBN 9781469649870 (pbk : alk. paper) | ISBN 9781469649887 (ebook)
Subjects: LCSH: Capital punishment—North Carolina—History— 20th century. | Capital punishment—North Carolina—History— 19th century. | Lynching. | North Carolina—Race relations—History— 20th century. | African Americans—Civil rights—History—20th century.
Classification: LCC HV8699.U6 N846 2019 | DDC 364.6609756—dc23
LC record available at https://lccn.loc.gov/2018021265

Cover image (detail) by David Simonton.

*A book about ending lives for three people just starting theirs.*
*To DMK, EAK, and CMK.*

# Contents

# Graph, Illustrations, and Tables

## Graph

## Illustrations

## Tables

# Introduction

## A History of the Present

Sunday morning, November 12, 1922, offered subscribers to the Raleigh *News and Observer* a range of informative and enlightening material. The first page featured stories of local and national Armistice Day celebrations; an interview with Benito Mussolini, who expressed his firm opposition to women's suffrage; and an account of a deadly earthquake and tidal wave in Chile. Turning the page, readers could take in the story of Carolina football's narrow victory over the Virginia Military Institute, read columnist Nell Battle Lewis's celebration of messy bookcases, and learn how to get rid of their fat without diet or exercise—one free trial treatment waited to be claimed! Toward the back of the Sunday edition's thirty-six pages was William Jennings Bryan's weekly Bible talk, this one on 7 Luke, in which Jesus rebukes a Pharisee and tells a sinful woman, "Thy sins are forgiven."[1]

Forgiven, too, were the sins of the Confederacy. The paper reported on World War I and Civil War veterans parading through Raleigh and mingling at a barbecue where Josephus Daniels, the *News and Observer*'s editor, called on them to heed the example of the "sturdy faith and nobility of Robert E. Lee."[2] There was a glowing review—written by a Confederate veteran and Democratic Party operator—of a new book on Jefferson Davis and a celebration of the recently deceased Thomas Nelson Page's "charming picture of the days of the Old South."[3] Like North Carolina itself in the 1920s, the paper was thickly veined with mannerly white Christian supremacy. In refusing to look to the future without absolving the sins of the past, the *News and Observer* that Sunday captured what was by then the well-established dogma of Old South nostalgia and Confederate hero-making.

This hero-making drew in the Ku Klux Klan, resentful ex-Confederates and their hangers-on seeking to push back the gains of emancipation who were later reimagined in D. W. Griffith's *Birth of a Nation* as defenders of white southern civilization. In this vision, the Klan was not a loose guerilla army terrorizing formerly enslaved people, responsible for scores of lynchings and firebombings and whippings. Instead, they were champions of justice in an unfairly besieged region, resisting tyranny from without and threats from within. Opening their newspapers on this Sunday morning, *News and Observer* readers had a taste of this revision in the form of three solid columns celebrating the Ku Klux Klan's defeat of "carpet-bagism, scalawagism, and negro rule."[4] The piece, like those sprinkled throughout the issue, justified and sanctified white violence, whether against people of color or against political rivals.

The author of this tribute was identified as Capt. J. J. Laughinghouse. Writing as the last surviving Reconstruction-era Klan member from his native Pitt County, John Joseph Laughinghouse declared of this victory, "No great achievement in all history was ever accomplished for civilization and humanity. A great courage, a dauntless spirit, a manly mission and high ideals were the actuating principles of those ex-Confederates of the Ku Klux Klan."[5] Laughinghouse, a tall, gray-eyed lad from Pitt County, was orphaned during the war and entered military school, later leaving to join the Second Regiment of the CSA's Junior Reserves. He was promoted to captain shortly before the end of the war.[6] Returning to North Carolina, he fostered a friendship with a former major general, Bryan Grimes, who had earned a reputation as a fairly capable but grasping officer in the Army of Northern Virginia and who, like the Confederacy itself, enjoyed the fruits of a concerted effort to burnish his reputation after death.[7] Grimes, committed to breaking up Republican control of state and local government, started the Pitt County chapter of the Ku Klux Klan and brought Laughinghouse along.[8]

Grimes inflicted violence and it was inflicted on him in turn. He complained that agitators—the pro-Union Red Strings? The Union League?—burned down the watermill on Grimesland, as he called his farm, and they came after Laughinghouse, too, poisoning his well.[9] The conflict reached a peak when Grimes was ambushed and killed while watering his horses at a creek about nine miles from his home. The murder incensed his friends and neighbors, who were among the "determined looking men" stalking around the murder scene looking for clues about the perpetrator.[10] Among them must have been Laughinghouse, who would later write, "Many years ago one of my best friends was foully murdered, and as soon as satisfactory evidence was obtained, I said, let's lynch him, but the older heads said no, we were bound to convict, and let the law take its course."[11] With Laughinghouse and his allies in the Klan acquiescing, a trial took place in December 1880. The alleged assassin, William Parker, had secured promises from a number of friends before the murder to serve as alibis, and he confessed the killing to at least two fellow inmates while jailed in Washington, North Carolina. "It is a little remarkable that all the direct testimony against Parker has come from himself," one journalist observed.[12] Moreover, Parker was known to be very poor, but after Grimes's murder he appeared in town with pockets full of spending money, wearing a new suit and riding a horse, both of which were known to have belonged to one W. B. Paramore, the same man convicted of poisoning Laughinghouse's well. It seemed clear to observers that Paramore and his brother had hired Parker to eliminate their hated rival.[13]

So "it was a surprise to almost every one" when—after the first attempt ended in a mistrial and a second trial was held in June—Parker received a verdict of not guilty.[14] Laughinghouse was outraged: the law had taken its course, yet a "packed jury turned the criminal loose."[15] Parker's acquittal—imagined as the alternative to the lynching Laughinghouse desired—seems to have crystallized Laughinghouse's worldview. Lynching was the solution to the problem of not just a court system vulnerable to political manipulation, but the laws themselves were overly permissive. Years later, he would explain in an editorial defense of lynching in the *News and Observer* that "the law making powers are solely responsible for the bad laws and therefore responsible for lynching." More than that, "lynching parties are generally composed of the bravest and best men who regret sorely the necessity of such action" but take it because "court procedure does not offer protection to the public against criminal classes."[16]

Laughinghouse missed his chance to demonstrate his merit after Grimes's murder, and he did not forget Parker or what he had done. Parker was free, but his freedom didn't make him wise. He lived at a distance for years, but ultimately could neither stay away nor keep his mouth shut. Nearly eight years after Grimes's murder in 1880, he made the fatal error of drinking too much and returning to town to boast that he had gotten away with murder. He was locked up for drunkenness and may have been asleep shortly after 2:00 A.M., when the street lights suddenly went out. A small mob, perhaps ten or twelve men, entered the jail and confined the night watchman, an African American man, to a cell. Parker was carried outside and seemed only then to realize his peril. As he began shouting "Murder!" he was bound and gagged.[17] His body was found around 3:30 A.M., hanging from a bridge over the Pamlico River, a bridge Grimes once owned before selling it to the county.[18] A card hanging above his head read, "Justice at Last."[19] Was Laughinghouse among the dozen men who kidnapped Parker and swiftly hanged him? The answer to that question now lives only in family lore.

What does this story have to do with the history of the death penalty in North Carolina? What does this meandering tale of the Confederacy, the Klan, murder, courtroom drama, and lynching have to do with the history of the death penalty in North Carolina? It is one small history of one death penalty, meted out belatedly and illegally. In being delayed and outside the strictures of the law it was in fact not unusual as far as death penalties went. But perhaps more directly, this small history flows into the larger history of the death penalty in this state. In 1909, Laughinghouse—an unreconstructed Klansman, lynch mob member, and lynching advocate—was appointed superintendent of the penitentiary system in North Carolina. As superintendent, he ran the prison system, from the camps and road crews, to the prison farms, to the State's Prison, home to death row. In 1910, the first person was executed there under state authority. Laughinghouse was there to see the death penalty in North Carolina evolve from a local matter to a state institution.

Laughinghouse did not do anything particularly notable or uniquely awful during his brief tenure there, which ended in 1913.[20] His enthusiastic advocacy of forced inmate labor was normal among prison administrators, and not just in the South.[21] He would go on to an ignoble stint enriching himself selling deferments as head of North Carolina's World War I draft board.[22] But if an institution's leader expresses its values, then Laughinghouse's beliefs reveal a grim picture of North Carolina's prison system and its goals: swift, satisfying punishment, violent control of the lives and bodies of people of color, and the construction of a past and future atop a foundation of white supremacy. This story, of course, begins long before J. J. Laughinghouse accepted the superintendent position, and even before North Carolina was a state.

On August 3, 1726, in Edenton, on the Albemarle Sound, colonial authorities met to address complaints from members of the Meherrin Indian nation that English colonists had been "molesting them in their Settlements and taking their Lands." The council ordered the complainants to return in October to resolve the issue. But a group of Meherrin men appeared later that month, this time bearing with them George Senecca, accused of murdering Catherine Groom, a colonist, and her infant children. The council convened an oyez and terminer—from the French for "to hear and determine"—and decided that Senecca must die.[23] "The fact appeared to have been very barbarous," wrote the chief justice. "I see no cause to recommend him mercy."[24] Senecca was hanged on the same day, August 26, 1726. His was the first recorded execution in what would become the state of North Carolina.[25]

More than a thousand followed him, both free and enslaved; men, women, and children, though mostly men; usually hanged on scaffolds constructed for the purpose, but sometimes burned. Most were executed following a murder conviction, but some died for arson, robbery, housebreaking, desertion, and for plotting insurrection. Darkened by the passage of time, these scaffolds stand dimly in our memory, sources of gruesome fascination but remaining misunderstood. Their distance is explained in part by the pressing needs of the present, as capital punishment abolitionists continue to work to end death as punishment. The death penalty's continued presence might explain why there are not more published histories on the subject, despite its gruesome magnetism. Historian W. Fitzhugh Brundage has observed that in the 1930s and 1940s, lynching was a source of fascination to sociologists because it was a pressing contemporary problem they hoped to understand in order to solve. Historians did not give lynching much attention until it seemed well-buried by time. The same might be true of the death penalty today.

Attorneys, activists, political scientists, and legal scholars have authored pressingly important, deeply researched work on death penalty law and procedure. Yet in many of these volumes, the American death penalty effectively begins in 1972, when in a lengthy, convoluted decision known as *Furman*, the United States Supreme Court invalidated existing death penalty statutes but offered a loose framework for what might pass constitutional muster. The result, ordained four years later in *Gregg*, was the current incarnation of the capital sentencing process, with its separate guilt and sentencing phases, and the introduction of aggravating and mitigating factors. Since *Gregg*, American states have been tinkering with the machinery of death, to borrow a phrase from Justice Harry Blackmun, seeking to align the death penalty with evolving standards of dignity.[26]

Long before *Gregg*, North Carolina was a prolific executioner with a notably harsh mandatory sentencing statute. Many more people were sentenced to death than were executed, but the narrative about punishment was as clear to contemporary observers in the 1920s as it is to activists at nonprofits today: the death penalty punished those people least able to defend themselves. Its targets were young men of diminished intellectual capacity and of little means, and African American men with white victims who braced themselves against white rage inside and outside the courtroom.

The death penalty was undeniably a popular source of entertainment for many, many people: enthusiastic crowds gathered by the thousands to watch public hangings in county courtyards, and later, packed themselves into the lime-green octagonal death chamber in Central Prison. In 1868,

labor of people of color and the need to justify how it was extracted. Laws in British colonies such as Carolina were harsh, and vestiges of the British criminal code persisted into the nineteenth century. A criminal convicted of a misdemeanor (a term that took hold in the mid-eighteenth century) in a colonial Carolina court could face humiliation and torment in the stocks, a public whipping, mutilation, or dismemberment; those convicted of felonies risked land forfeiture or death.[34]

The British codes were North Carolina's legal foundation, but enslavers' conflicting impulses to protect slavery as an institution but to inflict violence upon enslaved persons drove its evolution. The percentage of enslaved people as a part of the population was lower in North Carolina than in any other southern colony, but slave ownership was an essential source of wealth and influence. North Carolina's criminal codes in the colonial period supported the slave regime, in part by punishing, and otherwise empowering enslavers to punish, the enslaved severely. The death penalty was essential to North Carolina's slave system, so important that even as they used a variety of psychological and physical pressure points to extract labor from their enslaved workforce, enslavers were willing to lose some of that workforce in order to use their suffering to control their fellows. By one estimate, between 1726 and 1772, North Carolina executed more than one hundred enslaved people, a total that exceeded the number of white people executed in the colony's entire history.[35]

In 1715, colonial lawmakers created a separate slave court system that gave some white North Carolinians the right to kill convicted or runaway slaves. The law, renewed in 1741 in the fearful aftermath of South Carolina's bloody Stono Rebellion, directed the courts, on which sat only people with slave property, to try enslaved people "guilty of any crime or offense."[36] The judges' role was only to select a punishment and to make sure it took place. Enslavers often preferred to exert their own authority, and did so with whippings, brandings, and other punishments.[37] But when an enslaved person was accused of a particularly serious or troubling crime, owners needed a way to kill them without becoming murderers themselves. North Carolina was the last colony to do so, but its legislators did make killing an enslaved person a felony in 1775—on the second offense.[38]

The death penalty was so deeply rooted in racial slavery that it took more than 150 years from the colony's first execution until the state executed a white person for the murder of a person of color. As human property under law, enslaved persons could be subject to theft or violence, but not victims of crime. The white person in question was the glaring exception that proves the rule.[39] Daniel Keath appears to have been an exceptionally unpleasant person and a threat to his own community as well as to people of color—a bigamist, a known rapist, a deserter from the Confederate Army, who raped and murdered a child. In 1880, he became the first white person in the state executed for a crime against a person of color.[40]

Enslavers' reluctance to protect the lives of enslaved persons belies the claim by historian Guion Griffis Johnson that North Carolina's slave code was "surprisingly liberal" because the "slave was property, the most valuable moveable property which a person . . . was likely to possess."[41] The leniency Johnson thought she saw showed itself in the fact that the enslaved received trials at all, for instance, and that enslavers could defend an enslaved defendant in court; that in 1774 the General Assembly made it a crime to murder a slave, giving the perpetrator one year of imprisonment for the first offense but death for the second; and that as of 1816, slaves could not be tried for capital offenses without a grand jury indictment and could claim benefit of clergy in some cases, winning a milder punishment by proving that they could read; of course literate enslaved people risked thirty-nine lashes for trying to teach other enslaved people to read.[42] The extension of these rights to people considered property under the law was hardly leniency. Rather, it revealed the courts' role in shoring up slavery as an institution, protecting enslaved human property against violence by poor and middling white people, and resolving disputes between slave owners.[43]

To ease the strain of capital punishment on enslavers, and perhaps to encourage them to use the punishment when deemed necessary, the law sometimes provided for compensation for the death of enslaved people. In the decade before 1758, for instance, owners who lost enslaved persons to execution received on average nearly 20 percent more in compensation than those who sold them. The execution of enslaved persons, then, could have been profitable for enslavers worried about the diminished market value of someone considered troublesome; at least, as one observer noted, "'the planters suffer little or nothing by it.'"[44] The lower classes did. It was their job to fill the fund with taxes they paid on alcohol and at the polls. Enslavers enjoyed the fund until 1758, when the financial requirements of the French and Indian War nudged the colonial government to cap it. The number of castrations for capital crimes rose sharply.[45]

In the early nineteenth century, North Carolina continued to maintain capital codes, as did other southern colonies, written to protect elites' vast property holdings, an aim that differentiated southern law from its northern counterpart.[46] Northern colonies, influenced by Puritanism, modified English codes to harshly punish moral crimes but offer a degree of leniency toward those convicted of crimes against property. Alexis de Tocqueville believed that the Connecticut Puritans were unlikely to execute criminals, noting in *Democracy in America* that "never was the death penalty more frequently prescribed by statute or more seldom enforced."[47] Tocqueville traveled the Northeast at a time when death penalty reform was peaking. There had been some motion toward softening capital codes before the 1800s. In the 1790s, Virginia followed Thomas Jefferson's warning that the death penalty removed able bodies from the workforce and joined Pennsylvania, Kentucky, New York, and New Jersey in banning it, except for murder. The change applied, significantly, only to whites.[48]

Harsh as it was, North Carolina's law as written was considerably harsher than in practice. In 1815, it listed at least twenty-eight capital crimes without benefit of clergy:

> Arson; burglary, whether or not goods were stolen; murder; highway robbery; accessories before the fact in each of these four crimes; treason; housebreaking in the day time and taking off goods to the amount of 20 shillings; bestiality or sodomy; dueling; bigamy; stealing slaves or aiding them to escape; stealing free Negroes from the State and selling them; voluntary return of slaves transported from the State by sentence of court; rebellion of slaves or conspiracy to incite insurrection; free persons joining a conspiracy or rebellion of slaves; concealing childbirth; breach of prison by a person committed for a felony; counterfeiting notes of the Bank of North America; and the second offenses of manslaughter; forgery; horse-stealing; maiming by putting out eyes or disabling the tongue; counterfeiting or knowingly passing counterfeited bills of credit, public certificates, or lottery tickets; robbery except in a dwelling house or near a highway; larceny from the person to an amount of twelve pence or upwards; too great duress of imprisonment on the part of a jailor; embezzling or vacating records in a court of judicature; and embezzlement by a servant more than eighteen years old of his master's goods to the value of $10 or upwards.[49]

The colony, and then the state, did not execute many people for property crimes. Most African Americans and white people executed in colonial and antebellum North Carolina died for murder and rape.[50]

Concerned by North Carolina's long list of capital crimes, Governor William Miller told North Carolina lawmakers in 1815 that "the end of punishment is the prevention of crimes. If that end can be attained by a system which substituted the reformation of the offender in place of frequent capital punishments, there certainly is room for a change. All history attests the fact, that the progress of correct principles is slow, and that they must finally make their way 'by patient and diligent enquiry, and by fair, candid, and liberal discussion.'"[51] Change was indeed slow. As racism became increasingly entrenched in the slaveholding South, northern states monopolized efforts to reduce the severity of their capital codes. In the Northeast and Midwest, a relatively robust abolition movement succeeded in eliminating or limiting the death penalty in the mid-nineteenth century. In 1837, Maine instituted a one-year waiting period between conviction and execution, touching off a trend that saw Vermont, New Hampshire, Massachusetts, and New York follow suit. In 1846, Michigan abolished the death penalty for murder, followed by Rhode Island and Wisconsin.[52] By 1860, no northern state punished any crimes other than murder and treason with death.[53]

Though similar reforms came slowly to the South, shortly before the Civil War, some conscience-stricken North Carolinians, motivated in large part by their shame over "the bloodiest code of laws of any state in the Union," managed to push through some legal changes.[54] The state's revised criminal code of 1855 decapitalized a number of crimes, including daylight housebreaking, forgery, and burning public bridges. The crimes that remained capital on the eve of the Civil War were sins against the body (murder, rape, and stealing free people for sale as slaves), the soul (sodomy and bestiality), and property (arson, burglary, and so-called slave-stealing). By this time, between the end of the Revolutionary War and the beginning of the Civil War, North Carolina had hanged or burned at least 109 enslaved people for crimes such as murder, rape, and revolt. Eleven women were executed, just one of them white. Five of the women of color executed were burned, a punishment reserved almost exclusively for enslaved women who killed their masters. The record does not indicate any slave executions during the Civil War; of the twenty-four men who died on the gallows during the war, twenty-two of them were deserters, all hanged on the same April day.[55] As the Civil War ended, the use of the death penalty to terrorize people of color, to further empower the powerful, and to maintain class and racial hierarchies was deeply embedded in the state's criminal justice system.

The limited success of reformers in antebellum North Carolina shows the relative lack of interest in crafting and applying a consistent ideology of state punishment beyond maintaining the slave system and white prerogative. Instead, North Carolinians made judgments about individual cases based on their concerns about pain, cruelty, or reputation. In this way, they slowly backed away from the bloody legacy of British common law, tinkering with it until they found a system that met their desire for local control and relatively clear consciences. From the bottom ranks of society, some citizens protested when they thought a local court had meted out an overly harsh sentence, such as in 1812, when Wake County residents petitioned the governor to intervene in the case of an African American man sentenced to be hanged and burned.[56] At the top, elites such as Assemblyman Frederick Nash, who would become the state Supreme Court's chief justice, condemned "the black catalogue of sanguinary punishments which disgrace our criminal code." In 1817, he pledged to work tirelessly to urge his colleagues to "rescue our common country from the foul reproach of being the last of her sister States in laying aside that sanguinary code which we inherited from our mother county."[57] He left the General Assembly the following year.

As efforts were well underway outside the South to modernize penal systems with the construction of penitentiaries, state legislators made a number of passes at building a prison, all of which failed.[58] An 1801 effort to dig an underground prison fell apart. In 1816, the House and Senate disagreed over whether the penitentiary should be situated in Fayetteville or Raleigh and compromised by building it in neither location. In 1827, the House allotted $100,000 for a seventy-five-prisoner facility, but the Senate defeated the measure. The public joined the conversation in 1839, rejecting a prison plan by referendum, a vote they repeated in 1846. It seemed that North Carolinians simply were not interested in erecting an expensive building intended to contain criminals, most of whom, they thought, were already quite well contained on the property where, enslaved, they lived and labored. Punishing such people with imprisonment seemed a waste of resources.[59]

Indeed, many North Carolinians believed that laboring for someone else made men and women slaves. In the 1830s, when reform was sweeping the North and pressing southward, one North Carolina man thundered against the idea of a penitentiary where white men might work for the benefit of the state. Turning reformers' language against them, he attacked this "horrid tyranny, which would disgrace the most barbarous and savage times." North Carolina, without a penitentiary, would be a "symbol of Christian humanity and benevolence . . . for, in my opinion, a free-born American sovereign to be placed in this degrading institution is far worse than death by any torture whatsoever."[60]

## Punishment in North Carolina after the Civil War

After the Civil War, the presence of 350,000 formerly enslaved African Americans changed some white North Carolinians' minds about imprisonment; the end of slavery propelled the state into criminal justice reforms widely described as modern but which were intended to or had the effect of controlling African American life and labor. One such reform was a penitentiary. When the Reconstruction Act of 1867 compelled southern states to rewrite their constitutions as a precondition to reentering the United States, North Carolina legislators mandated the construction of a penitentiary. Once the governor found a site near Raleigh in 1869, the prison "'built itself,' so to speak."[61] Convicts built it themselves, in fact. Five hundred thirty-three men, more than a quarter under twenty years old, arrived in January of 1870 and slept through the winter in a set of temporary cells they constructed from pine timbers. The prison would take fifteen years to complete. By 1872 the project was losing money, so state authorities began leasing most of North Carolina's prisoners to private industries, keeping only the most dangerous criminals on-site. The state opened a farm, too, the first of its kind in the nation, where it grew tobacco. These measures slowed down construction considerably, but by December of 1884, inmates had constructed a "magnificent" prison that resembled a castle.[62] Legislators hoped to imitate Auburn Prison in New York, a model already condemned as outmoded by the American Prison Association fourteen years earlier.[63]

The prison became a visible symbol of the approach to crime enshrined in the state's 1868 constitution, which declared that the object of punishment was "not only to satisfy justice but also to reform the offender and thus prevent crime." The constitution also directed the construction of Houses of Correction, or work houses, and Houses of Refuge for juveniles. It required that male and female prisoners in jails be held separately and obligated the legislature to find a way to educate "idiots and inebriates" and care for the deaf, blind, mute, and insane. It also created a State Board of Charities and Public Welfare, the first organization of its kind in the nation, to oversee these goals and institutions, bequeathing it authority to offer "suggestions" for improvement. The constitution limited capital punishment to murder, rape, burglary, and arson. In an impulse that would linger unanswered for more than a century, the Committee on Punishments, Penal Institutions, and Public Charities recommended that death be the punishment for murder only.[64] Thus the constitution enshrined a set of rehabilitative impulses toward petty criminals and the needy and purely punitive ones toward people convicted of more serious crimes.

Members of the Board of Charities and Public Welfare embraced the letter of the constitution and the spirit of the reform movement, but they could only urge action, not make policy. In 1910, the board declared its members' belief "that no person, no matter what his age or past record, should be assumed to be incapable of improvement," and a commitment for further such improvement with "religious and moral instruction, mental quickening, physical development, and . . . employment." The mentally disabled could at least be made comfortable. Trying to seize upon the long moment of optimism at the beginning of the century, the board appealed to state legislators on behalf of the "feeble-minded": "They sit in utter neglect upon the door-steps of the County Homes. Their past, the future, empty nothingness, the present oft-times filth and physical discomfort, their rush-light intellects gradually going out."[65] Board members recommended a number of improvements: a classification system for prisoners, the abolition of convict labor, funding for the construction of juvenile institutions, efforts to indemnify the wrongly convicted, indeterminate sentencing that might reduce sentences for well-behaved inmates, and a parole system.[66]

Prison officials seemed devoted to making the prison system a science-minded site for rehabilitating prisoners, in the vein of the burgeoning field of criminology. In the early 1900s, convicts arriving at the penitentiary were stripped and washed and their physical characteristics, from their eye color to their shoe size, were recorded. Upon intake, policy directed that prisoners be confined for two days, where a variety of officials would "assure them of interest in their welfare; explain the object of incarceration; urge upon them motives to reform; explain their duties as prisoners; read to them the prison regulations and perform other acts as will serve to win the confidence of the convict and inspire them with hope for the future."[67] There was little such hope for capital criminals, who until 1910 mingled with the rest of the prison population in Raleigh before returning to their home counties for execution.

Religious services took place at the State's Prison (today known as Central Prison), the State Farm in Caledonia, and prison camps around the state. In 1909, a library was constructed and soon held at least five hundred books; white and African American inmates could read there on alternate evenings.

The *Prison News*, a newspaper published by inmates in the 1920s, told of religious revivals, performances, baseball games, and boxing matches. Inmates hosted a radio program on Saturday nights; as with other pursuits, the broadcasts were segregated, with white inmates going on the air one week and African American inmates the next.[68] Superintendents and wardens urged legislators to institute a parole system, and in 1935 North Carolina became one of the first states in the nation to do so. Prisoners worked for about twelve hours a day, depending on the season, with "the pure air and bright sunlight of God's world all around them."[69]

At state prison farms, convicts raised and slaughtered livestock (hogs subsisted on prison trash), grew soybeans, wheat, alfalfa, clover, corn, and oats, as well as vegetables. They grew flowers in a large greenhouse and sold them to local florists; formed and fired bricks; and built cement culverts and sewers. At one point, the prison maintained a license tag plant, a mattress factory, a tailor shop, and a soap plant. Prisoners wove curtains and printed government documents in a print shop. Female prisoners, who were overwhelmingly black, made clothing, bedding, and towels for convicts and washed these articles when they became dirty. They also earned money by washing and repairing clothes for Confederate veterans at a nearby home. The prison even sold postcards. Reflecting the importance attached to the prison system's self-sufficiency, superintendents described its economic health with more care than they described their inmate population. Executions often did not appear in prison reports; expenses always did.

These programs in the State's Prison coexisted with horrific cruelty and neglect in the state's work camps and prison farms.[70] Jailers and camp guards used beatings, solitary confinement in the "dark cell," and whatever else they could think of as punishment. North Carolina retained flogging longer than most states, and without any guidelines on its use, the decision—or impulse—to beat a prisoner lay entirely with camp guards and their supervisors.[71] Mistreatment of work-camp prisoners shocked observers, from the Citizens' Committee of One Hundred, which investigated jail conditions in the early 1920s, to North Carolinians who read about the brutality in their newspapers. Scandal erupted in 1935 when two black convicts discovered at a Mecklenburg County prison camp required amputation of their feet following prolonged confinement.[72] Those prisoners not living in the State's Prison or temporary work camps were confined in county jails, "dungeons" rife with "sickening odors," where the sexes freely mingled, often without adequate clothing or bedding and without much access to hygiene or food.[73] "Fortunately for our prisoners many of these buildings are seldom occupied," the State Board of Charities observed in 1912.[74] Jails, one historian speculated, held only those "who cared not to escape."[75]

The contradiction between an interest in rehabilitation and a relentless work program—or perhaps the interest in seeing a consonance between the two—existed at least in part from the state constitution's directive that the prison sustain itself. The prison was a commercial enterprise, with prisoners working as much to fund their own imprisonment as to improve themselves with honest labor. Even the reform-minded members of the Board of Charities and Public Welfare admonished prison administrators not to stray from this goal: "It is for 'community service' that the State and county institutions exist. They are the concrete forms of our ideas of economic welfare and are not created from charitable motives alone," the Board cautioned in a 1915 report.[76] Prison superintendents worried that the relentless drive to make the prison self-sufficient hamstrung their efforts to reform criminals. In the early 1900s, Superintendent J. S. Mann admitted his doubts "that a term of imprisonment here can have any permanent reformatory effect upon the ordinary inmate. The association is vicious."[77] His successors echoed his anxiety for years, as poorly supervised camps and a poorly maintained prison piqued concern. In 1913, Governor W. W. Kitchin recommended vacating the prison altogether.[78]

Work camps contributed substantially to the quest for self-sustainability. Camp prisoners, often men who had committed minor crimes, labored in pine forests, in mines and quarries, or on farms. In the early twentieth century North Carolina maintained forty road camps around the state, each controlled by a county. One inspector described the satellite prisons as "forty wholly independent state prisons, under forty distinct managements, with forty different and distinct sets of rules and regulations, and over which there is absolutely no state supervision."[79] Life in road camps was hard, so much so that one prison superintendent worried that the "unremitting toil and unendurable hardships" there would cause prisoners "to be worn out and buried within a few months, or, at the least, a few years."[80]

Of 2,800 inmates in the prison system in the years 1911 and 1912, all but 75 worked on county roads, railroads, or farms; those 75 worked, or languished, within the walls of the State's Prison. This ratio persisted for decades. In 1928, just 305 of nearly 2,000 prisoners were held in the prison; in 1940, of 9,275 people convicted in North Carolina courts, 8,320 were sent to the roads. The commitment to using convicts' labor was so complete that in 1930, the General Assembly gave control of the prison system to the State

Highway and Public Works division.[81] And while the state constitution forbade leasing convicts sentenced for serious crimes outside the prison, in 1926 the superintendent confessed that "it has long been the custom" to use physically fit convicts on the roads "regardless of their crimes." Death row inmates might have been laboring on the state's roads for years.[82] North Carolina is still known as the "Good Roads State."

The emphasis on convict labor continued well into the twentieth century. A 1950 report on the prison system listed a total of eighty-eight work camps, and condemned convict labor and its control by the Highway Commission. North Carolina is "alone and wrong" in its approach to criminal punishment, the report argued, and "virtually no effort is being made to rehabilitate prisoners under the present system." The report's grim assessment was true for the fifty years before that: "North Carolina is sacrificing long-range gains for short-range earnings by making the chief function of its Prison Department the maintenance of highways rather than the rehabilitation of as many offenders as possible."[83] Officials could only hope, as one did, that "as poor, perhaps, as North Carolina's prison conditions have been, many of the prisoners have been better off while in prison."[84]

The death penalty, which represents a rejection of the belief in criminality as a curable malady, undermined the growing attention to the connections between crime and other social pathologies, and a commitment to redemption. Severe and irreversible, the death penalty was irreconcilable with these principles, though it coexisted with them, and even flourished in their presence. It was mandatory for first-degree burglary and arson until 1941, and for first-degree murder and rape until 1949. Its severity, according to some North Carolinians, made the death penalty a "relic of barbarism" enshrined in and legitimized by a prison that seemed to exist primarily to confine death row prisoners until their executions.[85]

Furthermore, during this long period of time but particularly between the late nineteenth and early twentieth centuries, legal execution operated alongside illegal but permissible lynchings as part of an intimidation apparatus intended to keep African Americans in place as fearful and thus pliant agrarian laborers. The great weight of these killings remains freighted to the state. It is tempting to claim, in the absence of a desire for a clear view of the past or of the problems we wrestle with in the present, that the executions of the 1830s and 1930s are ancient history. But there may be nothing so modern as the cynical development of a racial ideology to justify the morally repugnant accrual of social and material profit.

If North Carolina and other death penalty states actually executed everyone convicted of first-degree murder, it is hard to imagine that the punishment would last much longer. Most people who commit first-degree murder are not sentenced to death, and most people sentenced to death are not executed. In this regard, the death penalty is no different than other punishments, which are meted out much less frequently than the acts they punish. But the death penalty is different; indeed, the Supreme Court held in *Gregg v. Georgia* that "death is different" because it is irrevocable and the procedural safeguards of the Bill of Rights cannot later intervene in light of new evidence or revelations, errors, or misconduct.[86] Individual death sentences are reversible, as we have seen amid a spate of exonerations lately. The death penalty, broadly, is reversible, as this history shows. But the many hundreds of executions in this state since its creation are irreversible. Each has left its mark on the history of North Carolina.

## Reading This Book

The book begins at the end of the Civil War and moves forward chronologically to the recent past. Chapter 1 argues that throughout the twentieth century, the consonance between the receding phenomenon of lynching and the consolidating capital punishment system would grow stronger, not weaken. Most studies of the relationship between lynching and the death penalty have been conducted by social scientists. Their methods have failed to substantiate the substitution theory, the idea that legal executions served as replacements for illegal lynchings. In doing so, even using the careful language of social science, these scholars have diminished if not dismissed the relationship between these complementary forms of social control. This chapter argues that lynching and the death penalty were in fact closely related: they were mimetic methods of racial subjugation that North Carolinians at the time saw as in conversation with one another. Lynching played a key role in transitioning the death penalty in North Carolina from the nineteenth century to the twentieth century. Legal hangings and lynching had less in common than might appear; the state-run death penalty and lynching had more in common than immediately apparent.

The relationship between lynching and the death penalty reveals racial subjugation as a principal goal of the criminal justice system, introducing anxiety about law and order, deeply marked by racism, as driving both phenomena. Chapter 2 takes up anxiety in a different sense, exploring the relationship between execution procedure, technology, and the idea of modernity the state's elites sought to cultivate. The story begins with sheriffs charged with conducting hangings and the new tasks they needed to master, including erecting a scaffold and successfully tying a noose. Sheriffs were relieved when in 1910 the state took over control of hanging from local law enforcement. But the anxieties about procedure endured, as electrocution, hailed as a swift and sure mode of execution, proved as torturous and protracted as any hanging. Lethal gas, which North Carolina adopted without study, would prove just as troubling. During this period the death penalty became slightly more discriminatory and was transformed from a community spectacle with broad participation by poor white and black men and women into a contained act of violence against African American men.

The politics of mercy, and the role of race in its application, are the subject of chapter 3. In recent years, support for the death penalty represents a near-canonical part of conservative politics. Yet for most of its history in this state and elsewhere, the death penalty did not carry the political weight it does today, and governors with the power to commute death sentences to life in prison did so frequently, with little political cost, and often with the support of residents. Their clemency softened the harsh mandatory death sentences that came with convictions of first-degree murder, first-degree rape, first-degree burglary, and arson. Jury members participated in the extension of mercy first by refusing to convict people they believed guilty to avoid a death sentence, a kind of jury nullification; by voting to convict and then writing to the governor to urge clemency action; or, later in this history, by handing down guilty verdicts with recommendations of mercy.

Chapter 4 takes on the decline of the death penalty and the voices that sought to hurry it into obsolescence. By World War II, this decline was under way, and North Carolina did not execute anyone between 1961 and 1984. This de facto moratorium can be explained not by the success of activists but by the rise of alternatives to death, most importantly life without parole. This chapter explores the failures of anti–death penalty activism and the success of efforts to replace it. Yet this is not a celebration of the move away from death as punishment. Life imprisonment was cold comfort to the many African American men who encountered all-white juries, relied on apathetic defense attorneys, and were otherwise failed by the criminal justice system. The death penalty declined not because North Carolinians acknowledged its many flaws, but because its many failures led them to search for an equally certain—if equally flawed—alternative.

The death penalty, by the 1950s, had lost its political weight in North Carolina. Never a hot-button political issue, it had, as described in chapter 3, declined quietly throughout the 1940s and 1950s. Its decline reflected the success, such as it was, of the substitution of life imprisonment for the death penalty, but also the seemingly settled nature of the race question in North Carolina and elsewhere in the South. Certainly, in the minds of participants in the nascent civil rights movement, issues of race were far from settled. But in North Carolina, aggressive, starkly racist white supremacy had mellowed in tone, and rhetorics of harmony resonated in middle-class black and white discourses. This changed following the United States Supreme Court ruling in *Furman v. Georgia*, as North Carolina joined its southern neighbors in scrambling to reinstate the death penalty, ultimately restoring the mandatory death sentence and setting up a showdown with the Supreme Court. Chapter 5 examines that retrenchment in the face of a host of new cultural and social developments in the state, at the heart of which was the renewed sense that the race question was not in fact settled at all. With the death penalty achieving new symbolic value, it returned to its position at the apogee of a system of race-based control that it had not occupied since the 1930s.

The death penalty in America can seem like an oddly ahistorical phenomenon. Death as punishment has been a persistent part of human existence since well before records can date its first instance. Executions have continued despite the American Revolution's upset of monarchical power. The death penalty has endured its own gruesome spectacles and a consistent drumbeat of opposition from newspapers and civic groups. It lasted through the Great Depression, during which many imagined a new American state dedicated to lifting up the struggling and impoverished. It lasted through two world wars fought in the name of democracy. It persisted despite the Black Freedom Struggle's successes in addressing institutional discrimination. It endured here even as our peer European nations rejected it. Throughout these many decades, the same kinds of people were executed with chilling consistency: people of color, impoverished people, the mentally incapacitated. The only category in which the punishment showed any degree of range was in age: in North Carolina and in the United States at large, we executed mothers and fathers, grandchildren and grandparents.

The death penalty's remarkable persistence, despite both direct pressure and considerable political and social reorganization, wavered in the 1960s. While the absolutist arguments for and against it remained static—

the Bible says do it versus the Bible says don't do it—when given the choice, jurors increasingly chose to meet potentially capital cases with recommendations for life imprisonment. Yet this behavior, too, was consistent. For generations, here in North Carolina and elsewhere, we have executed a very small number of people convicted of capital crimes. If there were as many executions as there were murders, or rapes, or burglaries, these executions would hardly be the crowd-drawing spectacles they were. They instead might be quiet, mundane affairs witnessed by a handful of family members and journalists. In other words, they might have looked like today's cloistered lethal injections, with none of the gravity of the state's taking of life but little of the spectacle, either.

When the Supreme Court finally weighed in on the death penalty in the 1970s, it not only did so confusedly, but also, in acting, it aligned death penalty abolition with other activist causes of the era, namely African American liberation, making abolition as essential to resist as any other government program seeking to address the legacies of enslavement. Mercy, which had always limited the number of death sentences and executions, and which whittled America's capital punishment into a scarcely used symbol, was now a weapon wielded by an activist Supreme Court and had to be opposed. But when the death penalty resurged, buoyed by new tough-on-crime rhetoric, it found itself once again limited by its human participants. Today the death penalty's small but meaningful story unfolds in a handful of counties in states such as Texas, Oklahoma, Florida, and Arizona. Even in those counties, people seem to prefer not executing.[87] The people executed are poor, people of color, lacking adequate representation, intellectually limited, even terminally ill.[88]

The historic death penalty, like its modern descendant, was a punishment hotly debated but rarely used, hugely significant to a very small number of people yet symbolic for most. It was one with seemingly immutable characteristics that express the worst legacies of a criminal justice system that came to maturity as an instrument of Jim Crow racial subjugation. It was one that has seemed often to be painful and nerve-wracking for all involved, demonstrating the psychic weight not just of being punished but of inflicting punishment, and often unjustly. These features persisted through the punishment's modest rise and fall, its resurgence, and today, its narrowness and irrelevance to most Americans. What do we do with such a constrained history, and such a stubborn one? We begin by seeking to understand the decisions that shaped it. In doing so, we can begin to understand one of our state's and our nation's most enduring institutions: death as punishment.

## A Note on Methods

The most widely used resource on the death penalty in America is M. Watt Espy and John Ortiz Smykla's list of executions between 1608 and 2002, known by researchers as the Espy File. The Espy File is available through the Inter-university Consortium for Political and Social Research (ICPSR) and the Death Penalty Information Center. For this book, I accessed the Espy File via the ICPSR and, using its data about North Carolina as a baseline, created an independent record of executions in the state. In doing so, I identified a number of specific and systematic errors of the kind noticed by other researchers.[89] Specifically, the Espy File misspells names or includes only a surname; misidentifies the crime for which persons were executed, often noting that a person executed for a murder committed during a robbery was executed for robbery, not murder; and mixes up burglary (entering an occupied domicile at night with intent to commit a felony, a capital crime) and housebreaking (an undefined offense).[90] The Espy File also does not include the race of the victim, essential information for understanding the death penalty in North Carolina and elsewhere. Despite these errors and omissions, the Espy File is a remarkable resource that should be celebrated for creating an essential baseline of knowledge about execution in the United States. Like any resource of its kind, it should be used with caution, as I believe I have done here.

# 1 The General Sense of Justice

## Lynching and the Death Penalty, 1880–1950

· · · · · · · · · · · · · · · · · · · · · · · · · · · · · · · · · · · · · · · · ·

When in 1907, historian James Cutler sought to understand the relationship between the death penalty and lynching in the United States, he concluded that lynchings occurred because of a communication failure: in his view, white people failed to grasp why black people could not attain whites' level of civilization. After centuries of social development, Cutler argued, whites were so very civilized that they felt compelled to inflict "tortures and cruelties" against African Americans who violated their norms. Likening the lynch mob to an "unreasonable father" who savagely punishes a child incapable of meeting or even understanding his father's expectations, Cutler offered a wan critique of lynching while insisting on the right of the mob to kill people of color: an unreasonable father is still a father.[1] And if the unreasonable father is a problem, the solution is certainly not to eliminate the father altogether. A child needs a father, after all. The solution, instead, is to make the father appear reasonable.

Cutler was not able to establish a one-to-one relationship between lynchings and the death penalty, or that each lynching that took place occurred in the absence of a necessary execution. Contemporary scholars have persuasively demonstrated that such a relationship did not exist.[2] He did assert, though, that if the death penalty were abolished, the number of lynchings would increase.[3] "Whenever unusually brutal and atrocious crimes are committed, particularly if they cross racial lines," he wrote, "nothing less than the death penalty will satisfy the general sense of justice that is found in the average American community."[4] Although he didn't phrase it this way, his claim suggests that lynching and legal execution, both of which disparately harm people of color, were in fact part of a sprawling system of lethal punishment that included mob lynchings, county and state executions, and other punitive deaths, such as those inflicted by organized white posses or white private citizens. Mob killings and the death penalty coexisted throughout the late nineteenth and early twentieth centuries, ultimately declining together after reaching modest peaks in the 1930s.

Lynching's primary function at the end of the nineteenth and the beginning of the twentieth century was to terrorize and thus control the African American community amid the consolidation of white supremacist political and social power. In the second half of the nineteenth century and the first half of the twentieth, lynching also provided a scaffolding on which to build a death penalty—one that disproportionately targeted African American men—that satisfied both those who thought black deviants deserved public, torturous death and those who believed they deserved something just as lethal but less spectacular. Throughout this period, angry white southerners used the threat of lynching to coerce the criminal justice system into hasty judgments against black defendants. As lynching receded, driven in part by unusually aggressive policing at the direction of North Carolina's governors, the death penalty took up its mantle, growing only more discriminatory as time passed. The drive to punish black communities did not wane; the forms this punishment took varied in their restraint and respectability. Lynchings and executions were both, to use sociologist Oliver C. Cox's phrasing, "culminating act[s] of continuing white aggression against the Negro."[5]

While historian Christopher Waldrep has revealed that there existed no clear-cut definition of lynching while the practice remained widespread—the National Association for the Advancement of Colored People (NAACP), for instance, debated the issue so as to give their annual accounting more credibility—observers then and scholars now have taken pains to distinguish between lynching and legal execution.[6] On its face, the distinction seems real and obvious: lynching is illegal murder, while execution is legal extermination. Yet looking only slightly deeper reveals that the similarities far outweigh the differences. In emphasizing these distinctions, in the words of Jacqueline Goldsby, we "*denominate* the violence, ordering and fixing its meanings in ways that delimit our capacities to interpret it."[7] The apparent special character of lynching has allowed us to overlook its regularity, its resonant impact on black communities, and its connections to other less spectacular forms of violence, including but not limited to the death penalty.[8]

Before examining this relationship more closely, we must ask why we feel the need to distinguish between lynching and the death penalty at all; they were both, in Cox's view, acts of aggression against black men. It seems that one reason is to understand the role of violence in the state. If the death penalty was, as sociologist David Garland and others have argued, essential to state stability and security, it is important to distinguish it from a form of killing not essential, and even harmful, to that security.[9] Considering the phenomenon from the perspective of state actors, lynching must be as harmful to social infrastructure as the death penalty is helpful. It seems the height of illegitimacy not because the mob usurps state power—white supremacy relies on informal policing—but because it reveals the fragility of the state's monopoly of force.[10]

But what if we are interested instead in state formation that condoned, even relied on, illegal violence to carry it toward maturity? This violence is both illegal—insofar as it consists of kidnapping, assault, and murder—and essential, carrying out the important task of enforcing a set of politically and socially fundamental rules. It is only when this violence becomes nonessential that its unacceptability can be recognized, even if it remains basically legal. Lynchings in the Jim Crow South and in North Carolina ultimately declined not because they were unacceptable, but because that kind of white-hot violence was no longer necessary. With lynchings declining in frequency, the state could continue its attacks on African Americans through a death penalty that felt more like an expression of state power than a blow against it. Jim Crow North Carolina did not just rely on violence and the threat of violence to function; that violence was fundamental to its existence.

## Lynching in North Carolina

At least some of this desire to differentiate between lynching and the death penalty must stem from the desire to push back against mobs' fashioning of lynchings so that they resembled legally sanctioned punishment. Lynching was made to resemble the application of legal, lethal punishment by those who perpetrated its violence: inasmuch as it was a punishment that awaited certain classes of people for offenses against certain other classes, lynching functioned like law. But more accurately, during the period between the end of the Civil War and beginning of World War II, the law also functioned like lynching: subjugating, constraining, and disrupting black communities. The invention and enforcement of new statutes to coerce black labor and rob African Americans of their political power after the Civil War demonstrate the law's role in holding fast to the privileges afforded by slavery.[11]

Moreover, North Carolina progressives used the distinction between lynching and the death penalty in support of a nakedly racist, usually unfair, often cruel death penalty that killed the innocent and guilty alike, submitted its victims to openly hostile trials, and consigned innocent people to a lifetime of forced labor even after their death sentences were commuted. When law-enforcement officers openly participated in the violent hangings of black men, so empowered by the governor's signature on a death warrant, they were the solemn officiants of legal hangings. When they clandestinely or semiclandestinely participated in such hangings, or openly participated afterward, such as in the case of the coroners who notoriously ascribed mob murders to "parties unknown," they were participants in illegal lynchings, legitimized by their presence.

Although its legislators joined their southern peers in blocking the passage of anti-lynching legislation at the federal level, by the early twentieth century North Carolina had the South's toughest anti-lynching laws, which were, remarkably, occasionally enforced.[12] For instance, in 1906, Governor Robert B. Glenn took a personal interest in the lynching of J. V. Johnson, a Confederate veteran killed after receiving a mistrial on a murder charge.[13] Within just a few days, the Anson County sheriff had made arrests, and with strong support from Governor Robert Glenn, solicitors secured indictments using an 1893 statute that made conspiring or attempting to break into a jail to kill a prisoner a felony punishable by as many as fifteen years in prison.[14] This law, and threat of indictment, appears to have offered little deterrent. While the trial of Johnson's lynchers was still under way, a mob in Salisbury brutally lynched three African American people, two men and a fifteen-year-old boy.

The ultimate outcome could only encourage those inclined to mob up. After convening a special term of superior court, Governor Glenn was reported to be actively involved in the prosecution, and the fact solicitors he appointed secured as many as twenty-five indictments, though three of the indicted lynchers never came to trial, as they fled the state.[15] Courtroom testimony in the first trial, that of one John Jones, was detailed and direct, naming mob members and their behavior—one, who rode rather than walked to the lynching site because of a sore foot, another who joined in because Johnson's alleged victim used to save him from bullies at school.[16] Facing a hostile reception, the prosecutors ultimately abandoned murder charges and sought convictions only for jail-breaking. The presiding judge, in light of this choice, amplified the state's argument, reassuring jurors that if the defendant were convicted of these lesser charges, there was no risk the murder charge would be sought.[17] Jurors deliberated for a half hour before acquitting Jones, who was received outside the courtroom with "jubilation."[18]

During the course of the trial a letter emerged, addressed to John Boggan, sheriff of Anson County. Boggan had testified as to the members of the mob, naming a number of them and identifying a man named Zeke Lewis as their leader. "'I talked to him and called him by name,'" testified the sheriff, who made some effort to prevent Johnson's abduction from jail. Now, Boggan was at risk for speaking out in court. "We, the crowd that done the noble deed on Sunday night want to tell you that we have no hard feeling toward you," the letter read. It noted that there were 343 men from five counties in the mob, and that while some of them might be fools, at least 274 were "settled men." These settled men were "not looking for trouble, but if you want trouble we can certainly give you all you want."[19] The note was an apt reflection of community sentiment. Lewis was acquitted and the presiding Superior Court judge advised the solicitor prosecuting the case to give it up: feeling in the area was in favor of the mob members, so much so that a community fund was financing their defense.[20]

Law enforcement moved with similar, similarly ineffective swiftness following the Salisbury lynching, soon making a number of arrests, which resulted in fifteen indictments. Of those, just one led to a sentence: George Hall, who wielded the sledge hammer that destroyed the jail's door.[21] Hall was unlucky to be an outsider from a neighboring county, and to have confessed his participation; one editorial declared that his conviction meant only that "a hill billie can be punished for a lynching . . . while then men who can command money and influence can not."[22] As Hall prepared his appeal, Governor Glenn issued orders to sheriffs and state guard units to aggressively deter lynch mobs, using their firearms as necessary.[23] George Hall served two years and four months before escaping prison in 1908. He was recaptured after nine months and returned to prison, but news of recapture spurred some to fret that, in the words of one editorialist, "justice has been nodding or has slipped a cog or two in making [Hall] the martyr for members of that lynching bee."[24] This argument gained traction: If no one else was being punished, why should we punish George Hall? A few days before Christmas, 1911, in light of similar petitions from Rowan County residents, Governor W. W. Kitchin issued the pardon, making George Hall a belated beneficiary of the lax approach to prosecuting people for participating in lynching.[25]

Perhaps the most forceful fallout from a lynching occurred in 1872, well before Robert Glenn's efforts to tamp down the practice. Govan and Columbus Adair were brothers, described by journalists as bootleggers who ran a so-called blockade distillery to resist government efforts to tax their liquor. When they were indicted for this behavior by a grand jury, the Adairs sought revenge against those who testified against them: Silas Weston, a man of mixed race, and his wife, Polly, who was white. With at least one accomplice who later testified against them, the brothers raided the Weston home, shooting those they found inside and setting the dwelling alight, killing Silas, three of his children, and Polly's son from a previous marriage. Disavowed by newspaper coverage as both Republicans and Ku Klux Klan members, Govan and Columbus were sentenced to death and hanged.[26] Although contemporary observers did not call the attack on the mixed-race, cohabiting family a lynching, it fits the profile of such an attack and appears as such in contemporary sources.[27] Ultimately, the political context—the Adairs' executions occurred shortly after the so-called Kirk-Holden War of 1870 and 1871, when Republican Governor William Woods Holden declared martial law to battle the Klan—and the form of the killing may have made it easier to pursue legal sanction. Had the murders resembled a lynching more closely, and had the Adairs not been stirring up other kinds of trouble, it is not certain they would have been punished in the same way.

Whatever disincentive to mob action it bore, the laws that briefly punished George Hall and took the lives of the Adair brothers were not written to preserve the lives and bodies of African Americans. Instead, they were written to preserve white rule in a still-precarious political environment. As state government, and particularly the Democratic Party, consolidated power, lynching itself appeared to ordinary white North Carolinians to be less necessary. North Carolina did not need lynching, one petitioner wrote to Governor Thomas W. Bickett in 1917: "The courts in the land are all in control of the whites, so there is never an excuse for a lynching."[28] The writer reveals a cynical awareness of lynching's importance in maintaining white supremacy in the state's political infrastructure, setting aside its defenders' assertions that lynching was necessary for the protection of white women.

Lynching, then, was one of a variety of mechanisms used to destabilize African American communities and their social, familial, and economic lives, including but not limited to explicit and implied threats of violence against individuals, constraints on movement, commerce, and civic participation, police violence and neglect, incarceration, debt peonage, and of course the death penalty. As John Dollard wrote nearly eighty years ago, "It must not be supposed that the major or perhaps even the significant part of white aggression against Negroes consisted of the few dramatic acts of lynching featured in the newspapers."[29] And if the formally constituted government was similarly bent toward disruption, then, in the words of Charles David Phillips, "it is only natural that violent state action and violent self-help"—in this case lynching—"should be intimately entwined."[30] The patchwork nature of legal protection for African Americans meant, as Jacqueline Goldsby writes, that "there was nothing *extra*legal about the mob murders of African Americans. Lynching functioned as a tool of domination meant to coerce . . . to deny . . . and to subjugate black people."[31] Lynching may have appeared to disrupt the state's claim to a monopoly of force, but in Jim Crow North Carolina, where all white citizens were drawn into the role of enforcers, lynching was the logical extreme of the daily policing of black behavior.

Lynching, in other words, was never a direct substitute for legal execution, just as harassing someone in the street is not a substitute for denying them a loan, or refusing to use someone's full name is a substitute for denying them service at your restaurant. These efforts at dehumanization work together. In this way, the death penalty and lynchings were symbiotic, feeding on one another until the death penalty was strong enough to stand on its own. Imagined as a developing organism, the death penalty learned two important lessons from lynching. First, it learned that to endure without sustained criticism it needed to take on a modern, professional appearance by using technologies that would mask pain or avoid inflicting it. In the early twentieth century, North Carolina joined other southern states in imposing restrictions on viewership of executions and seeking to improve the efficiency of the process. If lynchings were, as historian Ashraf H. A. Rushdy describes them, "the operas of white civilization," state-run executions were the soap operas—staged like lynchings but more contained and predictable.[32]

Second, in order to meet the demands of the mob, the death penalty revealed a renewed commitment to targeting young African American men, the same group of people who were targets of lynching and presumed to pose the greatest threat to a burgeoning white supremacist state. It was after the state of North Carolina took control of capital punishment

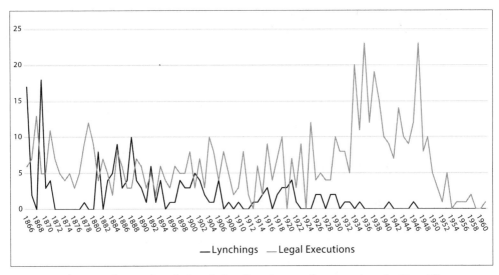

Lynchings and executions in North Carolina. Sources for execution: the Espy File; Daniel Allen Hearn, *Legal Executions in North and South Carolina: A Comprehensive Registry, 1866–1962* (Jefferson, NC: McFarland, 2015); Ancestry.com; Newspapers .com. Sources for lynchings: Beck and Tolnay, Newkirk, *Lynching in North Carolina*; Ancestry.com; Newspapers.com. For a detailed note on sources, please see appendix C.

from county sheriffs that the death penalty in the state reached a new height, though just barely, of discriminatory usage: between 1910 and 1961, 78 percent of those executed were black men, most for crimes with white victims. Between the end of the Civil War and 1910, 74 percent of those executed were African Americans, although their proportion of the population never exceeded 38 percent.[33] Adding American Indians, a full 80 percent of those executed were people of color and just one white person was executed for a crime against a person of color.[34] Just one white person was executed for a crime with a single black victim, though the circumstances illustrate the exception that proves the rule: the condemned man in this case was reported to be a habitual criminal, a horse thief, a bigamist, a swindler, a rapist, a drinker, and a deserter from the Confederate Army who was sentenced to death for the rape of an eleven-year-old girl.[35] State-run electrocutions and asphyxiations, styles of punishment that appeared more modern and humane than locally conducted hangings, in fact carried forward the brutal logic of lynch mobs deep into the twentieth century.[36]

## Antisocial News: Lynching Scholarship

Scholarship on lynching began sluggishly, as many white professional scholars ignored or underrepresented it for generations. Their silence may also be indicative of the fact that lynchings were occurring and were matters of contemporary concern at least until the second half of the twentieth century. But voices of color were not silent on the subject. Among the first to publish on lynching was African American journalist and activist Ida B. Wells-Barnett, who produced three pamphlets in the 1890s seeking to dismantle the lies that, for instance, white mobs lynched black men because of their rapaciousness, or that the mob acted only when legal procedures failed.[37] Following in Wells-Barnett's footsteps, NAACP assistant secretary Walter White used his light hair and blue eyes to pass as white and investigate lynchings on the ground. He wrote up his experiences and conclusions in *Rope and Faggot* (1929), a book that arrived just as lynching was capturing the interest of social scientists in the 1930s.[38]

That interest found form under Howard Odum at the University of North Carolina. In 1930, while at UNC and under the auspices of the Southern Regional Council and the North Carolina Commission on Interracial Cooperation (CIC), Odum and his research team produced finely grained demographic studies of communities where lynchings took place.[39] Working first under Odum and later as research director for the Southern Commission on the Study of Lynching, set up by the CIC, sociologist Arthur Raper published *The Tragedy of Lynching* in 1933. Echoing a 1931 report by the commission,[40] he described lynchings as a symptom of a disconnectedness from stable institutions: taking place in remote spaces, perpetrated by "unattached people" largely in the South, where law enforcement remained underdeveloped.[41] But even in places where institutions had grown to relative maturity, Raper observed "a silent acquiescence" to the practice, due to the indifference of law-enforcement officers and the general white public to the welfare of African Americans.[42]

At least part of the acquiescence—or complicity—observed by Raper stemmed from a belief among many white people, of course including North Carolinians, that black people were crime-prone and in need of heavy-handed correction. This was a deep-seated belief frequently nourished by newspaper coverage of African Americans. One study published in 1932 found that nearly half the articles about African Americans or the African American community published in seventeen major newspapers that year presented African Americans as "antisocial." Some newspapers published hundreds of "antisocial news" items over the course of two months: the New Orleans *Times-Picayune*, for instance, printed 708 negative articles about African Americans versus 345 items of "general news." The *Baltimore Post* published 344 and the *Washington Star* published 391 negative stories.[43] In his conclusion, the author of the study observed that the press was a mirror of public opinion, and thus has emphasized "what is bizarre and pathological in Negro life," both dehumanizing and pathologizing the community.[44] Even academic studies seemed to begin from an assumption of African American criminality. One piece by a doctor published in the *North Carolina Law Journal* and presented before the Medical Association of the Carolinas and Virginia in its first sentence asserts "the tendency of the negro man to commit rape against the white woman."[45]

Frank Shay acknowledged the work of Raper and others (though not Ida B. Wells-Barnett) in his 1938 study, *Judge Lynch*, a book that stands out for its depiction of lynching as starkly racist and its forceful assertion that lynching was not only a southern phenomenon, an idea to which recently historians have returned.[46] Shay, not an academic historian, was an exception. Historian W. Fitzhugh Brundage notes that contemporaneous academic scholarship tended to ignore or apologize for lynching, and as the practice itself waned at mid-century, so too did the interest of sociologists.[47] It was not until the late 1970s, in the wake of the civil rights movement, that numerous scholars began in earnest to take lynching as a subject of study. Since then, many historians and others have sought to understand lynching's genesis, often with state-based or regional studies.

While there exists a vast if fairly recent body of scholarly work on lynching and a wide-ranging body of work on capital punishment, surprisingly, few works exist on the relationship between the two, despite similarities in form and substance.[48] Fewer still address North Carolina.[49] Criminologist Margaret Vandiver summarizes the handful of such studies in her own monograph on the subject, concluding that the data, which diverge considerably across time and space, do not indicate a tight relationship between the two. Vandiver's work supports that of veteran lynching scholars Stewart Tolnay and E. M. Beck, who determined that lynching and the death penalty in the American South spring from the same "social forces" but were "largely independent forms of social control."[50] From a social-scientific perspective, the relationship may not be possible to explicate, but to the historian, and to those living in what Mark Twain called the "United States of Lyncherdom," the relationship was real and visible.[51]

It is not surprising that finding discernible, data-based explanations for lynching's rise and fall and its relationship to other forms of punishment has proved difficult. It was their very unpredictability, the fact that they might occur anywhere, at any time, and to anyone for any reason, real or imaginary, that enhanced lynching's terrible sway.[52] In his poem, "Between the World and Me," written in 1934 and published the following year, Richard Wright evoked the power lynching had to attack the wider black community in addition to the specific target. Stumbling across the remains of a lynching victim in the woods, the speaker finds that "the sooty details of the scene rose, thrusting themselves between the world and me."[53] The speaker is transubstantiated into the body of the lynching's victim, the charred bones "melting into my bones. The grey ashes formed flesh firm and black, entering into my flesh." The speaker perishes gruesomely, battered, tarred and feathered, and burned to death. The poem ends with his body reduced to ash and bone, awaiting the next passerby to terrorize. Wright's work embodies the generational trauma wrought by lynching and the terrifying way in which it spread among people of color, giving only white people the luxury of forgetting it.

Reliable data on lynching have been, until fairly recently, hard to unearth also because contemporaneous researchers relied on uneven newspaper accounts that sometimes proved to be inaccurate recitations of rumors. To this day, there are only three main sources historians have used to count lynchings between the 1880s and the 1960s (data were and are much harder to come by for the Reconstruction period between the end of the Civil War and 1877): Tuskegee Institute, the *Chicago Tribune*, and the National Association for the Advancement of Colored People. But it was not until the 1980s (or 1990s?) that E. M. Beck and Stuart E. Tolnay set out to address flaws in these data with a systematic comparison of reported incidents and newspaper coverage. The result, in addition to scholarship including their 1995 *A Festival of Violence*, was the most reliable source we have for counting lynchings. And they continued to reassess and update their data for North Carolina as recently as 2016; their findings, with additional confirmation efforts pursued by Tolnay and historian Amy Kate Bailey, are currently available online.[54]

This information, supplemented with work by Vann Newkirk and original research, provides a conservative estimate for the number of lynchings in North Carolina between the end of the Civil War and World War II, at least 175, not counting attempted lynchings or those that took place out of state at the hands of mobs from inside the state. North Carolina had the fewest lynchings and the lowest lynching rate in the former Confederacy.[55] That count also does not include those murdered during the bloody 1898 coup d'état in Wilmington—which claimed between 60 and 300 black lives— though it does include the 1929 murder of Ella May Wiggins, a white civil rights activist, during a labor protest. Nor does this accounting include attempted lynchings, and undoubtedly, the scores of unreported incidents that likely took place during and after Reconstruction. Just 29 of these victims were white and 8 were women. At least 6 were children. The overwhelming majority of victims, then, were African American men.[56]

In a 2013 article, historian Michael Trotti illuminated the challenges (and absurdities) inherent in counting lynchings.[57] The simple choice a scholar might make to measure lynching frequency by raw count instead of rates in relation to population can have a significant effect on what southern lynching patterns look like. Achieving a raw count is at best difficult, especially during Reconstruction and Redemption. Worse, it is overly reliant on white supremacist newspapers and their interests. Perhaps still worse, counting lynchings handles each lynching as one event, treating the lynchings of more than one person on one date as just one lynching and not as something bloodier, crueler, and with wider symbolic, social, and political resonance. Seeking to count lynchings is like counting pain—it is not entirely possible and it might not be a good idea to try because it can never account for the many varieties of human experience. If pain's complexity and intensity renders it "unsharable," as Elaine Scarry has argued, quantifying painful experiences further reduces their gravity.[58]

The issues raised by Trotti can be extrapolated to counting executions. The swift electrocution of an African American father and property owner, himself eligible to sit on a capital jury; the horrifyingly distended asphyxiation of a mentally disturbed African American teenager; the public hanging of a known ruffian and domestic abuser: these executions, each counting as one event, had immeasurably different effects on the executed persons and their families, on those who viewed the execution, and those who read about it. And of course the crimes for which they were executed had varied and painful effects on the victims' families and communities. Yet we count executions. We count them because rates and numbers are how we have historically sought to understand crime and punishment, and the comparison of historic and contemporary numbers allows us to draw some conclusions about trends. We count them because states count them. We count them because we do not yet have an alternative. And we count them because, just as anti-lynching activists believed in the 1940s, we know that one number is of huge significance: zero.

One alternative to counting is local history. The most finely grained and complete study of lynching in North Carolina remains historian Claude A. Clegg III's *Troubled Ground*, which examines the state's lynching history through the lens of the horrific 1902 and 1906 lynchings of five men and boys. Clegg demonstrates that although North Carolina was not the site of as many lynchings as its southern neighbors, the state's social and political infrastructure built and was subsequently buoyed by an ideology that encouraged systematic violence against African Americans. Emerging after the Civil War, this culture was widespread and robust enough to generate the 1898 coup that, with the active participation of the state's most widely read newspaper, the *News and Observer*, and at least five future governors— Charles Aycock, Robert Glenn, Locke Craig, Thomas Bickett, and Cameron Morrison—deposed, in a spasm of violence, the government of the city of Wilmington. As Clegg argues, with the complicity of politicians, collusion by law enforcement, and hysterical, racist demagoguery by the press, "a custom of such violence became further institutionalized."[59] This institutionalization was enduring enough that as late as 1957, an African American man imprisoned on suspicion of burglary was "whisked" away from the jail in Statesville, North Carolina, and confined in a secret location lest local anger turn lethal.[60]

North Carolinians can take little comfort from the fact that their state's lynching total is significantly lower than in Deep South states, for instance, or in the Southwest. Lynching in North Carolina was widespread enough to mean that African Americans from the sparsely populated western part of the state to the majority-black enclaves of the Northeast had good reason to fear it.[61] During the same time period, the state executed 315 people, or about twice as many as were lynched, almost all of whom were also black men. There were, however, some years when the number of lynchings far exceeded executions, such as 1869, when one legal execution and twenty-three lynchings took place, and 1888, in which ten lynchings occurred and no legal executions.[62]

If we follow Arthur Raper's formulation that lynchings took place in remote spaces—geographically, socially, and politically—then lynching would appear as the rural corollary to execution. The counties in North Carolina with the most executed persons, Orange and Durham, are home to the state's major public university (University of North Carolina at Chapel Hill, in Orange County) and one of the state's largest cities (Durham, in Durham

County). The counties with the highest lynching totals are Greene, a fairly rural, not particularly wealthy county near the Atlantic Coast, and Moore, a somewhat more densely populated county today known for its golf courses. But lynchings and executions appear haphazardly in time and space and there simply were not enough of either between 1865 and 1941 to create the weight needed for certainty; to echo the state's attorney general in an 1895 report to the governor, it is unwise to "draw conclusion from such meager data."[63] Greene County, for instance, earned its dubious distinction with the lynching of seven alleged rapists by so-called Regulators in 1867. Another lynching occurred in 1869, but then not again until 1917.

Conventional counts do not, but perhaps should, include attempted lynchings or deaths not deemed lynching at the time, such as that of Tom Bradshaw. In the summer of 1927, Bradshaw escaped police custody and for a time eluded a mob of police and private citizens, dubbed a posse by the press. But his pursuers eventually found and killed him. A coroner examined Bradshaw's body where it fell five hours after his death. According to newspaper accounts, the mob had dispersed but a crowd of two hundred materialized as the coroner made his examination, concluding that Bradshaw likely died from shock and exhaustion—and gunshot wounds. Some locals took photographs with handheld cameras. "As to who shot him," one reporter wrote, "there was silence, a deep understanding silence, one might almost say a satisfied silence."[64] Another concluded, "At any rate there has been no lynching, or any unseem[ly] violence, or any record of it entered in the annals of the county."[65]

Well into the twentieth century, lynchings remained the most frequent lethal sanction against African Americans that we know about. Between the end of the Civil War and the onset of state-administered executions in 1910, lynchings outnumbered legal hangings.[66] This period gave North Carolinians a chance to continue punishing African Americans for real and perceived bad behavior even as it sought to build legitimacy for its formal criminal justice system. As long as lynchings continued, which they did in North Carolina at least until World War II, the starkly racist death penalty was always the preferable option and North Carolinians' focus remained on the form, not the function, of lethal punishment. But more important, it meant that the state's dominant lethal sanction, the form of punishment it relied on as its most forceful response to deviant behavior, was lynching. As the death penalty grew into maturity after it was centralized and technologized in the early decades of the twentieth century, it overwhelmingly continued to punish the same people (African Americans) for the same crimes (murder, rape, burglary) against the same people (white victims) as did lynching.

## Lynchings and the Death Penalty: Alvin Mansel, Larry Newsome, and Harvey Lawrence

There is ample evidence that many North Carolina communities indeed understood lynching and legal executions as two styles of death penalty that worked individually or even in conjunction to attain a desirable result. The case of Alvin Mansel offers one such example. In 1925, Mansel was arrested on suspicion of the rape of a white woman near Asheville, North Carolina, in the Blue Ridge Mountains. A mob laid siege to Asheville's jail to get Mansel, doing considerable damage, but wily deputies had secreted the prisoner to Charlotte to await trial.[67] When the deputies returned with Mansel and a suspect in another crime for trial, they did so with two carloads of National Guardsmen, who escorted Mansel into the courtroom through throngs of white observers who had arrived early seeking seats inside. Black residents of Asheville had been urged by community leaders to stay out of sight.[68] The presiding judge ordered night sessions, and "in this matter," wrote one journalist, "the machinery of the court was speeded up."[69]

Mansel was tried in the presence of National Guardsmen armed with bayoneted rifles and convicted despite considerable evidence of his innocence: witness testimony suggested he could not have had the time to commit the rape, and while the victim described her assailant as a thirty-five-year-old dark-skinned black man, Mansel was light-skinned and just seventeen years old. Mansel's attorneys, funded by the African American community in Asheville, laid out the case for his innocence before the North Carolina Supreme Court, arguing that the verdict was directed not by the evidence in the case but by the threat of lynching:

Under the circumstances, we respectfully submit that the prisoner did not have a fair trial; that it was impossible in the presence of armed Militia to remove the idea from the public generally, including the jury, that the court was simply protecting the defendant to the end not that he should have a fair trial, but, that the law should have its course and that the law should execute him instead of the mob. The whole atmosphere of the Court House spoke out and said: "Let the law have him. It will do what ought to be done and let individuals stand back and let it have its way."[70]

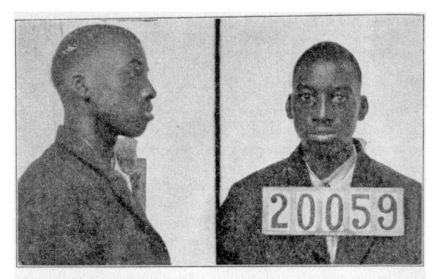

```
Prisoner:   Negro.   b. Pickens, S. C., July 10, 1909
Charge:   Rape
Sentence:   Death
Sentence Commuted to Life Imprisonment
Mental Diagnosis:   Feeble-minded
                    Chronological Age:   18 Years (1927)
                    Mental Age:   8 Years, 6 Months
                    Intelligence Quotient:   53.
```

A possible image of Alvin Mansel, as pictured in State Board of Charities and Public Welfare, *Capital Punishment in North Carolina*. Mansel survived a lynching attempt and a death sentence for a rape conviction, ultimately serving five years in a prison camp before being released.

The court rejected Mansel's appeal, but his apparent innocence attracted a good deal of attention: four thousand Buncombe County residents, including the rape survivor herself, wrote to Governor Angus McLean asking for clemency.[71] McLean listened and commuted Mansel's sentence to life imprisonment, writing, "I can think of no act more serious than the commission of or the crime of rape except the taking of life of an innocent person either with or without due process of law."[72] Soon Mansel's life sentence was reduced to a thirty-year term, and in October 1930, he left prison on parole.[73] He joined a family baking business in his hometown of Pickens, South Carolina, married, and started a family. Having been saved from death twice, once at the hands of a mob and once by law, Mansel died in 2001 after working as a doorman at the United Nations building in Manhattan, 825 miles and 76 years distant from his death sentence.[74]

In 1927, two years after Alvin Mansel's conviction, another black man suffered through a hostile death penalty process. Larry Newsome was attacked by relatives of his alleged victim during his murder trial. The Superior Court judge fired a pistol into the ceiling of the courthouse to break up the scrum. Newsome was hustled from the courthouse by armed sheriff's deputies while the judge trained his pistol on the would-be lynchers.[75] Represented by attorneys who declared during the trial that they were not defending him voluntarily, Newsome was convicted and sentenced to death but received a new trial on a technicality.[76] The mob then followed him to the new trial location, demanding of the new judge, "'Will you promise us if we don't kill him that he will be convicted and hanged?'" The judge would make no such promise, but again Newsome received a guilty verdict and a death sentence. Larry Newsome was a twenty-four-year-old African American man from Wayne County, North Carolina, not far from Raleigh. He had married his wife, the former Bertha Dobson, just the previous year.[77] He was executed in the electric chair in September 1928.

The case of Harvey Lawrence offers another example of the influence of lynch mobs on the course of legal sentencing. According to newspaper accounts, in April 1930, in rural Hertford County, North Carolina, a white couple allegedly discovered an African American man in their bedroom. The aged husband, who was convalescing in bed, managed to rouse himself and beat the attacker with his cane. When the sheriff arrived to investigate the break-in, the wife produced what she said was the attacker's hat; it was embroidered with the name "Harvey Lawrence." Soon, the sheriff arrested Lawrence, who sported a newly inflicted injury to his head, apparently received during the break-in, though Lawrence professed no memory of the incident.

Fearing a lynching attempt, the sheriff took Lawrence to the State Prison in Raleigh, rather than jailing him in Hertford County's jail in Winton. Confining an African American suspect in Raleigh's more secure State Prison was a common practice throughout the nineteenth and twentieth century in North Carolina. Suspects were described as being taken to Raleigh for "safekeeping," a phrase—initially used by sheriffs and other law-enforcement officers to describe the practice of jailing enslaved runaways until their enslavers paid out a reward and collected them—used to describe the imprisonment of suspects awaiting trial to this day.[78] A special term of court convened to try Lawrence and, anticipating a lynching attempt, local authorities secured the services of twenty-eight National Guardsmen.[79] The trial, conducted in the shadow of the lynching tree, concluded swiftly: after twenty minutes of deliberation, the jury of twelve white men had handed Lawrence a guilty verdict on the charge of first-degree burglary. The conviction carried a mandatory death sentence, and Lawrence, who according to newspaper reports was either seventeen or nineteen years old, was sentenced to death.[80]

In its appeal, Lawrence's defense argued that the presence of the armed soldiers created a "martial atmosphere" that swayed the jury to convict the defendant. "The populace here are evidently so satisfied of his guilt that they are ready to kill him here and now," the defense explained, before describing the jurors' mindset: he surely must be guilty of a capital offense, otherwise their demands could not be so pronounced. They want him killed; and if we do not find him guilty of a capital offense so that he may be legally executed, then we have made a gross miscarriage of justice, and the populace will hold us in contempt. To save our own reputations we must by our verdict take his life. Therefore we, for our verdict, find the accused guilty as charged, which finding carried with it a legal death sentence; and we have saved the State a lynching![81] The description suggests that attorneys saw them as related, even in the absence of evidence of a statistically sound relationship between lynchings and legal execution. The "one" death sentence replaced the "one" lynching for a single individual, as opposed to a functioning state or regional replacement. The attorneys' appeal also reveals the remarkable contortions that white southerners performed to justify a regime of racial violence under the law. In order to preserve the law a jury must disregard it; it must create the conditions for one kind of violence in order to prevent another. Jurors viewed the presence of the militia not as an effort to protect a defendant from the mob, but from the threat posed by the defendant or even to jurors who did not return the desired verdict. The North Carolina Supreme Court denied the appeal.[82]

Alvin Mansel, Larry Newsome, and Harvey Lawrence were of course not the only African American men facing lynching who instead received death sentences in the presence of the very mobs that sought their extermination. Newspaper coverage and trial transcripts provide an incomplete picture of the lynching threat that suspected rapists faced, but from the early 1900s to the late 1930s, at least eleven of the twenty-five black men executed for attacks on white women evaded mobs before their arrest or were saved from lynching by law-enforcement officers. One important difference between lynchings and executions in North Carolina was that executions took place when members of local law enforcement refused to cooperate

Prisoner: Negro. b. Wilson County, N. C., November, 1905(?)
Charge: Rape and Murder
Sentence: Death
Electrocuted Sept. 28, 1928
Mental Diagnosis: Subnormal in General Intelligence and
Decidedly Psychopathic
Chronological Age: 23 Years (1928)
Mental Age: 5 Years, 6 Months
Intelligence Quotient: 34.

A possible image of Harvey Lawrence. State Board of Charities and Public Welfare, *Capital Punishment in North Carolina*, detailed Lawrence's many disadvantages, including poverty, a lack of education, and a family history of mental incapacity.

with the mob; when they cooperated, someone was lynched.[83] There was, according to one Superior Court judge, a right way and a wrong way to administer criminal justice.[84] North Carolina newspapers occasionally denounced these hurried proceedings using a term that would gain coinage among activists. In 1920, O. J. Pederson, the editor of the *Sampson Democrat* in tiny Clinton, North Carolina, condemned the "virtual legal lynching" of an African American murder suspect. "It is simply lynching under legal form," he lamented.[85]

## Mobs Explain Themselves: Protecting White Women

The impulse for these "lynchings under legal form" and for mob lynchings flowed from the same source: the poisonous gendered dynamics of interracial contact. In her remarkable *Revolt Against Chivalry*, historian Jacquelyn Dowd Hall illuminated the development of the gendered narrative about lynching and the ways in which activists such as Jessie Daniel Ames tried to engage with it and reject it. Correctly surmising that white southerners would scarcely be swayed by appeals about the suffering of African American victims, Ames sought to persuade her audiences that lynching had nothing to do with protecting white women. She pushed back against a vast body of material averring the opposite. Among the chorus of voices that asserted the need to protect the virtue of white women from the animalistic passions of black men, which included editorialists, politicians, orators, and others, were the members of the lynch mobs themselves. The mobs maintained the pretext of anonymity, never speaking directly to the press, but they could rely on the press to amplify messages they left pinned to the bodies of their victims.

It was an open secret in the lynching South that interracial rape was not in fact the dominant factor in lynchings. The data easily refute the claim, shoring up the work of Ida B. Wells-Barnett and later Jessie Daniel Ames and her Association of Southern Women for the Prevention of Lynching, that lynching was necessary for protecting white female virtue or even avenging it with any great frequency. Suspected murder was overwhelmingly the mob's explanation for what they did. Of the lynchings in North Carolina for which we have some sort of explanation, thirty-four appear to have been prompted by murder, while twenty-six were in response to suspected rape or attempted rape.[86] These North Carolina numbers are echoed by national totals: white mobs most often targeted black men they accused of murder. The same is true of capital punishment: most executions followed convictions for first-degree murder. But the capital code also ostensibly existed to protect white female virtue. A rape conviction also carried a mandatory death sentence, as did a conviction for first-degree burglary, a crime that to hysterical whites carried the stain of sexual malevolence.

Mobs' obsession with co-policing white female and black male sexuality was echoed by capital punishment statutes as written and more so as practiced. The American colonies brought the bloody English code with them as they established early governments, but in North Carolina no one was executed for sassing their parents, for instance, or for stealing horses, both of which were capital crimes under the law. Following their loss in the Civil War, southern states rewrote their constitutions and criminal codes, both to respond to the federal government's preconditions for joining the Union and to seek methods for compelling newly free black labor. Included in North Carolina's constitution was a streamlined death penalty. Initially proscribing death for murder only, an amendment mandated a death penalty for conviction on four charges: murder, rape, burglary, and arson.[87]

Editorialists, even those who saw lynching as a blot on the state's reputation, often explained it as a symptom of the failure of this capital punishment infrastructure to meet the needs of the white community. After the gruesome lynching of three African American people in Salisbury in 1906, the *Union Republican* posted a short piece that identified the "remedy" for lynching: "upholding the laws, avoidance of delays, too many technicalities."[88] Indeed, North Carolina's elites, as represented by the editors of its many newspapers, were united not only in their condemnation of lynching but their belief that it stemmed from inadequacies of the criminal justice system, not to mention that it was a natural response to the tendency of black men to rape white women. Halting the occurrence of lynching was reliant, so the argument went, on black communities controlling the behavior of their criminal element and white communities supporting an efficient and certain criminal justice system.

## The Sanctity of the Home: The Death Penalty for Burglary

The death penalty for rape and burglary might have been heir to lynching culture had it not coexisted with the practice. Lynchings conducted in the imagined defense of white female virtue or as an enraged response to a real or invented attack operated in concert with statutory law, which identified rape and burglary as among the state's most heinous crimes. The fear of black male sexuality and the fetishistic obsession with white female virtue animated both lynching and the death penalty until, as lynching receded, the death penalty became the sole lethal sanction for interracial sexual contact.

The state's enduring commitment to harshly punishing sexual contact between African American men and white women extended to its treatment of executions for burglary. The standard for a first-degree burglary conviction, established by English common law, was intent: a burglar breaks into a dwelling place at night in order to commit a felony.[89] Those executed for burglary in North Carolina were always black, their victims were always white, and the crimes that resulted in executions almost always carried the hint of interracial sexual violence. First-degree burglary criminalized the presence of black men in homes occupied by white women. The connection between burglary and sexual threat was so strong that one condemned burglar won a commutation after Governor Locke Craig determined that there was "no element of rape in this case."[90]

The death penalty for burglary was widespread in the United States for many years, but by the mid-twentieth century, only Alabama, Delaware,

Kentucky, and North Carolina maintained that crime's capital status.[91] Until 1941 in North Carolina, first-degree burglary carried a mandatory death sentence. Thereafter, jurors could recommend a life sentence after conviction. Relatively few burglars died in North Carolina between 1909 and 1961: just ten men were executed for the crime, including three after the statutory change. Even if execution for burglary was rare, it was symbolically significant.

There is an enduring belief among law-enforcement professionals that a capital burglary statute protected "the sanctity of the home."[92] But only white homes, and the white women who lived in them, were sacred in North Carolina. In most cases in North Carolina, burglary amounted to the capitalization of attempted rape or the suspicion thereof, giving communities the opportunity to punish a black man for sexual aggression toward a white woman, but leaving a record of the white woman's intact virtue. *State v. Langford* gave solicitors and jurors considerable latitude by designating first-degree burglary as "the breaking and entering into the mansion house of another in the night time with the intent to commit some felony within the same, whether such intent be executed or not."[93] The latter portion of this definition allowed juries to guess at whether or not an indicted burglar intended to commit a crime worse than theft.

Of the eleven men who were executed for burglary in North Carolina in the twentieth century, seven died for a crime that contained suggestions of a sexual attack. A burglary charge might save the victim from the pain of testifying about a rape, and it seems likely that burglary was used as a proxy, as in the case of Willie Cherry, executed in October 1947. Cherry "shocked Eastern North Carolina" with his crime, and was indicted on two capital charges, the *News and Observer* noted, in a flush of modesty, without naming the second one.[94] Thirty years before, the newspaper showed even more restraint in reporting the execution of Lawrence Swinson, who died for burglary but had "several counts" against him.[95] In 1917, Lee Perkins was discovered in the bedroom of a young white woman. Two months later, he died in the electric chair.[96]

## Quick to Take a White Woman's Word: The Death Penalty for Rape

In 1977, the United States Supreme Court invalidated the death penalty for the rape of an adult woman, ruling that it constituted cruel and unusual punishment. Before the United States Supreme Court's 1977 ruling that a death sentence for the rape of an adult woman violated the Eighth Amendment, scores of Americans were executed for first-degree rape.[97] Into the 1960s, rape was a capital crime in fifteen states, nearly all of them in the South, and it was a federal capital felony as well. One study found that between 1930 and 1963, nearly 90 percent of those executed for rape in the region were black. North Carolina was a leader in executing black men for rape during this period, putting forty-one to death, compared to just four whites. Only Oklahoma and Georgia executed more people for rape.[98]

The use of the death penalty as a response to the specific or general threat of lynching suggests that North Carolina, with the avowed anti-lynching stance of its governors, was using rape executions to forestall lynchings spurred by suspicion of sexual violence. The specter of interracial rape dominated the imaginations of white men, many of whom imagined that interracial sexual contact constituted an assault on the white community.[99] A rape accusation against a black man by a white woman might spark a lynching, but if it was resolved in the court room, the accused was unlikely to encounter a sympathetic jury. For instance, one observer in 1929 noted that the jury trying Ed Dill "confronted by a choice between the testimony of a woman against him, and a formidable alibi attested by many negroes and the brother-in-law of the alleged victim, believed the unsupported testimony of the woman."[100] The African American newspaper the *Carolinian* called a rape charge by a white woman against an African American man the equivalent of an automatic death sentence.[101]

Between the end of the Civil War and 1910, when the state took control of executions from sheriffs, twenty-four men were executed for rape, just one of them white, a man who raped his own daughter.[102] In the cases in which race-of-victim information is available, the rape convictions that resulted in death sentences for black men involved white victims except in one case, when the victim was a child.[103] After delocalization, the number of African American men executed for rape jumped. Between 1910 and 1950, when the last such execution took place, North Carolina executed sixty-seven men for rape, almost 20 percent of the 356 people who were executed during this period. Nearly all of them were African Americans, and nearly all of them were convicted of attacks on white women. One 1929 study found that between 1910 and 1929, rape accounted for nearly a quarter of criminal convictions of African American men, versus just 4 percent for whites.[104]

There were very few exceptions to this rule of using the death penalty to punish African American sexual contact—or the suspicion thereof—on white women. Between 1910 and 1950, just five African American men died for raping African American victims. Their executions demonstrated that the death penalty for the rape of a black person was used only when the attacker had demonstrated particular desert, such as with long criminal records or the rape of a child.[105] After one such execution in 1937, the *News and Observer* implied that the prisoner was executed for the sum of a lifetime of crime, including a sexual assault on his eleven-year-old sister and a number of other women.[106]

White men, of course, received milder treatment. According to one journalist, "The best ticket a man [on death row] can hold is that of being a white man."[107] In the state's history, no white man was ever executed for raping a black woman, substantiating social scientist John Dollard's 1937 claim that African American women fell "into the category of unprotected women."[108] Furthermore, every white man who died for rape—there were just five of them—was convicted of an attack on a child. The first white man to die for rape did so ten years after the state took charge of executions, and there was a nearly twenty-year gap between the second and third such executions. North Carolina's black community bitterly complained about the state's failure to protect their women from white men, a passivity that "crucified justice on a cross of racial prejudice," and, they cautioned, taught white people a dangerous disregard for the law.[109]

Even white men convicted of rape benefited from vigorous efforts to remove them from death row; their black counterparts often died alone and rarely secured effective counsel. Take for instance Smithfield native Churchill Godley, who in 1920 became the first white man to die for rape in North Carolina. His victim was a nine-year-old girl, yet his wife and friends made "heroic efforts" to save his life. Their pressure spurred Governor Thomas Bickett, a former prosecutor, to give the case "'every possible consideration.'" In response to petitions from Johnston County and the urging of Godley's attorney, Bickett granted Godley a thirty-day reprieve for a psychological evaluation.[110]

Meanwhile, Bickett himself traveled to Smithfield, where he spoke with Godley's victim to assure himself that her testimony was credible. He asked the girl if she would "'tell Jesus just exactly what you are telling me now.'" The girl replied that she would, and Bickett decided not to intervene in Godley's execution. The *News and Observer* printed the text of his decision in full. The exceptional attention that the governor and the press gave to Godley's case, especially given Godley's partial confession, reveals the extraordinary consideration afforded to some white criminals, particularly when convicted of committing a crime branded as black. Bickett agreed, and used his decision to shore up the fiction that the death penalty in North Carolina was unblemished by racial prejudice:

> A great many good men have besought me to commute [Godley's] sentence, and I want these men to put to their own conscience this question: if a negro had been accused of committing this identical crime, and had been convicted upon the identical testimony offered against Godley, would these men ask for executive interference in behalf of the negro? It is my opinion that they would not. Justice and mercy know no color line, and when the governor is called upon to exercise the highest and most solemn duties of his office he must measure out justice and mercy alike with an even hand, to white and black alike.[111]

Godley died in the electric chair a week later, angry and denying the existence of God.[112]

Three more white men were executed for rape before the practice ended with the execution of Claude Shackelford on July 21, 1950. By 1950, with the threat of interracial rape receding, North Carolina's mandatory death sentence for rape had been defanged: juries were empowered to issue a binding recommendation for life sentences for first-degree rapists.[113] But Shackelford, who was the first man to die in North Carolina under a sentence imposed by a female judge, failed to win such a recommendation. Governor W. Kerr Scott maintained a careful vigil over Shackelford, once granting him a reprieve less than ten minutes before his scheduled execution when he heard of the appearance of new evidence as to the condemned man's guilt. The ten-year-old victim had signed a statement disavowing her testimony, but, it turned out, had been tricked.[114] He died in the gas chamber.

Capital rape dramatized the power of white women and, still greater, the power of the white men who charged themselves with white women's protection. In 1938, the black-owned *Carolina Times* complained about the lethal power of the white woman's word. After African American Frank Blackwell was jailed following an accusation of rape by a white teenager, the paper opined, "It is plainly another case of a white woman's word being used instead of simple reasoning and thorough investigations on the part of those who have the strings of law and justice around their fingers."[115] But white women could not always control the aftermath of such an accusation. Just days before Blackwell's confinement, the *Times* had noted that a white woman was unsuccessfully trying to recant testimony she delivered against an African American man condemned to death for burglarizing her home. "The same law that is quick to take a white woman's word when she condemns a Negro of such a crime should be equally as quick to take it when she attests to a Negro's innocence," the editor argued.[116] That the law failed to balance its lethal response to white female testimony with occasional restraint reveals that white women's power in this instance ebbed once the accusation left her lips.

## Too Formal, Too Abstract: Lynching and the State

Even as the death penalty system responded to the prerogatives of the mob, lynch mobs often signaled that they did what they did because of that system's inadequacies or sluggishness. Although many lynchings involved whites who, in the words of W. E. B. DuBois, mistook "self-reliance for insolence" and lashed out against political, social, or economic transgressions, the overwhelming majority followed the alleged or fabricated commission of what the criminal justice system might deem a crime if given the chance, such as rape, murder, or burglary.[117] Members of the mob, whether in preparation for the lynching or in post facto justification, often understood themselves as agents of justice avenging a crime the law was failing to address. Members of one mob pinned a note to the breast of their victim that read, "We take executive power in this case and hang this man, because the written law provided no adequate penalty for the crime. And be it understood, we have done this act and will repeat it under similar circumstances."[118]

This tendency of white mobs to perceive themselves as agents of justice reflects a national trend. As historian Michael Pfeifer demonstrates, "Whites who murdered African Americans . . . made a statement about the law." It was "too formal, too abstract, and too concerned with process" to meet the requirements of Jim Crow subjugation.[119] Their actions, as sociologist David Garland puts it, constituted "state sovereignty contested."[120] Taking Garland's claim one step farther, lynching both contested state sovereignty by doubly demonstrating the weakness of its institutions, which could not meet popular demand for lethal punishment nor prevent the lynching itself, and by strengthening the broader white supremacist system by terrorizing African American communities. It was only with routine Ku Klux Klan lynchings that Redemption government took hold in North Carolina; it was after an orgy of violence in Wilmington's 1898 coup that a white supremacist regime was installed in state government.

Members of lynch mobs were straightforward about their lack of faith in the formal system of law. For instance, in late December of 1885 a mob of masked men seized John Lee, who had been accused of murder, from jail. After killing Lee, one of the mob's members was collected enough to pen a note in a "business-like hand," writing, "'Merry Christmas and Happy New Year. To this tree hangs the body of John Lee. Until the packing of juries ceases this process of justice will be sought.'" Below the body lay a note with a request: "The editors of *The Rocket* and the *Spirit of the South* please copy."[121] The note demonstrated the mob members' absence of guilt, their rationality, their confidence that they had the support of the local press, and lynching's role in a public relations campaign to influence the legal system.

Lee was white, and indeed, white mobs who lynched white victims were likely to do so, if we credit their own explanations, because of their sense of inability of the law to punish them effectively. A mob of approximately one hundred people who lynched a white man who was witnessed, naked, in an attempt to sexually assault a child, pinned a card to the hanged man's coat with the following message:

We hang this man, not in passion, but calmly and deliberately, with a due sense of the responsibility we assume. We take the executive power in this case, and hang this man in accordance with the law of the land, because written law provides no penalty adequate to his crime. And be it understood, that we who have done this act will repeat it under similar provocation.

THE PEOPLE'S COMMITTEE.[122]

Coverage in the *Greensboro North State* betrayed the contortions taking place in the state as lynching numbers rose in the late 1800s. After publishing a prurient account of the assault, printing the letter in full, and averring the flimsiness of the legal response to attempted rape, the paper devoted four paragraphs to decrying lynching as a source of "destruction . . . strife and sorrow."[123] In condemning lynching as antithetical to the intentions of a modern state even as it lauded the mob for committing their murder "coolly and deliberately" the newspaper itself revealed both the impulse to act on a subculture of violence and suspicion, operating in opposition to state government, and the legitimacy of government itself. This posture suggests, perhaps surprisingly, that white mobs were in fact more confident that the law could handle African American deviants than white ones, that they had successfully trained formal law enforcement, with the threat of lynching, to act swiftly and with deadly force in response to serious crimes, or the perception thereof, committed by African Americans. If this is true, it might explain the decline of lynching after the mid-1930s, when deep economic suffering and attendant anxieties interrupted the phenomenon's decline.

If the torturous, psychosexual murder of black men was a strange way to remind African Americans of the superiority of whites, so too was it a strange way to enforce the rule of law. Yet far from undermining the law, lynching gave legitimacy to the more restrained but also racist death penalty system, making even the smallest gestures of restraint—such as permitting a demonstrably innocent black man to be tried for rape and sentenced to death rather than hanged without due process by a mob—signs of the beneficence and orderliness of Jim Crow justice. Lynch mobs, thinking they were reacting against the sluggish state's neglect of white prerogative, in fact gave the state's deeply racist, faltering, inconsistent, profit-driven penal system a reputation boost. This mindset was widely shared. For instance, the prosecutor in Will Exum's 1904 trial for murder told the jury that "lynching would be the result" if they did not hand down a guilty verdict, saying, "Strike down the strong arm of the law, and bloodshed will run riot in the land."[124]

The counter-narrative, one of many employed by white elites (and black elites, though they were more concerned about the impact of lynching on black people, their families, and their communities), was that lynchings advertised the weakness of local and state government and the unsuitability of white southerners to call themselves United States citizens at a time when many southerners hoped they were beginning to leave behind the shame of their loss in the Civil War. It is not an unpersuasive argument, and it fit well within the narrative laid out by anti-lynching activists, who warned southerners about how other Americans and those around the world saw them through the distorting prism of lynch law. But white southerners did not need to be convinced that people were paying attention to what they were doing when they lynched African Americans. On the contrary, they understood lynchings as public events whose ripples spread well beyond the space where they took place. Amy Wood has demonstrated the extent to which mobs and their enablers documented, disseminated, and even commoditized images of lynchings in order to extend their reach beyond the borders of their communities.[125] These images may have shocked many who encountered them, but more important, they normalized the "damnation, defilement, and dismemberment" of black bodies.[126]

Law-enforcement officers not uncommonly believed in the value of lynching, too. Although many sheriffs ably defended their prisoners and their sense of duty against lynch mobs and saved many lives as a result, law-enforcement officers often participated in lynchings in various ways before, during, and after the killing. Their actual participation in the murder was not necessary, but their cooperation before and afterward was essential, even if it meant only looking the other way when the mob removed their victim from his jail cell and in the aftermath of the killing, when investigations, if begun, were allowed to trail off without result. For instance, in 1927 an African American murder suspect named Tom Bradshaw collapsed and died after fleeing a mob of men and baying dogs through the pine forests near Bailey, North Carolina. A crowd numbering two hundred milled about as the coroner conducted his investigation, concluding that Bradshaw died from a combination of shock, exhaustion, and gunshot wounds. No one who gathered could, or would, identify the shooter or even anyone who had joined the chase. One reporter noted that among the crowd "there was a silence, a deep understanding silence, one might almost say a satisfied silence."[127] Thank goodness, another reporter noted, "there has been no lynching."[128]

The complicity of the formal criminal justice system played out in the courtroom as well. When suspects were not killed, their trials, often during specially convened terms of court called to preclude further violence, moved with remarkable speed, exchanging a death sentence for good behavior and allowing members of the white community to congratulate themselves for letting the law take its course. "Courts in southern states," an editorial in the *Carolina Times* wryly observed in 1938, "are not always as careful as they might be when a Negro stands before them, for trial, especially when he is accused of rape."[129] A black man saved from white mobs by determined law-enforcement officers or promises from governors could expect the mob to reappear at his trial, and again at his execution, blurring the line between mob and state execution. For instance, in 1911, Norval Marshall, accused of rape, was pursued by a posse. Captured on September 17, two days later Marshall was indicted, assigned counsel, tried, convicted, and sentenced to death. On October 27, after a one-week delay because the prison superintendent was out of town, Marshall was electrocuted.[130]

Indeed, this was how members of mobs understood their actions, even if the so-called crime they punished amounted to no more than aspirations of upward mobility by the underclass. It is tempting to reject the mob's pretensions and call them murderers; it would not be wrong to do so. After all, lynching someone for whistling at a white woman, or for his success at his business, or for defending himself and his family against a terrorist attack can hardly be considered a form of criminal punishment. It would be more accurate, perhaps, to describe lynchings as modern journalists describe organized killings, as "execution-style" murders conducted with a recognizable form and rationale. Although mobs often lynched their victims in response to alleged crimes, they also acted in retaliation for violating a set of conveniently imagined principles. Setting aside the rare instances in which white mobs lynched whites or black mobs lynched blacks, victims of mob violence committed offenses against the white supremacist order. A lynching was the most extreme of a set of consequences for racial transgressions, an unusual and cruel reminder to African Americans of their precarious social and economic position in the South.

But there is more than one good reason to try to tweak just slightly lynching's place in the law-enforcement system in Jim Crow North Carolina, and indeed in the death penalty process. First, lynching was not strictly legal in Jim Crow North Carolina: murder, whatever form it took and whoever its victim, was forbidden by law. But Jim Crow dramatized daily the critical, even lethal, gap between legal and permissible. Yes, Governor Robert Glenn aggressively pursued some members of lynch mobs, yet his successor pardoned the only person convicted as a result.[131] In the 1920s, Governor Thomas W. Bickett ended the practice of arming National Guardsmen with rifles loaded with blanks, a change about which the members of a mob in Graham learned only after the Guardsmen shot dead two of their number.[132] Yet even in North Carolina, where elites sought to cultivate the appearance of the rule of law and where politicians like Governors Glenn and Bickett gave credence to that claim, lynching was an important part of a crime control system that existed to constrain and compel African American people and their labor and to make an example of those who crossed lines of custom and law.

Second, the very idea of extralegal punishment—a form of criminal punishment administered outside the traditional confines of law enforcement, yet with some gesture to it—assumes the long-standing presence of bright lines dividing formal and informal law enforcement. Public torture lynchings emerged as new phenomena in the New South, but historically, community-based law enforcement was normal, even essential. Jim Crow depended on community policing to enforce its complex, race-based rules; as one black minister reported after escaping a lynching, a white resident of Murphy, North Carolina, told him, "'People in Murphy have their own laws for niggers, and that's lynching.'"[133] Before then, the night riders of the Ku Klux Klan, whose ranks often included law-enforcement officers, reconstituted white authority damaged by the Civil War. During slavery, groups of whites, variously organized and sometimes dubbed "Negro whippers," hunted down enslaved people who had fled or been outlawed, killing them for a bounty, whipping them, or returning them to their enslavers.[134] Those enslavers enforced laws and rules themselves on their plantations and in their homes and had the authority to kill enslaved people deemed their property by law during such punishment. In the early 1890s, when race-based lynching was reaching its peak, newspaper coverage of the hangings of two death row prisoners took care to note that the executions were legal.[135]

Third, and perhaps the most real to those living in North Carolina between the late 1800s and 1930s, lynching was the mechanism white communities used to compel actors in the criminal justice system to conduct their business in a fashion and at a speed that met the needs of that community. To members of the mob, lynching was one of two ways to reach an inevitable outcome: the death of the alleged criminal. Whether or not a lynching was technically legal was immaterial. The threat appears to have worked. North Carolina's history reveals more than a few instances of trials hastily convened and conducted following a lynching attempt. A particularly illuminating case is that of Tom Gwyn, who was arrested in 1919 on suspicion of rape.

Gwyn, a black man, was arrested for the rape of a white teenaged girl near Hickory, North Carolina. After thwarting a lynching attempt, local law-enforcement officers kept their charge, twice moving Gwyn in secret when wind of mob action blew their way. Meanwhile, though, the question of Gwyn's guilt had been settled in the public imagination. "There is no longer any doubt," penned a local journalist, "that he was the guilty brute."[136] Governor Thomas Bickett summoned police from around the state and deputized twenty-five soldiers to protect Gwyn at trial. Gwyn was indicted in absentia and snuck into the courtroom for jury selection. Arguments concluded within two hours and at 3:10, the jury recessed to deliberate. Ten minutes later, they returned a guilty verdict, which carried a mandatory death sentence. Gwyn was executed in Raleigh forty days after his arrest.[137] Gwyn's case demonstrates that white communities saw lynching as a punishment that was less desirable or acceptable than a death sentence that led to an execution, but one they were willing to undertake. Between the turn of the twentieth century and the 1930s, at least eleven of the twenty-five black men executed for attacks on white women evaded mobs before their arrest or were saved from lynching by law-enforcement officers.[138]

The use of the death penalty between the end of the Civil War and the early twentieth century demonstrates the surprisingly small effect that cataclysmic war and the termination of the slave system as such had on application of the death penalty in the South. Enslavement ended, but for the formerly enslaved, the death penalty did not. Tellingly, the black codes drafted after emancipation quite literally directed readers to substitute the words "persons of color" for "slaves and free negroes."[139] In other words, in the absence of new laws, law-enforcement officers and the courts were to look back across the chasm of the Civil War when making life-and-death decisions about people of color.

### A Proxy for the Public: Lynching and the Death Penalty

Lynching and the death penalty declined together after the 1930s; the fruit of the same tree, they withered as the tree did. It is hard to say a phenomenon waxed or waned when at its peak it never reached an annual total of more than ten. But North Carolinians lynched just three people in the 1930s and no one between 1935 and 1941, when the state's last recorded lynching took place. Lynching's violence, however, continued to exert its influence. So-called hanging trees remained standing in towns and cities for decades, providing daily reminders of the incident and in at least one instance, a macabre make-out spot for young couples.[140] Despite these grim reminders, African American memories of lynchings remain underdocumented, in part because lynching's trauma was so profound that some African Americans who experienced it, directly or indirectly, remained unable or unwilling to discuss it.[141]

Lynching also declined because North Carolina's governors were remarkably active in seeking to punish members of lynch mobs. After an attempted lynching in Northhampton County in 1947, when a grand jury refused to indict seven white men based on evidence uncovered and presented by the State Bureau of Investigation, Governor R. Gregg Cherry unearthed a statute more than a half-century old and assigned a state Supreme Court justice to serve as a magistrate to hold a hearing on the case. The jury refused to convict the members of the mob, and the case aroused a good deal of anger toward Cherry in eastern North Carolina, indicating that lynchings did not decline because the belief in mob justice had waned.[142] The state's governors were prepared to make the state refrain from lynchings, even if its residents did not necessarily wish to do so: as Governor Cherry said in a 1947 address, "This is a civilized state. Lynching will not be tolerated within its borders."[143]

As sociologist David Garland has argued, the persistence of lynchings in the American South—and even well outside the South, as recent scholarship on lynching subcultures has demonstrated[144]—reveals America's divergence from its European forbears in the development of mature and restrained criminal justice systems. America's rhetorical and real reliance on the power of "the people" continued to legitimize mob action against deviants even as the court system slowly matured. Ironically, it was that maturation, including the advent of layers of appeals, public counsel, and other legal steps between arrest and execution, that further infuriated mob members. Opinion leaders explained mob violence as symptomatic of an unsatisfying legal process; over time that process grew less and less satisfying as it grew more and more complex. Lynching was entirely conversant with, and stood the test of time alongside, the maturation of formal criminal procedure, identified by some observers as "civilization."[145]

If either a reliable but slow or a swift and sure death penalty system might have served as a replacement for lynchings, we will never know. Lynchings began a slow decline in the 1930s and 1940s, and while racist violence persists today, the practice as North Carolinians knew it in the years after the collapse of Reconstruction was over by World War II. It ended not because of fear of reprisal, which rarely happened, or shame, which was notable only for its absence. It ended because systematic racial violence had insinuated itself into government, which no longer needed the people to threaten it into giving them satisfaction.

In 1936, the *Fayetteville Observer* noted in an editorial that in the twenty-two executions that took place that year, "The State . . . acted as proxy for the public which would have lynched them had there been no system of courts and punishments established."[146] Along the same time frame, the use of the death penalty declined. In 1941, the General Assembly had removed the mandatory death sentence from first-degree arson and burglary convictions; in 1949, it did the same for first-degree murder and rape. The number of death penalties and executions plummeted as new legislation allowed people charged with potentially capital crimes to accept a sentence of life without parole in exchange for a guilty plea. The last person slated to be executed in North Carolina before the modern era of Supreme Court interventions died in the gas chamber in 1961.

There is nothing particularly antimodern about lynching in the context of the Jim Crow South. Of course elites condemned the practice as barbaric, but as described in chapter 2, lynching was a tool that benefited elites as they consolidated political power. Lynching gave elites a touchstone against which to measure progress toward rational government, and it benefited them both when it took place and when it did not. Lynchings that occurred allowed elites to condemn the practice and offer the legal criminal justice system as an essential alternative to lawlessness. Lynchings that were prevented even more forcefully demonstrated the government's commitment to law and order. And lynchings that did not take place allowed state attorneys general and their bosses in the governor's mansion the chance to boast about maintaining order.

In 1935, the state reached a new high in the number of annual executions. As usual, most of those executed were African American men with white victims, including a number of men sentenced to death for minor burglaries. It was clear that the state was, like the mob, violently asserting domination over the black community. In doing so, the state and the mob were in competition for primacy in this essential Jim Crow function, and it was a competition that ultimately strengthened state legitimacy. As historian Ashraf H. A. Rushdy wrote of mobs in the post-Reconstruction South, into the 1930s in North Carolina, "Those who believed in their continued right to form mobs and kill black Americans did so now with an added intent of explicitly contesting the state's right to proscribe that ability."[147] But as lynching declined, it became clear that the state's monopoly of lethal force was successfully consolidating and spectacular mob violence fractured and transformed into the mundane daily violence of Jim Crow.

Lynching, perhaps counterintuitively, played an essential role in that consolidation. Ensuring that legal executions in the state of North Carolina did not resemble lynchings became an important driving force behind reform efforts in North Carolina's General Assembly in the late nineteenth century. As detailed in the following chapter, disorderly spectacle troubled elite reformers considerably more than the racial character of lynching or public hangings (a few unheeded voices spoke out against its obvious victimization of African Americans with white victims). North Carolina's governors, along with their southern peers, never outrightly claimed that the experimentation led the state to abandon hanging and embrace new modes of execution. Yet to adopt sociologist David Garland's phrasing, the death penalty they set up was a mirror image of lynching, "designed to be an antilynching."[148] This "antilynching" responded to the same social influences as lynching, including, importantly, the white fear of black male sexuality and white fear of what it meant for the white supremacist experiment in North Carolina.

## 2  Without Howling, Without Squirming

Reinventing the Death Penalty in Jim Crow
North Carolina, 1910–1936

By the turn of the century, there were few voices willing to defend public hanging and many rising to condemn it, as one editorialist did, as "not in . . . harmony with nineteenth century civilization."[1] Before the Civil War, however, northeastern intellectuals debated the role of execution in a growing nation. The Calvinist preacher George B. Cheever used his remarkable oratorical gifts to frame execution as an essential institution in a modern state. In an 1843 speech soon published word-for-word in New York newspapers and later edited and expanded into a published tract, Cheever described the death penalty as among the only barriers between humans' depraved natures and "rape, murder, chaos in the streets."[2] Cheever's biblical justification for the death penalty may have made it seem like an archaic punishment, if not a timeless one. But his emphasis on certainty, severity, and order addressed his audiences' fears about the instability of a modernizing democracy.[3]

In the American South, including North Carolina, many whites looked to lynch mobs to provide them with this certainty and severity. The courts, many believed, were gummed up with appeals and technicalities that impeded the swift passage of justice.[4] Yet these very technicalities demonstrated North Carolina's growth as a modern state bureaucracy: guarantees of appeals, the assignment of attorneys to represent indigent defendants, the slow arrival of skilled defense attorneys who took up cases as civil rights matters. Yet ultimately it was not the development of this infrastructure with which North Carolinians measured the modernity of the death penalty. Instead, they judged it on its spectacle, a defining feature of the state's twin death penalties, lynching and legal execution, at least until reformers intervened, transforming the effect while compounding the starkly racial nature of the death penalty.

This chapter argues that the main driver of death penalty reform in North Carolina in the first half of the twentieth century was fear of spectacle that would expose its leaders as incapable of the kind of control necessary for maintaining a modern state. Spurred by spectacle hangings in the late nineteenth and early twentieth centuries and by their racially mixed audiences, they sought to maintain the practice of execution by containing it. Crucially, they increasingly limited and managed the audiences allowed to watch executions, transitioning the death penalty from a broadly public ritual observed by mixed-race audiences to one conducted clandestinely before all-white audiences. In doing so, they deeply embedded the death penalty in modern North Carolina as a practice that expressed and enforced its core organizing principle: that North Carolina was a place where the race question, when not settled by other means, would be settled with lethal punishment, and where African Americans were subjects of, never participants in, community sanctions. If lynchings, as discussed in chapter 1, expressed the excesses of post–Civil War racial conflict, in the early twentieth century the death penalty system expressed white North Carolinians' desire to continue this violence in a more orderly space.

In doing so, the death penalty in North Carolina assumed the place of lynching at the apex of a suite of tools used to subjugate African Americans. To borrow from historian Grace Hale, over the course of the twentieth century, legal execution contributed to generating a "collective, all-powerful whiteness" while seeking to make "the color line seem modern, civilized, and sane."[5] State-run execution addressed the professionalization problem with public hangings, attempting to rationalize their disorder and unpredictability and to update the symbolism of the death instrument, replacing the noose with something more expressive of modernity, more "in the line of progress."[6] This new style of execution, contained as it was, managed to remain public thanks to detailed reporting that disseminated details of prisoners' deaths that might not have been visible to a member of a crowd of thousands at a hanging. Technologically advanced, state-run execution, then, evolved not just from the public hanging that was its legal predecessor but from the illegal lynchings that laid its ideological foundation. That legal execution could subsume lynching as the sole lethal punishment for African Americans—setting aside legal police and citizen shootings—demonstrates that white elites felt comfortable that the color line was bright. The death penalty, like the race question itself, was settled.

## Efficiency, Economy, and Rational Progress: Jim Crow North Carolina

Political leaders in early twentieth-century North Carolina sought to make the state a site of what historian George Tindall called "business progressivism." This posture encouraged academics and politicians to collaborate to rebuild and strengthen essential institutions, not tear them down.[7] Angus MacLean, who sat in the governor's mansion between 1925 and 1929, declared that his state aspired to "efficiency, economy, and rational progress" in all areas of public life, including the death penalty system.[8] In seeking to rebuild and strengthen the capital punishment infrastructure, politicians signaled its importance to a Jim Crow North Carolina in which the race question was "settled": African Americans were socially and intellectually inferior, according to this supremacist infrastructure, and while they deserved protection against excessive violence, they did not deserve protection from systematic discrimination or the vote.[9]

Public hangings cut against MacLean's vision of efficiency, economy, and rational progress. Between the end of the Civil War and the early years of the twentieth century, hangings were often hugely popular social events. In 1879, by one count, ten thousand people attended a hanging in the tiny town of Hillsborough, far exceeding its population.[10] News coverage of the hanging of Tom Dula—today remembered hanging his head as Tom Dooley in the folk song—described large crowds, "males and females, whites and blacks, many being on foot and many in carriages." These attendees revealed a "morbid" interest in hanging, the article's author judged, as "so general among the ignorant classes of society,"[11] and as they mingled freely, perhaps drinking illegal liquor, they upset elites' vision of a settled color line.

The county sheriffs who performed hangings had a difficult job: execute a condemned prisoner in a way that balanced appropriate gravity with a nod to satisfying the public, and in a way that avoided errors and ensured a swift and quiet death. This was no easy task and the stakes were high. The prominence hangings took in the social and cultural life of a community sprang from not only their gruesome spectacle but also their rarity. There were 158 hangings between the end of the Civil War and the advent of the electric chair in North Carolina in 1910. Sheriffs serving their two-year terms in North Carolina's approximately one hundred counties, then, had widely varying experiences with hangings. Some conducted no hangings at all; some conducted as many as three at once. For both executioner and executed, a hanging was more than likely a once-in-a-lifetime event.

Hangings' infrequency and importance led sheriffs to rely upon one another to share knowledge of how to competently conduct a hanging, including how to tie a hangman's knot. Sheriffs who hanged more frequently offered advice to those doing so for the first time, such as before an execution in Asheville, when the sheriff from Charlotte contributed knowledge, particularly about how to tie the noose. The sheriff of Rowan County attended the hanging to learn about the process in anticipation of replicating it himself.[12] In 1879, the sheriff of Brunswick County spent an hour with New Hanover County's sheriff, practicing tying hangman's knots.[13] And sheriffs often joined one another to lend a hand during executions. Sheriffs from five counties—six counting the one where the hanging took place— were present to assist in the execution of two African American prisoners in Salisbury in 1902.[14] In other instances, sheriffs from neighboring counties tied the hangman's knot for the presiding sheriff.[15] Some sheriffs opted to secure nooses around the prisoners' necks before they approached the scaffold, allowing them the time and privacy to do the job to their satisfaction. In 1901, Ned Sellers and Dave Brown, sentenced to death for rape, emerged from the Elizabethtown jail with nooses already around their necks.[16]

Nooses used in successful hangings traveled among sheriffs inside and outside North Carolina like totems against bungling. For instance, a noose used for an execution in Wake County was used by one sheriff there in 1883 and another sheriff in 1890. It then traveled to Moore County and was subsequently used in two executions in Guilford County. On the eve of a double hanging for the murder of a "Jew peddler" in Franklin County, one newspaper reported that the rope was en route to Orange County for the hanging of a convicted murderer and then on to Alamance, where it was to be used to hang a man sentenced to death for rape.[17] In 1895, in planning for his first hanging, the sheriff of Edgecombe County traveled to nearby Wake to "get 'points'" from its sheriff and borrow the rope. He also secured the services of an avowed expert to construct a scaffold.[18] In at least one instance a scaffold was shared in the same manner, transported from one county to another for a second use.[19]

Reusing the rope presented perhaps obvious risks. For instance, in November 1901 witnesses at the Fayetteville jail gathered to watch the hanging of Louis Council. They listened as a Catholic priest, standing on the platform, declared Council innocent. Then the rope broke when Council fell through the trap, sending him sprawling to the ground beneath the scaffold. Council "regained his feet," climbed the scaffold for a second time, and

Peter Smith addresses the approximately one thousand people who gathered to watch him hang in October 1904 following a death sentence for rape. "They are done kicking me around now and I am ready and thankful to go home now," he said. "I am not frightened. Guilty men are scared." *Hanging, Last Man Executed at Marshall, NC, in Madison County* (N2423) in the E. M. Ball Collection, D. H. Ramsey Library Special Collection, University of North Carolina Asheville 28804.

submitted himself for a second hanging. Beyond celebrating Council's remarkable composure, newspaper coverage noted that the broken rope had been secured from a nearby county after a previous use.[20] Just a few years later, another sheriff betrayed his concern about a broken rope when he commissioned a noose woven from fishing line.[21]

### A Crass, Primeval Impulse: Limiting Viewership

As early as 1868, North Carolina's lawmakers sought to make formerly public executions if not private, semipublic. That year, lawmakers passed An Act to Regulate Capital Executions "at the ends of justice, public morals, and the preservation of order."[22] The act directed that sheriffs perform hangings behind an enclosure, but most ignored the law for many years.[23] Even sheriffs who did construct enclosures did little to limit spectatorship. When

Ben Williams entered the enclosure behind the Wake County jail shortly after noon in December 1906, for instance, "the waiting throng in the jail yard surged behind him like the crowd clamoring at the tent-gate of a circus," the *News and Observer* reported. "Flattened against the fenced enclosure of the jail stood dense humanity still, full of eyes. They hang on buildings, packed motionless. They stood sharp-defined against the sky on telegraph poles, in trees. From them came a murmur that indicated their silence. It was a moment of the strange appeal of death to the living, the common spectacle which will ever find its audience. Unvoiced, but strong and sinister, there went forth from the black figure on the gallows to the brains of the watching crowd, the message, the shudder, of mystery, of awe."[24]

The following year, a reporter reprimanded Durham residents who gathered for the city's first hanging. "Durham has run up against a new experience," he wrote. "It is a sordid thing, which she has escaped: a crass, primeval impulse . . . Durham is morbid, without knowing it."[25] Residents gathered despite ice and snow, milling around the jail hoping to catch a glimpse of the two condemned men.[26] Not long after Ben Williams's hanging, Attorney General Robert D. Gilmer urged the General Assembly to direct that the execution of condemned prisoners be carried out in the State's Prison rather than in county jail yards. Not only would such a change diminish the "mock heroism" of the condemned, Gilmer wrote, but it would also assure "a speedy death at the hands of persons familiar with the work, rather than a bungling execution at the hands of sheriffs who are totally unfamiliar with hangings."[27]

As important as bungling in the minds of reformers was the social threat posed by these gatherings of mixed-race audiences who trampled the color line as they enjoyed the execution spectacle.[28] In the minds of segregationists, African Americans in particular might absorb counterproductive messages from executions, especially if the condemned used his last words for something other than prayer. Such was the case with African American prisoner Henry Bailey, who in 1906 mounted the gallows unassisted, dressed neatly in black, and addressed the crowd. "The drift of his remarks was the frequent injustice given in the trials of negroes and [he] said in his own case that had [his white victim] killed him there would never have been a hanging." Bailey died of strangulation twelve minutes after falling through the trap, but his final words doubtless reverberated through the largely African American crowd.[29]

According to white supremacist observers, the most insidious elements in these crowds were African American women. Demonizing black women, particularly poor black women, was common practice in the post–Civil War American South. Popularly depicted as savage and sensual, unbound by moral or sexual strictures, and dangers to the white household, black women were at best denied the privileges extended to white women. At worst, white society sought to deny them personhood altogether and, in a cruel echo of the pressure on black women to keep house in a less dramatic sense, blamed them for creating the intimidating black men many white supremacists feared.[30] The social and legal inequity generated by enslavement and reasserted after emancipation sought to force women of color, particularly working-class women, to the bottom of the social hierarchy and to diminish their personhood as victims under the law.[31]

They were commonly demonized in public, too. Summoning the specter of black crime, reformer and idealogue, Rebecca Latimer Felton implicated "the black whore . . . brazen in her denial of moral laws," who raises black boys to be rapists.[32] Poor women of color also faced criticism from some middle-class African American women who explained the condition of "depraved" black women by pointing to the viciousness of slavery and white men.[33] Middle-class black men joined this chorus when they publicly worried about black women leaving their homes to mingle in an interracial public sphere, while the exclusion of black men from political life and constraints on their public life actually offered opportunities for women of color to seize some political territory.[34] In the late nineteenth and early twentieth centuries, middle- and working-class women of color entered civic life in strength, forming suffrage and mutual aid societies and otherwise asserting their humanity, citizenship, and control over their labor.[35] Some of the successes of working-class black women were overt, such as unionization efforts; others were clandestine, such as work slowdowns.[36]

As educated, middle-class women of color formed associations to strengthen their civic and social bonds, public hangings created surprising sites of community-building and political engagement.[37] At these events, working-class women of color could gather to defend black men and in doing so defend their own role in creating the community that so threatened Felton and her ideological allies.[38] Much of the evidence of the presence of working-class women of color at the public hangings of African American men appears in newspaper coverage in white-owned papers bemoaning their presence. For instance, in 1895 an ostensibly hard-news article in the *Henderson Gold Leaf* decried the conduct of African Americans, "especially the women," at a hanging. The air "reverberat[ed] with shrieks and shouts as the trap fell," the florid piece observed, continuing, "right thinking persons" must have "felt that such a spectacle was a disgrace to a civilized community."[39] Beyond criticizing their behavior, an editorial in the *Wilmington Messenger* called black women "the most dangerous element in many communities." According to the *Messenger*, led by these women, people of color at hangings showed a "decided inclination . . . to take sides with rapists and to become turbulent in the expression of their leanings and sympathies."[40] In one sense, black women did pose a real threat to Jim Crow society, though not in the way Rebecca Latimer Felton thought. Their efforts were particularly important because of the many often violent efforts to mute black men of color, including the hangings themselves.[41] By asserting their personhood and that of black men, working-class women of color asserted their protective roles. Like their predecessors who "participated from the gallery" after the Civil War, black women at public hangings claimed civic space and in doing so upset white supremacists.[42]

If women of color were at the heart of the disorder of public hangings, they were at the heart of the rationale to eliminate them. Containing civic engagement by women of color cleared the public sphere for white women, and white women only, to perform their particular version of femininity. In Jim Crow North Carolina, this femininity included their high value as victims of crime, especially as perpetrated by black men, a perverse reversal of black women's vulnerability to assault by white men, remarked on by white supremacist and African American observers alike.[43] White women on the other hand, presuming their adherence to certain standards, were the recipients of a great deal of protective energy, sometimes lethally so.[44] By expelling women of color from public hangings, elites sought to reassert these hierarchies. If women of color held so little value as victims under the law, why should they have such a prominent role at executions? Moving executions from county to state authority would answer that question. The transition expressed the state's aspiration to efficiency, and one made possible by a newly available source of lethal power: electricity.

### Westinghoused: The Advent of Electrocution

In the early twentieth century, electricity was in wide use as a therapy, used by doctors attempting to treat diverse ailments such as sciatica, gout, and arthritis. Its less curative properties were starkly illustrated when, in 1881, a drunk Buffalonian staggered into a terminal powering that city's vaunted arc lights and died on the spot. Not much later, *Scientific American* offered up electrocution as a way to swiftly slaughter cattle, and the Buffalo Society for the Prevention of Cruelty to Animals, taking the lead on the matter, recruited the help of Alfred Southwick, a dentist with a professional interest in pain management, to investigate. Southwick's experiments on dogs demonstrated electricity's lethal potential, and soon the governor of New York had asked him to widen his inquiry to its utility on human subjects. In contrast to another potential method of execution, a lethal injection, electricity was appealing to medical professionals because it meant they would not need to be involved in executions. Southwick's team also wrote to Thomas Edison, a death penalty opponent who nevertheless recommended that New York use alternating current (AC), instead of direct current (DC).[45]

Edison, whose cruel cunning has been overshadowed by his brilliance, owned most of the country's DC transmitters and hoped that if prisons began using AC current to execute people he might gain a competitive edge over his old employee and current competitor, Nicola Tesla, who developed AC, and his chief rival, George Westinghouse, who owned the patent on the technology. As the shift away from hanging was under way, Edison waged a public relations campaign on behalf of AC power's lethal virtue, traveling the country killing animals, persisting even after Southwick recommended the use of AC power in his report. Moreover, Edison testified in court as to the ease of death by electrocution after Westinghouse filed a suit contending that electrocution of condemned prisoners violated the Eighth Amendment's prohibition against cruel and unusual punishment. The United States Supreme Court ultimately rejected Westinghouse's claim, finding that "it is within easy reach of electrical science at this day to so generate and apply . . . a current of electricity of such known and sufficient force as certainly to produce instantaneous, and therefore, painless, death."[46] Edison gleefully suggested that when a person is put to death with electricity, they should be said to have been "Westinghoused."[47]

Electricity was all the more attractive for having seized the public's imagination in the late nineteenth century, provoking both fear and fascination. In Mark Twain's *A Connecticut Yankee in King Arthur's Court*, published in 1889, the time-traveling Hank Morgan uses "labor-saving" technologies learned in an armaments factory to do battle against the forces of barbarity in medieval England. Under siege in an elaborate fortress, Morgan decimates an attacking army of knights by powering on an electric fence. His distance from the battlefield permits him to safely enjoy the lethal efficiency of his ambush without encountering its gruesome results.[48] By 1931, Twain's novel had been filmed three times, by which time Americans would have grown used to strolling under electric streetlights and reading advertise-ments for electric gadgets in newspapers and magazines.[49]

As American readers were encountering *A Connecticut Yankee* for the first time, legislators in New York were installing an electric chair in Eastern State Penitentiary, the first in the nation. Alfred Southwick was in the au-dience at Auburn Prison, near Syracuse, on August 6, 1890, when the switch was pulled for the United States' first state-run death by electrocution. Be-fore the execution, Southwick grandly declared the moment "the culmina-tion of ten years' work and study," adding, "we live in a higher civilization from this day!"[50] But the execution failed to lived up to his expectations. The condemned prisoner, William Kemmler, lived through the chair's first current, and as the pong of burning flesh filled the death chamber, his body burst into flames.[51] George Westinghouse, also in attendance, quipped that "'the job could have been done better with an axe.'"[52]

To New South politicians, electricity promised to boost the state's indus-trial output. In his 1913 inaugural address, Governor Locke Craig declared, "Like the dervish in the Arabian tale, man has gotten hold of the casket with the mysterious juice that reveals to him the hidden treasures. The genii, in whose keeping are the streaming forces of the universe, have whispered to him their secrets. The world is pulsing with the currents of newly discov-ered energy."[53] North Carolina would soon become a leading producer of electric power in the American South.[54] Criminal justice reformers also embraced its promise. The potential of electricity to kill painlessly answered mounting concerns, inspired by and embodied in the Progressive movement of the late nineteenth and early twentieth centuries, that execution as prac-ticed was fundamentally antimodern.[55] A painless method of execution, lawmakers hoped, could not only burnish the reputation of the state but also reduce the risk of empathy with condemned prisoners by eliminating spec-tacle. Moreover, some thought that "death by lightning" might restore, "through its very incomprehensibility and mystery," the deterrent effect of executions, especially for African Americans, who they believed to be more tractable than whites.[56]

North Carolina had been moving toward consolidation of its death pen-alty system for many years. This process, dubbed delocalization by schol-ars, was central to the Progressive experiment: it demonstrated a belief in the competence of a central government, and sought to nurture the better angels of the public spirit by removing from view one of the more unpleas-ant by-products of maintaining order. Between the 1890s and the 1920s, state governments in the United States took increasing control over the power to execute. In 1890, local executions conducted by sheriffs accounted for 87.3 percent of the national total; in 1920, state-administered executions accounted for 88.3 percent of the total.[57]

In 1909, after a series of false starts, a Goldsboro legislator introduced a bill "to establish a permanent place in the State Penitentiary at Raleigh for the execution of felons" and "to change the mode of execution so that the death sentence shall be by electricity, and to provide an appropriation therefore."[58] The appropriation was essential for the perennially cash-strapped prison. That year, North Carolina became the sixth in the nation to adopt the chair.[59] The act also directed that the prison warden or a deputy, a physician, and at least twelve reputable citizens attend each execution. It opened the doors to other visitors as well: the prisoner's counsel was welcome, as were ministers and relatives of the condemned. Custom soon dictated that sheriffs distributed tickets by request to members of the injured community, giving sheriffs near-complete power over the composition of the audience. Although it did not appear in the legislation, prison officials would usually execute criminals around 10:30 on Friday mornings.

The death chamber was constructed on the first floor of the east wing of the main building of Raleigh's State's Prison. "Scarcely as large as an average-sized living room," octagonal, and painted lime green, the room received meager light from six long windows.[60] One door admitted prison officials and prisoners from inside the prison and another opened onto the lawn at the front of the building through which witnesses entered. Edwin Davis, the engineer who built New York's chair, was hired to do the same for North Carolina and worked so inefficiently that Governor W. W. Kitchin had to delay the state's first execution four times, prompting some to protest that the delays amounted to cruel and unusual punishment.[61] But Davis eventually got the job done, constructing an oaken chair fitted with leather straps to restrain the head, chest, arms, and legs.[62] Davis asked to perform the first electrocution himself; after all, he had done so before in a variety of states that used his services. Warden Thomas Sale refused.[63]

On March 18, 1910, at 10:15 A.M., Walter Morrison, sentenced to death for rape, left his death row cell and walked toward the death chamber. "A burly negro, 35 years old, over six feet in height, of a dark copper color"[64] with "nothing like as bad a countenance as one would expect to see in view of the fiendish crime of which he was convicted,"[65] Morrison wore a new brown suit, a denim shirt open at the neck, and new shoes. He passed the switchboard, a polished marble slab affixed with an ebony lever; pulling the lever would send an electric current into the death chamber along two

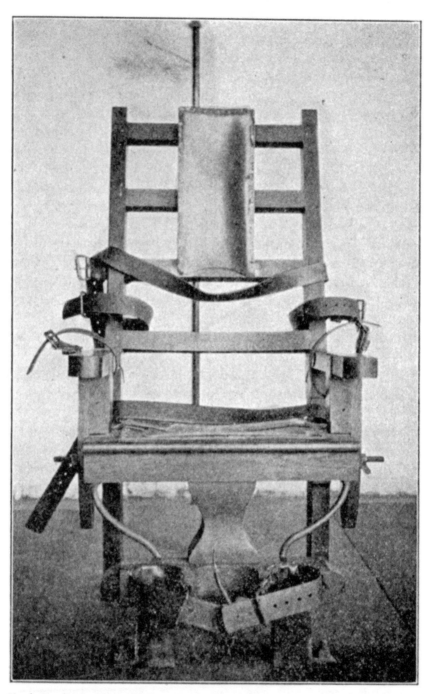

North Carolina's electric chair, as pictured in the State Board of Charities and Public Welfare's 1929 pamphlet, *Capital Punishment in North Carolina*. The chair was used until 1938, when the state began to rely exclusively on lethal gas. The chair is now in the possession of the North Carolina Museum of History in Raleigh.

overhead wires. One of these wires was to be connected to an "electro headhood," affixed to Morrison's head atop a wet sponge to conduct the current. Another wire would drop to Morrison's right leg, where it would complete the electric circuit at his bare calf. Before he walked by, prison officials covered the switchboard with a wooden case should he try to postpone his death by damaging the machine, and to shield it from view so as not to upset him.[66]

Entering the death chamber, "crying and praying in low choking tones,"[67] Morrison clutched a crucifix, a gift from a priest, who had baptized Morrison the previous afternoon in a bathtub in the prison basement.[68] The condemned man kept his eyes fixed on the crucifix, not looking up at the crowd of white spectators that sat on the other side of the metal chain. (A black preacher had applied for admission but arrived too late to attend.) "'Jesus please help me,'" Morrison prayed as guards strapped him into the chair, "'At last I mean to do what was right.'" He continued to pray, his attention focused on the crucifix, which he held between his knees, until Warden Thomas Sale threw the switch.[69]

The 1,800 volts rendered Morrison's body rigid, silencing his prayers. As the current flowed through Morrison's body, the arm holding the crucifix slowly rose, straining against the straps, and "until the current was withdrawn the Cross remained in this position."[70] Prison physicians listened to Morrison's heart after each round of electrocution and declared him dead after four shocks of about a minute each, "the usual resistance of a strong negro's body." The crucifix fell from Morrison's hand to the rubber mat beneath the chair, making no sound. Warden Sale would later note with Hank Morgan–like satisfaction, "The operation of the first electrocution was perfect, and I believe that death was almost instantaneous. The machine worked well and is entirely satisfactory."[71] None of the witnesses stayed to watch Morrison's body be taken from the chair. His family refused it, so "the usual disposition was made of it": it was given to a nearby medical school.[72]

Despite boosters' confidence in the chair's lethal efficiency, many prisoners were terrified of it, and while some responded with mute horror, others struggled with prison guards or cried out in fear. With witnesses gathered just feet away, there was little to disguise the distress of execution victims. Will Frazier's 1921 execution was not well-attended, but those who did show up were sickened, first by Frazier's shrieks, and then by the odor of burning flesh. "Not in all the grim history of the death chamber . . . have prison attendants been called upon to witness so harrowing a spectacle as did the negro present as he came shrieking out of death row," a reporter wrote. Blessedly for Frazier, he fainted soon after he was forced into the electric chair. Prison guards' hands shook as they secured the straps around Frazier's body, and even a death row veteran, accustomed to watching men pass his cell on the way to their deaths, "was cowed by the spectacle . . . his dark face an ashy gray." When smoke began to rise from Frazier's body, the spectators, "already shaken by the spectacle, turned sick."[73]

Frazier's gruesome death was not an outlier. At the September 1922 executions of Angus Murphy and Jasper Thomas, members of the nervous, giggly crowd wondered in whispers whether the four women in attendance could endure the spectacle in the cramped, hot room, made more intense by "the odor of burned flesh" that "suffused the room." The women, as at any social occasion, had been escorted into the death chamber first, and the warden directed them to a prime viewing spot just four feet from the electric chair. They retained their poise during the electrocution, but after Thomas's body was "dumped" into a wicker basket, the spectators, mopping their faces, hurried out, "some of them sickened."[74] Electrocution had proved to be as unsettling as hanging.

Following such grisly episodes, officials adjusted procedures to minimize the impact of obviously painful death on the execution audience, both by controlling the size and composition of the audience and by controlling what the audience saw. Little could be done about electrocution's effects on the human body, but prison officials could try to limit its impact on the audience. In the absence of clear guidelines for visitors or legislative directions for the execution process, wardens sought to assert some control over the proceedings, echoing the sheriff's haphazard efforts to manage local hangings. In December 1920, Warden Samuel Busbee reprimanded an audience that "laughed and jabbered incoherent nonsense."[75] After Daniel Nobles's grisly 1923 electrocution in front of more than eighty witnesses—his body changing color and, obscured by a cloud vapor, his chin and leg burning, the headpiece "crackling like a hickory fire"—Busbee announced that he would limit the crowd to thirty-six, would lock the prison gates at 9:00 that morning, and would bar people without tickets until after the end of the execution. Finally, Busbee moved to ban women unaccompanied by their husbands. In a measure of how state control limited the execution audience, the first woman to attend an electrocution had done so just two years earlier.[76]

In 1923, the General Assembly sought to complement these piecemeal procedures with an effort to bar press coverage of executions. The bill made it before the Senate Judiciary Committee in late February, but after receiving a report "without prejudice"—the noncommittal review that often doomed measures—the bill was tabled. Not long after the bill's failure, though, the legislature did manage to limit attendance somewhat. The new law limited the number of spectators "over and above privileged classes"—such as ministers, law enforcement officers, physicians, and members of the press—to six.[77] There is no indication that anyone heeded this new rule, though crowds never again approached the numbers of the early 1920s.

These policies reshaped the on-site execution audience, allowing the same people to watch again and again, drawing the community of white witnesses ever tighter: "As one after another is led out of death row down the narrow hall-way to the end, the semi-circle of faces that greets them is curiously unchanged," observed one journalist. "The regular, seasoned, witnesses are strangely numerous."[78] In 1919, Aaron Dupree died before "the usual crowd"; the same group showed up for the electrocution of Ralph Connor the following year. In 1923, "it was the usual throng that snickered and joked as it waited and then fell silent when the spectacle of death was brought in before them."[79] This usual crowd was clannish enough to scoff at a visitor who made the mistake of admitting that he was attending his first electrocution. When this newcomer asked the warden about a piece of the electrocution apparatus, a member of the crowd responded, "Ain't you never seen one before?"[80]

Anxiety about the failures of electrocution peaked in 1916, during the state's first double execution, when confessed murderer Ed Walker and his accomplice, Jeff Dorsett, died one after the other in the electric chair. "Good bye," said Walker confidently as he entered the execution chamber and seated himself in the electric chair. "I am going to meet my God." Warden Sale was known to "mope and worry" before executions, one journalist would later write, but on this Friday the warden was in "unusually good spirits," joking with witnesses.[81] His mood soon changed. As Walker's body convulsed under the current of the first electric shock, the power suddenly failed. "My Lord," gasped Sale, "what's happened?" The current returned as suddenly as it had left, though, and after a second shock, the prison physician declared Walker dead.

Sale was shaken and showed "signs of extreme nervousness" when he threw the switch on Dorsett. He then escorted twelve witnesses into his office, where they signed the two death certificates and watched as Sale fell forward "onto his face with a peculiar strangling noise in his throat," spilling the ink he was so carefully blotting. He never regained consciousness. Sale's death, and the implication that the grave task of presiding over executions took his life, revived the conversation about the suffering caused by execution, and the discomfort of prisoners, witnesses, and prison officials.[82]

There was no escaping that discomfort in the death chamber. The room was small, dominated by the imposing electric chair, and seemed to accentuate the weather outside. In the winter, it was cold and damp. In the summer, it grew hot and stuffy. The colder months dulled the room's odor, but in the spring and summer, the heat made "the odor of burning flesh . . . a constant accompaniment" because the electrodes affixed at the leg and head scorched the skin.[83] In 1931, Bernice Matthews and J. W. Ballard, convicted and sentenced together for murder, were both burned by the electric current. Matthews, a teenager, nearly lost his ear, and when Ballard's head caught on fire Warden H. H. Honeycutt emptied a shaving mug over it.[84]

## A Whiff of Sweet-Smelling Gas: The Transition to Asphyxiation

In 1935, state representative Charles A. Peterson, a physician, introduced a bill to change North Carolina's method of execution from electrocution to asphyxiation by gas. While the bill made its way through the legislature, Peterson attended the electrocution of Sidney Etheridge. Etheridge seemed determined to put on a show. A forty-four-year-old white veteran of World War I, Etheridge sent a note to the warden shortly before his execution asking that he be given whiskey so he could toast the black cat that he had eaten a quarter century ago to seal a pact with Satan. He enclosed an image of the cat, cut from the Sunday comic "Polly and Her Pals," with the note. He declined to meet with a minister, declared that the devil would join him for his execution, and refused to drink water before heading to the chair, rebuffing this common practice for condemned prisoners hoping to increase the conductivity of their bodies.[85]

Warden H. H. Honeycutt had to stop the electrocution when a "crackling of blue flame" ignited at the leg electrode. The leather strap that secured it had become wet, Honeycutt explained, which may have prevented the leg from burning at the point of contact. Despite this mishap, Peterson declared that electrocution was not as gruesome as he had expected—he had never seen one before. The fact that he introduced the legislation with only a "second hand" understanding of the spectacle of executions, convinced that lethal gas would be "more humane for witnesses," indicates the widespread discomfort with electrocutions as described in the press. Peterson was sure of the virtues of switching over to gas, and the *News and Observer* editorial board seemed to agree. The day after Etheridge's disturbing death, it excoriated "modern North Carolina" as too close to "old times of devil worship and torture and cruelty."[86]

The transition to execution by asphyxiation in a handful of western states boded well for North Carolina's own experiment. Gas was used for the first time in 1924, when Nevada executed a man for a gang murder. According to one witness, after a stern reprimand from the captain of the prison guards to "take it like a man," the prisoner inhaled "a whiff of sweet smelling gas like unto the odor of bananas" and died instantly and without pain.[87] The warden of the Carson City prison would later call gas "by far the simplest and most humane method yet devised."[88] Arizona adopted it in 1931, and Colorado followed in 1933.[89] In 1935, Peterson aimed to make North Carolina the fourth state in the nation, and the first east of the Mississippi, to make the change. North Carolinians, wrote one doctor, had "become tired of electrocuting and barbecuing their criminals."[90]

Peterson's bill passed the State House in early April 1935, buoyed by its sponsor's medical credentials, testimony from a number of physicians and dentists, and the support of one journalist who declared electrocution "'the worst possible way to do the worst possible thing' the state finds it necessary to do."[91] One supporter anticipated with satisfaction that gas executions would be "dignified," not "a big show like a circus." The vote also affirmed the fact that executions would continue in Raleigh, despite some sentiment to the contrary. One representative had sought to amend the bill by mandating the creation of a traveling gas chamber that, mounted on a truck, would stage executions in the counties where the crimes in question had occurred.[92] Another wanted to return to semiprivate hangings in county jail yards. Another derided the suggestion of a "peripatetic, perambulatory death house," saying, "I don't think they have public executions in any civilized country in the world." He was almost right: the United States' last public execution would take place two years later. Both bills failed.[93]

The chairman of the State Highway and Public Works Commission, which by the 1930s ran the state prison system, decided to simply build the gas chamber around the electric chair. Construction of the steel chamber, inset with an eight-foot observation window, began in October 1935.[94] Once the chamber was complete, the state commissioned construction of a new chair that could be used for either electrocutions or gassings; eventually, the chamber held three chairs. Robert Dunlop's electrocution, in January 1936, gave witnesses their first look at the new chamber, scheduled for later that month. One journalist noticed that witnesses, watching the death through heavy glass windows, with steel walls replacing a metal chain, could no longer smell burning flesh, nor hear the condemned prisoner's last words.[95]

The asphyxiation process itself added more distance between the executioner's hand and the condemned criminal. Instead of sending electricity directly into the prisoner's body, a switch released capsules into a container of acid. Early plans imagined cyanide "eggs" dropping into a jar of sulfuric acid suspended above the subject's head.[96] For perhaps obvious reasons, that plan was amended. Instead, the cyanide capsules, wrapped in cotton, would drop into a box positioned beneath the chair, dissolving in a mixture of sulfuric acid and water to create a deadly gas. Prisoners, of course, had to inhale the gas themselves. Afterward, ammonia would be piped in to neutralize the gas, which then would be vented outside.[97] "All this takes approximately one to two minutes," boasted the prison warden.[98]

The *News and Observer* closely followed the preparations for the state's first gassing. On Tuesday, it noted that Commissioner of Paroles Edwin Gill had interviewed Jimmy Lee "Allen" Foster, an African American teenager sentenced to death for rape, and could find no reason to intervene in his impending execution.[99] On Wednesday, the paper reported that Foster had been moved from a second-tier death row cell to one on the ground floor, where he ate and slept "just eight paces" from the death chamber. Foster, steadfastly denying his guilt, complained that "he 'never had a [chance]," and "pressed his flat nose flatter against the bars of his cell." He spoke at length with a reporter, complaining that he had been beaten by police, and insisting that knowing his death was imminent, he had no reason to lie about his innocence: "'If I had done it,' he said, 'I would say right now I done it, 'cause I know Friday's my day and I got to die then for something I never done. I know I ain't got a [chance], no matter what I tell, so I'd [just] go on and tell it if it was [the truth].'" He told the reporter that he had not seen his court-appointed lawyer long enough to learn his name.[100]

Death row was uneasy on Thursday night as Foster's final morning approached. "I stayed last night with the living dead," wrote *News and Observer* reporter John A. Parris Jr., who visited death row without the knowledge of the prisoners there on the eve of the first gas execution. "The night was long," he wrote. "The tenseness of death hung over these men who are about to die. There was that feeling of something going to happen—

something that couldn't be stopped. The lonesome wail of a train whistle outside in a world that seemed far away." Death row made for a mournful community. Prisoners sang hymns, and one of them, known as The Reverend, led them in prayer. "'You know your day is coming just the same as Brother Allen's,'" he said from his cell. "'Brother Allen goes tomorrow and I wish there was something I could do for him that would help him but all I know is to pray.'" He prayed, and Foster prayed with him, to "a God he found yesterday," Parris wrote.[101]

Meanwhile, "every detail connected with the operation of the new method of execution in the State has been checked and rechecked." While Parris described Foster as composed, praying in a voice "steady and firm," companion coverage revealed Foster as "openly terrified." He told one reporter, "'I feel mighty tough,'" but confessed that "'the soul can be ready, but the flesh ain't, and I'm worried.'" It was unclear whether the gas chamber would spare Foster's flesh. Prison officials gassed two dogs in preparation, and the animals howled as they died, though, one reporter noted, "they were killed quite dead." Prison officials hoped that the first human victim would be killed "without howling, without squirming."[102]

"First Lethal Gas Victim Dies in Torture as Witnesses Quail," wailed the *News and Observer* headline the following morning. The failure was not for lack of cooperation from Foster. He entered the gas chamber wrapped in a blanket; he wore only underwear to prevent the deadly gas from lingering in folds of clothing and threatening prison staff during the disposal of his body. He threw off the blanket and sat down unassisted, a boy wearing boxer shorts. When the ministers and prison guards had withdrawn from the chamber, and the door had been sealed, the executioner pulled the lever to release the cyanide capsules. Foster watched as gray fumes rose from beneath the chair, and when they reached his nostrils, he breathed them in, then out, then mouthed "Good bye" to the spectators. But "then he began to suffer. No man could look squarely into his eyes and fail to perceive that they were registering pain." For at least three minutes, Foster "suffered obviously and consciously" before he passed out, and it took another eight minutes before physicians confirmed that his heart had stopped. "This is just hell," said one witness who had seen more than fifty executions.[103]

The other spectators concurred, as did the medical professionals and prison officials in attendance. "We've got to shorten it or get rid of it entirely," said a Duplin County congressman. W. T. Bost, a journalist who witnessed dozens of electrocutions, two hangings, and two lynchings, declared asphyxiation the worst death of all. The Wake County coroner agreed:

# First Lethal Gas Victim Dies
## In Torture as Witnesses Quail

### WARREN SUFFERS POLITE REVERSE

**Gets Every Courtesy From House, But Few Votes For His Potato Proposal**

The News and Observer Bureau.
1232 National Press Building.

**By ROBERT E. WILLIAMS.**

Washington, Jan. 24.—Representative Lindsay C. Warren received many flowing compliments on the floor of the House today, but when a vote was taken on his proposal to make an appropriation for the compilation of data respecting the growing and marketing of potatoes, the House defeated it by a ...

### Execution of Negro, Taking 11 Minutes, Described as 'Horrible'

The State of North Carolina yesterday inaugurated the career of its new lethal gas chamber before more than 30 sickened witnesses.

For three full minutes and possibly more, Allen Foster, 20-year-old victim of the new chamber suffered obviously and consciously before he was overcome by the fumes of the hydrocyanic gas which rose from beneath his chair to flood the tiny white cell. Eight minutes more elapsed before physicians signified his heart had stopped.

"That's just hell," breathed one witness—one who had seen half a hundred electrocutions—as Foster writhed and retched in the straps which held him in the death chair. A chorus of assent, in which no voice of dissent mingled, greeted the remark.

### NEW COLD WAVE HITS NORTHWEST

**More Than 100 Deaths Attributable to Frigid Weather in Three-Day Period**

Chicago, Jan. 24.—(AP)— Fresh snows swept out of the Northwest tonight in the van of a new cold wave.

The double assault presaged a swift end to the brief respite from some of the most frigid weather of the century.

Although temperatures eased slowly upward during the day from South Dakota to New York, subzero and subfreezing conditions ...

Teenaged Allen Foster's death resulted in this chilling headline in 1936. State authorities did little study before constructing the gas chamber around the electric chair. According to observers, Foster entered the gas chamber without understanding what was coming. One story had him boasting of fighting the boxer Joe Louis before he inhaled the lethal gas. Courtesy of the *News and Observer* of Raleigh.

"This was one of the most terrible and horrible things I ever looked at," he said. One prison guard confessed that the gassing had "got me," reminding him of when his father suffocated to death during an asthma attack. The story received national attention. The *New York Times* picked up an article by Virginius Dabney, the editor of the *Richmond Times-Dispatch*, who noted the "storm of indignation" that ensued when the gas chamber "failed to function in accordance with expectations." The only witness who thought the execution affirmed the efficacy of gas was Charles Peterson, the bill's sponsor.[104] One columnist mocked the legislature: "I shall hope prayerfully," he wrote, "for no more legislative brainstorms that push our State back toward barbarism."[105]

The head of the prison wired his colleagues in Colorado, sure that Foster's eleven-minute death was unusual. A few days later, the Coloradans replied: no, eleven minutes is normal.[106] On the Monday morning following Foster's Friday execution, the *News and Observer* published a story claiming that scientific authorities agreed that electrocution was more humane. And worse, "the gas victim, whether or not he suffers any actual physical torture, such as would be produced by a burn, feels himself being slowly killed." In what may have been the first systematic study of gas execution, a nonprofit concluded that gas execution caused "internal asphyxia," a condition in which the body cannot absorb oxygen from the blood. Add to that the gas's paralytic effect, preventing breathing, and the subject might slowly suffocate, the heart continuing to futilely beat for as long as ten minutes after breathing stops. The best solution—more gas—would not be safe for the executioner and spectators, the report concluded. Electrocution, on the other hand, causes the almost immediate destruction of essential nerve centers, "horrible as the details may sound, electrocution is . . . beyond doubt the most humane method of executing criminals."[107]

However, members of the legislature, who had unanimously supported the Peterson bill, were not going to reverse course, impugn their own judgment, or embarrass their popular colleague. And after painting a narrative of steady progress toward a perfectible execution system, rolling back to electrocution would be a symbolically potent and hard-to-explain retreat, not to mention an expensive and cumbersome one. Governor J. C. B. Ehringhaus posed the question to a journalist two days after Foster's death: "'Do you think that a Legislature which passed such a law without a dissenting vote would completely reverse itself and repeal the law now?'" Ehringhaus, who did "not like to have the problem presented by North Carolina's new gas asphyxiations dropped on his shoulders," had no plans to do anything about the situation, and announced that he would not consider a blanket commutation or reprieves for current death row inmates.[108]

Foster's death prompted a reexamination not just of execution methods but of the question of pain. Newspaper coverage of the execution prompted a flood of letters into the governor's office. One man declared his opposition to capital punishment in early February, not least because "of the pitiably brutal failure of the General Assembly in its recent search for a more humane way of killing those condemned to death."[109] A doctor recommended another change in method: "Few people ever kill themselves with hydrocyanic gas," he wrote. "The legislature might save a great deal of money and make these deaths more dream-like if they would [use] an old Model T Ford and hitch the exhaust to a small gas chamber. This would please some of these sympathizers who are always howling for protection and good care of the criminals."[110] Ehringhaus's secretary replied to one correspondent, "You of course understand that Governor Ehringhaus . . . had no power at all with reference to making this substitution."[111] When the execution following Foster's using a different chemical mixture netted a more palatable result, one prison official declared, "Lethal gas has come to stay in North Carolina."[112]

### Notoriously Overwritten: The Spectacle in the News

Newspaper coverage meant that the death penalty remained public, and even found a wider audience, after its confinement in the State's Prison. Moreover, the number of people who read about executions in the *News and Observer* in the first half of the twentieth century was vastly larger than the total who attended public hangings. The paper, which enjoyed a steadily growing circulation from close to 15,000 in 1910 to 50,000 in 1935 to nearly 120,000 at mid-century, played an important role in opening up the death penalty to the public.[113] Articles about executions were "notoriously overwritten" by "cub reporters, [who], turned loose on an electrocution, reveled in the contortions and the smells."[114] Their attention to detail, both gruesome and technical, is notable for two reasons. First, it demonstrated that whatever broad cultural shifts the concealment of executions seemed to indicate, the public still had a taste for blood. It was a taste that could, in the early 1900s, be satisfied by photographs as well as text, and editors took advantage of both media.[115] An appetite for gore, it seems, was acceptable only among the right sort of people.

Reporters also took the opportunity to describe prisoners in starkly racist language that illustrated the essential racial hostility of the act of execution. Convicted rapist John Goss "looked the part of the picture that 'mean nigger' conjures up," reported the *News and Observer*. "Short, squat, thick-bodied, and with the face of a gorilla. Even the eyes were muddy with the diffusion of the color of his skin," the article continued, as if Goss's blackness had sullied the windows to his soul. After four shocks, an attendant pronounced that no life remained "in the black carcass," which was "dumped into a basket" to be taken to a local medical school for dissection. Condemned rapist Howard Craig was a "gorilla-like negro" who "crept like a wild beast upon his innocent, unimagining victim." Craig, "a powerfully built African," died in the electric chair in December 1914 as the victim's father watched.[116] Newspaper coverage of the execution of convicted rapist and murderer Theodore Boykin in 1952 transformed a "slender young Negro laborer" into a beast: "The fight-back instinct of the trapped animal surged to a climax" after guards strapped Boykin into the chair in the gas chamber, wrote a *News and Observer* reporter.[117]

As these reports reveal, the bodies of African American men were sources of fascination, fear, contempt, and envy for journalists. "Diminutive yellow" Jesse Brooks and "rotund brown" James Johnson were both electrocuted in March 1934.[118] One reporter described Fred Steele as "tawny, loquacious,"[119] while Leroy McNeill was a "tall, slender, and coal-black boy."[120] One reporter praised the composure of convicted murderer Dortch Waller, a forty-three year-old farmer, as he lowered himself into the electric chair in August 1935. The 2,300 volts that shocked Waller to death "tugged at the life within the body which officials said was one of the finest ever sent to State's Prison." Indeed, Waller had a "splendid body."[121] A reporter who covered the execution of Hector Graham marveled at Graham's size. Praising Graham for his gallant fight for his life, newspaper coverage noted that "the big Negro's voice fairly boomed as he pronounced 'my salvation.'"[122] On the other hand, Andrew Jackson, a convicted rapist and career criminal who was electrocuted in 1920, was "a great, stupid, unlettered animal" who was executed "for the worst crime in the catalogue of evil, and his great hulking body was trundled away to do its first service to society in the hands of medical students."[123] These descriptions reveal not just the fascination with blackness at the heart of white supremacy, but also reveal how a private death penalty allowed for a more concerted study of its subject.

Meanwhile, prison officials had been using a mask to conceal the faces of prisoners in the gas chamber, but its use was inconsistent. Behind a mask, the prisoners' face could no longer communicate fear or pain. At the 1939 asphyxiation of King Solomon Stovall, a reporter observed that audience members were "unable to see facial contortions of the dying man, and witnesses said the mask made it easier to watch the execution."[124] The change was, at least briefly, almost too effective. A few months later, Warden H. H. Wilson was having a different problem—trying to scrounge up the number of official witnesses required by law to sign the death warrant after an execution. Wilson wondered if the mask "took the sensationalism out" of executions and made it difficult to generate interest.[125] The thrill of executions, what made them important to the public, appears to have been their unpredictability and the violence that prison officials and lawmakers tried to eliminate.

A series of such gassings, which drew equally muted newspaper coverage, and a declining death row population, appeared to dull calls for further technical reform. In the 1940s, reporters turned their attention to the increasing legal twists and turns taken by death row inmates, who, as the United States Supreme Court increasingly involved itself in the death penalty process, were more often appealing their sentences. Legislators had moved from tinkering with the machinery of death to tinkering with the law, debating bills that relaxed mandatory sentencing guidelines and considering the question of abolition. The crowds that gathered at executions thinned as well. Sensational cases drew crowds, such as the more than one thousand people milled around outside the prison during a 1949 asphyxiation, but as legal challenges slowed the death penalty process, fewer executions took place, and those that did provoked less interest.[126]

## No Negroes among the Spectators: Crystallizing the Jim Crow Death Penalty

One popular theory of punishment posits that as states mature, their punishment style shifts from bodily punishments to punishments aimed at the soul; solitary confinement, for instance, replaces the guillotine.[127] In broad strokes, this characterization is true of the United States, the South, and North Carolina: the prison cell replaced the stocks. But the death penalty in North Carolina inverted that transition. Although crowds at public hangings came for a show, much of that show was directed at the condition of the prisoner's soul. Drunk or not, rowdy or not, the crowd witnessed to the prisoner's life and death. Whether observed rigorously or not, the time-tested execution rituals offered the chance for public absolution and the prisoner's soul was the subject of conversation.

In the death chamber in Central Prison, the smaller group of observers gathered not to witness the soul's progress but to view the impact of electricity or lethal gas on a body—eight out of ten times, that body was an African American one. It made the black body the source of a new kind of fascination, one that quietly dramatized the mechanisms of the modern state bent against blackness. The death penalty's quietude in the 1950s and the first years of the 1960s also demonstrated, whether or not state leaders recognized it, that technologies of concealment rather than technologies of display could be leveraged to achieve the goals of racial subjugation and, ultimately, labor coercion in the Jim Crow South. This is not quite the transition Foucault described in *Discipline and Punish*, in which he theorized that maturing states over time abandon bodily punishments such as public

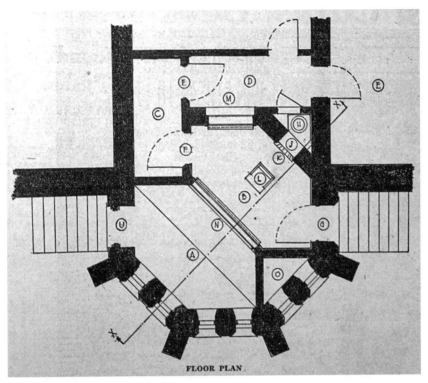

**FLOOR PLAN**

A diagram of North Carolina's death chamber shows where the condemned prisoner enters the room (E) and sits in the chair (L). Ticketed members of the public could enter via the stairwell at (U) and (G). A divider (N) was installed when the state converted from electrocution to asphyxiation. *Diagram of the Lethal Gas Chamber at Central Prison in Raleigh, N.C.*, University of North Carolina Libraries, accessed March 16, 2018, https://exhibits.lib.unc.edu/items/show/2805.

torture for psychological ones such as imprisonment. North Carolina, in fact, remained exceptionally committed to the violent, public coercion of African Americans, whether building the state's "good roads," cutting pine for turpentine, chopping onions on prison farms, or in another capacity.

Prison officials, politicians, and other reformers made the mechanics of execution the focus of their attention; in their minds, controlling the spectacle of execution was essential to presenting North Carolina as a modern state. The walled-off death chamber, the tickets and viewing restrictions, the gas chamber itself—all these structural and technical innovations were geared toward minimizing the state's discomfort as it strengthened the social and legal strictures of Jim Crow. By the 1930s, the death penalty, like the wider criminal justice system, had closed in on African American men while excluding meaningful participation and precluding public resistance by other people of color. The death penalty, then, both expressed and contributed to the rigid regime of racial subjugation that to many North Carolinians appeared to settle the issue of racial hierarchy. As they did so they pushed the death penalty out of the public square and onto the fringes of social and cultural life, eventually to be experienced by most as a media event and by its participants in a cramped execution chamber, in the wee hours of the morning, before a small group of observers. As the execution spectacle was constrained, the tangle of meanings that freighted public hangings fell away, leaving just one powerful symbolic message: the death penalty in Jim Crow North Carolina expressed the state's firm commitment to a criminal justice system created to control the bodies and lives of African Americans, but only as subjects, never as actors.

Crucially, in addition to limiting spectacle, state control dramatically whitened the execution process. Newspaper coverage of turn-of-the-century public hangings describes racially diverse, even black-dominated crowds, but witnesses at subsequent electrocutions, and later asphyxiations, were predominantly white. With the exception of the African American clergy, few African Americans who were not on their way to their deaths appeared at executions, so few that revealing rumors arose in the African American community that the condemned were not killed, but spirited away to work camps.[128] Not until 1934 did the first black reporter attend an execution.[129] When two African American men attended a 1934 execution as witnesses, a white reporter was surprised that they did not appear to react to the spectacle. "Neither Negro displayed any emotion over seeing a member of their race electrocuted," the reporter observed.[130]

This profoundly biased yet aspirationally modern system perfectly expressed the conflicted ethos of the New South in North Carolina and broadly; in the words of historian David Potter, like the New South itself the death penalty "could not bear either to abandon the traditions of the Old South or to forego the material gains of modern America."[131] One such tradition was lynching, in which white mobs killed people of color before ever-smaller all-white audiences.[132] In the ten years before *Furman v. Georgia* spurred southern lawmakers to reinvent their death penalty systems, North Carolina executed just fifteen people, thirteen of them African American. All the victims in these cases were white. One of these final fifteen was Ross McAfee, an "itinerant Negro farm worker." McAfee was put to death for "an attack on a young white housewife." McAfee seemed resigned to his fate, telling prison officials that he was "ready to go." Then, under the gaze of a crowd of reporters, observers, and officers from the scene of the crime for which he was condemned, McAfee was asphyxiated. One observer noticed that "there were no Negroes among the spectators."[133]

# 3  I Cannot Allow This Boy to Be Executed

The Essential Role of Mercy, 1910–1949

· · · · · · · · · · · · · · · · · · · · · · · · · · · · · · · · · · · · · · · · · · ·

It was after midnight in March of 1944 when a Mrs. G. V. Parker, eight months pregnant and in bed with her seven-year-old daughter, heard a key turn in the front door of her modest home in Wilmington, North Carolina. She thought her husband might have returned from his job at the nearby shipyard early. But whoever was in the house did not immediately enter the bedroom. "Who is that?" called Parker. "It is me," an unfamiliar voice replied. "Who is me?" she rebutted. "Jake," answered the voice, and the speaker entered the bedroom. Threatening to kill her child, the intruder demanded sex. As her daughter sobbed on the bed beside her, the intruder raped Parker. As soon as she could, Parker called the neighbors, reached her husband at the shipyard, and summoned the police. She described her assailant in great detail, telling police that "she was satisfied she could recognize his eyes."[1]

The next day, police took Parker to the "colored section" of Wilmington, where after some time she called out, "There he is," and became "much agitated and hysterical." Police apprehended the person in question, Ernest Brooks Jr., and brought him to the office of the superintendent of the New Hanover County Bureau of Investigation office for questioning. It was there that Brooks would later testify the superintendent told him that the authorities had his fingerprints (they did not) and that if he confessed, "it would be easier." Brooks did confess and was sentenced to death following convictions for first-degree burglary and rape. Brooks's attorneys raised some objections, arguing that Brooks's confession had been coerced, and that the jury's confusion—revealed by a lengthy preconviction question-and-answer session with an exasperated judge—should invalidate his sentence. The Supreme Court disagreed, however, and ruled that there had been no error in the Superior Court's decision. Brooks, the first son and namesake of a Wilmington longshoreman, was fourteen years old.[2]

Brooks's impending execution provided a moral test for the state's governor: would they hold firm to the need for a swift and certain death penalty, or would they decide that youth offered some protection and show mercy? The previous April, Governor R. Gregg Cherry had announced, in commuting the death sentence of a sixteen-year-old convicted of murdering a police officer, "I do not feel that the State of North Carolina should execute a child. We cannot hold him to the same degree of responsibility to which we hold an adult."[3] Although the April beneficiary was white and Brooks was African American, Cherry gave Brooks the same consideration. In his statement, Cherry took the opportunity to push a favorite issue: public schools and mandatory attendance. Part of Brooks's delinquency, said Cherry, arose "from the neglect of the State and society in general to provide a better environment for growth into a useful citizen." With the recommendation of the Superior Court judge, Cherry commuted Brooks's sentence to life imprisonment.[4]

*Time* magazine noted the rarity of Cherry's taking of responsibility. "Rarer still," the issue read, "in North Carolina there was no outcry."[5] On the contrary, letters of support arrived at Cherry's office from across North Carolina and the nation. A Mississippi woman interpreted Cherry's action as a "courageous stand in the face of the lynching sentiment rampant in this part of the country." One Durham resident wrote that "to have executed [Brooks] would have been a blot upon the state's name," and that commutation would help preserve North Carolina's reputation as racially moderate. And another man praised Cherry for his effort to resolve "an impossible situation," an execution that would have harmed "both white and negro society."[6]

But *Time* was mistaken to assert that approval for Cherry's action was unusual. It was far from unheard of for North Carolina, even in the twentieth century, to execute teenagers, but available records indicate that no one under sixteen was ever executed. And more to the point, in a state with a mandatory death sentence for as many as four crimes—murder, rape, burglary, and arson, all in the first degree—commutations like Cherry's were not just commonplace, but were essential to managing the image of the state and maintaining a death penalty that threatened to be too extreme in a state that was seeking to moderate its violence. Gubernatorial commutations were an essential safety valve to preserve the death penalty in some form, in part by lightening the burdens on juries in the absence, until near mid-century, of alternatives. And, commutations softened the impact of death sentences, seeking to square the community's need for vengeance with a more restrained approach to criminal justice.

By the time the state assumed from counties responsibility for executions in 1910, North Carolina's criminal legal system had developed to relative maturity. Counsel in capital cases, whether appointed by the court or hired by the defendant, while not always mounting a vigorous defense of their client, often brought appeals to the North Carolina Supreme Court after a conviction. While the United States Supreme Court would not rule on access to counsel for indigent defendants until the 1960s, every person indicted for a capital crime in North Carolina was represented by an attorney in Superior Court, and at least by the 1930s, many of those attorneys were pressing hard for reversals or new trials on appeal. Their appeals were sometimes so strident, in fact, that some North Carolinians objected to the number of exceptions—potential reasons for granting a new trial—granted capital defendants.[7] Superior Court judges took their jobs seriously, issuing grave and detailed charges to their juries, and while the opening and closing statements of solicitors and defense attorneys do not appear in trial transcripts, there is little evidence to suggest that they directly appealed to raw prejudice or vengeance.[8] Yet as we have seen, vengeance, openly demanded by angry mobs, played an enduring role in influencing guilty verdicts well into the twentieth century. Once that verdict was issued to satisfy an aggrieved community, the governor could reproduce the trial process with his own growing staff of investigators, and eventually a dedicated board, and modify the outcome, showing mercy even in light of apparent community condemnation.

Edwin Gill, a longtime public servant who would become pardon commissioner in 1933 as the need for such a position became apparent, insisted in a report that his office did not exist to retry the facts of a capital case. Its only task, he wrote, was to look for new evidence that might exonerate the condemned person or to discover mitigating circumstances. In their search for new evidence of innocence or factors that might mitigate a capital crime, the commissioner and his investigators consulted the trial judge, the solicitor, and the arresting officers; they pored over the trial transcripts and the North Carolina Supreme Court's response to the prisoner's appeal; sometimes they held public hearings in the injured communities; and they considered petitions arguing for or against clemency.[9] In short, staffers in the governor's mansion did indeed retry the prisoner, but without the mandatory sentencing laws, rigid requirements for submitting appeals, or other processes regulating the capital trial and sentencing process.

The commutation investigation was part of a post-sentencing process representative of a maturing legal system. No longer would convicted criminals be executed swiftly, in the heat of community anger and without an opportunity to dispassionately review the circumstances not only of the trial but of the crime itself. Furthermore, as they were limited to one term—and as the death penalty was not yet freighted with the profound symbolic weight it acquired after the 1972 *Furman v. Georgia* decision—governors would face little political blowback. Governors, then, were both insulated from community sentiment and possible vectors of it. Yet the governor's discretion ultimately moderated the death penalty, working in concert with new statutes and jury behaviors that ended the process altogether by the early 1960s.

This chapter presents the essential role of mercy in the administration of the death penalty in North Carolina during the first half of the twentieth century. Today, gubernatorial clemency is a rare and fraught process attended by a host of players, from voters expecting a tough-on-crime posture from their elected officials to well-organized advocacy groups. Commutations, let alone pardons, are rarely—and grudgingly—issued. But historically, in North Carolina and elsewhere, clemency was frequently used and was extended not just in light of errors or new evidence, but out of a general sense of mercy or propriety. Clemency saved many lives, but it also highlighted the racial character of the death penalty and the shortcomings of the mandatory execution statute it purported (or attempted) to mitigate. That mandatory statute persisted, ironically, because clemency prevented what would have been an intolerably lethal system. But even as clemency sustained the death penalty generally, by the early 1940s it had undermined it to the point where capital punishment in North Carolina began to fade away.

### As the Life of the Prisoner Is Involved: The Need for Clemency

As the state considered the creation of a Board of Pardons in 1913, editors at the *News and Observer* railed against the possibility. They explained in a January editorial that the reason the governor was so overburdened by requests for pardons was because governors around the nation had shouldered too much responsibility. It was a heavy burden because the chief executives were acting "as if the Governor was an appellate court, above the Supreme Court, and virtually bound to review all the cases which they are asked to take up, and this takes time." If governors had the courage to reject improper applications, criminals and their lawyers "would soon find out that the Governor is . . . not a judicial officer" and "the only hope for executive clemency would be in some after-discovered evidence or in some extraordinary condition."[10] But barring the development of such an extraordinary condition, judicial precedent and the letter of the law actually meant that the governor was indeed expected to act as a kind of judicial officer.

North Carolina's 1868 Constitution enshrined the long-held power of clemency in the office of the state's governor. While some states diluted clemency power by assigning it to a board, or preventing the governor from acting without outside consent, nearly half, including North Carolina, reserved it exclusively for their governors.[11] The only restrictions in the clemency process fell on the condemned persons themselves, who had to produce a written explanation of their request.[12] Executive clemency in capital cases made the governor the final gatekeeper between a prisoner and an error of justice. By at least 1911, after the state had taken control of executions, the state's governor had begun to issue reprieves to death row inmates so he could examine their claims. That year, Governor W. W. Kitchin gave condemned murderer Taylor Love a reprieve so his lawyer could have ample time to prepare a petition.[13]

The rigidity of North Carolina's criminal statutes and the imperfections of the post-conviction process created the need for a post-sentencing safety valve for a number of reasons. First, the state's mandatory sentencing laws threatened to fill up death row. Until 1941, North Carolina law set a mandatory death sentence for anyone convicted of first-degree burglary or arson. First-degree murder and rape retained mandatory death sentences until 1949. Second, sloppy or neglectful lawyers sometimes failed to properly file condemned prisoners' appeals. Although precedent directed that North Carolina Supreme Court justices look for "any error on the face of the record" in capital appeals, "as the life of the prisoner is involved," many appeals were dismissed because they were not properly filed, a task for which the often uneducated, even illiterate, defendants relied upon their court-appointed lawyers.[14] Such was the case with James Farmer and Albert Sanders, who held hands and "shouted loudly to Jesus" as they died in the gas chamber, side by side, in June 1947. The North Carolina Supreme Court was prepared to review their case—they were convicted and sentenced to death for beating a young World War II veteran to death—but their lawyers failed to properly file their appeal.[15] The state Supreme Court had a history of strict readings of appeals: in 1801, the court arrested judgment in a capital case because, as one justice later recalled, "the letter 'a' had been omitted from the word 'breast.'" This "deference to technical interpretation" made for an inflexible appeals process that tended to preserve lower court decisions, however flawed.[16] As one justice later wrote, "He who sleeps upon his rights may lose them."[17]

Third, as Commissioner of Pardons Edwin B. Bridges explained to Governor O. Max Gardner in 1929, North Carolina law did not a provide for new trials upon discovery of new evidence in criminal cases, although it did so for civil actions. This position was not uncommon. While some states, such as New York, created provisions for new trials in the late nineteenth century, as late as 1941 attorneys were decrying the statutory limits that denied condemned prisoners new trials in light of newly discovered evidence.[18] In these cases it was up to the governor to weigh the new evidence and decide whether to commute the condemned's sentence or pardon him altogether.[19]

A fourth factor that created the need for mercy was the law's murky stance on jury discretion, the privilege of juries to convict someone indicted on a first-degree charge of a lesser crime. In its effort to clarify its stance on the matter, the Supreme Court of North Carolina issued a series of conflicting rulings. In 1890, justices reprimanded a jury they believed had handed down a verdict of second-degree burglary when the evidence pointed to a first-degree crime. But a few years later, the court let stand a similar decision despite what it called the jury's "abuse" of discretion. This permissiveness stood for most of the twentieth century, although jurors passed down their verdicts based on the trial judge's charge, likely in ignorance of procedural precedent. And at least one judge told jurors that he would not accept a second-degree verdict for a prisoner indicted for a first-degree crime. In 1940, in a split decision, the court upheld that judge's decision. So, while jurors appeared to have some discretion, it was as likely as not that they were faced with the decision to acquit someone they felt was guilty rather than condemn the defendant despite believing the person to be undeserving of death.[20]

Even when the Supreme Court hinted that it was open to flexibility in sentencing, Superior Court judges might close that door. The case of Huzy Jackson illustrates the way in which gubernatorial clemency addressed a claim of actual innocence when the state Supreme Court would not. Jackson was convicted of rape in the spring 1930 term of the Rowan County Superior Court and given the mandatory death sentence. According to the defense's brief in their appeal to the Supreme Court, while the prosecutrix, as they called her, offered convincing evidence that she had in fact been raped, the perpetrator was not Jackson. In their appeal, the defense offered new testimony from Jackson's employer, who vouched for his whereabouts at the time of the attack, as well as emphasizing other exculpatory evidence that had arisen during the course of the trial. In its response, the court cited precedent to deny a new trial based on new evidence: "It is the settled rule of practice with us, established by a long and uniform line of decision, that new trials will not be awarded by this court in criminal prosecutions for newly discovered evidence."[21] Nor would the Supreme Court review a Superior Court judge's decision to deny a motion for a new trial. What they would do, however, was send the case back to the Superior Court for resentencing because the trial judge failed to sign the judgment, rigidity of a different kind offering Jackson a second chance.[22]

While this policy may seem cruel, it was rooted in the sensible desire to mark an end to the trial process. Anyone convicted of a serious crime would have every incentive to dig ceaselessly for new evidence, or create some, until they had left prison or been executed. But with Jackson, the Supreme Court of North Carolina tried to have it both ways, remanding his case back to Superior Court for judgment, asking that the judge reconsider Jackson's sentence and take into account the new evidence. But the Superior Court judge sentenced him again to death in November, ruling out the new evidence and setting an execution date in January of 1931. When Jackson's appeal again failed before the state Supreme Court, the decision then fell into the hands of Governor O. Max Gardner, who eventually commuted Jackson's sentence to life imprisonment. Jackson was paroled to South Carolina in 1943, thirteen years after his conviction, the beneficiary, then, of a stingy kind of justice—one that, its teeth sunk in, might release its grip just a bit in the face of incontrovertible evidence of innocence.[23]

The Supreme Court took slightly more assertive action in the case of Herman Casey. Casey was convicted and received the mandatory death sentence, on mostly circumstantial evidence, for a brutal murder in Lenoir County in September 1930. After Casey's attorneys filed an appeal on his behalf, they learned that before his trial, at least two members of the jury had agreed to convict Casey and send him to the death chamber. The attorneys secured affidavits from a number of Lenoir residents, including one who swore that a juror told him that "if [Casey] were turned loose they might as well throw away the electric chair and tear down the jail."[24] In the next term of Superior Court, Judge W. A. Devin refused to grant a new trial, opining that the result would be the same, and the North Carolina Supreme Court refused to order a retrial.[25]

That ruling gave state Supreme Court justices a chance to tussle about the matter. Justice Heriot Clarkson disagreed. Citing multiple precedents, he argued that the state constitution provided for new trials in civil actions and, by not providing the same guarantee for criminal cases, had left that power to the governor. To support his claim that considering new evidence was "contrary to our well settled rule of practice and procedure," Clarkson noted that Rules of Practice of the Supreme Court of North Carolina, a volume edited by the sitting chief justice, made this point "in bold type," and added some capital letters to strengthen his argument: "NEWLY DISCOVERED EVIDENCE IS NOT CONSIDERED IN CRIMINAL CASES." Common law and the Constitution both directed that the governor assume this responsibility, Clarkson argued, and there was no reason for the court to take power "more efficiently performed by the Executive."[26]

Justice J. W. Brogden, dissenting, complained of the fact that "courts have power to rehear cases and to entertain motions for newly discovered evidence where a nickel's worth of property was concerned," but were "powerless and impotent where life is concerned." He added, "If the courts have power to hear in misdemeanors, but no power to hear in capital felonies, then it is manifest that criminal procedure is more concerned with the mote than the beam."[27] Perhaps encouraged by a split judiciary, Casey's lawyers appealed again, and Casey was granted a new trial, ultimately receiving a second-degree murder verdict, and a sentence of twenty-five to thirty years in prison. *State v. Casey* provided precedent for Superior Court judges, at their discretion, to grant new trials to capital prisoners seeking to avoid execution even as the process affirmed the role of the governor in assessing post-conviction guilt.

Even after the *Casey* ruling, North Carolina's courts proved reluctant to rehear cases in light of new evidence. For instance, in 1944, lawyers for William Little, sentenced to death for rape, presented Superior Court Judge Henry A. Grady, not a supporter of the death penalty, with a letter from a doctor attesting that the plaintiff had not actually been sexually assaulted. He also delivered letters from jurors stating that had they known the results of the medical examination, they would never have convicted Little.[28] But despite this indication that Little may not have been guilty, and that a jury might not have convicted him, Grady refused his request for a new trial. Little's appeal to the Supreme Court of North Carolina failed as well, when his lawyers neglected to perfect it.[29] He was executed in 1947, praying as he died.[30]

Resistance by the Supreme Court to accept new, potentially exonerating evidence on capital cases; lawyers who failed to follow through on appeals; mandatory sentencing laws; and uncertainty about jury discretion created a confusing legal environment where the governor was expected to step in to resolve cases rejected by the Supreme Court. In 1924, the *Concord Tribune* described the procedure that was well in place by then. In an editorial that complained of the long, often-delayed path of the death penalty in the state, the paper described how a condemned man might appeal to the Supreme Court, wait months for consideration, receive a rejection, and then appeal to the governor. To give the condemned man "a square deal," the governor "cannot turn a deaf ear to the petition."[31]

Indeed, North Carolina's governors took seriously the responsibility of evaluating clemency applications. Most such applications came from the relatives of prisoners with short sentences, men whose wives needed them to return home as breadwinners during tough times, or with sick relatives, or who were decent people who had been away from home for too long. But the applications on behalf of condemned criminals required the most careful attention. A condemned prisoner who had lost an appeal to the Supreme Court, or, as frequently happened, found his or her appeal dismissed because it was never perfected, saw in the governor a last resort. Family members and friends, residents of the county where the crime took place, lawyers, judges, and members of the jury might all write to the governor urging mercy. The governor weighed new evidence of guilt or innocence, the circumstances of the crime, the condition of the victim, the injury to the state and the community, and the mental and physical health of the prisoner.

### Ain't Done Nothing No How: Explanations for Commutation

By the beginning of the twentieth century, this heavy (or important) responsibility had grown significantly more demanding as the powers of the governor grew with the size of the state's prison population. In 1910, the first year of state-run executions in North Carolina, the state prison system held 670 convicts; by 1925, that number had more than doubled; and by 1940, the total was approaching 9,000.[32] In 1925, responding to the increased demands on the governor's commutation power, the General Assembly gave the governor a pardon commissioner. In 1929, the legislature replaced the independent commissioner with a governor's executive counsel and gave them the salary of a Superior Court judge.[33] By 1935, that counsel, now charged also with evaluating parole requests and investigating and preventing potential lynchings, had a full staff of investigators, who sought exculpatory evidence, held public hearings, and prepared reports for the governor. This was an aggressive, systematic hunt for reasons to commute.[34]

The decision of the governor, such as those made in Superior and Supreme Court decisions, was subject to public pressure, argument, evidence, and questions of fairness. But unlike court decisions, it was bound by neither precedent nor procedure, beholden to a sense of justice unencumbered by mandatory sentencing guidelines or narrow definitions of premeditation and insanity. Sometimes, governors commuted or reprieved sentences based solely on (often arbitrary) personal motives. For instance, Marcus Edwards, after being condemned for the murder of his wife in 1918, willed all his property to his child. Governor T. W. Bickett admired this gesture, and said so when he commuted Edwards's sentence.[35] Governor Cameron Morrison granted Bob Benson a reprieve, adding two months to his life, so the governor could vacation with an easy mind.[36]

There was a general class of persons less likely to be sentenced to death for serious crimes: white people, who represented just 25 percent of condemned prisoners in the early twentieth century despite representing approximately 70 percent of the population. There were other semiprotected classes. In one sample of twenty-nine beneficiaries of commutation, longtime Commissioner of Paroles Edwin Gill found that two people won commutations for their youth, three for mental disability or limitation, seven because the governor deemed that the prisoner had caused no serious injury, and seventeen because of "doubt as to guilt or degree of guilt." In other words, twenty-four of twenty-nine commutations were granted because of questions as to whether the severity of the crime for which a prisoner was convicted matched the severity of the sentence, or because the prisoner had not committed a crime at all.[37] Other explanations, such as youth, mental condition, and sex, demonstrate how the death penalty in North Carolina was intended to punish the person and not the crime, and that a criminal act, however ghastly, was shorter-lived than the reputation of the criminal.[38]

Insanity, mental disability, or incapacity motivated about 30 percent of all commutations between 1909 and 1953.[39] As Governor Angus McLean explained in 1926, "The State of North Carolina should under no circumstances take the life of one of its citizens who is not capable of understanding the consequences of his acts." The citizen in question was James Jeffreys, a "low type moron," who upon learning of his commutation, said, "'Ain't done nothing no how.'"[40] However, as North Carolinians learned in a 1929 state publication, *Capital Punishment in North Carolina*, edited by activist and journalist Nell Battle Lewis, mental incapacity was hardly an obstacle to execution. Her account details more than two dozen death row denizens with severely diminished mental capacity or profound mental illness. Not all these men were executed, but many were.[41]

After a commutation such as James Jeffreys's, which acknowledged mental disability but did not confer the legal status of insanity, the criminal was likely to be confined in the State Hospital for the Dangerous Insane in Raleigh;[42] if they were black, they would be sent to the segregated State Hospital for the Insane, later Cherry Hospital, in Goldsboro.[43] Institutions such as these hospitals had existed for decades. The first was established in Raleigh in 1856, and the separate facility for those deemed dangerous was at least intended to be built in 1898,[44] though it does not appear to have opened until the mid-1920s.[45] There, many inmates could expect castration or eugenic sterilization. North Carolina, led by the declaration "the feeble-minded breed feebleminded [and] we pay the cost,"[46] was prolific in this area for many years.[47]

Commutation for mental incapacity might lead to a parole. For example, eighteen-year-old condemned murderer William J. Dunheen, denied a new trial by the North Carolina Supreme Court, was scheduled to die in the gas chamber in December 1945. Governor R. Gregg Cherry extended reprieves as he and others studied the case. In May, a team of five psychologists persuaded Cherry that Dunheen was mentally ill. His brother had epilepsy, Cherry noted in a statement, and his father and two of his uncles had been confined in mental hospitals. Dunheen himself, though admitted to the army in July of 1943, had spent most of his time in uniform in the hospital, eventually receiving a medical discharge. Dunheen's crime was horrible, Cherry said, but "I cannot, under the constitutional power given me, permit the execution of a mentally ill man. I am, therefore, asking the relatives and friends of the cruelly murdered young girl to be encompassed with the mantle of mercy and believe with the medical authorities and with me, that this youthful defendant is far from a normal human being in mental makeup."[48] Dunheen was eventually paroled in 1958.[49]

Sending mentally ill prisoners such as Dunheen to an institution rather than the death chamber aroused indignation in some quarters. As *News and Observer* editors complained, "The law gives the breaks to the most dangerous criminals—the crazy ones."[50] It was a persuasive argument that struck at the heart of the death penalty's purpose: should it, like incarceration, remove a dangerous person from among those he or she threatens? Should it strike back, with finality, at a violent criminal? Should it be a dispassionate, yet lethal, response to a terrible crime? North Carolina's governors, and before them solicitors and juries, preferred to answer these questions on a case-by-case basis.

Youth, just as a diminished mental capacity, was understood to reduce culpability long before the United States Supreme Court ruled that executing minors was unconstitutional.[51] British common law, which, undisturbed, prescribed punishment for North Carolinians for many years, judged that only children under seven years of age should be absolved of responsibility for actions that would otherwise be considered criminal. Children between seven and fourteen could be held responsible if deemed appropriate, and a number of children, the youngest of whom was ten years old, were executed in the United States before 1900. But by the early twentieth century, many states, including North Carolina, were beginning to treat youthful offenders differently from adults, seeking to protect their futures, and their bodies, with the creation of juvenile courts and the construction of juvenile detention facilities.[52] Giving children special consideration, however, did not prevent North Carolina from becoming a leader in executing teenagers. Between 1910 and 1961, the state electrocuted or gassed sixteen teenagers between the age of sixteen and eighteen.[53]

Very few young women made it far enough in the death penalty process to need a death sentence commuted; in general, women were less likely to commit serious crimes. In 1916, the State's Prison in Raleigh and various satellite work camps held over 850 men but fewer than 50 women. Ten years later, the male prison population had ballooned to more than 1,300, but the female population had grown by just one inmate, and in 1940, the male population was approaching 10,000, while the female population was 150.[54] The death row population was similarly male. Of the 660 people admitted to death row between 1910 and 1961, just six were women, only one of them white. In a measure of the protection womanhood offered even to African Americans, four of these women eventually won commutation. While some men, such as those convicted of rape, were commuted because the governor and others believed that their victims were not chaste enough to merit retribution, some condemned women won their lives because they were considered too ladylike to die in the death chamber.

Ida Ball Warren was one such woman. In 1916, Warren became the first woman in North Carolina sentenced to death under the state-run death penalty system. She made it there because she resolved a romantic quandary by enlisting her paramour to murder her husband.[55] She and that paramour, Samuel P. Christy, bungled the murder of Warren's husband a number of times: they put arsenic in his soup, mercury in his wine, plotted to shoot him and leave his body on the railroad tracks, and sought to lure him to his death at an accomplice's house. Finally, the husband hastened matters along by interrupting an assignation. In the ensuing fight Christy killed him with a monkey wrench.[56]

Christy later told law officers that Ball had entranced him. "'I became a perfect love slave to her,'" he said. "'I was in her power deeper than I really thought at the time, I guess.'"[57] There was little question of Warren's guilt, despite her efforts to implicate Christy and portray herself as an innocent bystander, but the judge had difficulty giving Warren a death sentence. Speaking from the bench, he told the people in the crowded Winston-Salem courtroom that he wanted them "to realize something of the ordeal of the court being forced to pronounce the extreme penalty of the law upon a woman."[58]

After the North Carolina Supreme Court rejected Warren's appeal, it fell to Governor Locke Craig to decide whether to let the sentence stand. Craig issued a lengthy statement explaining his decision in the context of its gravity: "When a petition for pardon or commutation is placed before the Governor he must act. He cannot avoid the responsibility. His action is the orderly process of the administration of justice, provided in the Constitution. His judgment is the final decree of the people and the law pronounced by the ultimate tribunal." But, he went on, "as the Governor of the State of North Carolina it is not my judgment that the majesty of the law demands that this woman, unworthy and blackened by sin though she be, shall be shrouded in the cerements of death, dragged along the fatal corridor and bound in the chair of death. . . . The killing of this woman would send a shiver through North Carolina."[59] When Craig commuted Warren's sentence, Christy enjoyed a kind of secondhand mercy. Eventually both parties were sentenced to over twenty years in prison,[60] but both were released after fifteen years. By 1931, Warren had a job with the YWCA in Raleigh.[61]

Among the unlucky women who did not receive the same consideration as Warren were African Americans Bessie Mae Williams and Rosana Phillips. Phillips followed her husband, Daniel, to the gas chamber in 1943 for the murder of the couple's landlord. The trial revealed that Daniel had killed the man with an axe; Rosana, in assisting with the disposal of the body, made herself culpable for equal responsibility. She might have won more pity from the jury had she not married Daniel after the murder and honeymooned with him on the victim's money. As the death date approached, the *News and Observer* reported that Rosana was hopeful for a commutation, certain that a reason for mercy would arise. When it did not come, parole officials hoped that in sending Rosana's husband Daniel into the gas chamber first, they might spur a confession that would exonerate Rosana and give the governor an excuse to commute her. But Daniel went to his death with only the customary prayers on his lips, and Rosana followed.[62] The following year, nineteen-year-old Bessie Mae Williams died in the gas chamber for her confessed participation in the robbery and brutal murder of a Charlotte taxi driver. A female accomplice, fourteen at the time of the murder, won a commutation from Governor J. Melville Broughton, but the governor explained that this commutation was due wholly to her age, and Williams could not expect similar mercy.[63]

Ida Ball Warren's trial captivated North Carolinians in the early twentieth century, but it did not become the sensation that an arson trial did in 1931. On March 12, 1931, a gang of determined arsonists torched two residence halls at Samarcand Manor, a school for delinquent girls in Eagle's Nest, causing more than $100,000 worth of damage. Police charged sixteen suspects the following day. It did not matter that the suspects were adolescent girls, nor that they were white. Indeed, some reformers at the time viewed such persons as "an unredeemable lower class of feebleminded poor."[64] If convicted of arson, they would receive the death penalty. The trial touched off a statewide discussion of North Carolina's flimsy effort at serving its neediest citizens and laid bare many residents' enduring distaste for poverty, especially when mingled with sex. News and Observer columnist Nell Battle Lewis put her new law degree to work for the first time defending the girls, using the opportunity to publicize the cruel corporal punishments they endured while in the state's care, and revealing her clients' sexual histories to illustrate their difficult childhoods. The press and the public vacillated between pity for the victims of rough treatment and revulsion against these depraved young women, who seemed to embody a dangerous new style of sexual, aggressive womanhood.[65]

The girls' behavior while awaiting trial heightened observers' anxieties. At the Robeson County jail, one group of girls destroyed their cells, tearing up their bunks and setting fires. Another, in jail in Carthage, torched their beds and attacked a firefighter called to quench the blaze. After being transferred to the Moore County jail, they set fire to it, too.[66] A week later, the girls were to be tried for first-degree arson, but a plea bargain spared their lives, as well as ensuring North Carolina did not sully its reputation. Far from death, the twelve girls convicted received sentences for their second-degree arson convictions ranging from eighteen months to five years. Like

Ida Ball Warren, the Samarcand girls, when facing execution, were treated with a deference they might not have enjoyed in any other circumstance, despite embodying the kind of femininity that many white North Carolinians found distasteful.

Like Warren and Christy, condemned prisoners who won commutations had a fairly good chance of eventually leaving imprisonment. If a former death row inmate served his time quietly, he might eventually see his sentence reduced to a period of years, and finally, receive parole. For instance, in 1936, when he was twenty years old, Reed Coffey was sentenced to death for the murder of his uncle. As Coffey's death date approached, evidence of his innocence and his strenuous protests spurred the Paroles Commission to launch an investigation, which netted him a commutation about a year after his conviction. But while Paroles Commission investigators believed that Coffey was innocent, it was not until November of 1940, four years after his commutation, that Governor Clyde Hoey reduced Coffey's sentence to a term of twenty to thirty years. After fourteen and a half years, Coffey, a "nearly model prisoner," not to mention an apparently innocent man, finally earned a parole.[67]

Others received commutations because of doubts about the degree of their guilt. First-degree murder, for example, required premeditation and malice, hotly debated terms, but ones that excluded killings during fights, for example. Kenneth Taylor was an African American man who killed a "woman of poor reputation" in a "house of bad character" during a quarrel. Governor Hoey commuted Taylor, rebuffing the jury's judgment by explaining that "I do think he killed under sudden impulse rather than in cold blood."[68] Gary Thompson, an African American man sentenced to death for a 1935 burglary, won a commutation a few hours before his execution after Governor Ehringhaus was "'informed by officials and responsible citizens . . . that this crime involved no serious injury to either person or property.'"[69]

Perhaps the best example of a prisoner who received gubernatorial clemency as a result of a claim to innocence was also one of the only people in North Carolina, among a number of apparently innocent people condemned to die, who received a pardon. William Mason Wellman, referred to by his nickname "Mace" in coverage in white newspapers, stood trial for the rape of a white woman in Iredell County, North Carolina. Wellman, an African American man, was arrested in Washington, D.C., in April 1942, two months after the assault. Wellman fought his extradition to North Carolina, producing evidence and a witness who attested that Wellman was working at Fort

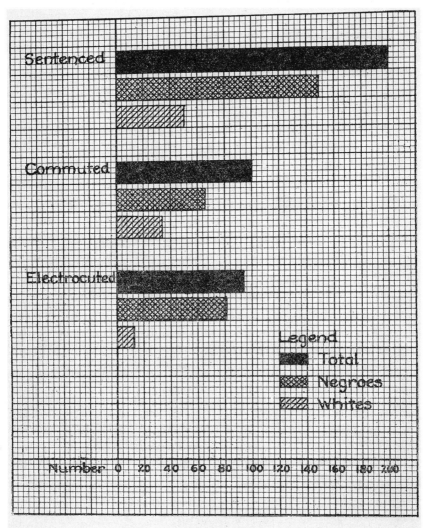

GRAPH I
DISTRIBUTION OF SENTENCES, COMMUTATIONS AND ELECTROCUTIONS OF
PERSONS CONVICTED OF CAPITAL CRIMES

A hand-drawn chart by Nell Battle Lewis reveals that in the early years of North Carolina's state-administered death penalty, African Americans were sentenced to death in such disproportionate numbers that they were both commuted and executed in higher numbers than whites. From State Board of Charities and Public Welfare, *Capital Punishment in North Carolina*.

Belvoir at the time of the assault, approximately 350 miles away. At the trial, his attorneys failed to produce this argument: it was his word versus the survivor's.[70] Based solely on her testimony, and after just fifty minutes of deliberation, Wellman was convicted of first-degree rape and sentenced to death.

Wellman took advantage of his automatic appeal to the state Supreme Court to again insist that he was nowhere near Iredell County when the rape took place, but the court simply acknowledged that his evidence was in "direct conflict" with the testimony of the survivor and refused to grant an appeal.[71] That decision sparked a cascade of petitions and hearings in which citizens urged Governor J. Melville Broughton to commute Wellman's sentence, if not to pardon him altogether. Over the course of eight months, Broughton heard from the survivor's attorney, who argued that Wellman perpetrated the rape in an act of revenge against her, and the playwright Paul Green, among others, arguing for mercy.[72] C. C. Spaulding, the president of Durham's North Carolina Mutual Life Insurance Company, seen as a leader in the African American community, warned Broughton that executing Wellman would "be nothing but a legal lynching."[73] In April 1943, approximately one year after his arrest, Wellman received a full pardon.[74] Nearly thirty years later, Wellman would return to North Carolina to receive $986.40, the maximum allowable compensation for his wrongful conviction.[75] He died in Washington in 1975.[76]

Neither innocence nor incapacity, however, guaranteed mercy. Records from W. Kerr Scott's 1949 to 1953 term, more carefully kept than those of his predecessors, log the cases of those who did not receive mercy. Ernest Liles was executed for committing rape on November 22, 1950, just two days after his lawyer revealed new evidence that his accuser had not been raped. Covey Lamm, sentenced to die for murdering his wife in early March 1950, was executed toward the end of that year despite what appeared to be a consensus that he was "unbalanced." And while Judge Henry A. Grady told Governor Scott that he had no formal recommendation in the case of James Edward Lewis, condemned for murdering his wife, he added, "Here is a case where you and I can save the life of a miserable fool . . . I think we should do it."[77] Scott did nothing.

Although executive clemency originated as a monarchical power and remained in the hands of the governor alone, the process allowed citizens to maintain contact with the punishment process, whatever its disposition, during a period of accelerating professionalization. The sociologist Elmer Johnson found that appeals from "responsible officials," members of the jury, or community members figured in more than half of commutation statements between 1909 and 1954, an illustration of the enduring depth of community involvement in the death penalty process. A community's silence could doom a convicted murderer, but recommendations by respected citizens and others were certain to win a condemned prisoner a close examination by the governor and his staff.[78] As Governor Angus McLean wrote in one commutation statement, "It is inconceivable that all these citizens should speak with one voice in appealing to me for clemency if it were not for the fact that they earnestly believe the infliction of the death penalty would be a grave injustice under the circumstances of the case."[79]

One apparent result of clemency decisions such as McLean's was that North Carolinians appeared to feel that they had a real voice in whether death sentences were carried out. As a double execution slated for Good Friday in March 1951 approached, a number of citizens wrote to Governor W. Kerr Scott requesting a delay. "I believe this is an outrageous date to have an execution," huffed Bitsy Clem of Raleigh. Asking Scott to postpone the execution to "a more proper date," Clem added, "I, firmly believing that you are a Christian, know that this is a small favor to ask one for the sake of Christianity."[80] Another petitioner made the same request. "It seems ironical that an execution should be set for this day," wrote Gerry Dickinson. "It certainly is not in keeping with the significance of the day or the week." He added his hope that Kerr would select "a more suitable time" for the double asphyxiation, perhaps not the anniversary of the day Jesus was executed.[81]

As often as North Carolinians sought reprieves or clemency, just as often they complained that the governor's interventions put up roadblocks along the path to justice. One 1949 missive ably summed up the many complaints about gubernatorial commutations in a letter to Governor W. Kerr Scott. The writer, in urging Scott not to alter the death sentence of wife-murderer James Creech, argued that clemency eroded support for courts and trampled on the rights of, and removed the protection of the law from, law-abiding North Carolinians:

We do feel that you are indebted to us as well as all other law
abiding citizens in North Carolina, and that debt is this: Protect our
daughters in married life by ridding the Governor's Mansion as the
(scape goat center) for criminals, stop it from the Hobby (as the last
four years seem to have been) for commuting, paroling, and pardoning

criminals, and turning them back on society as almost unpunished murderers or other types of low violators. It is embarrassing and regrettable to feel that the time has come when a small citizen must speak out in defense of the rights granted us by the laws of our state, and in turn denied us to a great extent by the powers vested in our Governors, and which has been to our thinking overexercised during the last four years. If we cannot have a Governor who will stand pat on the execution of the law, and have more respect for our courts and quit intervening in so many (especially murder cases) we just as well close our court houses and quit spending our State's perfectly good money to convict criminals.[82]

Concern about the deleterious effects of commutation were not limited to law-abiding citizens. In 1944, Alex Harris, the forty-nine-year-old tenant farmer executed for one of four murders he committed during a holdup of a gas station, advised Governor Cherry against commuting him, actually externalizing the logic—sound or not—against using clemency. "'I know I ought to pay the penalty,'" he told his chaplain. "'If I should come out of this with a commutation of sentence, and ten years from now the Governor would see fit to parole me, other people might think they could do the same thing and get away with it.'"[83]

Another source of worry was the effect of an increasingly formal clemency process on the path of punishment. Deliberations extended the time between conviction and execution, which even by the early years of the twentieth century was alarming North Carolina's judiciary. The justices of the Supreme Court, themselves often blamed for attenuating legal process, blamed a sluggish trial and appeal process for the state's relatively high homicide rate and the incidence of lynching. In 1914, in rejecting condemned murderer Jim Cameron's appeal, Chief Justice Walter C. Clark added a lengthy aside on behalf of "organized society," which must object to the "slow and cumbersome" path of justice that saw Cameron still alive eight months after receiving a death sentence. Clark complained that while the state had a death penalty, "the punishment [for murderers] is too often a moderate fine paid by the murderer, or his friends, to his counsel in the shape of the fee and a far heavier fine laid upon the taxpayers in the form of a long, tedious, and futile trial."[84] It would, of course, only get worse. As the legal process became more protracted, justices continued to call for clarification and cleanup. After Earl Neville was saved from a lynch mob by the governor's promise of a speedy trial, Clark warned that the governor risked reneging on his word by no fault of his own, due to the slow progress of Neville's appeal, sent on its meandering path "by the easy indifference of officials."[85]

## Is Murder Less Deadly than Whooping Cough?
## The Acceleration of Sympathy

Indifference was certainly a factor in the death penalty process, but the true culprit was sympathy. North Carolinians were often predisposed to pity capital criminals, or at least to extend them more consideration than the law dictated. They established a precedent of executing relatively few of those condemned to die in the very early years of state-run electrocution. In 1912, the warden of the State's Prison reported to the General Assembly on the fates of the twenty-five men sentenced to death since the adoption of the electric chair in 1910. Two received new trials on appeal, one winning acquittal and the other a second-degree conviction; eleven were commuted; and twelve were executed.[86] The effect of commutation on the death penalty process was profound. For the first three decades of state-imposed death penalty in North Carolina, nearly as many prisoners were commuted as were executed. One commissioner of paroles reported that between 1910 and the end of that administration in January 1937, 183 people had been executed, but 149 commuted.[87]

North Carolina's newspapers chided state officials with regular articles and cartoons illustrating the shortcomings of the death penalty process. In 1928, one journalist laughed that the motto of death row should be, "While There Is Life There Is Hope," because when someone "takes up residence in the shadow of the electric chair, [he] holds a ticket in the strangest lottery known to man."[88] The following week the *News and Observer* published a cartoon of a scowling man emerging from shadow, a gun in his hand. "Chair?" he asks. "Bah!" Below the gun is a caption: "N.C., 1910–1926. Tried for Murder, 3,065. Executed, 63."[89]

Locke Craig commuted more people than he permitted to be executed, as did Cameron Morrison. With the exception of J. C. B. Ehringhaus, during whose administration fifty-nine men died in the electric chair and gas chamber and twenty-nine won commutations, most governors commuted nearly half of the condemned criminals whose cases they considered, and just a few years into the twentieth century, they were considering almost every capital conviction.[90] Before Ehringhaus took office, in fact, only about 30 percent of white murderers and rapists sent to death row would eventually die in the electric chair; African Americans convicted of murder or rape were 20 percent more likely to be electrocuted. White people convicted of burglary, though just three were sent to death row, were all commuted, as opposed to just 64 percent of African American men.[91]

Adding to commutation's effect on death row, in the first half of the twentieth century the number of people admitted to prison for potentially capital crimes dwarfed the number of those condemned to death. According to the unevenly kept records of the State's Prison, 61 first-degree murderers entered the prison system between 1909 and 1916, in addition to 121 burglars, at least 9 rapists, and 11 arsonists, amounting to a total of 202 potentially capital prisoners. During these years, 29 people died in the electric chair. Similar statistics exist for other periods during which record-keepers chose to note the number of prisoners entering the system and differentiated between first-degree murderers and other killers. For example, in the year ending on June 30, 1932, just one of 16 men admitted to the prison system for a rape conviction received a sentence of more than five years; only one of 30 killers received more than five years. Between 1927 and 1930, 41 arsonists were imprisoned, and not one died in the electric chair.[92] North Carolinians were finding ways around mandatory sentencing laws.

With help from Ehringhaus and an active execution season in the late 1940s, the percentage of executed capital criminals inched upward, but not so much that in 1941 the *News and Observer* could not claim that "the mandatory death sentence isn't mandatory."[93] The paper was right: executive clemency spared a large number of North Carolinians sentenced to death, transforming the death penalty into just one of a variety of responses to capital crime. At any given time, many of the inmates on death row could expect to be "let out into the yard," as the slang went, moved into the general population, and maybe even paroled.[94] And these were the unlucky men who were actually sent to death row after being convicted of a murder, a rape, or a burglary. Most people convicted of these crimes never received a death sentence because before the sentencing phase of the death penalty process, North Carolinians prevented the state's rigid laws from taking effect.

As early as 1924, the death penalty process in North Carolina was raising questions about its certainty such as, "Is murder less deadly than whooping cough?" So asked Frank Smethurst in a 1924 Sunday piece in the *News and Observer*. He noted that since 1910, when the state abolished public hangings, courts addressed 1,168 capital cases, but just 127 convicts entered death row. Of those 127 condemned men, only 67 were executed. According to Smethurst, someone indicted for a capital crime in North Carolina in the early years of the electric chair had between a 5 and 6 percent chance of being executed. As he wrote, these were odds that "would make a gambler blush."[95] According to North Carolina's attorneys general, who left behind an incomplete record of the capital cases they brought before Superior Courts, the number of such cases actually exceeded Smethurst's calculation, not including second-degree crimes. The attorneys general reported on capital cases in their yearly reports to the state legislature—reports in which they may have grouped all sex crimes under rape, inflating the number of capital cases on record, but also omitted some data and appeared to transpose numbers for certain crimes—recording 1,269 capital cases between 1909 and 1924, driving the odds of electrocution even further down.[96]

North Carolina's mandatory death sentence created a new kind of deterrent, not to criminals contemplating a burglary or a rape, but to solicitors charged with prosecuting them, juries charged with convicting them, and judges charged with sentencing them. It is not possible to count the number of acquittals resulting from discomfort with mandatory death sentences, but North Carolinians sensed that the laws prevented convictions. Echoing an ongoing national conversation among lawyers and academics, the *News and Observer* worried that jurors were giving "undue weight" to their doubts in capital cases because they refused to accept the responsibility for execution. The result was that undeserving people went free.[97]

Acquittal was one way jurors, judges, and lawyers avoided mandatory sentences. Another path was trying to reverse their own decisions after they were made. It was a powerful sign of the confounding status of the law that with some frequency, the same people who sent someone to death row sought to bring that person back, agreeing to use one law to skirt another, trusting that executive clemency could be used to get around mandatory sentences. These appeals represent a remarkable stage in the death penalty process: an after-the-fact effort at nullifying a verdict by the very people who produced it. Commissioner of Pardons Edwin B. Bridges explained the move in a 1929 letter to Governor O. Max Gardner: "Often Judges of the Superior Court, after giving more mature consideration to the sentence imposed on the prisoner," he wrote, "feel that sentence was too severe and recommend that the prisoner's sentence be reduced."[98]

Such was the case for George B. Plyler, the kind of man who did not seem to deserve special treatment—after all, he was a drinker, and a schemer, and confessed to arranging a neighbor's death. As Plyler testified in court in 1911, he had grown fearful of this neighbor, Carter Parks. Plyler had insulted Parks by murdering his brother-in-law, and then, by trying to kill Parks himself. After this failed murder attempt, Plyler began to worry that Parks might seek revenge and Parks would probably pull it off—Plyler was a small man, and had only one eye. Getting out ahead of Parks's imagined plot, Plyler offered three men a gallon of liquor each to kill Parks before Parks killed him. They accepted, and soon afterward, Plyler was arrested, tried, and sentenced to death. His dedication to self-preservation led him to implicate his hit men. It was this gesture of civic responsibility, coupled with urgent appeals for his life, which won him a letter of recommendation from his trial judge. Plyler was "properly convicted," Governor W. W. Kitchin wrote, but since the judge who tried him recommended clemency, he commuted Plyler's sentence.[99]

Sometimes, judges made decisions during capital trials that led them to strike a deal to ensure a convicted criminal would not die. The result was a bargain that saved a life and underscored that the symbolism of the death penalty did not require an actual execution. In 1942, for instance, one Superior Court judge called solicitor Thomas Johnson into his chambers after a rape conviction and death sentence. The judge told Johnson that he was setting aside the death sentence and reversing course, allowing his client to plead to a lesser charge. Johnson resisted, telling the judge that "the publication of [the client's] death sentence would have a very salutary effect in the community in which the prisoner lived." He convinced the judge to pronounce the death sentence, with the understanding that they would recommend life imprisonment in a follow-up letter to the governor. As Governor Broughton considered the prisoner's application for clemency, Johnson wrote to Commissioner of Paroles Edwin Gill. He had assured the judge that "there would be no difficulty," he wrote, and "naturally, if the Governor declines to follow our recommendation, I am left in a somewhat embarrassing situation."[100] The man was not executed, and was paroled in 1958.[101]

These efforts on behalf of capital criminals constituted informal recommendations of mercy at a time when the law did not formally allow juries this privilege. In 1923, for example, Governor Cameron Morrison considered commuting the death sentences of Eugene and Sidney Gupton, convicted of first-degree murder in Edgecombe County and sentenced to death. Morrison explained that although the case was a "horrible one," he was reluctant to disregard the recommendation of the Superior Court judge, the prosecutors, and the trial jury that the brothers receive life imprisonment for their crime. The jury convicted them, but, whether out of ignorance of law or an understanding of practice, added a nonbinding recommendation of mercy.

The judge had to hand down a death sentence, but, he explained in a letter to Morrison, "'If I had had the power I should have shown some regard to the request of the jury.'" The judge was powerless, but Morrison was not: he commuted the Guptons' sentences.[102]

Alex Harlee won a commutation, and eventually an indeterminate prison sentence, after the trial judge, solicitor, and entire jury wrote to Governor Morrison recommending clemency. George Williams and brothers Fred and Frank Dove were sentenced to death for the 1922 murder of a rural mail carrier; records show that the three men were commuted in 1923, and denied parole two years later. But in 1929, seven years after another man confessed to the crime for which they were sentenced, they won full pardons "upon the strong recommendation of the trial judge, the trial solicitor, the arresting officers, the private prosecution, the prosecuting witness, a number of jurors and practically all the officials who heard the trial, who are of the opinion that the prisoners are entirely innocent of the crime for which they are charged."[103] The trial judge made a particularly strong push for clemency. "'I have prayed to the God of all truth, knowledge, and judgment, without whom nothing is true, or wise, or unjust to direct me,'" he wrote. "Each of us, with Robert E. Lee, believes that 'duty is the sublimest word in the language.'"[104]

Despite the frequent success of these pushes for mercy, such efforts did not guarantee clemency. In 1937, before the law made such recommendations binding, jurors recommended mercy for nineteen-year-old Robert Brown as they convicted him of first-degree murder. The governor declined to commute his sentence, revealing that the law's flexibility bent it in both directions.[105] The *Charlotte Observer* would have applauded Hoey's resolve. In 1924, the paper had condemned jurors' efforts on behalf of condemned criminals, worrying that that such post-conviction appeals meant "that the work of the court is nullified and public confidence in the courts is shaken." A juror's "good sense is smothered under the froth of sentimentalism," the paper complained.[106] Days later, the *News and Observer* echoed this complaint, noting that "it may seem strange that men who would convict another man could turn right around and ask the Governor to aid the prisoner, but that happens many times."[107]

### This New Mercy Law You All Passed: The Birth of Discretion

Recommendations to the governor were an essential way for judges and juries to skirt mandatory sentencing laws and apply a degree of practicality, or mercy, that the law did not allow. The *News and Observer*'s editorial board believed that the practice highlighted the shortcomings of North Carolina's judicial system, and in a 1939 editorial, urged lawmakers to follow the examples of judges and juries and take a "practical approach . . . to the whole problem of capital punishment." Instead of relying on technicalities to free wrongly condemned prisoners, the editors reasoned, why not vest in judge and jury the kind of discretion only the governor could wield? The paper hoped that by doing so, the General Assembly might reverse "a prolific inspiration of cynical attitudes toward the whole judicial process."[108] Eventually, "after nibbling at the subject for years," the legislature took this advice, essentially codifying the relative leniency that jurors and others had been extending to serious criminals for decades.[109] First, in 1941, the General Assembly relaxed the state's mandatory sentencing laws, allowing juries to formally recommend mercy for first-degree burglars and convicted arsonists. According to the amended law, convicted arsonists and burglars "shall suffer death," but, "if the jury shall so recommend, the punishment shall be imprisonment for life."[110]

In 1949, the General Assembly again amended the state's general statutes, this time making capital punishment in first-degree murder and rape cases discretionary: now, juries had discretion over sentencing for all four death-eligible crimes. Legislators did so at the recommendation of the Special Commission for the Improvement of the Administration of Justice, a group led by North Carolina Supreme Court Justice Sam Ervin and Harold Shepherd, dean of the Duke University Law School. In its report, published in 1948, the commission noted that North Carolina was among just four states with a mandatory death penalty and that "quite frequently, juries refuse to convict for rape or first-degree murder because, from all the circumstances, they do not believe the defendant, although guilty, should suffer death. The result is that verdicts are returned hardly in harmony with evidence."[111]

The change meant that willful, premeditated killing, or a killing committed in the act of another felony, such as a robbery, remained punishable by death. But "provided, if at the time of rendering its verdict in open court, the jury shall so recommend," the punishment would be life in prison. The law directed the same for rape, burglary, and arson.[112] Of course, the law was just giving a procedural nod to what juries had been doing for decades. For instance, in 1923, Judge Frank Daniels of Edgecombe Superior Court wrote to Governor Morrison, recommending a commutation for convicted murderers Eugene and Sydney Gupton. "Dear Governor," he wrote, "The jury accompanied their verdict of guilty of murder in the first degree with a recommendation to the mercy of the court. Under this verdict, I could impose only the death sentence. If I had the power, I would have shown some regard to the request of the jury."[113] After 1949, judges such as Daniels would be able to do so, and juries, instead of recommending mercy for the governor after handing down a guilty verdict, could make a legally binding recommendation in the courtroom. One first-degree murderer wrote from a prison farm to "My Dearest Mr. Governor Scott," thanking him for "this new mercy law you all passed."[114]

The 1949 legal change left the jury "totally unconfined," to the point where after the ruling, the Supreme Court of North Carolina at least twice awarded new trials to defendants when the court believed that the judge, in charging juries to look at "'facts and circumstances,'" had improperly limited jury discretion.[115] Furthermore, judges could not explain to juries the implications of their decision to recommend mercy; the Supreme Court of North Carolina granted a new trial in the early 1950s because when, mid-deliberation, a juror asked the judge if the defendant might receive parole if given a life sentence, the judge said that he could not answer the question but failed to instruct the jury to put it out of their minds altogether.[116]

In 1953, another law allowed those indicted for capital crimes to plead guilty, and if their plea was accepted, to receive a life sentence instead of the death penalty.[117] In concert with jury discretion, this measure hastened the decline of the death penalty in North Carolina: between 1939 and 1948, about twenty people each year received death sentences, but between 1959 and 1968, that number fell to just two per year.[118] As one journalist put it, "Laws providing for the offering of pleas in capital cases tend to decrease events of capital punishment."[119]

By the late 1940s, prosecutors were trying to secure convictions in capital cases by reassuring juries that a death sentence did not ensure a death. For instance, in a 1948 appeal to the North Carolina Supreme Court, convicted murderer Clyde Little's defense attorney complained that the prosecuting attorney had instructed members of the jury that as in all first-degree cases there would be a string of appeals "and that not more than sixty percent of prisoners convicted of capital offenses were ever executed."[120] Between 1957 and 1961, no more than three men waited on death row at any time. In 1961, the state executed its last prisoner for more than twenty years. As the death penalty appeared to expire in North Carolina, the prison population swelled with inmates who accepted life sentences rather than risk execution, anticipating recent trends in criminal justice.[121] Yet even as North Carolinians witnessed the inception of mass incarceration, they rejected death as punishment, ultimately weakening the strictures of mandatory sentencing and relieving the governor of his role as the ultimate arbiter of capital punishment. The shift from post facto commutation to preemptive mercy resulted in a near quarter-century experiment in not executing.

**Intelligent and Civilized Sentiments**

Activism, Discretion, and the Decline of the
Death Penalty, 1941–1961

· · · · · · · · · · · · · · · · · · · · · · · · · · · · · · · · · · · · · · · · · · · · · · · · ·

On an October morning in 1947, Earl O'Dear ate a breakfast of ham and eggs, toast, and coffee.[1] Described by journalists as "a surly mountain youth," O'Dear was one of five men awaiting execution in Raleigh's Central Prison. He finished his last meal with a dessert of cherry pie and ice cream, and when he was done, he used the wooden spoon to jam the lock on his death row cell door. The stunt won O'Dear forty more minutes of life. He spent them watching prison guards extracting fragments of the spoon from the lock, as two of his fellow death row inmates entered the gas chamber, each taking one of two chairs. Once the lock was clear of debris, O'Dear was escorted from his cell and took his seat in the gas chamber next to Robert Messer, his accomplice in the hammer slaying of a taxi driver and his wife. In about thirteen minutes, as his mother and father wept at the prison gates, O'Dear was dead. Before the day was over, Willie Cherry, an African American man sentenced to death for burglary for entering the home of a white woman, became the fifth man executed by the state of North Carolina in a single day. Governor W. Gregg Cherry said that he hoped the executions of the young men, aged between twenty and twenty-six, would deter mounting juvenile crime.[2]

The five executions received national attention and prompted a little bit of soul-searching in editorial pages. "What does it profit the State of North Carolina to inflict capital punishment?" asked the *Asheville Citizen-Times* in an unsigned editorial. "Does the death penalty actually have the effect of deterring . . . capital offenses?"[3] Hugh Wilson, warden of Central Prison and veteran of eighty-three executions, also worried about the death penalty's failures as a deterrent. His solution was to return executions to the counties and make them public.[4] But the question was largely settled: the execution of O'Dear, Messer, Cherry, Jethro Lampkin, and Richard McCain amounted to a final spasm of state violence preceding the decline of death as punishment in North Carolina. In 1947, largely due to the October 3 executions, North Carolina reached a peak in the number of annual executions in the state not touched since 1936. The state would not reach that level again: in 1949, ten people were put to death but throughout the 1950s a total of just eighteen people died in the gas chamber.[5]

This chapter explores the slow dismantling of the death penalty in North Carolina between the mid-1930s and the early 1960s. It focuses on two forces pushing the death penalty to the margins: vocal abolitionists who sought to undermine the rationale behind death as punishment, and ordinary jurors, who, when given the chance to punish without death, took it. As activists such as journalist Nell Battle Lewis or playwright Paul Green worked for decades to rally public attention to the death penalty's many flaws—keeping the many forms of anti–death penalty discourse in the public sphere—and as attorneys such as Caswell J. Gates fought capital charges in courtrooms, the state legislature whittled away at the mandatory death sentence, allowing jurors to make formal recommendations of mercy in arson, burglary, rape, and murder cases, giving defendants life sentences rather than death. As juries took advantage of this option, the death penalty fell out of use and activists in the late 1950s would be forgiven for thinking that politicians had finally come around to their argument that the death penalty had no place in a civilized state.

## For Want of Good Moral Character:
## North Carolina's White Juries

Although African American men served occasionally, and undoubtedly under considerable pressure to vote with the majority, North Carolina's juries were composed largely of white men until the 1960s.[6] If the jury was a "political institution" and "the most energetic means of making the people rule," as Alexis de Tocqueville suggests in *Democracy in America*, in Jim Crow North Carolina, it was a political institution tasked with energetically reinforcing white power.[7] Jury composition varied county by county, with the General Assembly making slight modifications to the general arrangement. The county Board of Commissioners created lists of eligible voters drawn from rolls of residents who had paid tax the previous year, wrote those names on scrolls of paper, and secured those scrolls in a locked, partitioned box. In New Hanover County, for example, a 1909 act of the General Assembly directed that the county sheriff keep one key and the chairman of the Board of Commissioners another, to be accessed no fewer than twenty days before the fall and spring terms of Superior Court, where serious criminal cases were heard, at which time a child no older than ten would draw thirty-six scrolls from one side of the box and place them in the other side. The people named on those scrolls constituted the jury pool, from which the jury of twelve was drawn.[8] These names were overwhelmingly white, despite the statistical improbability of such homogenous jury pools. Although the Civil Rights Act of 1875, sustained by the United States Supreme Court's decision in *Strouder v. West Virginia*, forbade racial discrimination in selecting jurors, there was no meaningful enforcement mechanism to ensure people of color served.[9]

The case of Raleigh Speller illustrates the lengths some courtrooms would go to exclude jury service by African Americans. Speller was an African American man sentenced to death for rape in Bertie County in 1948, just one year before the state made such a sentence discretionary. His attorneys won two retrials before reaching the North Carolina Supreme Court. They argued that African American jurors had been unconstitutionally excluded from the jury pool, and presented solid evidence supporting their complaint: the clerk of court in Bertie County, which was 60 percent African American, testified that over the course of his seventeen years of service, an African American person had never been selected for jury service. In his words, it was "common knowledge, and generally known, that Negroes do not serve and have not served on grand or petit juries in Bertie County."[10] The court rejected this claim. Its decision noted that there had been "no intentional or purposeful discrimination against the colored race in the selection of jurors." Indeed, the exclusion of eligible African Americans was on its face racially neutral. As the clerk of court explained, during jury selection, the names of all eligible jurors were placed in a box and drawn, by a child under ten years of age, one by one and without overt racial identifiers. However, the names of white people were written in black ink and the names of African American people were written in red. When a red name was drawn, the prosecuting attorney would dismiss that juror "for want of good moral character or sufficient intelligence."[11]

Raleigh Speller's case would ultimately come before the Supreme Court of the United States, grouped with two other North Carolina cases that each demonstrated the starkly discriminatory character of the criminal justice system.[12] One was that of Clyde Brown, an illiterate African American youth, arrested for the rape of a white high school student, held without charges for five days, during which time he confessed; held an additional eighteen days without a hearing, he remained unrepresented by an attorney at that hearing. The other case heard in conjunction with Speller's was that of Lloyd Ray and Bennie Daniels, whose appeal protesting their involuntary confessions and discriminatory jury selection was rejected because it was submitted one day late.[13] In a "kaleidoscopic production" of a decision, the court denied relief to all four.[14]

Like the Daniels case, Speller and Brown's impending execution attracted some activist energy from the anti–death penalty population in North Carolina. As the executions approached, David Andrews, a white Methodist minister, sent a note to Governor James Umstead telling him that he was going to wire the local papers about his "protest against all capital punishment in North Carolina" and to make a "final plea" for executive clemency. He then sat down on the steps of the capitol, announcing that he would hold vigil for twenty-four hours, until the execution the following morning. The photograph that appeared on the front page of the *News and Observer* the following day was a powerful one—Andrews, just twenty-eight years old, sat with his back to the capitol, his legs crossed and a halo of sunshine on his high forehead. He would fast during his protest, he said, but would accept water if someone offered it; Andrews was confident there was a toilet he could use in the capitol building. He was stoic about the effects that this "Gandhi-like fast" might have on his body—"'it certainly won't do me any good,'" he told a reporter.[15]

He protested just about long enough to get hungry. After seven hours, he announced he was leaving. He called the papers to let them know. "'I have thought this over and now feel I have made my own protest effectively,'" he said. "'I intend now to carry on an educational campaign and then see what can be done in the next Legislature to change the laws.'" Andrews's protest, designed to persuade Umstead to commute two death sentences, failed. This failure, colored by optimism, typifies the movement, which, especially by the 1950s, had endured its share of shortcomings. Direct protest abandoned, Andrews returned to his desk to write some letters.[16] Among Andrews's correspondents was Paul Green. Later that year, Green began work on a play about a young minister who struggles to balance his family obligations with his desire to plunge himself into anti–death penalty activism. The main character is an amalgam of Green and Andrews, a man whose "sensitive imagination pictures the whole misery of the thing."[17]

The composition of juries had an impact in the courtroom. Between 1930 and 1940, sociologist Howard Garfinkel found that North Carolina jurors approached homicide cases differently depending on the race of the offender and the victim. African Americans who were accused of committing crimes against whites received the harshest treatment, with jurors acting on a compulsion not just to see that "Justice is done" but also to "get the nigger who is responsible for this." Juries trying African Americans who committed crimes against other African Americans felt no such compulsion, evaluating the defendant's character and weighing the consequences of acquittal and conviction. Jurors asked, "Murder? Another one? Who is the man? Where is he from? Whom did he kill? Are we going to try him or did he enter a plea?"[18]

While confirming that white jurors widely believed that African Americans were inherently criminal, the study also revealed that average white North Carolinians did not feel an urgent need to punish criminality unless it spilled over into the white world. This indifference deepened over the course of the legal process. In Garfinkel's findings, for example, more than 90 percent of African Americans arrested for murdering other African Americans were indicted for first-degree murder, more than any other offender-victim group. But as the trial proceeded, the chance that one African American charged with killing another would be sentenced to death steadily dwindled. Just over 50 percent indicted ended up being charged with first-degree murder, meaning that between the indictment and the trial, the prosecuting attorney accepted a plea or recommended a different charge. Ultimately, just 3 percent of those indicted were convicted of first-degree murder.[19]

Garfinkel's work exposes the biases that sent some murderers to the electric chair but others to chain gangs. It suggests a loose, personal system that coexisted with the dictates of the law, leaning on it at times, bending it at others, and sometimes discarding it altogether. Even this description may imply more order and rationality than existed. Some whites, when not exploiting it, were prone to ignore African American criminality, not to mention the African American community at large. As social scientist John Dollard observed in his 1937 study of Indianola, Mississippi, African Americans were "marked by a kind of 'second-handedness.'"[20] White officers sometimes arrested African American criminals, sometimes not; white juries sometimes convicted them, but sometimes they did not; white stakeholders in the legal process seemed sometimes to care about the idea of justice, but sometimes felt comfortable indulging their desire to inflict pain on African Americans.

Further, Garfinkel's research suggests that the administration of justice—in the form of a thirty-day stint in a work camp or the law's severest penalty—depended on a combination of simple bias and reference to Jim Crow standards of behavior for African Americans. Garfinkel argues there was a sacred element to defending white prerogatives in the courtroom when African Americans committed crimes against whites, whereas when they committed crimes against one another, "there is little sense of administering a sacred trust."[21] In those instances, juries and other participants in the legal process seemed to elevate the character of the defendant, gauging his or her reputation as the most important factor in the conviction process. Jurors decided whether or not they liked the defendant. If they did not, he would die.

Such was the case for Taylor Love, an African American man who murdered another African American and died in the electric chair in December 1911. Love was executed because he had a "generally bad reputation," and his "previous bad record" ensured a "violent end to a violent life," a journalist explained in the *News and Observer*.[22] Lewis Moody demonstrated his particularly bad character with a particularly brutal murder; Governor J. M. Broughton refused to commute his sentence because of the violence of the crime and Moody's cruelty in telling the victim's wife about it afterward.[23] Fleet Jack Wall, executed in the spring of 1941, was "declared to be a bad character," and one observer reprimanded him for "staring sullenly at the floor" as guards strapped him into the chair in the gas chamber.[24]

But the case of Fleet Jack Wall illustrates that one factor was more important than character for North Carolina's white juries. Wall had become convinced that his wife was unfaithful to him and had tried to kick her out of the home they shared. He drank, she did not leave, and after he had finished his whiskey and moved on to rubbing alcohol, he killed her. Of the sixty-nine African Americans who were executed for killing other African Americans between 1910 and 1961, thirty-four of them died for murdering their wives or girlfriends. Four were hired to kill their victims, five were guilty of brutal multiple murders (all of which included women), and twenty-six died for murdering other black men, either in particularly brutal fashion or in the course of committing another felony. Thus at least thirty-nine of the sixty-nine African Americans arrested for murdering other African Americans, including Fleet Jack Wall, were convicted of killing women. Garfinkel's claim that white jurors shrugged at black homicide seems most accurate when describing the trials of African American men who killed other African American men.[25]

Garfinkel notes that only a fraction of the African Americans convicted of murdering other African Americans were convicted of first-degree murder, thus earning a mandatory death sentence. These murderers of women, then, were considered particularly abhorrent. The murder of a wife or girlfriend seems to have upset jurors' sensibilities, which according to Garfin-kel, in the case of black-on-black murder, include a "lack of persuasion as to its specific criminality."[26] Jurors trying African American men for mur-dering African American women seem to have been somewhat more con-vinced that their actions merited punishment, as in the case of white-on-white crime. African Americans who rejected the domestic strictures that policed their behaviors as effectively as the threat of white violence needed to be removed from the community. And black women who tried to build lives with black men deserved some degree of protection, though only as ideas, as we have seen how they were treated when they testified to the own roles and the humanity of African American men in public (see chapter 1).

White law demanded that these people die although their crimes did not directly damage the white community, and they were not alone. In 1918, for instance, Baxter Cain, an African American man, found a substitute, another African American man, for his shift as a night watchman at the Southern Public Utilities Company in Salisbury. He showed up later, shot his sub to death, and took $70 from the company's safe. He used some of the money to buy himself a new wooden leg, and one of the bills he used to buy the leg implicated him. Of the sixty-nine African Americans executed for murdering other African Americans, just twenty-six, including Cain, were convicted for the simple murder of other black men, from respected citizens to numbers-runners.

Although executions during this wider period substantiate Garfinkel's ar-·gument that character was key in determining punishment for intraracial crime, they also add a new dimension to his work; they show that in North Carolina courtrooms, white jurors and the governors who signed or declined to sign death certificates had some sense of a commitment to punishing Af-rican Americans for crimes against other African Americans, and they were certainly committed to punishing white perpetrators for crimes against white victims. But they were less interested in punishing white people for crimes against people of color. Between the end of the Civil War and World War II, just six white people were executed for crimes with African Ameri-can victims, with four of those instances taking place during Reconstruc-tion, when the state's formal apparatuses were more supportive of African American personhood than they would become during Jim Crow. Just two white men in the twentieth century were executed for crimes against Afri-can Americans.[27] And, that the punishment functioned this way was no secret. James Allison, a white man sentenced to death for murder, knew it. In 1911, he slashed his own throat before being transported to death row, and again attempted suicide after he arrived, "saying he would not be the first white man electrocuted in North Carolina." He was: "First White Man Is Electrocuted," read the headline the following day.[28]

## Breaking Down the Ancient Landmarks: Opposition to Capital Punishment

American opposition to the death penalty flowed from the same Enlightenment energies that informed the American Revolution: to some thinkers, many of whom were inspired by Cesare Beccaria's 1726 *Essay on Crimes and Punishment*, execution exerted the kind of monarchical power they wanted to banish.[29] Beccaria believed that imprisonment was more effective at reducing crime than execution, in part because execution tended to model violence rather than prevent it. Using this argument, influential American intellectuals such as Benjamin Rush were able to push reform through their state governments. Rush managed to diminish the use of the death penalty in Pennsylvania, defining second-degree murder and paving the way for other states to do the same.[30] Thomas Jefferson tried but failed to ban capital punishment in Virginia.[31]

Those engaged in the debate about the death penalty in nineteenth- and early twentieth-century America attacked or defended the punishment using the theological, scientific, sentimental, and pragmatic arguments that would endure into the twentieth and twenty-first centuries. Given the relative infrequency of the death penalty, the argument was remarkably heated, and repetitive enough to make another detailed recital unhelpful. Opponents might cite biblical proscriptions against killing and New Testament lessons about mercy; proponents could counter with the law of the Torah and Jesus's death on the cross. Turn-of-the-century enthusiasm for science and medicine drove many to view crime as a medical problem, not one for the gallows. Less science-minded were those who sought to dramatize the pain and anguish attending execution, whether in death itself or in the miserable lives of the condemned. Amid these discussions, the utility of the death penalty as a deterrent was a continual source of lively debate.[32]

One prominent contributor to the conversation in the Northeast and Midwest was Edward Livingston, the man responsible for the South's flirtation with abolition in the nineteenth century. After leaving the mayoralty of New York City in disgrace and debt, Livingston rebuilt his career in New Orleans. Newly elected to the U.S. House of Representatives, he drafted a code of laws that would have abolished the death penalty. Livingston's principal concern was the risk of executing innocents, the only solution for which was banning execution altogether. Louisianans, however, were not interested, and by the time they considered his proposal, Livingston had left the state. His ambitions, which soon took him to Washington, D.C., may have limited his ability to persuade Louisianans, but his ideas, which he introduced on a national stage as well as in Louisiana, influenced lawmakers as far away as Maine, a state that limited executions in 1837.[33]

Maine was not alone. By the 1820s and 1830s, buoyed by literature and poetry that romanticized the criminal, dissected their final moments, and lamented the way in which hanging precluded the full bloom of guilt into repentance, an anti–death penalty movement was stirring. Anti–capital punishment societies sprang up around the country, and state legislatures in New York, Massachusetts, and Ohio considered abolition. By mid-century, in a sort of compromise between pro- and anti–death penalty forces, fifteen states had made their hangings private. Other states pressed ahead with banning the death penalty altogether, and between 1846 and 1897, six states, from Rhode Island to Colorado, rejected the death penalty.[34] Despite the disruption of the Civil War, these victories gave reformers momentum entering the twentieth century. The American League to Abolish Capital Punishment, founded in 1925, sought to transform state abolition groups into a national network, and while it largely failed, nine states and Puerto Rico abolished or restricted the death penalty between 1907 and 1930. But these changes were short-lived: only one of the states that abolished the death penalty during this period, Minnesota, kept it off the books, and between 1901 and 1939, during a period that included rising rates of violent crime and rising hysteria about them, eight states that had previously banned the death penalty restored it.[35]

. The states that abolished the death penalty in the early twentieth century were a diverse group that included North Dakota, Kansas, Washington, Arizona, and Tennessee. The only common characteristic they shared was a relatively small nonwhite population, which might help explain why they abolished the death penalty but not why most of them reinstated it.[36] The small nonwhite population removed an obstacle to public outcry that might have followed abolition—whites did not feel threatened—and at the top, prominent citizens or powerful politicians worked for it, often with the support of the press. In Kansas, for example, Governor Edward W. Hoch explained that it was because of his insistence that the legislature abolished the death penalty in 1907. Closer to North Carolina, Tennessee's

Duke Bowers, a wealthy retiree, pushed so hard for abolition in 1915 that the short-lived act that ended the death penalty bore his name.[37]

North Carolina seemed to be a good candidate for abolition. The state's leaders supported, or at least showed interest in, humanitarian reforms such as parole and the abolition of corporal punishment. In a broader sense, the state embraced Progressive social welfare programs, from public health initiatives, to the construction of mental health facilities, to juvenile prisons. Many elite North Carolinians also embraced temperance, which, though perhaps sour and judgmental, indicated sympathy for an underclass struggling with social and economic change.[38] The state's political leaders clung to convict leasing longer than in some southern states, but prisoner treatment became a cause for reformers, and the stripes and the lash were eliminated in the early years of the twentieth century.[39] North Carolina also boasted a number of socially prominent death penalty opponents who might have used their influence to inspire a ban.

The possibility of abolition, too, arose frequently enough to suggest that getting rid of the death penalty was not entirely out of the question. According to a 1938 *News and Observer* article, "Nearly every session of the Legislation sees an attempt to change the status of capital punishment."[40] Even so, the absence of these bills in the legislative record reveals that they rarely passed one, let alone both, houses of the North Carolina General Assembly. In 1919, Congressman W. O. Saunders championed an attempt to eliminate the death penalty altogether, winning support from some of his conservative colleagues who believed that death sentences led jurors to free dangerous criminals.[41] Saunders defended his bill in biblical terms, warning against snuffing out God's creation, and asking, "What is the Christian thing to do?" The bill passed the House after Saunders agreed to a compromise between two legislators, one of whom favored total abolition, and another who wanted instead to return to "good, old-fashioned hanging," that would deter crime and lynch mobs.[42] The compromise, which abolished the death penalty for arson and burglary only, passed by a comfortable 80–18 margin.

The editorial board of the *News and Observer* was optimistic about the Saunders bill. On the day after it passed the House, an editorial appeared applauding the vote, which, the board wrote, "will commend itself to the most intelligent thought in the State." The move showed that "the trend away from capital punishment is making itself felt in this State. Eventually, capital punishment will be abolished in all the States." At the same time, the editorial conceded that "the average person will be pardoned for confessing to ignorance as to whether a State benefits from having capital punishment abolished."[43] And it was, of course, these average citizens who made up the majority and made their support for the death penalty felt in the state senate.

Debate was vigorous and the gallery was filled when state senators debated the measure, presenting varied arguments, many of them for retention. One created a vivid picture of an idyllic mountain home that required protection by a muscular punishment system. "When it comes to encouraging crime in North Carolina . . . I am not a Progressive," said another to applause. Another claimed the death penalty was a deterrent, another that it was ordained by God. "Let the murderers stop first," one senator declared. The bill's proponents were somewhat less evocative in their orations, which may be why the *News and Observer* declined to describe their arguments in detail. The debate concluded with two senators voicing their opposition "to breaking down . . . the ancient landmarks." When the debate ended, "the remains" of the bill "were laid to rest" at the Capitol by a vote of 17–26.[44]

The Saunders bill was one of many attempts in the legislature to ban the death penalty; it is also the attempt that appeared to make it the furthest until the early 1940s, when the General Assembly relaxed the mandatory death sentence for arson and burglary. But these legislative efforts, though sometimes informed by an anti–death penalty movement, or pursued by legislators recruited by activists, often progressed only as far as the legislator who believed in them could push them. Anti–death penalty activists did not seek, in an organized, deliberate way, to craft and pass legislation until the 1960s. Until then, they combined advocacy for individual death row prisoners with persuasion, in hopes that convincing enough North Carolinians to oppose the death penalty would result in convincing legislative action. But opposition to the death penalty in principle and opposition to the death penalty for an individual are two very different positions.

The history of anti–death penalty activism between 1910 and 1961 in North Carolina unfolds much like an argument on the subject, a back-and-forth that moves from moral and religious persuasion, to logic, to an effort to inspire empathy. Henry L. Canfield, a Universalist minister, emerged as one of North Carolina's leading abolitionist voices in the 1920s, averring that execution was immoral and unjust. Nell Battle Lewis, a journalist who took up Canfield's mantle in the 1930s and 1940s, derided the death penalty's uselessness and stupidity, a stupidity that to her reeked of barbarism. And Paul Green, who began years of anti–death penalty work in the 1930s, personalized the punishment, using storytelling to render condemned men as characters in a too familiar tragedy. As these white advocates sought to spark a conversation about a punishment that disproportionately targeted African American men, African Americans themselves sought to condemn the death penalty's unfairness to their community while distancing themselves from African American criminals.

The debate rested more on personality than persuasion. When a condemned criminal's community spoke out for his life, drawing attention to the criminal as a social being, he received special consideration that at least half the time resulted in a commutation. Those most prone to mercy were judges, jurors, and governors who confronted capital criminals face to face, and were unable to reduce these criminals' lives to matters of principle. Just as the application of the death penalty rested on personhood, so too did the debate over its existence. Bills to abolish or change the death penalty were often personal projects; and the movement against the death penalty in twentieth-century North Carolina was powered neither by an organized lobby nor a grassroots network, but by the intense energy of a few people who could see from top to bottom and did not like what they saw.

## Intelligent and Civilized Sentiments: Henry Canfield's Pious Protest

In 1925, one minister wrote to another suggesting that they "join hands with all those who desire to see this barbarous custom of capital punishment ended."[45] The letter's recipient was Henry L. Canfield, who had two years earlier—evidently more quietly than he had hoped—founded an organization dedicated to ending the death penalty. Canfield was an Ohio-born Universalist minister and omnivorous activist who found his way to North Carolina the early 1920s and right away began sermonizing and speaking in support of pacifism, reproductive control for women, and the development of African American schools. In 1923, following but not in overt response to the Sacco and Vanzetti case, Canfield and others formed the Greensboro Society for the Abolition of Capital Punishment—over the next decade, press coverage called it by various names—a group devoted to the "abandonment" of the death penalty and other criminal justice reforms.[46] Progress was slow: three years later, they met in Greensboro to draft a constitution, and they did not elect leadership until 1928. Meanwhile, Canfield and his allies held meetings and gave talks, seeking to sway the public toward abolition, and to inspire the formation of similar groups, to develop "such pressure for the removal of the death chair from the paraphernalia of punishment as will make it impossible for a western legislator to withhold support from any bill looking to the dismantling of that engine of annihilation."[47] To achieve this goal, a committee crafted these arguments, disseminated them with literature, and recruited speakers to spread the message.[48] Members paid fifty cents in dues to cover stationery and other costs.[49]

There are few existing records of the league's activities. They met once a year in the Guilford County Courthouse to make plans for the coming year. At one such meeting one of Canfield's colleagues attacked the death penalty as a moral failure that ignored those most in need. "In the field of moral delinquency," he said, "where we are supposed to exercise the greatest charity, is the very field where we perpetuate vindictiveness and savagery." Canfield hoped that rather than springing from a moral revolution, abolition of the death penalty might inspire one. A better way of punishing criminals would [be to] "gradually" encourage "intelligent and civilized sentiments in the public mind instead of nurturing man's all too prone tendency to be vindictive and cruel to his fellow man."[50] A shortage of money stalled this effort, but Canfield spoke regularly against the death penalty. In the late 1920s, he delivered a series of lectures on a Greensboro radio station, including one that questioned the value of punishment itself. "What a sickening hodge-podge the State makes of administering its archaic, irrational, and inhuman laws relating to capital crime!" Canfield wrote to the *Daily News*. "It is expert in straining out the gnat and swallowing the camel."[51]

In 1926, the *Winston-Salem Journal* printed an editorial in which Canfield claimed that juries, reluctant to send criminals to their deaths, were choosing instead to set them free. "As civilization advances," he argued, "it becomes more and more difficult to get a conviction for first-degree murder."[52] The following year, Canfield advocated a legal change that would take three decades to accomplish: making the death sentence optional. But some supporters of capital punishment believed that jury discretion, expressed legally or by jurors who refused to commit, encouraged a distressing sentimentality that could be exploited by prisoners of means. "The greatest force working for the abolition of the death penalty is the discrimination in its enforcement," a *Greensboro Daily News* editorial complained in 1927. "Those not in position to work up sentiment in their behalf, without influence sufficient to bear, are more likely to suffer the extreme penalty than those in a position to command powerful influence."[53] In other words, mercy might be reserved not for the most deserving, but for those with the most means.

By the mid-1930s, Canfield was on a relatively short list of North Carolinians who were dues-paying members of the American League to Abolish Capital Punishment, a New York–based organization led by the famous Clarence Darrow that produced abolitionist literature. Throughout the 1930s, Canfield continued to write and speak on the issue but, despite his energy, had little success galvanizing opinion among lawmakers or the public. A high school student's letter to Canfield expressed the situation for death penalty opponents in the state. The student had requested materials to prepare an argument against the death penalty for a classroom debate, and in return Canfield sent the student some pamphlets and a book from the Greensboro public library. She wrote back after the debate, thanking Canfield. "The affirmative team won," she lamented, although those arguing against the death penalty argued well. She added, in a statement truer in the classroom than the courtroom, "There is victory in defeat."[54]

Canfield often addressed the death penalty's ineffectiveness as a crime control tool, but his convictions sprang from his religious faith. Many North Carolinians shared that faith, though they were more likely to be Baptists than Universalists. "God is sending you a message through me," wrote Nomira Waller, a Durham woman, to Governor Ehringhaus in 1933. "These are not my words but His Words; not my thoughts but His Thoughts," she added in a preface before launching into an eighteen-stanza poem that filled five pages with anti–death penalty references from the Bible. Waller's poem lays out one of the biblical conflicts that bedeviled religious North Carolinians as they weighed death as punishment: the law of Moses versus the teachings of Jesus. As Waller writes, so-called Mosaic law, spelled out in Exodus, appeared to demand lethal punishment.[55]

The phrase "an eye for an eye," often quoted by defenders of the death penalty in twentieth-century North Carolina, first appears in Exodus. God told Moses that when two people who are fighting injure a pregnant woman and "harm follows, then you shall give life for life, eye for eye, tooth for tooth, burn for burn, wound for wound, stripe for stripe."[56] The prescription arises again more broadly in Leviticus, when God tells Moses, "Anyone who kills a human being shall be put to death."[57] It returns in Deuteronomy alongside a vote of confidence for deterrence. Perjurers should be punished with the punishment their false testimony might have produced, God tells Moses. "The rest shall hear and be afraid, and a crime such as this shall never again be committed among you. Show no pity: life for life, eye for eye, tooth for tooth, hand for hand, foot for foot."[58]

But, as Nomira Waller pointed out, Jesus appeared to speak out against death as punishment a number of times. Waller cites Colossians, and Matthew 5:38, addressing vengeance directly. "You have heard that it was said, 'An eye for an eye, and a tooth for a tooth,'" Jesus said, according to Matthew. "But I say to you, do not resist an evildoer. But if anyone strikes you on the right cheek, turn the other also."[59] And John recorded that Jesus saved an adulterous woman from a mob, saying, "Let anyone among you who is without sin be the first to throw a stone at her."[60] However, some Christians interpreted Jesus's death on the cross as a tacit condoning of the death penalty and of the government's power to impose it. If Jesus did not believe in the power of the state to execute criminals, he would not have reassured another condemned man who complained about his fate, saying, "Today, you will be with me in Paradise."[61] Paul explained in his letter to the Romans that state authorities wished only for good behavior from their citizens. "But if you do what is wrong," he added, "you should be afraid, for the authority does not bear the sword in vain! It is the servant of God to execute wrath on the wrongdoer."[62] North Carolina's preachers said as much to their congregations. In 1935, one minister told his congregation that "God has delegated to government the authority to execute the death penalty."[63] Or, as one man put it in a letter to the *News and Observer*, "And kings, and governors, and judges, and sheriffs, and policemen, and jails, and penitentiaries, and the gallows, and the electric chair are the agents through whom God punishes evildoers—even in the taking of human life."[64]

This sentiment appears to have been widespread. In 1935, a Presbyterian pastor wrote to Governor Ehringhaus, urging him to resist the push for abolition because a ban on the death penalty would violate "God's divine plan for the continuity of life, the sustenance of life, and the protection of life." He added, "Nothing short of the death penalty can meet the demands of justice."[65] This letter and the many others that appeared in the *News and Observer* and newspapers across that state reveal the intractability of religiously inspired positions on the death penalty—"I sometimes wonder what the Devil will do with so many in Hell," wrote one woman[66]—but also the commanding presence of religion in the private and public life of many North Carolinians in the early part of the twentieth century. Ehringhaus agreed. In response to a letter urging him to commute a condemned inmate's sentence, he wrote that there was nothing he could do. "I did not make the law," he wrote. "The law of capital punishment even is as old as the Book from which we derive inspiration and hope of salvation."[67]

## Champion Idol-Smasher: Nell Battle Lewis
## in the 1920s and 1930s

Opponents of the death penalty never lacked for support on the state's editorial pages and from the press of North Carolina. In the front lines was Nell Battle Lewis, a columnist for the *News and Observer* who savaged the death penalty in her Sunday column, "Incidentally," for years. Lewis's columns were biting, sarcastic indictments of the death penalty and its supporters. Her voice determined both the movement's style, and substance, for many years. Lewis was such a forceful critic of the death penalty—and of the Ku Klux Klan, the social strictures on women, racial discrimination, and ultimately, Communism—her family feared for her mental health.[68]

A member of an influential North Carolina family that included three presidents of the University of North Carolina, Lewis graduated from Smith College before World War I and, frustrated that her education there did not challenge her enough, headed to the front to participate in the war effort. Back home, she returned to Raleigh and a career as a journalist: she began on the *News and Observer*'s society pages, but by 1921 her wide-ranging, politically charged columns were being picked up by other North Carolina papers as well as the *Nation*, the *Baltimore Sun*, and the *American Mercury*. She ran for office, too, becoming her county's first female candidate for the General Assembly in 1928.[69] According to her editor and publisher, Josephus Daniels, she was the state's "champion idol-smasher and hell-raiser,"[70] and another admirer credited her for leading "the great Gulliver South"[71] out of backwardness.

Lewis believed that the death penalty was barbaric, unbefitting of a Christian state, that it did not deter crime, and that it was used needlessly against a deeply dispossessed underclass. In short, she thought the death penalty was a stupid punishment. "Our infliction of capital punishment boils down to this," she wrote, "we kill these criminals because it's the simplest thing to do; because the revamping of our theory and practice of punishment requires high intelligence and considerable cerebration. So—why bother about it!"[72] The early adoption of the gas chamber, and prison officials' lack of understanding of how to properly use it, prompted Lewis to condemn the state, the first east of the Mississippi River to use gas, as "the dumbest commonwealth on the hither side of that storied stream."[73]

According to one biographer, Lewis cherished her role as "the village atheist" but she believed in the potential for a society that adhered to core Christian values and reserved special contempt for a Christian state that

Nell Battle Lewis, called a "champion idol-smasher" by her editor at the *News and Observer* of Raleigh. Lewis spent years attacking the death penalty in her column "Incidentally," in the *News and Observer*. Image from the Kemp Plummer Lewis Papers, #3819, The Louis Round Wilson Special Collections Library, University of North Carolina at Chapel Hill.

executed its criminals.[74] As she wrote, "An eye for an eye and a tooth for a tooth, and a life for a life is a law that, as I understand it, was superseded once and for all nineteen centuries ago."[75] In other words, Jesus had revised and updated Mosaic law. "As Christians, we at least profess to believe" in the teachings of Jesus, she wrote in 1935. And "Jesus, first of all, was practical, and that what we now call idealism is in the end the only practical way of carrying on the affairs of men."[76] Her celebration of Jesus's practicality reveals that Lewis's Christianity was less bound up in scriptural interpretation than it was in her conviction that a civilized state should not execute its citizens. Reading reports of men dying in the electric chair, praying to God instead of appealing to politicians, she remarked, "We're a great crowd of Christians we are!"[77]

Lewis sought to shame North Carolinians without too much condescension: her gaze was often sidelong, rather than down her nose, and her acid tone could never be mistaken for stuffy preachiness. But she was sometimes directly and unapologetically patronizing; you cannot call a punishment barbaric without calling its supporters barbarians. Reacting to the rush for tickets to the execution of a condemned rapist in 1922, Lewis wrote that such "morbid curiosity" was "a product of the unenlightened public opinion which countenances the death penalty, and which is its real *raison d'être*. Such opinion is one of the most striking examples of the primitive character of the group mind." She did, however, join in the collective responsibility for executions when she added, "We are still barbarians, however civilized we may think of ourselves as individuals."[78]

Her quest for civilized punishment deviated from fellow reformers' hopes for a technological solution to execution's disturbing messiness. When the gas chamber replaced the electric chair, she described a variety of medieval tortures before asking her readers, "Can't you imagine, when any of these earlier instruments of punishment were abolished, the great howl that went up from the diehards—the indignant wonderment at what the world was coming to, the ponderous apprehension that lawlessness would increase mightily. We are going to look and sound just as foolish a few hundred years from now."[79] When state lawmakers tiptoed around the margins of the death penalty in 1935, replacing electricity with gas, she mocked the change mercilessly. "Oh, the wonders of modern science!" she wrote. "Lethal gas is more 'humane' than the electric chair, but both methods are equally lethal. . . . Oh, well, we grow softer in North Carolina. In the good old days, we used to burn prisoners at the stake."[80]

Whether or not the death penalty was barbarous or stupid was a matter of opinion. But no one disputed that only lower-class and otherwise underprivileged North Carolinians ended up in the death chamber. Lewis hammered on this point, and it resonated. Unlike arguments about barbarity, it did not insult death penalty supporters. Unlike arguments about racial discrimination, it did seek to convince white supremacists to consider the interests of people of color. Unlike religious arguments, the class issue was easily explained and easily illuminated. Lewis did so in a 1935 column when she wrote, "The people we kill are the people who can't save themselves, the ones who haven't money or influence; the ones, in general, who have come from the poorest sort of environment and who have the poorest sort of heredity."[81]

In 1923, Lewis described prison reformer Thomas Mott Osborne's contribution to the North Carolina Conference for Social Service in words that might have described her own work. According to Lewis, Osborne "told a vivid human interest story . . . arresting not only because of the logic of the theory advanced, but chiefly because of its bulwark of fact. The point of view Mr. Osborne presented was that of the prisoner, the man behind the bars, sitting in surly judgment upon the society which has condemned him."[82] Lewis was acutely interested in the point of view of the prisoner, an interest she nurtured in work for the State Board of Charities and Public Welfare (SBCPW). With considerable contributions from Lewis, the SBCPW published "Capital Punishment in North Carolina," a pamphlet that drew on research by the African American director of the Division of Work among Negroes. Though written in a restrained style, the book argued persuasively against the death penalty and served as the foundation for Lewis's future columns on the subject.

The first half of the book describes the history of North Carolina's death penalty, from the gruesome executions of the eighteenth century to the first electrocution in 1910, and reports damning statistics without judgment, describing the death row population as mostly African American, illiterate, and unlucky. The second half of the book adds names, faces, and stories to this statistical picture, offering a rare personal dimension to a history studded with numbers. It describes, with pictures, twenty-six capital criminals and the lives that led them to death row. These men represent only a small sample of the nearly two hundred people sent to death row between 1910 and 1929, but their experiences shed light on a death row populated by the poor, the abused, the uneducated—an invisible underclass, with the court a conduit from the darkness of poverty to the darkness of death row.[83]

One young African American man, identified as Case J, showed up at a one-room schoolhouse from time to time near his home in South Carolina, but never received a consistent or formal education. He learned to read and "do a little writing," and prison doctors, fond of the Binet-Simon scale, assigned him a mental age of seven years. Following farmwork around the Carolinas, eventually ending up near Charlotte, he was at a fish fry there in 1927 when some sheriff's deputies raided the party. One of the deputies ended up dead, and J confessed to the murder after he was beaten in a Charlotte jail.[84] Case D was a white man with blue eyes, salt-and-pepper hair, and a mustache. He was "easily influenced" and generally known as being of a "low mentality." His employer, a hosiery mill owner, had hired him and his family, but soon, finding them "of too low order to fit in," kicked them all out of town. According to his testimony, he helped dispose—in grisly fashion—of the body of someone killed by a hunting companion. But his friend was convicted of second-degree murder and he of first-degree. He was sentenced to death.[85]

The careful studies of these men reveal the way in which scientific and medical methods, not least the sociology pioneered by Howard W. Odum and his colleagues at the University of North Carolina, were animating efforts to understand crime and punishment. One can see, too, the influence of the Progressive movement of the late nineteenth and early twentieth centuries, when the state sought to take responsibility for the deserving poor. That responsibility came to define Lewis's posture toward capital punishment and that of those who followed her. As she wrote in 1924, "'The State,' they say, does the killing. But we are the State. . . . It was a human being for whose unnecessary and barbarous death you and . . . I and everybody else in North Carolina are responsible. And may God forgive us for it!" Lewis was not the first to recognize that the death penalty was most embraceable in the abstract. Temperance advocate Charlotte Story Perkinson voiced her opinion on the matter in 1928, when she wrote, "No, the jurors do not want the blood of any man on their hands, no matter how guilty he is, the Governor doesn't want it, the wardens couldn't stand it," and people "shouldn't have the right to impose any such duty upon any human being."[86]

Lewis continued to emphasize the conclusions drawn by *Capital Punishment in North Carolina*, the "pitiful stories of the ignorant, the friendless, the underprivileged, and in very strong probability, the mentally defective and the psychopathic dying in North Carolina's electric chair, whose victims the General Assembly is too busy to consider," she wrote in 1935.[87] After 1929, Lewis used "Incidentally" to frame the death penalty as a punishment

Prisoner: Negro. b. Abbeville, S. C., April 9, 1905
Charge: First Degree Murder
Sentence: Death
Electrocuted February 17, 1928
Mental Diagnosis: Subnormal in General Intelligence and
                  Decidedly Psychopathic
                  Chronological Age: 23 Years (1928)
                  Mental Age: 4 Years, 6 Months
                  Intelligence Quotient: 28.

Prisoner: Negro. b. Cumberland County, N. C., June 1, 1887
Charge: First Degree Murder
Sentence: Death
Electrocuted December 9, 1927
Mental Diagnosis: Definitely Feebleminded.

*Capital Punishment in North Carolina* (1929) was published by the State Board of
Charities and Public Welfare (SBCPW), which at that time held responsibility over the
prison system. The SBCPW's commissioner, Kate Burr Johnson, recruited her friend,
Nell Battle Lewis, to edit the pamphlet. Lewis took the opportunity to dramatize the
death penalty's disproportionate weight on the "friendless" in her state.

for the mentally compromised. By the mid-1930s, Lewis was "plucking again the familiar string on the old harp," as she put it, about punishment's sluggishness in catching up with the growing body of knowledge about the human mind.[88] "I don't believe I've ever summarized my position," she wrote in 1935. "It's simply this: CRIME IS A SYMPTOM OF SICKNESS."[89] Her conviction eventually provoked a lengthy response from University of North Carolina historian H. M. Wagstaff, who wrote to Lewis in "an attempt to phrase my feelings about your most interesting column—which I always read":

> It is when Miss Lewis comes to the one thing she is most serious about does she peeve her readers. Here she loses all perspective and becomes maudlin. She is a crusader against social ills and has made up her mind that abolition of capital punishment is the Jerusalem that must be wrested from the hand of the infidel. . . . She regards capital punishment as an evil folkway that has survived without logic or reason. She backs up her thesis with the contention that crime is the fault of the state, traceable to neglect of this or that class, and the non-application of the right social cures.[90]

Wagstaff went on to deride the idea that neglect plays any role in warping the criminal mind, mocking the idea that "a John Dillinger, a Hauptmann, a Homer Van Meter, a Pretty Boy Floyd" might be the product of difficult childhoods. Instead, he wrote, these notorious criminals exploited the very sentimentality that Lewis displayed, and knowing that "society had become pudgy, tolerant of crime," they did what they wanted.[91]

Wagstaff accurately describes Lewis's posture, if not her attitude. She did see crime as a "psychiatric rather than a legal problem," a position she defended in this way: "My opposition to the death penalty is much like the opposition I'd have to a doctor's killing his patient. . . . To kill the socially ill . . . is much too simple a way to deal with the complex problem of crime. It's something like the doctor saying: 'This man has smallpox; he is dangerous to others, so I'll kill him because that is the surest way of getting rid of him and keeping him from harming the rest.'" She concluded that at a time when "Mr. Wagstaff and I are long since dust," crime would be the domain of the physician rather than the judge.[92]

Lewis was never optimistic that North Carolina's government would offer people convicted of crimes treatment rather than punishment. "I wish I thought that I would live to see the day," she wrote in 1937.[93] She had her moments of optimism, though. In 1936, after the protracted asphyxiation of Allen Foster horrified people around the South, she predicted that their revulsion would "crystallize into a strong and active sentiment" for abolition.[94] Early in her career, she observed that though "much of the howling about North Carolina's 'Progress' is the veriest twaddle," an "honest, disinterested, and determined" opposition to the death penalty had arisen.[95] It had, but it never crystallized into an organized opposition with a strategy. She was right that such horrific executions provoked strong reactions; she was wrong that they would galvanize into meaningful, measurable shifts in public opinion and policy.

Elite opinion, however, was on Lewis's side. Her newspaper, the *News and Observer*, frequently criticized the death penalty, and it was joined by papers such as the *Greensboro Daily News*, the *Asheville Citizen*, and the *Winston-Salem Journal*. As one *News and Observer* column said, the arguments to ban execution seemed persuasive, "and the strongest arguments" against abolition . . . "are that it would involve expense and trouble."[96] But even death penalty opponents wondered what to do with people who committed their crimes in the thrall of mental illness. In 1935, the *News and Observer* published a column arguing, "It is time that society began to realize that the crazy killer is a greater menace to its safety than the sane killer."[97] Years later, another column finished this thought: "If we as a people are going to kill men, the ones to destroy are those mental monsters who threaten the innocent with the vilest crime. Yet those are the very ones we save. . . . It would be more humane to destroy such creatures, not as a measure of vengeance, but as a matter of sanitation."[98] Such a eugenic program amounted to what Paul Green would later call "pruning"—removing dangerous elements from society.

The influence of Lewis and her fellow journalists is difficult to measure, but if polling offers any clues, their sway was limited. Polling outfits did not conduct a concentrated survey of North Carolinians about the death penalty during Lewis's lifetime, but Gallup and Harris polled nationally, and the results generally showed strong support for the death penalty, at least for murderers. A 1936 Gallup poll asking, "Do you believe in the death penalty for murder?" found that 61 percent of Americans did.[99] The following year, a poll asking a similar question showed that 65 percent of Americans favored the death penalty for murder, and whether or not the condemned criminal was a woman did not significantly affect that support.[100] Pollsters, however, did not ask about alternatives to the death penalty, such as life without parole, until the 1960s, finding that when given the alternative, a plurality of Americans favored life without parole as an alternative.[101] In earlier polling, respondents were not given the option, nor the option to declare themselves undecided, or qualify their responses in any way.[102]

Not long after the publication of this polling, and perhaps despite it, abolitionists' hopes reached a high point. A columnist noted a growing number of people opposed to the death penalty "in principle."[103] "Our congratulations for Mr. Roper!" wrote one North Carolinian after the congressman introduced an abolition bill in January 1939. The bill quickly died, however.[104] The failure of the Roper Bill, the last credible push to abolish the death penalty before its opponents found success in limiting it, revealed how little progress death penalty abolitionists made in the early decades of the twentieth century. As he helped kill the bill in committee, one representative explained why he and others clung to the death penalty: "adherence to the old Mosaic law . . . the need to eliminate undesirables from society, and to retard crime by the example of death."[105] Lewis may have shared the bafflement of one respondent in a letter to the *News and Observer*: "We are supposedly not living under the Mosaic dispensation," she objected. Furthermore, life imprisonment removes undesirables from society as effectively as death, and, writing well into Prohibition's introduction of higher crime rates and more visible lawbreaking, "does not our own staggering crime rate give positive proof before our very eyes that capital punishment does not prevent crime?"[106]

In 1931, Lewis took her anti–death penalty advocacy off the editorial pages and into the courtroom, using her legal training to defend sixteen girls against arson charges. The girls, ranging in age from thirteen to nineteen, faced execution for setting fire to their beds in the Samarcand Manor, the state's training school for delinquent girls. Lewis managed to bargain the charges down to a noncapital offense, but twelve of the girls received sentences as long as five years for their uprising.[107] Later that year, after she suffered what appears to have been a nervous breakdown, Lewis took some time off and returned to the paper a changed person, now turning her sarcasm against her former allies. She died in 1956, when the death penalty's decline was well under way; a *News and Observer* paperboy found her body in her driveway. By then, she had abandoned most of her progressive positions, and her progressive friends, for aggressive anti-Communism and skepticism of the occult.[108] The death penalty was one subject, though, that Lewis did not entirely reverse course on even as she grew more conservative. In lieu of abolition, she urged legislators to soften the application of the death penalty, allowing jurors to decide between life imprisonment and death as punishment and eliminating the death penalty for burglary and arson.[109] This notion drew on her years of urging that North Carolina's citizens take responsibility for the death penalty. Her recommendations would eventually become law, but years after she had stopped arguing forcefully for them.

## We Try to Consider Each Case on Its Merits: Executing the Friendless

An enduring complaint about the death penalty, one that Lewis made frequently, which would be taken up by Paul Green, was that the electric chair and the gas chamber were reserved for members of the underclass. Two cases illustrate this issue. The first case was that of W. B. Cole, a wealthy white mill owner who went on trial in 1925. The second was that of James Creech, also white, who had two years of college education and decent standing in his community when he faced a jury in 1949. Both illustrate the open secret that the resources to retain an attorney rather than rely on one appointed by the court and that the presumption of innocence that attended wealth and status, particularly wealth and status gilded by whiteness, were predictors of leniency. More than any other class, white men of means could kill or rape without consequence.

The Cole case caused a sensation. Wealthy, white, and president of the Hannah Pickett Mill, W. B. Cole was the rare capital defendant who had appeared in the newspapers before his trial.[110] According to newspaper accounts, Cole left his office to fire three bullets into his victim, William Ormond, as Ormond sat in his car on Main Street in Rockingham, in the south-central part of the state not far from South Carolina. Cole then returned to his office, placed his pistol on his desk, and waited for police. The fact that Cole "remained silent" after his arrest suggests that police officers were unwilling to coerce a confession out of him.[111] Reporters speculated that Cole resented Ormond's attention to Cole's daughter, and reported that Cole had threatened Ormond's life in a heated exchange of letters. Cole was a prominent citizen but Ormond, a World War I veteran and the son of a Methodist minister, was no slouch either.[112] The three hundred cars that drove in his funeral procession passed Cole's house.[113] Newspapers anticipated a sensational trial, and one that would test the state's commitment to justice despite public sentiment. "Calm consideration requires the dismissal of identity," read one editorial in the *Asheville Citizen-Times*. Could North Carolina "stand firm against the beat of emotion's surging waves"?[114]

As the trial began in late September, the volume of telegraph activity created by reporters filing stories on it necessitated a special arrangement with Western Union, and hotels in Rockingham were filled to capacity.[115] Onlookers brought bag lunches into the courtroom so as not to lose their seats.[116] The stakes were clear, according to Jonathan Daniels, who covered the story for the newspaper his family owned, the *News and Observer*. "The trial has raised throughout North Carolina the question whether or not a rich man can be sent to his death in the State's Prison here. Cole is rich and will be defended by the ablest lawyers in the state," he wrote.[117] Of course, the high-profile case attracted ambitious prosecutors, too, among them Clyde Hoey, who would later become governor.[118]

Daniels and his colleagues from around the region gave the Cole case front-page coverage. The *Rockingham Post-Dispatch* devoted nearly its entire paper to the trial for a week, transcribing the proceedings for its readers. During an "intense moment," Cole testified that the decision to kill Ormond came to him during prayer. He knew then, he explained, that he must murder Ormond to protect his daughter's reputation. In addition to resting on the claim of temporary insanity, his defense relied "on the grounds of this 'unwritten law' . . . which would justify a killing to hush slander."[119] After twenty-one hours of deliberation and much prayer, the jury declared Cole not guilty of first-degree murder. When one observer thanked the jury, saying, "'Any of us would have done the same thing Mr. Cole did,'" one juror responded, "'Yes, yes, that's what we decided.'" The presiding judge would later say—if he did not chuckle approvingly it is easy to imagine he did—that he thought the jury, "'a fine body of upright citizens, probably used the heart more than the head.'"[120] In other words, the jury and the state failed the test of the *Asheville Citizen-Times*. Declared sane thereafter, Cole faced a civil suit by Ormond's family but was a free man.[121]

The verdict thrilled the "better people" of Rockingham, who "received it with rejoicing."[122] But the less wealthy and connected were upset. One Chapel Hill man warned that "whirlwinds and rebellions will be visited upon us through the power of [God's] mighty wrath," as a result of an unjust verdict.[123] A Burlington man wrote that the people of North Carolina were "indignantly shocked" at this "case of financial power overturning justice."[124] The verdict was "an outrage,"[125] a "travesty of law and order."[126] Some newspapers tried to reassure North Carolinians that they could trust their legal system, damning it with faint praise. "There has been a lot of talk that we might as well burn the courthouse down, and open the penitentiary and jail doors, but no such expression should be indulged in by intelligent people," read a column in the *New Bern Sun-Journal*. "Just because the church is full of hypocrites, the schools presided over by modernists . . . there is no reason why these institutions should be torn down."[127]

Court officials had feared violence in response to the verdict, but, according to Jonathan Daniels, those who believed Cole guilty were "moved more to cynicism at the courts than violence toward the defendant."[128] The voices of North Carolinians, both members of the elite and ordinary citizens, vindicated Daniels's observation. In 1934, a professor wrote to Governor Ehringhaus, complaining that the people on death row were "without exception poor, ignorant, feeble-minded, or Negro. That is the only class ever executed. Not one of those has ever had a normal opportunity due to our social wrongs and injustices." Ehringhaus bristled at the suggestion, replying, "I cannot agree with your suggestion that only the friendless class are ever executed," noting that some friendless felons were released from death row as a result of public pressure. "We try to consider each case on its merits," he concluded.[129]

The role of class in capital trials showed itself again twenty-five years later in the murder trial of tobacconist James Creech. Creech argued that he had been drinking heavily and thus did not have his wits about him when he aimed a shotgun at his wife and, in his words, "blowed her brains out."[130] Creech, "a Mason and a Methodist,"[131] had able defense, including future governor J. Melville Broughton, but lost his defense and his appeal, and in late January 1949, was preparing to meet death in the gas chamber. As W. Kerr Scott considered commutation, letters flowed into his office. Henry A. Grady, a Superior Court judge who delivered many death sentences in his twenty-six years on the bench, wrote to Scott urging him to let Creech's death sentence stand:

> It has been my observation that money and political influence have been able to save the lives of practically every person that I have sentenced to death. The poor Devil who had no money and no influence, *walked the plank*, and the general public said "well done." The many with money and influential friends got by with a life sentence, which in a few years, was reduced and he finally walked out, a free man. Such things have been disgusting to me. . . . I am not in favor of capital punishment; but *it is the law*, and the rich, the poor, the high, the low should all be measured by the same yard stick, and it seems that you now hold that stick, and that you are going to wield it safely and sanely.[132]

Scott took Grady's advice and refused to commute Creech, making him the unlucky exception to prove the rule. In response, he received an outpouring of support from North Carolinians who praised, in one instance, "the splendid way in which you have upheld the dignity of the law of God and man in this case."[133]

In 1949, the *Asheville Citizen* noted that Creech was "a minority of one," being the first person executed with more than a high school education. The *Citizen* was wrong—George Keaton, executed in 1934, spent two semesters at the Tuskegee Institute[134]—but it was correct to point out that "the rule of execution . . . usually applies to the uneducated, and even in some cases to what we suspect has been the moronic."[135] Like the *Citizen*, by the late 1940s, newspapers around the state had taken up Nell Battle Lewis's criticism of the death penalty's disproportionate use against the state's poorest citizens. In a 1947 editorial, the *Greensboro Daily News* urged its readers to "go over the list of criminals who have paid the death penalty in North Carolina and see how closely and sickeningly they conform to the pattern of neglect, of low educational, health, economic, and social standards."[136] It was an observation that indicted the state both for neglecting its neediest citizens, and for giving up on them once they showed signs of neglect.

Frustration with the death penalty's uneven application persisted as the punishment entered its decline at mid-century. In 1949, a woman who did not want to identify herself wrote to Governor W. Kerr Scott about Tom Wood, a man awaiting execution for murdering his wife. "One case I know of a man kills his wife (in Harnett County)," she wrote. "His father has money + he has fine, upstanding citizens for character witnesses, when he was tried they were all there everyone of them. Does he die? No of course not, he's Mr So + so he has nice friends and money. He gets off with a few years, (which he will probably never serve). But Wood, he has no money, he has no nice friends, clothes or anything just a hard working man who gets the book thrown at him (not the Bible either)."[137]

### Something of a Squared Deal: Paul Green, Humanity, and Race

Nell Battle Lewis admired Paul Green's work. She praised his play, *The Devil's Instrument*, as a work in which "North Carolina finds her voice."[138] Indeed, Green built a career on imagining the unheard voices of his state's residents, including white laborers and African Americans. He paired his keen ear with a soft heart, and his interest in the death penalty was sustained by his ability to empathize with death row prisoners. As Lewis lost focus on the issue in the mid-1930s, Green took up her mantle as the state's foremost opponent of the death penalty, exchanging her caustic criticism for appeals to North Carolinians' empathy. Though he embraced Lewis's belief that the death penalty was barbaric, Green pled for change rather than deriding stagnation, seeking to inspire abolition by giving life and personhood to condemned criminals, raising their voices as if they were characters in one of his plays. He found some success but ran into the same roadblocks as his predecessors: preventing an execution was not the same as changing public opinion on the principle of lethal punishment.

Green grew up in rural North Carolina, attended the University of North Carolina in Chapel Hill, fought in World War I, and returned home to a long career as a playwright and activist.[139] He had shown an interest in the human and racial elements of the death penalty in North Carolina and elsewhere, yet he was not an abolitionist. As he wrote, "I am not entirely against capital punishment as such," but "I am absolutely opposed to it as it is being carried out in North Carolina."[140] He decried the death sentences of the so-called Scottsboro Boys, eight African American youths sentenced to death for rape in Alabama in 1931, yet showed disdain for supporters of the youths who approached the case in political rather than human terms. He wrote a scathing letter to Theodore Dreiser in 1932 reprimanding him for using "the bones of seven [sic] negro boys to hammer the drums of social revolution."[141]

Green sought to explore the death penalty in human terms in his artistic work and, eventually, as an activist. In 1927, he won a Pulitzer Prize for *In Abraham's Bosom*, his play about an African American tenant farmer who murders his white landlord in a dispute about crop storage and is sentenced to death in the electric chair. In 1934, Green lobbied for the commutation of an African American tenant farmer who murdered his white landlord in a dispute about crop storage and was sentenced to death in the electric chair. The man was Emmanuel "Spice" Bittings, also a World War I veteran, who admitted to the murder but insisted he did so to defend himself and his children.[142] Sentenced to death following his counsel's mishandling of evidence substantiating his self-defense claim, Bittings found hope for life in the Bittings Defense Committee, an interracial coalition which included prominent African American businessman Louis J. Spaulding.[143] The committee retained African American attorneys, M. H. Thompson and C. A. McCoy, for Bittings's appeal.[144]

Bittings had an influential advocate in Green, who wrote to Governor Ehringhaus, urging commutation and asking for the condemned man "something of a squared deal."[145] Ehringhaus listened, and his Paroles Commissioner held four hearings to reevaluate Bittings's guilt. At the fourth hearing, though, Bittings's wife and children testified that Bittings shot his victim in the back. Their testimony, which surprised and horrified Green, may have doomed Bittings, and he died in the electric chair in 1934 after a failed suicide attempt on death row.[146]

Green's sensitivity and imagination found rich expression in the letters that he collected from condemned prisoners. The collection, though it was never published, was Green's companion to *Capital Punishment in North Carolina*. The letters paint a vivid picture of the emotional life of death row inmates, some anxiously awaiting their final moments, others embracing God and the promise of eternity in heaven. Monroe Medlin wrote to his mother, telling her, "Well, Mom, this is the last letter I am writing you. Keep it until you die which I hope you will never die."[147] Gurney Herring told his children, "Your daddy died in the gas chamber. . . . So, children, please remember this—be good and think about the way your daddy died for being so disobedient to God's laws. Please mind your mother."[148] Most of these letters, though, were directed at the condemned prisoners' peers, echoing the professions of faith and salvation once delivered on the gallows. "So you see, friends," wrote Emmet Garner, "you may be in prison and shut off from the word but God is always near and want to help you."[149]

This emotionalism on behalf of killers and rapists bothered some North Carolinians. The seeds of a countermovement for victims' rights appear in pro–death penalty arguments as early as the mid-1920s. Those who opposed the death penalty were often accused of a sentimentalism that was misplaced except when considering victims of capital crime and their families. In 1926, a Statesville resident wrote to the editor of the *Greensboro Daily News*, "The horror of the scene of the execution arouses such pity and sympathy, the crime of the murderer and the righteous judgment of the law is forgotten." Opponents of the death penalty such as Nell Battle Lewis urged North Carolinians to attend an execution; if they did so, she was certain, they would turn against death as punishment. This letter-writer suggested the inverse: that "if those who oppose capital punishment could be at the scene of an intended murder armed and see the murderer about to dispatch his victim," they would kill the to-be criminal "with the approval of conscience and law."[150]

In an argument that anticipated the victims' rights movements of the 1960s, 1970s, and 1980s, one North Carolinian pointed out in a lengthy defense of the death penalty published in the *News and Observer* in 1925, that the sympathy for some recently executed criminals was misplaced. "What about the victims?" he asked. "Quiet, peaceable, law-abiding citizens, attending to their own legitimate affairs, shot to death by murderous hands without the opportunity to send any 'pitiful farewells' or to give any information to loved ones as to why they never returned."[151] Another letter-writer in 1939 complained that crime victims' "hurts are caused through no fault of their own and the sob-sisters don't care how much they suffer before they die."[152]

In addition to trying to inspire pity for condemned criminals, Green also frankly addressed the racial character of the death penalty, which he described as "the frightful business of murdering ignorant Negroes."[153] This belief revealed itself in his efforts to save the life of William Mason Wellmon. Wellmon was an African American resident of Alexandria, Virginia, condemned to death 1941 for the rape of a white woman in Iredell County, North Carolina. Wellmon was sent to death row despite the fact that he produced a signed paystub that proved his presence in Virginia at the time of the crime. After Wellmon's appeal was rejected by the North Carolina Supreme Court, Green led a clemency delegation to Governor Broughton's office, where he was opposed by the prosecuting attorney. The next day, he wrote to the attorney in an effort to persuade him of Wellmon's innocence. "It is a nightmare they have been through," he wrote of the survivor and her family. "We all share in their suffering and sorrow," but "the cause of justice and race relations throughout the South would . . . be bettered by an act of clemency." He closed with warmth: "I hope you'll give me a ring when you're down this way and we can get together for a meal."[154]

Governor Broughton did extend clemency—according to one account, Wellmon was seated in the gas chamber at the time[155]—and later pardoned Wellmon. His decision drew out some racist bitterness.[156] A letter to Broughton accused him of racial pandering: "All the people here know that this whole case was planned from the very beginning by the Negroes," wrote the anonymous critic. "It appears that you are more interested in the Negroes than you are in justice. . . . If we women cannot get protection from the court we will see that our men give it to us. I would sign my name, but I am afraid that your office would let the Negroes have it, and they would perhaps attack my family. They seem to have full run of your office."[157] Broughton received some animus, and Wellmon received some paltry recompense. In 1971, the state of North Carolina paid him $986.40 to compensate him for the income he lost while he sat on death row for eight months.[158]

With his pardon, Wellmon became among just six people, convicted of three separate crimes before the modern era of the death penalty began in the 1970s, who were pardoned and freed, rather than having their sentences commuted to life imprisonment or being granted retrials. As discussed in chapter 3, it was much more likely for commutations to be used to address exonerating information post-trial. Joining Wellmon were brothers Fred and Frank Dove, convicted of murder with help from coerced testimony, who were pardoned in 1928 after their trial judge, prosecutor, and others urged Governor Angus McLean to do so.[159] And Gus Langley, a white man sentenced to death for murder in 1932 on the basis of perjured testimony from a cellmate, was pardoned by Governor Ehringhaus in 1938.[160]

For all its viciousness, the letter to Broughton was quite direct. Years later, Marion Wright, a white lawyer and journalist who led an organized death penalty abolition movement in the late 1960s and 1970s, complained that "the race issue" was responsible for support for the death penalty, "though no one will openly admit that fact."[161] For that reason, Wright sought to keep his own anti–death penalty activism as the head of North Carolinians against the Death Penalty separate from the civil rights movement.[162] But African Americans themselves well understood the racial animus behind the administration of the death penalty. Whether or not they drew attention to the issue was another question.

### "Money and Time and Sacrifice": African American Anti–Death Penalty Activism

The death penalty posed a complex challenge for civically engaged African Americans. On one hand, it presented to many African American observers a crystalline vision of biased Jim Crow justice. On the other, that bias fell most heavily on African American men often framed in the white press as vicious avatars of African Americans more generally. To expend social or political capital on condemned prisoners might weaken advocates' positions on economic justice, segregation, employment, or other pressing elements of the color line affecting the daily lives of people of color around the state. Despite this risk, many African Americans did take action against unjust death sentences and capital procedure, in the courtroom, in the black-owned press, and in their neighborhoods.

Many did so despite exclusion from party politics. For most of the period in question, which precedes the 1965 Voting Rights Act, most African Americans in North Carolina were not voters.[163] Nor did they preside as judges or often sit on juries, and there were relatively few African American attorneys in comparison to their white counterparts. African American attorneys could receive sterling legal education at Durham's North Carolina Central University and schools such as Howard University or Columbia; Elreta Melton Alexander-Ralston, an African American attorney who co-founded an integrated firm in Greensboro, received her JD from Columbia in 1945.[164] Durham attorney Caswell J. Gates, who earned his law degree at Boston University, was of such stature that at least one young attorney actually paid Gates so that he might work under him.[165] Alongside African American attorney Herman L. Taylor, Gates defended Allen T. Reid on a capital burglary charge in 1949 and teenaged cousins on trial for their lives in 1950. As one African American journalist wrote, Gates and Taylor "struggled against Jim Crow on both sides: They were Negroes and their clients were Negroes."[166]

It was not until the death penalty was in free fall that law schools in North Carolina began accepting black students. Floyd McKissick, who went on to prominence as an activist in the Congress of Racial Equality (CORE) and as a founder of Soul City, began taking classes at the University of North Carolina at Chapel Hill after a lawsuit led by Thurgood Marshall and the National Association for the Advancement of Colored People (NAACP). Yet as important as were Alexander-Ralston, McKissick, and Henry Frye—who in 1983 became the North Carolina Supreme Court's first African American chief justice—the presence of African American voices in the state's death penalty system was fairly constrained in the Jim Crow era. This somewhat muted presence is at least partially explained by archival practice: it is not surprising that in a state organized to sustain white wealth and influence, the papers and letters of African Americans were at best unevenly collected and preserved. Yet it is also reflective of choices some African American activists made about the possible effects of death penalty activism on the interests of the black community. And African Americans in any given place faced the very real threat of violent retribution should they seek to lend aid to someone facing a death sentence or reach outside their area for help.

Some influential African Americans, as represented by the newspapers they published and read, focused with uplifting their community as a whole over saving the life of a convicted murderer or a rapist as an expression of principled opposition to the death penalty. Sometime caution on capital punishment did not mean that black activists or those taking action for the first time stayed quiet. Black-owned and published newspapers such as the *Carolinian* in Raleigh, the *Carolina Times* in Durham, and the *Future*

*Outlook* in Greensboro spoke out forcefully on segregation in public facilities and schools, demanded the hiring of African American policemen, railed against police brutality, celebrated African American soldiers, educators, athletes, and clergymen, condemned lynching, and more. Louis E. Austin, who ran the *Carolina Times* between 1927 and 1971, was a lifelong, vociferous advocate for racial justice in print and in his daily life. Yet although he mounted campaigns against police murder he did not publish with any frequency on capital punishment.[167] It was not until the death penalty's later period, as in the 1950s when such cases were fewer and more sensational, that papers such as Austin's the *Carolina Times* consistently drew attention to injustices in capital trials.[168]

Moreover, when they did speak out, they risked undermining the standing of the law-abiding African American community at the expense of the life of one deemed to be criminal. To address this problem, North Carolina's African American newspapers couched their opposition to an unfairly imposed death penalty in strong anticrime language, a technique that precluded blanket opposition to the death penalty. The editor of the *Carolinian*, for example, condemned rape "as one of the most detestable and inexcusable of all felonies. It agrees with the southern white man and any other man worth his salt in calling for severe treatment of every case of actual rape, but entirely regardless of the ramifications of racial lines."[169] The *Carolinian* made discriminatory rape convictions a focal point, reinforcing the case-by-case approach of death penalty opposition among activist African Americans.[170]

North Carolinians of color feared direct retaliation, too. For instance, in 1918, four Raleigh-based members wrote to acting NAACP secretary James Weldon Johnson to tell him about convicted rapist Earl Neville, who escaped two lynching attempts before receiving a hurried trial and a death sentence. "Extreme secrecy will be necessary as to agency," they concluded. "If you could send a discreet white person here to investigate, the matter could be unraveled. We cannot do it. Any action on our part would prejudice the case and provoke bad blood."[171] As late as 1943, African Americans in North Carolina were warning NAACP officials that having a black lawyer defend a black man accused of rape "would be suicide."[172] Yet NAACP representatives did take risks to investigate injustice. For instance, members of the Asheville branch traveled fifty-five miles to Rutherfordton to speak with Charlie Hopkins, accused of murdering a postal worker and whose case aroused anger among some white people in Asheville. When they judged his story of innocence credible, they urged the national branch to assist them in securing Hopkins's freedom.[173]

Yet the NAACP did not always respond affirmatively to such petitions. Its leaders were selective and pragmatic in its advocacy for African Americans facing execution and its push for punishment for whites who committed crimes against African Americans. Instead, it depended on branches in Durham, Raleigh, and elsewhere that were not always well-funded or well-organized. The result was a not-always-tenable simulacrum of an arrangement: the national organization relied on the local branches for information they could not always provide, and local branches relied on the national organization for money it could not always provide. In 1939, Executive Secretary Walter White lamented having to decline assistance more than once because of a lack of money when he offered an Asheville NAACP member $25 to fund an appeal. When the Asheville contact asked for more, White declined, writing, "Negroes must realize . . . that justice like everything worthwhile costs money and time and sacrifice" and reprimanding North Carolina's African Americans for their paltry contributions to NAACP coffers.[174]

Communication with the national branch could be slow, and requests from North Carolinians for the national office's energies usually resulted only in the office exercising its policy of asking a local branch to take charge of the case. And as NAACP special counsel Charles Houston told the mother of a condemned man, the NAACP was "unable to take every case which is presented to us and our rules limit us to cases of persons who our investigation leads us to believe are persecuted on account of race or color."[175] Persons believed to be guilty could expect little help, whether or not their arrests and trials were marred by violence or misconduct.

These concerns and policies did not keep the NAACP out of North Carolina altogether. The national office offered legal advice, sent investigators to North Carolina a number of times, and telegrammed governors asking for commutations. In 1923, the organization sought to prevent the extradition from Pennsylvania of Dock McCoy, accused by North Carolina authorities of murdering a white man, for fear that he would be "lynched or railroaded to death" upon returning to the state.[176] Then-assistant secretary Walter White kept up correspondence with allies at the black-owned North Carolina Mutual Life Insurance Company and the historically black Saint Augustine's University to seek out local intelligence and support for McCoy. Their cooperation won a limited victory when McCoy was extradited but protected by the state militia during his trial and sentenced only to twenty years imprisonment.[177] In the 1940s, Thurgood Marshall and others fought to prevent the extradition from Washington, D.C., of William Mason Wellmon, who was sentenced to death in North Carolina but eventually pardoned. The organization also helped win a commutation, and eventually parole, for Charlie Pugh, who was sentenced to death for rape in 1940.[178] The effort to save Pugh's life came from members of Durham's middle-class African American community, namely L. J. Spaulding of the North Carolina Mutual Life Insurance Company and William J. Walker, who later sat on the board of the Mechanics and Farmers Bank. Wellmon and Pugh were precisely the kind of sympathetic—and innocent—prisoners who could expect support from the NAACP.

Whatever the risks, particularly to local membership, some employees in New York saw the benefit to successfully intervening in dramatic cases. Just before his execution for a 1931 murder, Chevis Herring confessed and exonerated his brother, Ernest, who had also been sentenced to death. "This is a most stirring case," wrote Walter White to a colleague, Robert W. Bagnall, then the NAACP's director of branches. His letter reached Bagnall in Raleigh: "This is so striking a case," White wrote, "that our entrance into it and a victory gained as a result would be especially timely just now."[179] Bagnall managed to rally the director of the Division of Negro Welfare at the State Board of Charities and Public Welfare to the cause, and the two men visited death row together, becoming convinced of his innocence. Yet money remained an obstacle. Herring's attorneys wrote to White asking for support; White turned around and wrote to Will Alexander of the Commission for Interracial Cooperation.[180] Ultimately the NAACP sent the young attorneys $100, with a promise of a further $150.[181] Meanwhile, Governor Oliver Gardner equivocated on Ernest's fate and a judge dismissed a motion for a new trial based on Chevis's confession, declaring that it was "probably not true."[182] Ultimately, though, Gardner believed Ernest and commuted his sentence from death to life imprisonment. It was a decision, one editorial gushed, that "would go far toward changing the opinion in northern circles that the friendless negro, facing doom, has no chance in the South."[183] The NAACP and Herring's attorneys exchanged letters for four years until the NAACP was able to pay the additional $150 promised; the Great Depression made it difficult to cover costs.

In this case and others the NAACP deliberated over or involved themselves in in the 1910s, 1920s, and 1930s, the organization's influence was limited and less systematic than the efforts that followed the incorporation of the Legal Defense Fund (LDF) in 1939.[184] But by then the LDF's rules were in place: the NAACP would act if there was evidence of "color discrimination" and if a "fundamental right of citizenship" was at stake.[185] Thus Thurgood Marshall cautioned petitioners from Raeford, North Carolina, who wrote to him about the fate of seventeen-year-old Nathaniel Bryant and his uncle, William Young, who were sentenced to death for first-degree murder and burglary in 1939. Writing on prison stationery, Bryant and Young themselves addressed a letter to "Mr. White, sir your honor," pleading for help "for us two colored boys" and arguing that the police tricked them. Bryant's mother, Nora, also wrote, explaining that "the police said that if they say that they kill the man that they was going to be light on them and if they say they did not do it they was going to put it on them inaway."[186] Marshall declined to aid, telling Nora Bryant that the case did "not come within the rules of this Association."[187]

As these pleas indicate, North Carolinians of color believed that the NAACP could be an effective advocate in the face of unrelenting discrimination. When two Vance County teenaged boys, Florida Bullock and Beaufort Kelly, were arrested on suspicion of attempted rape, both their African American attorney and the father of one of the boys wrote at once to New York. "We don't have but a little time, but we have so much to do," wrote Durham attorney Caswell J. Gates, earning a rebuke in return for seeking to arrange representation for the defendants.[188] Bullock and Kelly's situation reveals the way in which the criminal justice system in Jim Crow North Carolina sustained white rage against African Americans. Bullock insisted on retaining a white attorney, who informed the court he would not be joining Kelly in any motions; African Americans were struck from the jury; the teenaged accuser would assert only that she had been "beaten by those 'niggers.'" Inside the courtroom, Gates "could hear vibrating . . . the G__ D__ S__ B's__, we'll fix them"; outside, Gates and his legal team were assaulted and fired upon.[189] The teenagers were sentenced to life imprisonment, to work on the state's roads.[190]

The hostility between white people and people of color in Vance County underscores the limited contact between white and African American North Carolinians opposed to the death penalty. In the first half of the twentieth century, whites opposed the death penalty from a paternalistic position, and saw themselves as more persuasive advocates for African American lives than African Americans themselves. Activist Charlotte Story Perkinson, a white woman, provided an example when she lamented that the death penalty illuminated African Americans' need for white stewardship. She added that sterilization, which would cure African Americans of their habit of "promiscuous breeding," would preclude many executions.[191]

## Sleepless Nights: Juries End the Death Penalty

While mandatory death penalty relegated juries and even judges to fairly minor actors in the death penalty process, it made solicitors, and later district attorneys, hugely powerful players: the absence of discretion means that a prosecutor's decision to seek a conviction on a first-degree murder charge, for instance, could result only in a not guilty verdict and freedom or a guilty verdict and a death sentence. North Carolina introduced discretion in the 1940s, but prior to this change, there were just a handful of efforts to rebalance the process. Some of the first attempts took place in 1917, when a state senator introduced a bill that would allow juries to sentence capital criminals to life imprisonment.[192] The bill failed. There was little action until the idea gained traction as the number of annual executions rose into the 1930s. In 1935, Representative Charles Jonas, a Republican from Lincolnton, not far from Charlotte, introduced such a bill that January.[193] Not even a week later, the bill was tabled and cruelly dismissed by one Burlington newspaper: "Variety of Minor Bills Tossed into Assembly Hopper," read the headline.[194] In 1937, Governor Claude Hoey noticed that North Carolina was executing more than comparable states; the previous year the state had set a new record with twenty-three executions. "Under our present laws," Hoey told reporters, "a man must be sentenced to death if he breaks into an occupied dwelling after dark to steal food from a kitchen." The state's paper of record, the *News and Observer*, joined by at least three others, encouraged Hoey to move on his revelation.[195]

As the 1939 session began, Attorney General Harry McMullen, who had been a supporter of former governor Robert Glenn's anti-lynching posture, recommended to the General Assembly that they substitute either jury discretion or a punishment of life imprisonment for the mandatory death sentence for first degree murder, rape, burglary, and arson.[196] The Hoey administration sponsored such a bill in February, alongside a measure that would have designated lynching as a form of murder. The former languished in committee but ultimately made it to the floor of the state senate at the end of the month. The original bill gave judges discretion over sentencing following the jury's verdict. The version that passed gave discretion to juries alone and included language binding judges to their decision and it limited discretion to burglary and arson cases.[197] The bill received an unfavorable report from the House's judiciary committee, rendering it dead on arrival.

In 1941, the bill returned from the dead and the process began anew. The final law, enacted in the General Assembly's 1941 session, made a minor grammatical change and added a dependent clause to the state's Consolidated Statutes. The section, which read, "Any person convicted . . . of the crime of burglary in the first degree shall suffer death." This simple statement was "hereby amended by changing the period at the end to a colon." After the colon now came the following: "Provided, if the jury shall so recommend, the punishment shall be imprisonment for life in the state's prison."[198] The General Assembly did the same for arson, codifying the absence of lethal sanction for this crime.[199] North Carolina's newspapers shrugged in response. The bill would have the effect of "practically abolishing the death penalty in North Carolina," noted the *Robesonian*. Pointing out that the measure was intended to address "border-line cases where the death penalty is too severe," the unsigned editorial quipped, "but in such cases the governor commutes the sentence anyway."[200]

In 1949, the General Assembly again acted, relaxing the mandatory sentencing statute for first-degree murder and rape, including the rape of a child.[201] Capital punishment supporters grumbled. "When we applied the rule to burglary and arson four years ago," complained a state senator, "the proponents said they wouldn't ask for any more. I'll bet my hat the next time they will be requesting abolition of all capital punishment."[202] Two weeks later, the new statute was used for the first time, when a jury recommended mercy for Watson Stover, a white man, following his conviction for first-degree murder of a woman described in the press as his lover.[203] That spring, a Superior Court justice advocated eliminating capital punishment altogether. The General Assembly "made a grievous error," said Hoyle Sink, citing what he saw as an increase in rapes since the move.[204] "Under the present law, it is impossible to render fair and impartial justice."[205]

A conversation about abolishing capital punishment simmered gently in North Carolina's newspapers as juries began choosing life sentences over death. Competing for space with news of Julius and Ethel Rosenberg's death sentences, and with Dr. Samuel Sheppard's trial for the murder of his wife, were stories of men receiving life imprisonment upon being convicted of serious crimes by juries who were not willing to hand down a death sentence.[206] Newspaper accounts of attention-grabbing trials began taking note of when potential jurors were struck from the pool for their objection to capital punishment—for instance, "a number" of potential jurors excused in January of 1952, more than half of those summoned into a jury pool in Elizabethtown later that year, most of those dismissed in a Tarboro rape trial because of their opposition to capital punishment, and "the overwhelming majority" of those dismissed in a 1955 murder trial sent away for their discomfort with the death penalty.[207]

In 1953, the General Assembly passed a law permitting defendants in arson, burglary, rape, and murder cases to plead guilty before trial in exchange, if the state accepted the plea, for life imprisonment.[208] The bill created an opportunity for a representative of the state to reach an agreement with a defendant's attorneys, that they would not pursue a death penalty, drawing the solicitor—the equivalent of a district attorney—into a widening coalition of mercy-givers in state government and taking some of the pressure for clemency off the governor. It was ratified in the General Assembly, despite objections that it moved North Carolina closer to blanket abolition.[209] The 1953 change was important because prior to the revision, people indicted on capital felonies could not plead guilty—that plea would result in the receipt of a mandatory death sentence without a trial by jury. That year, just five people were executed, all of them convicted years earlier; there would be no additional capital convictions resulting in executions until 1955, when the solicitor refused to accept Richard Scales's guilty plea and Scales was sentenced to death for the murder of a woman and her daughter; and between 1953 and 1961 just six more men would die in the gas chamber.[210] Death row became a lonely place: between 1957 and 1961, no more than three men waited on death row at any time.

### When Put to Them as Individuals: Personal Responsibility and the End of Executions

Paul Green sought to treat African Americans as persons. In doing so, and in focusing on their cases, he contributed to saving lives, but not to the grand mission, inaugurated decades earlier by Henry Canfield, of convincing the public that the death penalty was wrong in all cases. The lack of legislative success in abolishing the death penalty stemmed in part from a lack of faith that criminals given life sentences would actually remain in prison for the rest of their lives. One man wrote to the *News and Observer* to complain that "life imprisonment doesn't mean a thing. The man so sentenced will soon be out, and I don't remember seeing where anybody who had a sentence of life died in prison."[211]

Moreover, North Carolinians understood the difference between supporting the death penalty in the abstract and handing down a death penalty from the jury box. They were prepared for de facto abolition, and activists like Green, Lewis, and Canfield deserve credit for making the reality of the death penalty unavoidable. The number of executions was on the decline after a high point in 1947, and after 1953, when the legislature decided that indicted murderers and rapists could plead guilty in exchange for a life sentence, it dropped precipitously. No one was executed in 1954, and North Carolina saw just one person executed each year in 1955, 1956, and 1957. After two more executions in 1958, none in 1959 or 1960, and one in 1961, abolitionists appeared to get what they had been seeking: the end of executions in North Carolina. In October 1961, Theodore Boykin became the 362nd person put to death by the state since Walter Morrison died in the electric chair in 1910.[212] Both men were African Americans, and both were executed for rape.

Executions ceased, though, not because activists persuaded a majority of North Carolinians that execution was ethically unacceptable, un-Christian, or foolish. Executions ceased because, as people had been observing for decades, it was much easier to support the death penalty when not in a position of actually inflicting it. In 1925, the *News and Observer* published an editorial that, acknowledging that the majority of citizens supported the death penalty for serious crimes, argued that "when it was put to them as individuals," jurors were reluctant "to say that a fellow man shall be electrocuted." As the editorial pointed out, "Many thousands who would oppose the repeal of the law will refuse to render a verdict that will carry it into effect."[213] More than a quarter century later, another editorial worried that North Carolina juries were offering binding recommendations of mercy not because of the nuanced presentation of the defense but because they might "save [themselves] some sleepless nights."[214] The 1953 law put that reluctance into practice.

A 1938 opinion piece aptly illustrated the way in which responsibility floated at the margins of the death penalty process. Killing a murderer is wrong, wrote Walter A. Cotton, but if "I join eleven other persons in a jury box, all of us basking under the pleasant fiction that we have formed no opinion about the case, and pronounce the same man guilty, all is well. For a brief time we are not individuals; we are the state." But Cotton did not think so. "The fallacy in all this is revealed vividly when we try to assign to any one person the responsibility for condemning a man to death," he wrote.

The prosecutor protests that he is just doing his job by making a strong case; the jurors blame mandatory sentences and the judge does the same: "All I can do is pronounce the sentence. The Supreme Court can examine only the record, and the governor, if he finds no new evidence, can do nothing but withhold clemency. So the circle goes round and round," Cotton complained. "Can we persuade ourselves into believing that we escape our individual responsibility by blaming the existence of capital punishment on society? Is society some abstraction, or is it not all of us grouped together?"[215]

It was. North Carolinians as a group continued to support the idea of death as punishment. In 1953, North Carolinians, like most Americans, continued to support the death penalty in principle. Gallup asked Americans that year if they favored the death penalty for murder, they did: 64 percent responded yes and just 25 percent no. Others had no opinion or qualified their answer.[216] But by 1960, support had fallen to 53 percent, opposition had risen to 36 percent, and the number of undecided respondents had risen to 11 percent.[217] Support had softened nationally but remained somewhat strong. In North Carolina, the impulse to reform remained weak. As novelist Doris Betts wrote shortly before Theodore Boykin's 1961 asphyxiation, "North Carolinians do not seem to be thinking much of future alternatives to the death penalty. We are a rural state and a fundamentalist one, still suspicious of doctors with long names who can get anybody off by saying he's crazy, and offenders who are 'mollycoddled.'"[218]

Just as North Carolinians used jury discretion, legally sanctioned and not, and executive clemency as problematic safety valves for a flawed death penalty process, so too they valued the persistence of the death penalty on the books as a still more problematic safety valve for the misapplication of mercy. If executive clemency answered the question "What if we condemn an innocent person?," the death penalty, in existence even after it ceased being used, answered the question "What if we encounter a criminal so evil that we need to ensure their death?" North Carolinians wanted to preserve the death penalty for this reason, even after they found themselves using other punishments instead. In 1956, as the death penalty was, temporarily, waning, the *News and Observer* published an editorial arguing that "either this State should . . . make the death penalty the rule or it should stop making such punishment the rare and almost irrelevant exception." Years later, the state would indeed make the death penalty the rule, but until they were spurred forward by the United States Supreme Court, North Carolinians seemed to prefer for execution to be "rare and almost irrelevant."[219]

# 5  An Emotional Craving

The Revival of the Death Penalty
in North Carolina, 1961–1984

· · · · · · · · · · · · · · · · · · · · · · · · · · · · · · · · · · · · · · · · · · · ·

"I'm sorry for the hurt that I've caused," Velma Barfield told an interviewer in 1984. "Today if it were possible I wish that I could take every bit of hurt on myself."[1]

Barfield was a "plump, hazel-eyed grandmother who read her Bible daily," a white woman who crocheted dolls for her grandchildren.[2] She was also a serial murderer who had poisoned and killed four people, including her mother, in Lumberton, North Carolina. While awaiting trial, Barfield experienced a religious awakening. Sentenced to die, she became a maternal figure on death row, winning respect and admiration from supporters including the daughter of evangelist Billy Graham. Graham himself praised Barfield for the "'big impact' she made on inmates' lives before her execution."[3] The spectacle of her trial and approaching execution drew national attention, with papers from Philadelphia to Los Angeles running Sunday features on the "Death Row Granny," as people around the country waited to see if North Carolina would become the first state to execute a woman in more than twenty years.

In her 1978 trial, Barfield was prosecuted by Joe Freeman Britt, the district attorney for Robeson County, who was called a "hurricane" and a "showman" in the courtroom by one peer.[4] Not long after his death in 2016, a report by Harvard Law School's Fair Punishment Project named Britt the deadliest district attorney in the United States, winning a total of thirty-eight death sentences over a fourteen-year period.[5] A 1975 profile noted that twenty-four of the thirty-four states with death penalty statutes had fewer people on death row than Britt's tiny 16th District.[6] Britt brought a hard-charging style into the courtroom, augmented by his six-foot-six frame and his disregard for courtroom rules.[7] Although Barfield pleaded not guilty on the grounds of insanity, Britt successfully framed her as a "cold-blooded, deliberate murderer" who took pleasure from attending the funerals of her victims. It took the jury just over an hour to convict Barfield and in the new, bifurcated sentencing procedure that split the assessment of guilt and the determination of punishment into two phases, it took another three hours the following day to hand her a death penalty.[8]

Barfield received a number of stays of execution as she appealed her sentence to the North Carolina Supreme Court and sought a hearing in the United States Supreme Court. Her efforts to obtain a writ of certiorari, which would allow judicial review, failed repeatedly in both courts. Then the United States District Court for the Eastern District of North Carolina and the Fourth Circuit Court of Appeals denied her motions for a rehearing. Just days before her November 2, 1984, execution date, Barfield again petitioned for a rehearing, claiming her drug addiction during the trial rendered her incompetent, but this motion and another to the state Supreme Court were rejected.[9] All the while, Barfield's attorney and allies fought for clemency, hoping to reduce Barfield's sentence to life imprisonment without the possibility of parole.

The source of that clemency, sitting Governor James B. Hunt, a Democrat, was locked in a fierce battle for a Senate seat with incumbent Republican Jesse Helms. Members of both campaigns insisted that the election, scheduled to take place just four days after Barfield's death date, would have no bearing on the clemency decision. As an avowed supporter of the death penalty, Hunt was more likely to lose enthusiasm than votes should he decide to commute.[10] Moreover, he had declined to commute the sentence of James Hutchins, who earlier that year became the first person in North Carolina executed after *Furman,* sentenced to death for killing three police officers. As Barfield's execution approached, the governor's office was flooded with letters, approximately two-thirds of them in favor of commutation.[11] Always a churchgoer, she was born again in prison and became an important friend and ally to her fellow inmates and even guards at the women's prison. Perhaps most important, she was a woman, and in all of North Carolina's history, the state had executed just six women, all but one of them African American. In fact, the last and only white woman to be executed in North Carolina died on the gallows in 1833, an event notable enough it inspired a folk song, "The Ballad of Frankie Silvers."[12]

But Barfield's attorneys were not optimistic. They met with the governor to lay out their case, emphasizing her recent diagnosis as bipolar and new details about her childhood, which was rife with sexual abuse. They did not leave the meeting optimistic, later recalling that Hunt was "cool, detached, and formal."[13] Moreover, Hunt seemed uninterested in the entreaties from allies such as the warden of the Women's Prison, where Barfield was incarcerated, and members of the Margie Velma Barfield

Support Committee. He was looking for new criminal evidence or revelations about misconduct rather than evidence of Barfield's personal transformation.[14] The attorneys' pessimism bore out: soon thereafter, Hunt declined to offer Barfield clemency, calling the decision one of the most difficult in his eight years as governor.[15]

In the wee hours of November 3, about three hundred anti–death penalty protesters gathered to hold a vigil outside Central Prison, where Barfield waited on so-called death watch. She had described a previous stay there, before a reprieve, as a "real trauma."[16] Her supporters carried candles, waiting for Barfield's 2:00 A.M. execution. Death penalty supporters, according to a Barfield supporter, chanted "Kill the bitch!"[17] They also sang the famous line, "Na-na-na-na, hey hey hey, goodbye" and called Barfield a "Mondale liberal," a moniker with which conservative Republican Jesse Helms had labeled his Democratic rival Jim Hunt.[18] In doing so they connected Barfield's fate with a wider political contest over the legacy of the civil rights movement.

The impermeable political lines had been drawn: Barfield was either a monstrous serial killer or a grandmother who herself fell victim to drug addiction and mental illness. The question was no longer whether or not Barfield had changed, but whether her conviction and sentence were properly applied. The era of compassionate commutation was over. The "Death Row Granny" was executed with a lethal injection in the wee hours of November 3, 1984, becoming the first woman to be executed in the United States in twenty-two years.[19]

With the notable exception of Velma Barfield herself—a white woman—the Barfield case exemplified the death penalty in the post-*Furman* era. The case involved a prosecutor with exclusive authority over whether or not to seek the death penalty; a politically sensitive clemency decision; a cascade of appeals and post-conviction motions; and, crucially, white victims. Even Barfield's identity may have played a role. As one criminologist wrote in an editorial following the execution, Barfield became "a symbol of equal opportunity in state murder by becoming the first woman executed in the United States in twenty-two years and more significantly, the first woman to be executed in North Carolina in forty years. There is irony in such 'equality.'"[20] Barfield's defense attorney contended that being a white woman, counterintuitively, made her more likely to receive a death sentence in an atmosphere of heightened concern about executing black men. "Velma's statistically OK to kill," he told one reporter. "'She's white, she's middle-aged, she's a woman. Executing her would help even the score.'"[21]

Evening the score: this mentality not only explained Barfield's execution but the posture of many North Carolinians in the 1960s, 1970s, and 1980s. That idea not only kept the focus of the post-*Furman* debate on the race of the condemned prisoner but also occluded the much more important role of the race of the victim in death penalty determinations. The first two people executed in North Carolina after *Furman*, a white man and a white woman, gave the appearance that the state had moved beyond its troubled past, and was now willing to execute a new kind of person. It would take until 1999 for North Carolina to execute a black person. However, the race of victims in death penalty cases remained constant: those convicted of killing white victims continue to receive death sentences at a significantly higher rate than those with nonwhite victims. Just eight of the forty-three people executed between 1961 and 2006 were executed for murdering black victims. In the death penalty's second act—after its gradual decline, and after the Supreme Court briefly banned it because its haphazard application could be explained only by racial bias—race remained the key defining feature of its usage. And its deep entanglement with racial bias is explained by its history, even after the successes of the civil rights movement.

## Capital Punishment and the Civil Rights Movement

The executions of Velma Barfield and James Hutchins marked the beginning of what death penalty scholars and attorneys know as the "modern" or "late modern" period of executions in North Carolina and the nation.[22] The biggest difference between this modern era and the historical period, which stretches back into the early 1600s, is in fact not *Furman* at all but the southern civil rights movement, which fundamentally reordered the relationship between citizens and the state, a relationship shaped by enslavement and post-emancipation efforts to hold fast to its economic and social products.

In the two decades between the execution of Theodore Boykin in 1961 and James Hutchins in 1984, the United States and North Carolina experienced the classical phase of the Black Freedom Struggle, including Freedom Summer, the March on Washington, the Civil Rights Act, and the Voting Rights Act. North Carolina was in the vanguard of nonviolent direct action, boasting the famous sit-ins at the Woolworth's lunch counter in Greensboro in 1961, but also the lesser known 1957 sit-in at Durham's Royal Ice Cream Company. But amid these pushes for reform, state actors were also on the vanguard of the resistance. Democratic senator Sam Ervin claimed a leadership role in consolidating the "Southern Manifesto," southern politicians' anti-integration screed disguised as principled opposition to federal over-reach.[23] Also signing on was Ervin's junior colleague W. Kerr Scott, who served as governor between 1949 and 1953 and presided over twenty-three executions, most of them of African American men with white victims.

At the beginning of the 1960s, the state boasted a well-developed apparatus of racial suppression, with voter disfranchisement key to maintaining white control of state institutions and their output.[24] Its African American population was the fourth largest in the United States and the difference between the population of white registered voters and black eligible voters was second only to Mississippi's. By 1968, African Americans had effectively been purged from electoral participation: the state had the fewest elected African American officials in the nation.[25] Yet it took work to maintain the white political regime, especially as a growing network of activists strained against it, often under the auspices of a well-developed network of NAACP branches.[26] That work was done by politicians, vigilantes, and their allies.

White North Carolinians revolted against the civil rights movement along with their fellow white southerners. Following the 1954 *Brown* decision, Ku Klux Klan membership in the state was exploding. After the Civil War, in North Carolina and its southern neighbors, the Ku Klux Klan operated alongside a motley assortment of white vigilante groups seeking to curtail Republican political power and terrorize African American people and communities. But it was in the 1960s that it reached its peak—in reaction to the civil rights movement—with the North Carolina Realm of the United Klans of America accounting for more than half of all Klan membership in the South, more than ten times as many members as in Louisiana.[27]

When students from North Carolina A&T State University touched off a national sit-in movement in 1960, the Klan gathered at their protests, but were already well-infiltrated by federal and state law enforcement and posed little threat. More numerous and more consequential were the Klan's sympathizers, middle-class whites who believed the civil rights movement threatened their personal liberty.[28] When the Civil Rights Act was pending before Congress, a group called the Freedom Fund took out a full-page advertisement in the *Statesville Record and Landmark*. Without mentioning race, the ad warned readers that the bill was "the most dangerous legislation ever proposed and would destroy our freedom of choice and our private enterprise system."[29] In 1968, one North Carolina man wrote to his senator, Sam Ervin, complaining about efforts to ameliorate the lives of people of color. "I'm sick of 'poor' people demonstrations (black, white, red, yellow, purple, green, or any other color!)," he wrote. "I'm sick of the U.S. Supreme Court ruling for the good of a very small part rather than the whole of our society."[30]

In the 1950s, under Governor Luther Hodges, North Carolina successfully resisted integration using a variety of legal and administrative tactics. The Pupil Reassignment Act of 1955 gave authority over public education to local school districts, thus exploding the number of potential targets for lawsuits should advocacy organizations seek to use the courts to force integration. The state's Pearsall Plan, enacted in the wake of *Brown* in 1956, gave residents the right to close their public schools should desegregation occur and to use public funds to send white students to private schools. Tom Pearsall, pulled from retirement to lead the plan's development, hoped to "preserve our public schools" by allowing just "a minimum of integration, appealing for separation of the races by choice for most of the state."[31] Hailed as "moderate," the plan maintained rigid racial segregation in North Carolina for more than a decade after *Brown* even as it appeared to bolster the state's reputation as a buoy of civility in a sea of violence.[32]

Backlash against the civil rights movement, galvanized by racial resentment, spurred the transformation of North Carolina from a state that voted for Democratic presidential candidate Lyndon B. Johnson in 1964 to one that gave 70 percent of the vote to Richard Nixon, who won the state, and Barry Goldwater. Both Nixon and Goldwater ran hard on restoring "law and order." As he campaigned for the presidency in 1968, Richard Nixon imagined an America threatened by rising crime rates and a more generalized miasma of violence as represented by antiwar protests and so-called riots in places like Detroit and Los Angeles. His late-campaign advertisements depicted a middle-aged white woman walking anxiously down a darkening street or mashed-up images of hypodermic needles, weapons, demonstrations, and other unrest. These advertisements conjured up an urban threat to suburban America, a creeping darkness poised to assault white communities, echoing older, more clearly articulated warnings about the sexual threat posed to white women by black men.[33] Without harsh punishments to deter this encroachment, white communities were vulnerable. This vulnerability was magnified, in the minds of many anxious observers, by the Supreme Court, which was defanging law enforcement with rulings such as *Mapp*, *Miranda*, and *Gideon v. Wainwright*.[34] The death penalty was one tool white North Carolinians used to "even the score" after the victories of the civil rights movement and Supreme Court intervention.

Among the mechanisms for maintaining racial segregation was busing, which in North Carolina often meant closing African American schools and sending their former students to white schools. Activists pointed out that the state's busing schemes amounted to retaliation against the African American community for seeking to dismantle an unconstitutional system.[35] When white students were threatened with busing, it became known as "forced busing" and was condemned as "the most insanely, stupid, idiotic, and illogical crackpot program ever promulgated in a civilized country in the history of human civilization."[36] As busing moved to the symbolic center of civil rights movement backlash, politicians running for local, state, and national office signaled their conservatism by criticizing busing, often intertwining it with law-and-order rhetoric. One candidate for United States Senate in North Carolina who left the Democratic Party for the GOP, ran on "forced busing and law and order with justice."[37] He lost the Republican primary to Jesse Helms, who ran on rigid opposition to busing, boasting in one advertisement that he "ha[s] never been namby-pamby about it."[38]

Opposition to busing, then, was the first and most obvious way to push back against the changes the civil rights movement wrought. But anti-busing and law-and-order reactionary politics linked easily in the minds of many North Carolinians to whom *Furman* was yet another example of the Supreme Court forcing change on unwilling communities. First *Brown*, then *Brown II*, then *Furman*, then *Roe v. Wade*: each of these decisions, to their detractors, elbowed public sentiment out of the public policy realm and illegitimately allowed the federal government to interfere in local affairs.[39] Particularly as the war on crime escalated into the 1970s, the death penalty was becoming shorthand for conservative political ideology itself. Ironically, it did so as it became somewhat less overtly racially biased. Its symbolism was becoming more important than its role in the criminal justice system.

## Why Keep the Law on the Books?
## Capital Punishment in the 1960s

As hysteria about crime was beginning to brew, use of and support for the death penalty was actually declining. As discussed in chapter 4, the death penalty lost ground in North Carolina and nationally throughout the 1950s and early 1960s due to a combination of factors, including but not limited to broadened jury discretion, falling murder rates, and a shift in public opinion.[40] By the early 1960s, capital punishment in North Carolina appeared to be fading out of use and out of mind. Gallup polling reveals that support for the death penalty fell between the 1930s—the era of the Public Enemy and widespread police violence, including the murder of notorious gangsters like Clyde Barrow and Bonnie Parker, John Dillinger, Pretty Boy Floyd, and others—and the 1960s. Support for the death penalty dropped alongside executions themselves, reaching a low of 41 percent in May 1966.[41] Emerging revelations about the systematic execution of Jews and other marginalized peoples in the Holocaust using a gas chamber no doubt contributed to this decline.[42]

In North Carolina, Governor Terry Sanford went on the record as an opponent of the practice and was vocal enough about the issue that condemned prisoners noted his position in their appeals for clemency.[43] Editorialists declared the death penalty practically over, observing that in North Carolina and elsewhere, juries were increasingly reluctant to hand down death sentences, offering verdicts of "guilty with a recommendation of mercy." Prosecutors complained that the law would not let them do their jobs and make the case for a death penalty. All that remained was to decide whether or not to ban the practice by law, or let it continue to wither on the vine. Considering this issue, one columnist posed two questions: "If the death penalty is not to be invoked, why keep the law on the books? On the other hand, if it is so seldom invoked as a practical matter, why bother to repeal [it]?"[44]

A handful of legislators sought to address these questions by banning the death penalty. In 1961, local papers in North Carolina kept careful track of a bill, introduced by a General Assembly member from Wake County, home of the state capital Raleigh, that would have abolished capital punishment in nearly all cases, reserving an exception for when someone serving life for a formerly capital crime committed another capital crime while in prison.[45] A delegation of religious leaders, including from the North Carolina Council of Churches, spoke in favor of abolition at a public hearing in May, summing up generations of opposition to capital punishment: it brutalizes people rather than serving as a deterrent, it preys on the poor and dispossessed, it is used mainly in the South, and it is antithetical to the spirit of rehabilitation. The Pulitzer Prize–winning playwright Paul Green added that most of those who were executed were "murky-minded, confused, badly trained, disorganized souls—pitifully weak people."[46]

However, at the public hearing before the House Judiciary Committee, no one spoke in favor of the bill, and the committee consigned it to its own death by opting against voting on it or modifying it.[47] In a voice vote in early June, the General Assembly tabled the bill.[48] "Of all the useless hearings ever held, this one takes the cake," complained one North Carolinian.[49] North Carolina's policymakers had little taste for the death penalty, but appeared to have little taste for repealing it. However, at least some General Assembly members remained optimistic that the state would still manage to ban it, or else that the Supreme Court would step in and take care of the problem. Every two years, legislators brought abolition bills to the General Assembly, and every two years those bills failed.[50] Yet the vote total was narrowing, and supporters of abolition were growing confident. Representative Howard Twigg, whose district included Central Prison, told the Associated Press his abolition bill would likely pass in the 1973 legislative session.[51] Editorialists shared his optimism: "Justice and humanity will be better served when this state and 49 others substitute life terms for death penalties," wrote the *Asheville Citizen-Times* in 1971.[52] And then came *Furman*. Instead of doing abolitionists' job for them, it reinvigorated death penalty supporters.

### Furman v. Georgia

On June 30, 1972, the United States Supreme Court rendered its 5–4 ruling, which it would later concede was confusing,[53] on the case of *Furman v. Georgia*. In a brief per curiam ruling on the death sentence of William Henry Furman, whose case was bundled with two others for the court's consideration, the majority found that "carrying out of the death penalty in these cases constitutes cruel and unusual punishment in violation of the Eighth and Fourteenth Amendments." Each of the five justices in the majority wrote a separate concurring decision. Just two justices, Thurgood Marshall and William Brennan, found that the death penalty was unconstitutional in all instances. Three concurring decisions by William O. Douglass, Potter Stewart, and Byron White found that the death penalty, in the words of Justice White, "provide[d] no mechanism" to address the capriciousness in which it was applied.[54]

Justice Potter Stewart's concurring opinion produced one of the more memorable lines from the lengthy decision when he noted that the death sentences under review were "cruel and unusual in the same way being struck by lightning is cruel and unusual."[55] Yet just a few sentences later, Stewart actually contradicted himself when he wrote, "My concurring Brothers have demonstrated that, if any basis can be discerned for the selection of these few to be sentenced to die, it is the constitutionally impermissible basis of race."[56] Therefore the death penalty operated like a lightning storm, but with lightning that disproportionately struck African American people. Potter then set aside race on the grounds that discrimination "has not been proved," but rested his concurrence on the death penalty being "wantonly and freakishly imposed."

Potter's nod to racial discrimination would have surprised very few people. Race, of course, was widely known to play a major role in the imposition and carrying out of death sentences, a point which activists underscored in their work to abolish it. Agitating for abolition in the 1930s, Paul Green had called the death penalty system "the business of murdering innocent Negroes."[57] Journalist Nell Battle Lewis edited a pamphlet, "Capital Punishment in North Carolina," for the State Board of Charities and Public Welfare, which printed photographs of African American death row inmates. One of Lewis's colleagues at the *News and Observer* noted in a 1928 editorial that "the best ticket a man [on death row] can hold is that of being a white man."[58] In a 1941 study, sociologist Guy B. Johnson, while acknowledging the difficulty in retrieving accurate data, estimated that 80 percent of African American men sentenced to death for killing white victims were executed, versus just 65 percent of those with black victims.[59]

With *Furman*, the U.S. Supreme Court undermined the rationale for the death penalty but did not dismantle it, allowing states the opportunity to create a mechanism for consistency rather than forcing them to abandon it. Thus *Furman* left the door open for a revised death penalty to endure; indeed, the ruling suggested that eliminating discretion would nudge the punishment over the constitutional threshold. Spurred by a new pro–death penalty movement,[60] states raced through this open door, revising their death penalty statutes with "unprecedented speed and vehemence."[61] Even states that had recently dismantled their death penalties hurried to reinstate them. In California, for instance, death penalty boosters got a referendum on the ballot to restore the punishment, which had been ruled unconstitutional by the state Supreme Court. New Hampshire and Oregon also took steps toward reinstatement. In more familiar territory, southern politicians soon spoke up in favor of the death penalty. Georgia governor Jimmy Carter averred, with reference to parole, that "seven years" was not a long enough sentence for a murderer.[62] Meanwhile, the ten people on North Carolina's death row were resentenced to life imprisonment.

## Evolving the Other Way: The Response to *Furman*

The response to *Furman* among politicians, particularly southerners, was swift and decisive. Law enforcement officers warned that the ruling would increase violent crime. The National Association of Attorneys General voted in favor of a resolution calling on state and national legislators to draft new death penalty statutes that would withstand Supreme Court scrutiny. President Richard Nixon expressed his enduring belief in the value of the death penalty as a deterrent, despite the absence of supporting evidence.[63]

The possibility that death might no longer be available as a punishment seemed to have galvanized public opinion, which throughout the 1960s had been fairly stable, though evenly split. That split gave politicians the opportunity to support or oppose the practice. But *Furman* sparked a major swing toward capital punishment, giving politicians considerably more incentive to support it. A Harris Poll, for instance, showed a ten-point swing in favor of capital punishment over the course of just a few years, with 48 percent of respondents in 1969 saying they "believed in" the death penalty rising to 59 percent by 1972.[64] Gallup showed similar results when it reported support for the death penalty at 57 percent, the highest level of support in two decades.[65] As historian Stuart Banner quipped, the "evolving standards of decency" that led the Supreme Court to declare capital punishment cruel "were evolving the other way."[66]

The social violence of busing, as imagined by its opponents, complemented the more direct violence posed by violent crime. Unfortunately for abolitionists, the violent crime rate began to rise just as the death penalty appeared to be receding. Starting in 1961, the number of homicides, rapes, armed robberies, and other violent crimes climbed steadily until the 1990s.[67] The impact of this trend on Americans, southerners, or North Carolinians is unclear, particularly as support for the death penalty increased only modestly in the late 1960s. After *Furman*, though, support for the death penalty increased, and compounding that shift, opposition decreased.[68] These national polls are blunt instruments, as the death penalty operates on a county-to-county level, but if nothing else they demonstrate the tenuous relationship between public opinion and the use of capital punishment.

Law enforcement officers in North Carolina reacted forcefully, and sometimes with only thinly veiled racial dog-whistling, to the *Furman* decision. The police chief of Statesville forecast an increase in crime and derided the death penalty's replacement, life in prison. In a possible reference to Warren Kimbro, a member of the Black Panther Party sentenced to life imprisonment for murder but released before serving his full sentence, the chief claimed to "remember a couple years ago when a Black Panther leader murdered someone . . . and was awarded a scholarship to Harvard University."[69]

In contrast, the ten men on North Carolina's death row celebrated the decision, which they heard about on the radio. Raleigh's Central Prison relaxed its policies to allow journalists to interview death row inmates, one of whom said that he reacted to the news by clapping, dancing, and yelling. They celebrated because *Furman* meant they were to be resentenced to life imprisonment; some did not celebrate, they told a reporter, because they were confident in their existing appeals.[70]

The immediate reaction to the ruling among North Carolinians fell along emerging ideological lines, at least judging from letters to the editors of a number of newspapers. The antiwar Left saw the question through the lens of broadening personal liberty while the conservative Right mourned the loss of harsh punishment as representing a cultural collapse. Editorials in major papers such as the *Asheville Citizen-Times* and the *News and Observer* of Raleigh generally favored the decision, whereas smaller papers denounced it. A survey of letters to the editor revealed significantly more letters opposed to *Furman* than supporting it, though the editorial staff may have used those letters as a counterweight to the paper's own position.

One of the few letters in support of *Furman*, published in the *Asheville Citizen-Times*, hoped the ruling would focus attention on the death and destruction of the Vietnam War.[71] On the other side of the political spectrum, the *Citizen-Times* published a lengthy missive attacking the Supreme Court for interpreting the Constitution to "suit their own personal ideas" and snidely bemoaning the idea that in using capital punishment, Americans "have been living a lie all these 200 years."[72] The *Statesville Record and Landmark* noted that the day after the *Furman* decision, the proprietor of a roadside establishment was murdered. It published an ironic fairytale, imagining the wolf in "Little Red Riding Hood" had posthumous representation from the American Civil Liberties Union and Students for a Democratic Society, and the woodman was punished for killing the wolf.[73]

Another letter-writer averred that "violent crime is rampant across our nation and stern measures must be applied for the protection of our citizens."[74] Yet another mocked people who "loose [sic] many sleepless nights worrying about the possibility that our system of justice might misfire and execute an innocent man (a possibility for which there is no previous precedent in all of American jurisprudence)" as opposed to worrying about innocent people murdered by criminals who received lenient treatment. The letter-writer added that "civilization simply cannot survive unless it is protected from its traitorous and uncivilized elements."[75] In imitation of the national tough-on-crime rhetoric, a white Durham teenager began a "Combat Crime" campaign, seeking 5,000 letters in support of capital punishment for delivery to Congress.[76] She received 25,000.[77]

In the absence of focused polling, it is not entirely possible to determine the position of the African American community, insofar as it can be considered as a unitary community with a particular perspective. Yet from all indications, reaction to the Furman decision among African Americans was, in a general sense, more positive.[78]

The African American press had a longstanding tradition of opposition to the death penalty because of its racist outcomes. Black papers regularly editorialized about lynching, closely followed the progress of and impediments to federal anti-lynching legislation and followed up lynching reporting with stories about the victims' innocence. Moreover, they pointed out inequities in the law and legal custom, not least the tendency of white jurors to value the testimony of whites, particularly white women, over African Americans.[79]

After *Furman*, Durham's long-standing African American–owned and –published *Carolina Times* called capital punishment a "barbaric and sadistic practice of state-sponsored murder" that was "applied in a way that discriminated against black Americans."[80] In 1976, the *Carolina Times* aligned itself with the Urban League when it published an op-ed by its president, Vernon Jordan, calling for a death penalty ban. In the tradition of the *Carolina Times*, the editorial approached a racially sensitive issue by highlighting the non–race-specific problems with it: its ineffectiveness as a deterrent and its finality. On the latter point, Jordan suggested that someone who is "black, poor, friendless" would be much less likely to benefit from the kind of efforts that might result in a lesser sentence, clemency, or a pardon.[81] The *Future Outlook* praised African American representative Henry Frye, a death penalty foe.[82]

## "The People of North Carolina Want Justice": The State's Legislative Response

The cultural and social preconditions for a return of the death penalty were as prolific in North Carolina as they were in many southern states. Although many faith organizations went on the record against capital punishment in the 1970s, in the evangelical religious imagination God appeared to be as enthusiastic about mortal vengeance as He was about saving souls. And the death penalty's history offered much to those committed to bending the criminal justice system against communities of color, an imperative now more pressing than ever in light of the new threats to white supremacy posed by black activism and political engagement. While southern states had ceased executing prisoners along with the rest of the country in 1968, even after *Furman* juries continued to send prisoners to death row in record-setting numbers: in 1975, nearly three hundred people received death sentences, the highest number yet recorded. Just three years after *Furman* emptied death rows around the country, the number of prisoners awaiting death reached a historic peak.[83]

In North Carolina, legislators immediately announced their plan to introduce legislation to bring the state's death penalty into line with the Supreme Court's ruling, but opponents expressed certainty that the efforts were "'doomed to failure.'"[84] Yet the question was already in motion in the courts. In 1973, the North Carolina Supreme Court stripped the state's discretionary death penalty statute of its discretion, leaving death as the mandatory punishment upon conviction of a capital crime. In *State v. Waddell*, the court severed the 1949 amendment from the statute and instructed judges to impose death sentences for anyone convicted of murder, rape, burglary, or arson—just as they had before 1941. Writing for the majority, Associate Justice J. Frank Haskins opined, "The Legislature . . . may wish to rewrite these statutes altogether to give expression to what it conceives to be the public will."[85] After *Waddell*, North Carolina's death row population spiked to 120, making it the largest in the nation.[86]

Following the court's lead, legislators sought to revise the death penalty statute, pursuing three possible paths. Seventeen bills divided into three basic groups: replacing the death penalty with life imprisonment, or abolition; imposing a mandatory death penalty for first-degree murder and rape; or imposing a mandatory death penalty for first-degree murder only.[87] Ultimately, the state House and Senate were unable to agree on whether or not rape should be capital, but in both chambers, members voted overwhelmingly for the death penalty in one form or another.[88]

Legislators' support for a death penalty of some kind reflected the dramatic shift in public opinion that had taken place from the 1960s to the 1970s. But the anti–death penalty movement may have reached its peak as the General Assembly debated how far to extend the punishment. In December 1973, under the mandatory statute as stripped down by the North

Carolina Supreme Court, three young African American men were sentenced to death for the rape of a white woman in Tarboro, North Carolina, about seventy-five miles east of Raleigh.[89] The men refused a plea deal, insisting on their innocence, and their case raised the ire of local and national activists. Following days of protests in Tarboro, the Reverend Leon White, who led the North Carolina–Virginia Commission for Racial Justice, led a march from Tarboro to Raleigh that drew two hundred people on Super Bowl Sunday.[90] The Tarboro Three ultimately spent two years in prison before taking a deal, pleading no contest to a charge of assault with intent to rape and accepting a six-year suspended sentence.[91] As of 2011, Vernon Brown and his accuser still live in Tarboro.[92]

Less than a month after those protests, the state Senate took up the question of a mandatory death sentence for murder and aggravated rape. The House approved the bill 102 to 9, on April 8, 1974, returning to the mandatory sentencing statute that was the law in the state since before it was a state and was codified in the 1868 constitution.[93] Legislators were careful to add severability to the statute revision, which meant that should the courts strike down the new law, people sentenced to death would receive life imprisonment.[94] In response, Southern Christian Leadership Conference president and former Martin Luther King adviser and friend Ralph Abernathy declared that North Carolina is "not only number one in basketball but number one in legalized killing."[95]

Abernathy was joined on July 4 by Angela Davis, representing her National Alliance against Racist and Political Repression. They led a 4,000-strong march in Raleigh—organizers claimed 10,000 attended—demanding an end to the death penalty. The alliance had identified North Carolina as a place where "repression of Black and Native American activists has been most intense."[96] Local leaders such as Leon Brown and Golden Frinks did not attend, fearing that these outside agitators would harm their own efforts. The protesters carried signs past Central Prison, housing 45 of the 123 death row prisoners in the nation. They carried signs, too, past members of the American Nazi Party, Klansmen in full regalia, and members of a right-wing group called the Rights of White People Party, who broke for coffee after the demonstrators passed by.[97]

Just ten days later, the glare of national and international attention shone even brighter on North Carolina during the trial where Joan Little faced the death penalty for murder.[98] The jailer of the Beaufort County jail, where Little was being held awaiting trial for a breaking and entering charge, used an ice pick to coerce Little into oral sex. Desperate, Little managed to grab the pick and stabbed the man before escaping. Fearing the law that allowed citizens to kill declared outlaws, Little surrendered to the State Bureau of Investigation.[99] A nineteen-year-old high school dropout with a criminal record, Little became a vessel into which local white men poured out their spite for and fascination with women of color. Journalist James Reston Jr. interviewed people in Washington, the Beaufort County seat, who universally disdained Little, and black women more broadly, as promiscuous. "'Hell,'" a car dealer told Reston, "'to them, fucking is like saying good morning or having a Pepsi-Cola.'"[100] Perhaps not surprisingly, Little recalled a Washington, North Carolina, that was "behind the rest of the world."[101]

Little assertively defended herself. She forcefully avowed her right to self-defense and the strength of her moral character. The dead man had used damaging stereotypes about black women to coerce Little, telling her as she resisted that no one would believe her claims of rape. Yet, as her attorney sought to demonstrate during cross-examination, the strength of her resistance demonstrated her character and dismantled the prosecution's claim that she had seduced and murdered the jailer in order to escape.[102] Activists across the county took up her defense. The ubiquitous Angela Davis spoke in her support, Bernice Johnson Reagon wrote a song entitled "Joan Little," and Rosa Parks formed a defense committee in Detroit.[103] The Free Joan Little movement included grassroots activists as well as celebrities,[104] while in the courtroom her defense received a boost from African American women testifying to similar sexual assaults by the jailer. She was acquitted and spared the gas chamber, but the case drew even more attention to the role of race in the death penalty system and in the wider criminal justice system in North Carolina.[105]

To its supporters, a mandatory sentence for only first-degree murder and aggravated rape, such as the rape of a person under twelve years old, would obviate the "unusual" nature of capital punishment.[106] Supporters also hoped it would address the race question by removing discretion, punishing the crime and not the person.[107] This viewpoint overlooked the role race and poverty may have played in arrest, effectiveness of counsel, conviction, and other matters. Even so, supporters praised the bill as a step toward fairness, while death penalty opponents saw it as a step along the way to complete abolition, bowing to what they saw as overwhelming public support for capital punishment. "A man who is starving will accept half a loaf," said one representative. Another added, "I am confident that the gas chamber at Central Prison will never again be used."[108]

This was certainly the hope of Jesse Fowler, an African American man sentenced to death under the new statute for murdering a man who broke his nose.[109] The United States Supreme Court agreed to hear Fowler's appeal, which sought to persuade the court that the death penalty in and of itself violated the Eighth Amendment's prohibition against cruel and unusual punishment.[110] Anthony Amsterdam, the Stanford professor and attorney who argued *Furman* before the Supreme Court, took the responsibility of oral arguments for Fowler, facing off with Deputy Attorney General Jean Benoy and United States Solicitor General Robert Bork, who argued for North Carolina. Amsterdam argued that the very arbitrariness of the death penalty was the only thing that made it tolerable. Justice Thurgood Marshall pressed Benoy on racial discrimination in North Carolina's criminal justice system, asking him to name a single black official. Benoy failed to summon a name, but told Marshall there was a "Negress" who was a judge in Guilford County.[111]

Fowler was the subject of national attention as the press waited anxiously to see if his case would resolve the uncertain death penalty.[112] Meanwhile, the mandatory statute was filling death row beyond capacity. It became so crowded that Fowler had to share a six-by-nine-foot cell with another man convicted of murder. The men were permitted to leave the cell for two hours each day and were allowed two showers per week.[113] But the poor health of Justice William O. Douglas disappointed those eager for a resolution. He was not expected to hear oral arguments after suffering a stroke on New Year's Eve, but gaunt and pale, he was wheeled into the chamber on April 21. When illness prevented him from participating in adjudicating Fowler's case, however, the court was deadlocked.

Joining Fowler on death row was Sam Poole, another prisoner whose case became a national issue. In May 1973, a white woman reported that a black man had broken into her home in Robbins, North Carolina, and entered her bedroom while she slept. She was not harmed, nor was anything taken from her home. Police found a button on her bedroom floor, which they later claimed belonged to Poole, who was charged with first-degree burglary. The state's new statutes mandated a death sentence upon conviction, so in an echo of death sentences handed down in the 1920s and 1930s, Poole was sent to death row for entering, and then leaving, a white woman's home. Noting that the person who burgled Daniel Ellsberg's psychiatrist's office received a sentence of just six months, Angela Davis, speaking at a rally in Raleigh, called Poole's sentence indicative of the "gimmick" of North Carolina's "New

South image," and the conviction was ultimately overturned by the state Supreme Court.[114]

The true test of North Carolina's new mandatory statute, following in the footsteps of *State v. Fowler*, came in the case of James Woodson. Woodson was convicted of felony murder and sentenced to death for his role in a convenience store robbery that turned lethal: he was sitting in a car outside while his accomplices committed murder.[115] The apparent unfairness of Woodson's mandatory death sentence—one of the two gunmen received a plea deal to serve twenty years in prison—gave the United States Supreme Court a chance to rule on the constitutionality of the mandatory death sentence.[116] With John Paul Stevens replacing Justice Douglas, the court considered Woodson alongside four other capital appeals, one of which was *Gregg v. Georgia*.[117] In *Gregg*, rendered 7–2, Justice Potter Stewart famously declared since "death is qualitatively different" from imprisonment, death sentences needed to be responsive to the particular circumstances of the crime and its offender. The court thus ruled that Georgia, Florida, and Texas had successfully applied guided discretion in order to avoid arbitrariness.

At the same time, in *Woodson* and *Roberts*, in much closer 5–4 rulings, the court ruled that North Carolina and Louisiana, both of which used a mandatory sentencing procedure, had not. Mandatory sentences could not attend to the particulars and were thus not constitutional.[118] In his dissent, Justice William Rehnquist, nominated by President Nixon, appeared to mock the idea of an "evolving standard of decency to which the plurality professes obeisance," the standard that animated the consideration of the death penalty under the Eighth Amendment.[119] Rehnquist also noted that the court appeared to contradict itself in recommending standards, when just five years earlier, it held that the absence of standards was constitutional.[120] Rehnquist's dissent, in which he was joined by another Nixon nominee, Harry Blackmun, as well as Warren Burger and Byron White, demonstrated the power of public opinion in driving the behavior of Supreme Court justices.[121]

North Carolina's response was fairly typical not just of southern states but of the nation at large. Eventually, many whose statutes were affected by *Furman* rewrote them so they again could begin using execution as punishment. Florida restored the death penalty just six months after the Supreme Court ruling. Thirty-one states had restored the death penalty by the spring of 1975.[122] But many of these states rewrote their statutes along the lines laid out by the Modern Penal Code (MPC), a tract developed in 1962 by the American Law Institute, an influential nongovernmental organization, intended to assist state legislators in the difficult task of achieving some degree of legal consistency from state to state. Despite the MPC's position that punishment was for "treatment and correction," in "a fateful interaction of theory and political concern," its authors included guidelines for a restricted death penalty system in a bracketed portion, including aggravating and mitigating factors and a blueprint for a bifurcated sentencing process.[123] These guidelines became the basis for many states' revised statutes.[124]

However, a number of states, including those considered under *Gregg*—Texas, Georgia, and Florida—rested their death penalties on the basic premises laid out by the MPC, yet made them harsher. Georgia rejected mitigating factors and added two additional aggravating factors. Texas rejected aggravating and mitigating factors altogether and instructed jurors that a death penalty was warranted if they judged there was a "probability" that the defendant might "commit criminal acts of violence" in the future. And Florida, though it cleaved fairly close to the MPC, altered both mitigating and aggravating circumstances.[125] The dwindling death penalty was separated from the resurgent death penalty by only a few years, but those years contained the classical phase of the civil rights movement. In reaction, southern states were showing a degree of retributive zeal that was, from a legislative perspective, absent a decade earlier.[126]

In *Gregg*, the United States Supreme Court approved these harsher statutes. North Carolina was not alone in losing its mandatory death penalty: the "legislative deluge" that followed *Furman* included seventeen other states, as widely dispersed as Rhode Island and Nevada, which also instituted mandatory death penalty laws.[127] At the time, that law had sent 117 people to death row in North Carolina, the most in the nation; they would now be resentenced to life imprisonment. According to prison staff, death row inmates in Central Prison were "jubilant," but the reaction was more muted at the Correctional Center for Women. Joe Freeman Britt, the district attorney who secured Velma Barfield's death sentence, said he was "surprised" at the ruling but willing to continue his work under new guidelines.[128]

Republican candidates for governor immediately called on sitting governor Jim Holshouser to call a special session of the legislature to revise death penalty statutes, with one warning that without a death penalty, the state was at risk of a new murder spree.[129] The same candidates stressed their support for the death penalty in campaign advertisements, such as Coy Privette's, which also stated his opposition to the Equal Rights Amendment, "forced bussing," and inheritance taxation.[130] Just one of the seven candidates for their parties' gubernatorial nominations, Democrat George Wood, claimed to oppose capital punishment.[131] Meanwhile signs of the national resonance of capital punishment were clear: the Democratic Party omitted it altogether from its platform.[132] The Republican position reflected that of a solid majority of North Carolinians; a 1976 poll in the *News and Observer* of Raleigh found that more than 66 percent of respondents favored a new death penalty law, while just over 21 percent opposed it.[133]

Not long after the November 1976 elections, the Utah Supreme Court granted condemned prisoner Gary Gilmore's request to "die like a man" in front of a firing squad rather than in the gas chamber like the man who preceded him.[134] But the United States Supreme Court stayed Gilmore's appeal, leading him to attempt suicide in an effort to shorten his time on death row.[135] He was resuscitated and rehabilitated to prepare him for his execution as dozens of men called the Utah state prison warden requesting permission to join the firing squad. By December, Gilmore was healthy enough to conduct a hunger strike to press the courts to set aside his appeal, argued by Anthony Amsterdam on behalf of Gilmore's mother. On Sunday, January 15, the firing squad awaited news in an old tannery known as the Slaughterhouse inside the prison. Minutes after a stay of execution was lifted, five men pointed their .30-30 deer rifles at Gilmore and shot him dead.[136] The death penalty in the United States was back.

But it was not quite back in North Carolina. State attorney general Rufus Edmisten personally opposed the death penalty,[137] and had led the effort to draft a new statute, incorporating bifurcated sentencing in imitation of systems in place in Florida, Texas, and California.[138] The original plan envisioned two separate juries but eventually North Carolina settled on using just one jury in two phases. Most of the seven other bills under consideration included some version of Edmisten's plan, though one aimed for abolition while another sentenced only killers of police and state officials to death. Public hearings in February 1977 featured academics castigating draft bills for their vagueness and cautioning lawmakers that a return trip to the Supreme Court was likely if they did not carefully constrain the punishment.[139] Public hearings brought out many opponents of the death penalty but few supporters.[140] There were many supporters in the House, however, which in early May 1977 approved a tentative bill 77–33 that would give juries, in separate hearings, the choice between a death sentence and life imprisonment for first-degree murder and murder committed during the commission of another felony.[141]

Later that month, the Senate voted 38–12 to approve the House bill with one amendment, which gave the defendant the right to the final argument during the sentencing phase of the trial. Both the support and opposition to the bill that emerged during debate revealed the power of public opinion. "'How sad that society has confused Divine justice with public revenge,'" mourned a Democrat from Charlotte. But a fellow Democrat rejoined, "'The people in North Carolina want justice and the only way we're going to give them justice is to put this bill in force.'"[142] Senator James McDuffie, another Democrat, explained, "Murderers deserve no mercy."[143] The bill returned to the House, where it passed easily.[144]

Gesturing at the guidelines of the Modern Penal Code, the statute, which went into effect on June 1, 1977, established today's bifurcated sentencing process.[145] In this process, the jury hands down a verdict of guilty or not guilty. Then in a separate hearing, the same jury evaluates so-called aggravating and mitigating factors. Eleven aggravating factors are enumerated in the statute, including a previous conviction for a violent felony, whether the capital felony in question was committed while undertaking another serious crime, or whether the capital felony was "especially heinous, atrocious, or cruel."[146] Mitigating factors include a clean record, whether the defendant committed the crime while under duress, as an accessory with a "relatively minor" level or participation, or while subject to "mental disturbance."[147] After weighing these factors, the jury must return a unanimous sentencing recommendation of life imprisonment or death.[148] The law, which codified the process of personal evaluation jurors had been using for decades, also provided for an automatic North Carolina Supreme Court review of death sentences. The legislature passed it in 1977.

Execution was back in North Carolina, and with it, some observers thought, a new mood. "Judges and justices sense it. Prosecutors and defense lawyers sense it. Educators and ministers sense it. The public knows it and the majority probably approves of it," observed one journalist. "The mood is one of retribution—at once an emotional craving and an ancient legal concept recently given legal credence by the U.S. Supreme Court."[149] It was certainly evident in a raft of letters sent to the *Daily Times-News* by students at Burlington's Southern Middle School. The letters, at least those published by the paper, were almost unreservedly in favor of capital punishment and revealed a strong belief both in deterrence and retribution. "Another reason that bugs me more than anything else," one student wrote, "is many people say that the death penalty is cruel and unusual punishment, but what about the innocent victims!"[150]

The death penalty in 1977 was also a newly minted political hot button issue: for decades, North Carolina's governors had avoided talking about the issue. In the 1980s, to win an election there and elsewhere required vocal support for the death penalty.[151] This new climate resulted, in 1984, in North Carolina's first execution in more than twenty years. Since 1977, North Carolina has executed forty-three people, enough to place it ninth nationally. Of states that regularly execute criminals, just three (Florida, Texas, and Alabama) hold more condemned prisoners than North Carolina, where as of July 2017, 152 people sit on death row.[152]

The commitment to the death penalty was strong enough among North Carolina legislators that immediately after voting for the new statute, the state senate took up consideration of a bill that would recapitalize rape.[153] A judiciary committee narrowly refused to let the bill up for a vote, explaining that they would wait for word from the United States Supreme Court.[154] That word came in the form of *Coker v. Georgia*, in which the Supreme Court ruled that the death penalty for the rape of an adult woman was "disproportionate punishment."[155] A female state senator who was among those blocking the proposal declared the decision "marvelous"; her male counterpart who supported the bill reacted less positively.[156] In October, a Lumbee Indian man named James Calvin Jones became the first person in North Carolina sentenced to die under the new statute. The prosecutor on the case was Joe Freeman Britt.[157]

## Less Painful, More Dignified, and Less Expensive: A New Method

In the late 1970s, states were searching for an alternative to electrocution. For all the claims that lethal injection was humane, the more salient fact appeared to be the expense of updating and maintaining long-unused existing facilities. In Virginia, one legislator estimated it would cost $2,000 to update the state's electric chair but just $1 per lethal injection.[158] The American Medical Association forbade its doctors from administering the lethal drugs, but states steadily passed lethal injection protocols throughout the late 1970s and early 1980s.[159] In 1982, Texas became the first state to use lethal injection for the execution of an African American man sentenced to death for murdering a car salesman. The execution made use of sodium pentothal, commonly known as truth serum, to render the man unconscious, then pancuronium bromide to paralyze muscles and respiratory function, and potassium chloride to stop the heart.[160]

As the state's first execution since 1961 approached, North Carolina's General Assembly passed a bill that allowed condemned criminals to choose whether they would die with this increasingly popular lethal injection or asphyxiation with gas. Public discussion rehashed the debate about pain and humanity that would have been familiar to North Carolinians one hundred years previous. Injection was "basically the same procedure for making people well in hospitals," said the bill's sponsor, a Democrat.[161] He noted, too, that the gas chamber evoked images of Nazi Germany, further noting that lethal injections were "less painful, more dignified, and less expensive." Opponents worried that the appearance of painlessness would in fact "sugar-coat" execution and make it more likely that jurors would opt for the death penalty.[162] Others sought to return to public hangings in order to maximize execution's deterrent potential.[163]

The final bill passed the buck to condemned prisoners, giving them the choice of asphyxiation in the gas chamber or lethal injection. James Hutchins chose lethal injection, as did most of those who followed him into the death chamber, but Ricky Lee Sanderson chose gas in 1998.[164] As his victim's father watched, Sanderson "turned beet red," straining against the leather straps that held him down and gasping in the deadly gas.[165] After Sanderson's death, the General Assembly voted to restrict the execution method to lethal injection only, and in 2000, the death chair was packed away and sent to the North Carolina Museum of History.

### Contests of Prosecutorial Resolve: A Newly Political Death Penalty

In the wake of Velma Barfield's 1984 execution, *Newsday* published a Sunday think piece entitled, "After Velma Barfield: Are Executions Gaining Acceptance?" The execution, the article opined, was a sign: that Americans were more willing than ever to execute women, that they rejected the idea of rehabilitation and clemency, and that generally they were more open than ever to capital punishment.[166] More than "gaining acceptance," the death penalty after Velma Barfield's execution was an obligation for virtually any politician outside of the handful of states that eliminated capital punishment at opportune times. This was a new, political death penalty; or, as one political scientist dryly put it, as a result of *Furman*, "political attitudes toward capital punishment became more polarized,"[167] with campaigns becoming "contest[s] of prosecutorial resolve."[168]

A powerful example of this political obligation, broadly, is then-candidate Bill Clinton's departure from the campaign trail to Little Rock during the 1992 presidential nominating contest to be nearby to handle issues connected with the scheduled execution of Ricky Ray Rector, a brain-damaged African American man sentenced to death for killing a police officer.[169] One British paper observed that "both Democrats and Republicans want to be seen to take a firm stand against violent crime in an election year," leading Clinton, then battling adultery claims, to "boost his reputation by refusing clemency" to Rector.[170] In North Carolina, even governors who opposed capital punishment tended to signal they would follow polling. James Holshouser, a Republican who served from 1973 to 1977, told one journalist he was personally opposed to the death penalty but would be "sensitive" to the public's support for it.[171] Democrat James B. Hunt, who was governor from 1977 to 1985 and again from 1993 to 2001, was known as a capital punishment supporter who would "follow the law" on the matter.[172] When he ran for his second stint in the governor's mansion in 1992, Hunt warned about rising crime, called for building more prisons, and boasted that he "toughened punishment" during his previous service. He added that he "successfully supported" the death penalty when it was in limbo.[173]

Democrat Mike Easley presided over twenty-seven executions during his 2001 to 2009 term, even as polls showed 65 percent of North Carolina voters supported a moratorium.[174] Fellow Democrat Beverly Purdue described herself as a "real strong supporter of the death penalty," although she signed the 2009 Racial Justice Act, which allowed death row inmates to contest their sentences based on claims of systematic racial discrimination.[175] Governor Pat McCrory, the Republican who followed Purdue into office, showed his own strong support for the death penalty by signing the General Assembly's reversal of the law.[176] Roy Cooper, a Democrat narrowly elected in 2016, and his Democratic attorney general both support the death penalty. These governors also denied clemency using the rationale established by James Hunt in 1984: no new exculpatory evidence, no mercy.

This bland if consequential support for the death penalty meant, in short, the end of executive clemency. Executive clemency in the death penalty's premodern period—between the colonial period and the 1960s—was an essential safety valve for a mandatory punishment instituted in a Jim Crow state. Three kinds of clemency had been reduced to one. No longer was clemency extended in the name of "unrestrained mercy" and no longer was it extended to preserve the death penalty only for the worst of the worst offenders. It could be used only in a "quasi-judicial" manner upon discovery of new, exculpatory evidence or demonstrated misconduct on the part of the state.[177]

Before *Furman*, unrestrained clemency meant actually innocent or dubiously culpable African American men and women could enjoy release from their unjust sentence, if not actual justice. And as governors felt free not only to reinvestigate and relitigate cases but also to act out of a sense of mercy, they could commute based on their sense of desert in a wider social context. Therefore, women like Ida Ball Warren, and apparently innocent teenagers like Alvin Mansell, lived beyond their death dates. And as explained in chapter 4, African Americans women were the disproportionate beneficiaries of executive clemency precisely because the criminal justice system discriminated against them so rapaciously. Oddly, then, in line with conservative thinking in North Carolina in the early 1970s, a mandatory death sentence was in fact fairer, but only because the arbitrary and possibly capricious decision of the governor mitigated some of its cruelest effects.

After *Woodson*, and as death penalty statutes expanded to guarantee appeals to the state supreme court, the death penalty became more of a process and much less of a certainty, allowing governors to imitate Jim Hunt's deference to the process and obviate any moral responsibility they might feel to intervene. That process, though, remained racially discriminatory under the new sentencing guidelines, as a host of studies have demonstrated. North Carolina's modern death penalty has received a great deal of attention from researchers, whose results, while drawn from different data sets over different periods of time, share the conclusion that, in the words of one such study, "extra-legal" factors—that is, race and gender—held a "controlling" influence over the death penalty process.[178]

Between 1980 and 2006, the state of North Carolina executed more white people than black people—twenty-eight whites and thirteen African Americans, as well as an American Indian and a man of Syrian descent—suggesting on its face that the new sentencing guidelines and other procedural changes had ameliorated the nakedly racist process that preceded them. For instance, death penalty scholars Michael Radelet and Glenn L. Pierce found that nearly 80 percent of those executed in North Carolina during this period were convicted of killing white people. This is despite the fact that black people are disproportionately more likely to be victims of homicide.[179] A more fine-grained study found that in Durham, a major city in the state, black murder suspects are more than twice as likely to face the death penalty as white murder suspects, particularly if their victim or victims are white, and more so if they are white women.[180] The power of white femininity, and the state's effort to leverage it, thus continued.

The post-*Furman* death penalty also marked, amid a cacophony of dog-whistle rhetoric, the emergence of a victim-focused death penalty. For decades, the language used by North Carolina's law enforcement officers, politicians, and journalists about the death penalty was relatively unmarked by vengeance. Their restraint importantly had little bearing on the comportment of those who attended the trials and executions. As this book has presented, those groups—sometimes armed mobs—were often angry and vengeful, their rage animated by racial animus. But as framed by local and regional papers, the death penalty was a simple repayment of debt to the state, as opposed to a mechanism through which injured parties extract vengeance or closure. For instance, Will Hopkins "paid to the last tittle the price that the law requires for murder."[181] After the electrocutions of condemned African-American teenagers J. W. Ballard and Bernice Matthews, the *News and Observer* reported that "the State had collected its debt in full."[182] McIver Burnett "paid" for his rape conviction "with the only currency that he had."[183]

After the execution process became private in 1910, witnessing of executions by family members of victims was rare enough to merit mention by journalists, and in October 1925, Governor Angus McLean told prison warden J. H. Norman to refuse entrance to "all members of the families of injured parties," saying, "The execution of a criminal is the most solemn thing in the administration of the law, representing the sovereignty of the people, and there should be nothing about an execution to indicate revenge. An execution ought not to be permitted to be looked on as an act of personal satisfaction for a wrong."[184]

In contrast, newspaper coverage of the executions of James Hutchins and Velma Barfield shows the emergence of a victim-focused narrative that had not been part of capital punishment rhetoric. As Hutchins approached his scheduled execution, the *Asheville Citizen-Times* interviewed the families of his three victims, who hoped Hutchins's death would "relieve them of some of the anger they felt" about their relatives' deaths.[185] "I'm about to be as happy as a bug in a rug," said another in anticipation of the execution.[186] Coverage of Velma Barfield's execution revealed a similar focus on victims' families.[187] That year, President Ronald Reagan inaugurated his Task Force on Victims of Crime and created the National Crime Victims Week, and Congress complemented his actions with the Crime Victim Fund.[188]

The victims' rights movement did not emerge with Reagan's decision; like the resurgence of the death penalty itself, it responded to the due process revolution of the 1960s, emerging with the creation of Americans for Effective Law Enforcement in 1966.[189] As a political entity sought to undermine the law, even as it imagined itself strengthening it, by offering the families of victims of serious crime the chance to add to the already heavy emotional weight of the sentencing decision of a jury. The desire for satisfaction, most boldly expressed by angry lynch mobs one hundred years before that movement, was thus formally reintroduced to the death penalty process in the form of victim impact statements. Just as members of lynch mobs saw themselves as spurring the law toward a more gratifying outcome, so, too, did the victims' rights movement seek to elevate the needs of a harmed individual or individuals over the needs of society or even to deny that society's very integrity.[190] One influential leader in the victims' rights movement described criminal justice as a zero sum game: any benefit to a criminal visits further harm on his victims.[191]

A death penalty process steeped in the rhetoric of victims' rights, paired with a tradition of valuing white victims, and rebuilt on the backlash against the civil rights movement revealed the importance of the death penalty, or support for the death penalty and other harsh punishments, as a way of laying down a kind of lethal color line. The *Furman* ruling put down in writing—and not for the first time—the racially disproportionate outcomes that the death penalty in North Carolina yielded. But as this long history demonstrates, in North Carolina, discretion was never intended to prevent discrimination. The discretion of the 1940s and 1950s, which sent a dwindling number of black men to their deaths, was replaced by a new kind of discretion, bent not toward mercy but toward vengeance.

Considered in this way, the death penalty can be considered a countermovement, against the personhood of people of color in colonial North Carolina; acting to divide enslaved people from one another and lift up white people above them; pushing back against the disorderliness of emancipation and the questions it raised about labor, citizenship, and personhood. And when the second Reconstruction arrived in the form of the civil rights movement, it stood ready to resist, both in word and deed, as it continued to work against African Americans and other people of color as well as signal allegiance to a certain set of reactionary political positions. The stillness of the gallows belies its force.

# Conclusion

## A History of Failure?

· · · · · · · · · · · · · · · · · · · · · · · · · · · · · · · · · · · · · · · · · · · · · · · · · · · ·

Even as North Carolina's death penalty lay dormant in the 1960s and early 1970s, it remained a part of the criminal justice system. The threat of a death sentence was enough to spur prisoners facing capital trials to accept a sentence of life without the possibility of parole.[1] When capital trials took place, such as in the case of Joan Little (see chapter 5), they revealed the same unhealthy tangle of race, gender, and poverty that had informed the punishment for generations. In 1968, as race-related violence seemed to peak as backlash to the civil rights movement intensified, a teenaged African American girl, tried as an adult, was given a mandatory death sentence upon conviction for the murder of a grocer during a robbery. Marie Hill received her sentence on the basis of a confession she gave to her arresting officer, without counsel present, but which she later recanted. Her appeals process would eventually be taken up by Julius Chambers with help from the NAACP Legal Defense Fund and support from North Carolinians Against the Death Penalty, the newly formed North Carolina Committee on Racial Justice, and the Save Marie Hill Committee, headed by Golden Frinks of the Southern Christian Leadership Conference. She awaited the outcome in solitary confinement in North Carolina's Women's Prison.

While Hill waited, North Carolinians in the media relitigated her case in revealing ways. One editorial aged her up, calling her "a teenager in years only." Evoking the white frustration of an era when white men and women were being forced to relinquish some of their structural privilege, the columnist argued that the victim was "just as dead as if a twenty-five-year-old white male had shot and beat him to death. Would there be a 'saving committee' in this case? I wonder."[2] The local chapter of the NAACP disagreed, releasing a statement speculating that such a white person would have been tried not as an adult but as a minor, and that Hill was prosecuted because "reactionary whites" needed a "scapegoat" for so-called urban violence.[3] The Reverend Ralph Abernathy declared in the wake of Hill's sentencing that the death penalty was "designed to kill off blacks."[4] Yet despite Hill's unwilling role in the emerging culture wars, many believed that Governor

Robert Scott would commute Hill's sentence.[5] Whether or not they knew it, such a commutation would fall well within historical bounds and precedent, especially as it would undoubtedly take age and sex into consideration. But Governor Scott never had to act. In 1971, the United States Supreme Court instructed the North Carolina Supreme Court to, in turn, instruct the Edgecombe County Superior Court to resentence Marie Hill to life imprisonment.[6] She was since released, after having served nearly twenty years.

The case of Marie Hill reveals the complexity of the history of the death penalty in North Carolina: the value placed on white victims and the lack of consideration for African American personhood; the deep-seated narratives about race and gender, the demonization of black women, and the papering-over of white misbehavior; the need for post-conviction relief from a governor or a court; the narratives about race and justice circulating in the state's press; and most of all, the inability or unwillingness of the actors in the state's criminal justice system to minimize the role of racial bias.

It was not until 2009 that the state of North Carolina sought to do something about that bias. It passed the Racial Justice Act, which attempted to excise racial discrimination from death row. The RJA, as it came to be known, allowed death row inmates to challenge their sentences by demonstrating that race played a significant role in seeking or imposing a death sentence. Kentucky had passed a similar measure in 1998, but North Carolina's law differed in a significant way: death row prisoners in Kentucky had to demonstrate specific, racially motivated discrimination against them in the course of their capital proceeding. In North Carolina, prisoners could use statewide statistics to demonstrate a pattern of racial discrimination. Bring on the academics.

Aided by careful, methodologically sound research, these academics were able to demonstrate such patterns with ease.[7] Most of the prisoners on Central Prison's death row, white and non-white, filed claims and judges began hearing them. Those hostile to the measure complained that these motions not only would gum up the death penalty process, but also that white prisoners' motions violated the spirit of the law—a record of racial discrimination should have benefited white men before entering death row, not after. In making this argument, the RJA's foes oddly affirmed the influence of race on the death penalty system: fine, the death penalty was racist, but in seeking to address that racism, we must not give additional benefits to its white beneficiaries. At the same time detractors argued that claims filed by white prisoners demonstrated the RJA was a Trojan horse, designed not to address racial bias but to give inmates on death row, in the words of state senator Thom Goolsby, a "desperate, last-ditch attempt to snag . . . a get-out-of-jail-free card."[8]

The first claim to come under consideration was filed by Marcus Robinson, sentenced to death for murder in 1994. Robinson, an African American man sentenced to death for murder at age twenty-one, claimed that African American jurors had been excluded improperly from his jury and demonstrated bias against potential jurors of color statewide. The Superior Court judge agreed, vacating Robinson's sentence and resentencing him to life without parole.[9] Three other prisoners successfully appealed their sentences using the same body of academic research. Yet in 2012, North Carolinians elected Republicans to state office in a wave, giving the party the governorship and both houses of the General Assembly for the first time in generations. The GOP governor, Pat McCrory, and the state legislature quickly set about dismantling the RJA, first diminishing its effectiveness and then repealing it altogether.[10] In 2015, the North Carolina Supreme Court vacated the previous ruling and remanded the case to Superior Court, where a different judge agreed with prosecutors' claims that the RJA's repeal meant it could no longer serve as grounds for clemency. Marcus Robinson and his four fellow successful petitioners were returned to death row. In March 2018, the North Carolina Supreme Court announced it would hear appeals from three of the four prisoners, including Robinson. Two other death row prisoners who filed RJA claims that were not ruled on are waiting the court's decision.[11]

Whatever the determination of the court, these prisoners face an uncertain future, as the RJA was not the only mechanism preventing executions from taking place in North Carolina. None have occurred since 2006 because the North Carolina Medical Board decided to punish physicians for participating in executions as required by law. When the legislature repealed the Racial Justice Act, the repeal bill both barred the Medical Board from disciplining practitioners who participated in execution and declared that "the infliction of the punishment of death by administration of the required lethal substances . . . shall not be construed to be the practice of medicine," thus letting participating doctors and others off the hook for their participation in the execution ritual.[12] In 2015, the House of Representatives sought to navigate around physician participation by passing the Restoring Proper Justice Act, allowing a medical professional other than a physician to monitor a lethal injection.[13] Despite this legislation, the Medical Board continues to assert that physician participation in execution is unethical.[14]

A separate case further complicates the process. In 2007, four death row inmates sued the state, claiming its three-drug lethal injection protocol—one drug to render the prisoner unconscious, one to paralyze the voluntary nervous system, and another to induce cardiac arrest—inflicted cruel and unusual punishment in violation of the Eighth Amendment. The state moved to a one-drug protocol before the inmates' case was heard and the petitioners are awaiting a ruling.[15] As a result, there is no certain process for physicians or nonphysicians to monitor.

This life-or-death drama echoes decades of similar anxiety about the death penalty process, its rituals, and its participants and like the history described in this book, it led to the end of the death penalty in this state. When North Carolina last ceased executing, in 1961, it did so because juries had been given by law the power previously held only by the governor: to extend mercy to those facing execution. This behavior was a concession, perhaps, to the instability of the decades-old system of sentencing many people to die and relying on the governor to eventually commute their sentences to life imprisonment. It may have made death as punishment more democratic, recognizing that the kingly power of commutation should be dispersed somewhat among a jury of twelve. In the 1960s, with jurors handing down fewer and fewer death sentences, capital punishment in North Carolina receded rather than being swept away. Yet it is not clear that public opinion "became enlightened by humane justice," to borrow Justice Joseph McKenna's phrase from the *Weems* decision.[16] If those jurors tell us something about public opinion, it is that support for the death penalty was waning at mid-century when there was a viable alternative—life imprisonment.

When North Carolinians and Americans began to view life imprisonment as soft—as crime control became a matter of national politics in the 1960s and 1970s—support for the death penalty surged. Public opinion in North Carolina is difficult to gauge, but national Gallup polling from the 1930s indicated strong if not ironclad support. Softening support for the death penalty in the 1940s and 1950s reversed itself in the mid-1960s and reached new peaks in the 1990s, when law-and-order rhetoric and policies were embraced by both major political parties.[17] The correlation with the civil rights movement and its aftermath is hard to ignore. Recent studies have demonstrated that white people are more likely to support the death penalty than people of color and that support for the death penalty correlates with racial prejudice.[18] The irrational, emotional character of death penalty support is on the one hand understandable because of the fearful reactions

Americans have to the threat of crime in a general sense, and the profound, legitimate emotional response to being a victim of crime or losing a loved one to crime. On the other hand, it reminds us that capital punishment is one area of American law enforcement and politics—of many, it must be said—that gives overt attention to the emotional satisfaction of the white majority rather than the needs of the wider community as a whole, and with nary a gesture toward measured outcomes. The death penalty, then, in its obstinate state of confusion and with its archaic violence, reveals itself as a persistent avatar of white rage condoned for generations by North Carolina's governing powers.

## Anxiety and Uncertainty

The debate about the death penalty in North Carolina has stretched and wavered across generations. Today's bifurcated sentencing process, along with other legal and procedural changes that followed the *Furman* decision, echoes earlier eras of soul-searching. Worried about who was being executed and why, North Carolinians came to address the death penalty's suitability for people with mental illness and children, and its effects on people experiencing poverty and people of color. Some considered the pain the punishment inflicted, and its effect on its subject, while others reckoned with the spectacle's effect on its viewers. They worried about its place in a civilized state, in a Judeo-Christian state, in a modern state. Anticipating United States Supreme Court Justice Harry A. Blackmun's chilling phrase, they repeatedly "tinker[ed] with the machinery of death."[19] For North Carolinians one hundred years ago, like North Carolinians today, the death penalty was a source of uncertainty. Are we executing the right people? Is the death penalty fair? Are we doing it right? Nationally and in North Carolina, we are still asking these questions. In doing so, we participate in a routine that dates back at least to the post–Civil War era: executing people while worrying about it. And the reason we worry is because the death penalty is a failure. This is no great revelation. Its failure has been transparent and consistent since the first noose broke.

A string of exonerations reveals that the concern over killing the right people is justified: Jonathon Huffman, freed in 2007 after twelve years on death row; Levon Jones, freed in 2008 after the star prosecution witness admitted to lying on the stand; Glen Chapman, released in 2008 following revelations of widespread misconduct during his trial. Most recently, two intellectually limited brothers, Henry McCollum and Leon Brown, were pardoned and released in 2014 after spending thirty years on death row for a crime which they did not commit. They were prosecuted by the ghoulishly vigorous Joe Freeman Britt, and received death sentences based on coerced confessions. Before they were revealed to be innocent, in 1994, Supreme Court Justice Antonin Scalia cited the case of McCollum and Brown in arguing for the necessity of the death penalty and brushing away concerns about its cruelty by suggesting that a death by lethal injection was preferable to being murdered, echoing the lazy argument some make that people in prison are spoiled by receiving daily meals and access to television.[20]

As North Carolina and indeed much of the United States has largely shored up its commitment to capital punishment, the rest of the Western world has discarded it. In the 1970s, 1980s, and 1990s, America's presumed ideological partners—at least until the presidential election of 2016—such as Australia, Canada, and the United Kingdom, abolished the death penalty. Indeed, the European Convention on Human Rights, first adopted in 1983, bans capital punishment outright. New signatories to the International Covenant on Civil and Political Rights and members of the European Union must abrogate the death penalty before joining.[21] Why then does the United States retain the death penalty, at a federal level and among its states? Why are politicians in North Carolina today seeking its restoration? The answer might be that for all its failures as a crime-fighting weapon, as a tool of state power, as a way to give closure to victims, and from a technical perspective, it has succeeded in channeling lethal white rage that modern values constrain or should constrain. Support for today's death penalty sends a powerful signal to members of one's political tribe.

Legal scholar William Berry argues the opposite in one sense, that rather than the satisfaction of the death penalty's violent excess, "procedural exceptionalism"—Americans' belief in the efficacy of its legal process— explains the United States' retention of the death penalty despite its rejection by other western nations.[22] Contradicting Berry's framing is the fact that the lengthy appeals process has been instrumental in revealing the errors and misrepresentations rife in capital trials. Moreover, the time and expense that these procedures take provide ample argument against retention.[23] Moreover, the death penalty's peak in North Carolina and elsewhere in the 1930s came at a time of mistrust and frustration with law enforcement's failure to control Prohibition-related crime and a rising generation of criminal heroes, from Al Capone to Bonnie and Clyde; notably, many of these folk anti-heroes were shot and killed by law enforcement officers rather than formally executed. And further, for decades, the death penalty easily coexisted with lynching, which signaled distrust in the formal criminal justice system's capacity to act with appropriate speed and viciousness.

If North Carolinians, even Americans, as a general class trust their criminal justice system to operate capital punishment fairly, and that trust today explains retention, it hardly explains retention in North Carolina in the 1880s, the 1920s, or the 1940s, when many white southerners in the post–Civil War era saw government as a hostile invader. Nor does it fully explain the punishment's swift return in the 1970s. Given that the imposition of individual death sentences is a local matter decided first by prosecutorial discretion and then by members of a jury, the explanation is complex. But on a statewide level, the decision to make the punishment available and the general support for that decision flow from the punishing impulses and essential vulnerability of white supremacy. The threat to white supremacy posed by the very presence of free people of color, then by voting people of color, by mobile people of color, and those seeking the vote, a seat on a jury, elective office—all of these populations strained against a modernizing Jim Crow North Carolina, which responded with lethal violence. Finally, when in the 1970s the United States Supreme Court threatened to take away white North Carolinians' right to use capital punishment, the state government responded with a renewed commitment to the death penalty that exists to this day. As this conclusion is being written, members of North Carolina's General Assembly are demanding once again that the state resume executions.[24]

Any history of the death penalty is a history of failure. It often begins with the failure of the state to support children, parents, and families as they struggle with poverty, mental illness, or a lack of education compounded by state neglect or the outright hostility of state actors, particularly toward persons of color. These failures are further compounded by the failure to mount a coherent or vigorous defense and the subsequent failure of jurors to see the defendant as deserving of mercy. Then the governor, advised by people inside and outside of government, must fail to see anything special in the case or in the defendant that might merit commutation. And finally, the death of the prisoner amplifies those collected failures, as society responds not with justice, but with a shrug: "We tried a little bit, and now we have stopped trying."

The death penalty operates in constant opposition to itself, grinding out its lethal outcomes even as it fails to accomplish any of its intended purposes beyond exacting vengeance. It fails quietly when it provides the families of victims no closure or satisfaction after a horrific tragedy and the long years of suffering they experience in its wake.[25] It fails spectacularly when innocent people are executed. Even for those lucky enough to win an exoneration and freedom, it fails by depriving them of years of life in freedom and leaving them deeply marked by imprisonment and the anticipation of death. This failure is not unusual. Many institutions fail, and many American institutions—even our governments—exist in a state of near constant failure. That failure is ameliorated when good actors armed with good data make incremental improvements, sometimes reactive and sometimes glacial. In North Carolina, this history of incremental changes and attempts at improvement failed to visibly minimize evidence of the pain of execution. As legislators switched from hanging to electrocution, then from electrocution to asphyxiation, then from asphyxiation to paralysis and cardiac arrest, it was never clear in which direction progress and modernity lay: toward the swift and uncertain, or toward the silent and indeterminate.

Similarly incremental changes in sentencing laws in order to make them more responsive to community needs strangely resulted in the rejection of death as punishment. As serious crimes such as arson and burglary, and ultimately murder and rape, were no longer punished with a mandatory death sentence, juries handed down guilty verdicts and sentences of life without the possibility of parole. Both this change and the change in execution method diminished the death penalty: as a spectacle of justice, as a tool of community vengeance, and in its frequency of use. Slowly but fairly surely, North Carolinians set aside capital punishment and worried little about the consequences. The death penalty became a threat to compel life sentences rather than a real sanction, lurking behind the state's criminal justice system but ceasing to wield deadly force. When it returned in the 1970s, it did so on a tide of fury, but with no more evidence supporting its use as a crime control tool than existed a decade before. In the words of scholars Phoebe C. Ellsworth and Samuel R. Gross, "People feel strongly about the death penalty, know little about it, and feel no need to know more."[26]

State officials and their allies have abetted that absence of curiosity by nudging executions toward darkness and silence. As executions were shunted from public view—at least after the 1940s—they became less frequent, too, even more so than they already were. Not-executing has always been a prominent if undramatic feature of the death penalty: most people sentenced to death, in the era of the gallows as in the era of the needle, were not executed. Today, nationally and in North Carolina, not-executing seems to be the death penalty's current incarnation: the stay of execution granted to the Missouri man who anticipated a difficult process; not-executing in Oklahoma as state officials sought a new method, ultimately settling on nitrogen gas inhalation; the attempt to execute a man in Alabama whose veins could not accommodate a needle; over a decade of not-executing in North Carolina.[27] Since 2006, thirteen condemned prisoners have died from natural causes, making age North Carolina's new agent of execution.[28] As the history of the death penalty suggests, it is both possible to not-execute and to follow not-executing with a hard, lethal turn. Whether North Carolina's 143 death row prisoners will be executed or not remains unknown.

# Acknowledgments

I owe a great debt to many people who sustained me and my work as I slowly and not-so-steadily pursued it. I will undoubtedly omit some of them here, and I trust their animus will drive me furiously toward my next project. I am grateful to W. Fitzhugh Brundage, whose intellectual acuity and vast knowledge contributed immeasurably to my development as a historian. (My immaturity is entirely my own.) I so appreciate the intellectual and technical interventions of Jacquelyn Dowd Hall, John F. Kasson, Tim Marr, and David Garland, all thinkers of inimitable clarity and creativity. I owe an additional debt to Jacquelyn Hall for her trust in me as I transitioned from graduate student into postgraduate life at the Southern Oral History Program. I am grateful for the editorial direction of Brandon Proia at University of North Carolina Press, for the friendship and support of Mark Simpson-Vos, and to the editors of the press's Justice, Power, and Politics series, Heather Ann Thompson and Rhonda Williams. I owe a great debt to Sarah Boyd for her discerning questions and comments on matters large and small and the grace with which she made them. Margaret Vandiver offered incisive responses, both broad and specific, on this manuscript, greatly improving it, and I also owe thanks to an additional anonymous reader for their essential observations. Dr. Barbara J. Fields's "People of the Old South" class set me on this path many years ago, and if I did not express my great respect for her thinking and writing, I would be remiss. Thank you to Donald G. Mathews for his remarkable example and generous feedback on my early work, and to Michael Trotti and Bruce Baker for their comments on later work. I have benefitted immeasurably from the friendship and mentorship of Malinda M. Lowery and Della Pollock. A very warm thank you to Bob Anthony, Sarah Carrier, Jason Tomberlin, and their colleagues at the North Carolina Collection; to Matt Turi, Tim Hodgdon, and their colleagues at the Southern Historical Collection at the University of North Carolina at Chapel Hill; and to Gene Hyde of Ramsey Library at University of North Carolina Asheville. My thanks to Elijah J. Gaddis for collaborating with me on the teaching of and research on lynching that contributed to this book. I am grateful to Frank R. Baumgartner for connecting me to the community of death penalty scholars in North Carolina and for his intellectual generosity. Thank you to the archivists at the State Archive in Raleigh. Many thanks to Lucas Kelley, who conducted some essential late-project research on my behalf. Historians Leonard Lanier and Susan Barringer Wells shared generously of their time and knowledge about North Carolina history. I am indebted to my current and former colleagues in the Department of American Studies at the University of North Carolina who supported me as I pursued this project to completion: Robert C. Allen, Gabrielle Anna Berlinger, Daniel M. Cobb, Elizabeth S. D.

Engelhardt, Marcie Cohen Ferris, William R. Ferris, Benjamin E. Frey, Bernard L. Herman, Sharon P. Holland, Glenn Hinson, Joy Kasson, M. Michelle Robinson, Patricia E. Sawin, Jenny Tone-Pah-Hote, Keith Richotte Jr., and Rachel A. Willis. I so appreciate the scholars I had the chance to work with during my time as a student in the University of North Carolina's graduate program in history, including but not limited to: Matt Andrews, Matthew Brown, Catherine Connor, David Cline, Joshua Davis, Joe Fletcher, Raphael Ginsberg, Elizabeth Gritter, Max Krochmal, Ethan Kytle, Pamella Lach, Cecilia Moore, Robyn Paine, Brad Proctor, Blain Roberts, David Silkenat, Aidan Smith, Rose Stremlau, Kerry Taylor, Dwana Waugh, Jacqueline Whitt, and Timothy Williams. Many thanks and much appreciation to the wonderful people at the Center for the Study of the American South and to those I worked with at the Southern Oral History Program: Barbara Call, Ayse Erginer, Joey Ann Fink, Patrick Horn, Elizabeth Lundeen, Willie J. Griffin, Elizabeth Millwood, Rachel F. Seidman, Emily Wallace, and Jessica Wilkerson. Thank you to my writing partner, Anna Krome-Lukens, for her collegiality and intellectual generosity. Thank you to my unfailingly supportive parents, Anne and Jonathan Kotch, and to my brothers, Alex and Noah Kotch, for their enthusiasm and curiosity. My third brother, Rob Pringle, keeps my head above water. Hey, Daniel, Efrem, and Cora! Love you. I could not have done this or many other things without leaning on Anne Olivar, whose intelligence, strength, and generosity are essential to whatever small success this book represents. Finally, I wish to thank Mogwai, Kurt Vile, The War on Drugs, Hiss Golden Messenger, and Run the Jewels for keeping me focused on my work as I banged away on my keyboard.

# Appendix A

Executions in North Carolina, 1865–1909

A note on sources: most of the information in these appendixes was initially drawn from M. Watt Espy and John Ortiz Smykla, "Executions in the United States, 1608–1972," commonly known as the Espy File, and supplemented with newspaper accounts, court records, death certificates, census records, data from the North Carolina Department of Corrections (https://www.ncdps.gov/Adult-Corrections/Prisons/Death-Penalty/List-of-persons-executed), and information from Daniel Allen Hearn's *Legal Executions in North and South Carolina*. This volume, published in 2015, added substantially to the information and sourcing available and contributed one hundred newly identified executions to Espy's log. It is a work revealing great diligence and care, yet is marred by the author's self-professed dismissal of "political correctness" and the resultant infelicitous language. However, Hearn's work remains the best resource for additional information and sourcing information for these executions. For a research note on the Espy File, see the Introduction and chapter 1. Occupations are taken from death certificates. The general lack of care as to the personal information on the certificates might lead to a number of conclusions: that "laborer" was a default choice made by white preparers about African Americans whose occupations they did not know; or that African American men without steady employment were called laborers. In at least one instance, that of Baxter Cain, his job as a night watchman for the Southern Public Utilities Company was an important element of his case, yet written on the occupation line of his death certificate was the word, "labor." A cross symbol (†) denotes a female executor subject. The race of the victim was often reported in newspaper coverage. Sometimes it was hinted at or ignored, the latter most often in cases when all parties involved in the capital crime were white. The race of victim for a burglary conviction refers to the race of the family living in the dwelling that was entered. Some of the information here varies across sources: the spelling of names and the ages of executed persons often differ in newspaper accounts and on death certificates, and both sources often refer to executed persons by their initials or nicknames. The information here is as accurate as possible, but reflects judgment calls about which sources to rely on when determining name, age, and occupation. Occupations marked as unknown mean the subject's occupation was not noted in newspaper coverage or on their death certificate. Blank spaces indicate unknown information. Additional victim information includes whether or not the victim had a relationship with the killer or assailant and the age of the victim; people fifteen or younger were marked as children. A plus sign (+) indicates multiple victims. The word "law" denotes a law enforcement officer. WM = white man; WF = white woman; BM = black man; BF = black woman; NM = Native American man. These are crude designations that do not fully reflect racial identity.

TABLE 1 Executions under county authority in North Carolina, 1865–1909

| Date | Name | Race | Age | Sentenced for | County | Occupation | Victim(s) |
|---|---|---|---|---|---|---|---|
| **1866** | | | | | | | |
| June 8 | James Nixon | B | | burglary | Jones | unknown | W |
| June 8 | Donaldson Ruffin | B | | burglary | Jones | unknown | W |
| June 8 | Richard Williams | B | | burglary | Jones | unknown | W |
| June 29 | Charles Parks | B | | murder | Mecklenburg | unknown | BF (wife) |
| September 7 | Henry Queary | B | | rape | Cabarrus | unknown | WF |
| December 21 | Augustus Williams | B | | robbery | New Hanover | unknown | BM |
| December 21 | Lewis Williams | B | | robbery | New Hanover | unknown | BM |
| **1867** | | | | | | | |
| April 26 | William Johnson | B | | murder | Chatham | unknown | WM |
| June 14 | Green Hodges | B | | rape | Mecklenburg | unknown | WM |
| July 12 | John Brinkley | W | 30 | murder | Lenoir | unknown | WM |
| August 16 | Lewis Albritton | B | | murder | Craven | unknown | WM+ |
| August 30 | Franklin Smith | W | | rape | New Hanover | unknown | WF (child) |
| September 20 | Banvester Haywood | B | | murder | Craven | unknown | BF |
| November 29 | Anderson Marslettur | B | | murder | Halifax | unknown | BF (wife) |
| **1868** | | | | | | | |
| January 3 | Willis Weatherly | B | 20 | murder | Rockingham | unknown | BM |
| January 3 | Squire Woods | B | | murder | Rockingham | unknown | BM |
| February 14 | Needham Evans | B | | murder | Craven | unknown | WM |
| February 14 | Washington Hicks | B | | robbery | Pitt | unknown | WM |
| February 14 | Richard Jackson | B | | murder | Pitt | unknown | WM |
| February 28 | William Parker | W | 17 | murder | New Hanover | unknown | WM |

| Date | Name | | Age | Crime | County | Occupation | |
|---|---|---|---|---|---|---|---|
| April 3 | Jim Knight | B | 43 | murder | Edgecombe | unknown | WM |
| April 3 | John Taylor | B | 32 | murder | Edgecombe | unknown | WM |
| May 1 | Tom Dula | W | 36 | murder | Wilkes | farm laborer | WF |
| May 19 | Reuben Wright | W | 60 | murder | Stokes | farm laborer | BM |
| May 22 | George Washington | B | 17 | arson | Lenoir | unknown | unknown |
| June 27 | Rufus Ludwig | W | 21 | murder | Rowan | unknown | WF (wife) |
| November 6 | Tom Ryan | B | | murder | Martin | unknown | WM |
| **1869** | | | | | | | |
| January 1 | Augustus Holmes | B | | murder | Edgecombe | unknown | BM |
| June 4 | Augustus Baker | B | | murder | Halifax | unknown | BM |
| June 4 | James Thomas | B | | murder | Halifax | unknown | BM |
| August 6 | John Smith | B | | murder | Orange | unknown | BM |
| October 1 | Benjamin Douglass | B | | murder | Moore | unknown | BM |
| **1870** | | | | | | | |
| January 14 | Lewis Hines | B | 39 | rape | Edgecombe | farm laborer | WF |
| April 1 | Bob Gunn | B | | murder | Orange | unknown | WM |
| April 1 | Tom Young | B | | murder | Orange | unknown | WM |
| August 26 | Andrew Tarpley | B | 14 | rape | Alamance | domestic servant | WF (child) |
| November 4 | William Stimson | B | | rape | Wake | unknown | WF (elder) |
| **1871** | | | | | | | |
| February 3 | Dumer Harget | B | 21 | murder | Carteret | unknown | BM |
| March 17 | Henderson Oxendine | N | 47 | murder | Robeson | farmer | WM |

(continued)

TABLE 1 Executions under county authority in North Carolina, 1865–1909 (continued)

| Date | Name | Race | Age | Sentenced for | County | Occupation | Victim(s) |
|---|---|---|---|---|---|---|---|
| May 5 | Madison Youngblood | B | | murder | Johnston | unknown | WM |
| June 2 | Ned McLendon | B | | rape | Richmond | unknown | WF |
| July 14 | Henderson Young | B | | murder | Mecklenburg | unknown | WM |
| July 21 | Lewis Coppedge | B | 17 | murder | Anson | unknown | WM |
| July 21 | Ned Myers | B | 54 | murder | Anson | unknown | WM |
| October 27 | Alfred Mackey | B | | murder | Columbus | unknown | WM |
| October 27 | William Parker | W | 50 | murder | Guilford | unknown | BM |
| November 3 | Mack Swann | B | | rape | Johnston | unknown | WF (elder) |
| December 15 | Pompey Lyon | B | 31 | murder | Orange | unknown | BM |
| **1872** | | | | | | | |
| July 12 | Govan Adair | W | 25 | murder | Rutherford | farm laborer | B+ (family) |
| July 12 | Columbus Adair | W | 27 | murder | Rutherford | farm laborer | B+ (family) |
| August 9 | Newton Chandler | W | 26 | rape | Gaston | unknown | WF |
| August 23 | Nathaniel Caldwell | B | 30 | murder | Mecklenburg | farm laborer | BF (child) |
| November 8 | York Lattimore | B | 42 | murder | Rutherford | farm laborer | BM |
| November 8 | Jerry Thompson | B | 24 | murder | Rutherford | farm laborer | BM |
| December 13 | Thomas Johnson | B | 21 | rape | Davidson | unknown | WF |
| **1873** | | | | | | | |
| January 16 | Orren Mercer | B | 35 | murder | Edgecombe | unknown | BM (infant) |
| May 6 | George Lea | B | 28 | rape | Caswell | unknown | WF (elder) |
| June 6 | Bayless Henderson | W | 26 | murder | Jackson | unknown | WM |
| June 30 | Aaron Stroud | B | 16 | rape | Orange | unknown | WF (child) |
| August 8 | Hardy Jones | B | 63 | murder | Craven | farm laborer | BM |

| Date | Name | Race | Age | Crime | County | Occupation | Victim |
|---|---|---|---|---|---|---|---|
| **1874** | | | | | | | |
| January 16 | Joseph Baker | W | 28 | murder | Mecklenburg | unknown | BM |
| June 26 | John Ketchey | W | 30 | rape | Rowan | unknown | WF |
| July 24 | John Blake | B | 24 | rape | Wake | farm laborer | WF |
| October 30 | George Berry | B | 28 | murder | Columbus | unknown | BM |
| **1875** | | | | | | | |
| March 5 | Aaron Bonner | B | 19 | rape | Beaufort | unknown | WF |
| May 28 | George Cunningham | W | 29 | murder | Buncombe | unknown | WM |
| August 27 | Cornelius Williamson | B | 17 | murder | Northampton | unknown | WM |
| September 3 | Lawyer Brown | B | | murder | Onslow | unknown | WM |
| October 1 | William Hall | W | | murder | Buncombe | unknown | WM |
| **1876** | | | | | | | |
| May 23 | Burwell Newsome | B | 18 | rape | Bertie | unknown | WF |
| June 1 | Isaac Berry | B | 45 | murder | Caldwell | unknown | BF (wife) |
| December 22 | William Messimer | W | 22 | murder | Rowan | unknown | WF |
| **1877** | | | | | | | |
| January 22 | Simon Ragland | B | | rape | Edgecombe | unknown | WF |
| November 2 | Hillman Morgan | B | | murder | Franklin | unknown | BM |
| November 2 | Nathan Overton | W | 33 | murder | Edgecombe | unknown | WM |
| November 2 | Noah Taylor | B | 31 | murder | Edgecombe | farm laborer | WM |
| December 21 | Hilliard Morgan | B | 35 | burglary | Wayne | unknown | WM |

(continued)

TABLE 1 Executions under county authority in North Carolina, 1865–1909 (continued)

| Date | Name | Race | Age | Sentenced for | County | Occupation | Victim(s) |
|---|---|---|---|---|---|---|---|
| **1878** | | | | | | | |
| January 18 | Arden Nelson | B | 22 | murder | Bertie | unknown | WM |
| April 12 | John Shallington | B | 28 | murder | Greene | unknown | BF |
| May 24 | Henry Roberts | B | 30 | murder | Cleveland | unknown | BM |
| June 14 | Harris Atkinson | B | 38 | murder | Wayne | farm laborer | WM/WF |
| June 14 | Noah Cherry | B | 64 | murder | Wayne | farm laborer | WM/WF |
| June 14 | Robert Thompson | B | 42 | murder | Wayne | unknown | WM/WF |
| October 25 | James Laxton | B | 43 | rape | Caldwell | unknown | WF |
| November 8 | William Rainey | B | | murder | Warren | unknown | BM |
| December 6 | William Jefferson | B | 31 | rape | Warren | unknown | BF |
| **1879** | | | | | | | |
| February 14 | John Edwards | W | 65 | murder | Johnston | unknown | WM |
| May 9 | Richard Leach | B | 29 | burglary | Bladen | unknown | W |
| May 16 | Henry Andrews | W | 29 | burglary | Orange | farm laborer | W |
| May 16 | Louis Carlton | B | 33 | burglary | Orange | day laborer | W |
| May 16 | Henry Davis | W | 32 | burglary | Orange | unknown | W |
| June 13 | Jessie Davis | B | 41 | rape | Franklin | unknown | WF |
| June 20 | Edward Foy | B | 19 | rape | Carteret | unknown | WF |
| June 25 | Robert Jones | B | 45 | murder | Edgecombe | unknown | WM |
| July 11 | John Davis | B | 29 | murder | Brunswick | unknown | BM |
| August 15 | Robert McCorkle | B | 60 | murder | Catawba | unknown | WM |
| August 29 | Thomas Bowman | W | | murder | Guilford | unknown | WF (wife) |
| October 31 | Robert Boswell | B | | murder | Orange | unknown | BF (wife) |

**1880**

| Date | Name | | Age | Crime | County | Occupation | |
|---|---|---|---|---|---|---|---|
| January 9 | Allen Mathis | B | 28 | murder | Pender | unknown | BM |
| January 30 | Joe Gillespie | B | 23 | murder | Iredell | unknown | WM |
| May 7 | Henry Horne | B | | burglary | Mecklenburg | laborer | W |
| June 11 | Robert Outerbridge | B | | murder | Bertie | unknown | BM |
| July 9 | Alex Howard | B | 40 | murder | Sampson | farm laborer | WM |
| September 3 | Stephen Richardson | B | 35 | murder | New Hanover | laborer | BF |
| September 24 | Peter Leach | B | 27 | murder | Robeson | laborer | BM |
| October 22 | Charles Pearson | B | 23 | murder | Catawba | unknown | BM |
| December 17 | Daniel Keith | B | 33 | murder | Cleveland | farm laborer | BF (child) |

**1881**

| Date | Name | | Age | Crime | County | Occupation | |
|---|---|---|---|---|---|---|---|
| April 29 | Marshall Baxter | B | 24 | murder | Mecklenburg | farm laborer | BM |
| October 28 | Allen Johnson | B | 25 | murder | Mecklenburg | unknown | BM |
| November 4 | Henry Lovett | B | 22 | murder | Columbus | laborer | BM |
| November 18 | Augustus Smith | B | 21 | rape | Johnston | unknown | WF (child) |

**1882**

| Date | Name | | Age | Crime | County | Occupation | |
|---|---|---|---|---|---|---|---|
| January 13 | Matilda Carter | B | 22 | murder | Rockingham | house keeper | BM |
| January 13 | Joseph Hay | B | 25 | murder | Rockingham | farm laborer | BM |
| January 13 | Eldridge Scales | B | 26 | murder | Rockingham | unknown | BM |
| January 27 | John Morris | B | 28 | murder | Lincoln | unknown | BM |
| May 19 | Stephen Effler | W | 21 | murder | McDowell | unknown | WF (wife) |

(continued)

TABLE 1 Executions under county authority in North Carolina, 1865–1909 (continued)

| Date | Name | Race | Age | Sentenced for | County | Occupation | Victim(s) |
|------|------|------|-----|---------------|--------|------------|-----------|
| July 11 | Philip Faison | B | 33 | murder | Sampson | farmer | BM |
| December 29 | Iverson Slade | B | 23 | murder | Caswell | laborer | BF |
| **1883** | | | | | | | |
| March 23 | Jerome Holt | B | 23 | rape | Alamance | laborer | WF |
| June 1 | Robert Henderson | B | 20 | murder | Granville | unknown | BF (wife) |
| August 27 | Henry Jones | B | 22 | murder | Wake | unknown | WM (law) |
| December 14 | Bert Ellis | B | 23 | murder | Cleveland | unknown | WF |
| December 20 | Gilford Soon | B | 40 | rape | Lenoir | unknown | WF |
| **1884** | | | | | | | |
| February 29 | Benjamin Gilliam | B | 28 | murder | Pamlico | saw mill worker | BM |
| May 2 | Enoch Brown | B | 40 | murder | Halifax | unknown | BM (wife) |
| **1885** | | | | | | | |
| February 23 | Irving Lang | B | | murder | Pitt | unknown | BM |
| July 17 | Eaton Mills | B | 46 | murder | Halifax | farmer | BM |
| August 7 | Tom Gee | B | 60 | murder | Cumberland | unknown | WF |
| August 7 | Joseph Howard | W | | murder | Cumberland | unknown | WM |
| August 7 | Tom McNeill | B | 23 | murder | Cumberland | unknown | BM |
| December 7 | Isaiah Richardson | B | | burglary | Gates | unknown | W |
| December 7 | Edward Saunders | B | 19 | burglary | Gates | unknown | W |
| December 7 | John Swanner | B | | burglary | Gates | unknown | W |

| Date | Name | Race | Age | Crime | County | Occupation | Victim |
|---|---|---|---|---|---|---|---|
| **1886** | | | | | | | |
| May 21 | Louis Kilgore | B | 40 | murder | Henderson | house servant | WF |
| June 1 | George McNair | B | 15 | rape | Onslow | none | WF (child) |
| July 2 | Frank Gaston | B | | rape | Rowan | unknown | WF |
| July 9 | Andrew Lambert | N | 40 | murder | Swain | farmer | WM |
| July 29 | George Moore | B | | rape | Mecklenburg | unknown | BF (daughter) |
| November 11 | Alliday Wren | B | 27 | burglary | Chatham | unknown | W |
| **1887** | | | | | | | |
| March 11 | Henry Artis | B | 35 | murder | Wayne | farmer | BF (daughter) |
| June 18 | Albert Taborn | B | 26 | burglary | Granville | farm laborer | W |
| July 12 | Archibald Martin | B | | murder | Richmond | unknown | BM |
| **1888** | | | | | | | |
| July 11 | Stephen Freeman | B | | rape | New Hanover | unknown | WF |
| July 13 | James Byers | W | 40 | murder | Wilkes | unknown | WM |
| July 19 | William Houston | B | | murder | Forsyth | unknown | BF |
| **1889** | | | | | | | |
| January 25 | John Yancey | B | 43 | murder | Caswell | farm hand | BM |
| January 29 | Amma Ellis | B | 31 | murder | Sampson | unknown | BM (father) |
| February 27 | Howard Anderson | W | 27 | murder | Wayne | laborer | WM |
| May 3 | Ely Ward | B | 26 | burglary | Northampton | farm worker | W |
| May 13 | Lee Carson | B | 33 | burglary | Cleveland | unknown | W |

(continued)

TABLE 1 Executions under county authority in North Carolina, 1865–1909 (continued)

| Date | Name | Race | Age | Sentenced for | County | Occupation | Victim(s) |
|------|------|------|-----|---------------|--------|------------|-----------|
| July 11 | William Weddington | B | | murder | Union | unknown | WM (law) |
| November 29 | Matthew Banks | B | 16 | rape | Pasquotank | none | WF (child) |
| **1890** | | | | | | | |
| January 10 | Claude Parrish | W | 39 | rape | Wake | unknown | WF (daughter) |
| February 7 | Elijah Moore | B | 26 | murder | Guilford | laborer | BF |
| February 7 | Manley Pankey | B | 19 | murder | Montgomery | unknown | BM |
| February 7 | John Wilson | W | 39 | murder | Yancey | unknown | WM |
| March 28 | William Shackelford | W | 42 | murder | Chatham | unknown | WM |
| October 10 | Stephen Jacobs | N | 45 | murder | Robeson | unknown | WF |
| **1891** | | | | | | | |
| July 2 | Henry Brabham | B | 21 | murder | Mecklenburg | unknown | WM |
| September 29 | Ben Bostick | B | 20 | murder | Moore | unknown | WM |
| December 11 | James Johnson | B | | murder | Bladen | unknown | BF (child) |
| **1892** | | | | | | | |
| January 22 | Caroline Shipp | B | 20 | murder | Gaston | none | BM (infant) |
| May 13 | John Cox | B | 21 | murder | Jones | unknown | BM |
| July 14 | Charles Blackman | B | 25 | murder | Guilford | unknown | BF (wife) |
| October 20 | Marion Headon | B | | murder | Guilford | unknown | WM |
| October 20 | Charles Reynolds | W | 25 | murder | Guilford | unknown | WM |

| | | | | | | | |
|---|---|---|---|---|---|---|---|
| **1893** | | | | | | | |
| February 17 | John Hambright | B | | murder | Cleveland | unknown | BM |
| December 1 | Sam Neely | B | 15 | burglary | Gaston | laborer | W |
| **1894** | | | | | | | |
| January 5 | Dan Gilchrist | B | 19 | murder | Richmond | unknown | BM (father-in-law) |
| February 8 | Peter DeGraff | W | 24 | murder | Forsyth | laborer | WF |
| July 13 | Calvin Coley | W | 20 | murder | Franklin | unknown | WM |
| July 13 | Thomas Coley | W | 24 | murder | Franklin | unknown | WM |
| August 3 | Orange Page | B | 45 | murder | Wake | unknown | BF (elder) |
| August 10 | Bob Madkins | B | 19 | rape | Alamance | unknown | WF |
| **1895** | | | | | | | |
| May 3 | George Mills | W | 29 | murder | Wake | keeping house | WF (niece) |
| July 25 | Anderson Brown | B | 33 | murder | Rowan | tobacco factory | BF |
| July 25 | Whit Farrand | B | 34 | murder | Wake | unknown | WM (law) |
| December 4 | George Washington | B | 18 | murder | Edgecombe | unknown | WM |
| **1896** | | | | | | | |
| February 13 | Thomas Covington | W | 26 | murder | Catawba | unknown | WM |
| June 19 | Edward Fairley | B | 19 | rape | Robeson | unknown | BF |
| July 2 | Henry Dowden | B | | murder | Halifax | unknown | WM |

(continued)

TABLE 1 Executions under county authority in North Carolina, 1865–1909 (continued)

| Date | Name | Race | Age | Sentenced for | County | Occupation | Victim(s) |
|------|------|------|-----|---------------|--------|------------|-----------|
| **1897** | | | | | | | |
| February 8 | Monroe Johnson | B | 40 | burglary | Mecklenburg | unknown | W |
| September 1 | Doc Black | B | 23 | rape | Greene | unknown | WF |
| September 1 | George Brodie | B | 20 | rape | Vance | unknown | WF |
| November 10 | Wiley Wright | B | | murder | Wayne | unknown | WM |
| November 17 | Edgar Purvis | B | | murder | Harnett | unknown | WM |
| December 23 | Robert Ryan | W | 41 | murder | Guilford | unknown | WF (wife) |
| **1898** | | | | | | | |
| April 1 | John Evans | B | 21 | rape | Richmond | unknown | WF |
| May 12 | Hatton Perry | B | 17 | rape | Beaufort | unknown | WF (child) |
| May 27 | Mit Sadler | B | 20 | murder | Cleveland | unknown | WM |
| November 11 | John Mays | W | 39 | murder | Surry | unknown | WF |
| November 26 | John Brooks | B | 20 | rape | Brunswick | unknown | WF |
| **1899** | | | | | | | |
| January 18 | James Booker | B | 22 | murder | Wake | unknown | BF |
| May 18 | Joe Jackson | B | 50+ | rape | Mecklenburg | unknown | WF (child) |
| August 24 | Julius Alexander | B | 49 | rape | Mecklenburg | unknown | WF |
| October 19 | Avery Kale | W | 19 | murder | Catawba | unknown | WM |
| November 10 | Elijah Joyner | B | 27 | murder | Pitt | unknown | WM |

| Date | Name | Race | Age | Crime | County | Occupation | Victim |
|---|---|---|---|---|---|---|---|
| **1900** | | | | | | | |
| February 8 | William Truesdale | B | 24 | murder | Mecklenburg | unknown | BF |
| February 9 | Reuben Ross | B | | rape | Robeson | unknown | WF |
| March 15 | Robert Fortune | B | 21 | murder | Nash | unknown | WM |
| March 15 | John Henry Taylor | B | 23 | murder | Nash | unknown | WM |
| August 31 | Thomas Jones | B | 29 | murder | Wake | unknown | BF+ |
| September 3 | William Edwards | B | 27 | murder | Rowan | unknown | WM (law) |
| September 28 | Chauncey Davis | B | 27 | Arson | Edgecombe | unknown | BM |
| September 28 | Archie Kinnaults | W | 21 | murder | Sampson | unknown | WM |
| **1901** | | | | | | | |
| February 1 | John Ruffin | B | 17 | rape | Alamance | unknown | BF (child) |
| September 13 | William Monroe | B | 20 | rape | Mecklenburg | unknown | WF |
| November 2 | Louis Council | B | 28 | rape | Cumberland | unknown | WF |
| **1902** | | | | | | | |
| February 26 | Ben Foster | B | 23 | burglary | Buncombe | unknown | W |
| February 26 | Frank Johnson | B | 25 | burglary | Buncombe | unknown | W |
| February 26 | John Rose | B | 24 | murder | Wilson | unknown | WM |
| April 14 | Frank Shaw | B | 36 | murder | Robeson | unknown | BF (sister-in-law) |
| July 8 | Archie Conley | B | 23 | murder | Rowan | farm laborer | BM |
| July 8 | Dick Fleming | B | 35 | rape | Rowan | brakeman | WF |
| November 25 | Calvin Elliot | B | 20 | rape | Lincoln | unknown | WF |

(continued)

TABLE 1 Executions under county authority in North Carolina, 1865–1909 (continued)

| Date | Name | Race | Age | Sentenced for | County | Occupation | Victim(s) |
|------|------|------|-----|---------------|--------|-----------|-----------|
| **1903** | | | | | | | |
| May 22 | John Broadnax | B | 16 | murder | Rockingham | farm laborer | WM |
| September 10 | Wilfred Roseboro | B | 24 | murder | Iredell | farm laborer | WF |
| December 1 | Cyrus Dixon | W | 22 | murder | Jones | farm laborer | WM |
| **1904** | | | | | | | |
| February 25 | Will Boggan | B | 31 | murder | Anson | farm laborer | WM |
| February 25 | Jabel Register | W | 29 | murder | Columbus | unknown | WM/BM |
| May 19 | Alfred Daniels | B | 33 | murder | Jones | timber cutter | WM |
| May 19 | Frank Davis | W | 30 | murder | Lenoir | farm laborer | WM |
| June 15 | Adam Hunt | B | 26 | murder | Person | unknown | WM |
| September 9 | Jesse Allen | B | 20 | rape | Granville | unknown | WF (child) |
| October 28 | Ben Clark | B | 25 | murder | Cleveland | unknown | WM (law) |
| November 16 | Dave Brown | B | 34 | murder | Bladen | day laborer | WF |
| November 16 | Neil Sellers | B | 34 | murder | Bladen | farm laborer | WF |
| December 17 | Reuben Johnson | B | 21 | murder | Washington | unknown | BF (wife) |
| **1905** | | | | | | | |
| April 6 | Walter Partridge | B | 16 | rape | Cumberland | unknown | WF |
| July 20 | Daniel Teachey | W | 33 | murder | Duplin | laborer | WM |
| September 2 | Joseph Hammons | W | 49 | murder | Forsyth | unknown | WF (wife) |
| September 2 | Ashton Moore | B | 19 | rape | Sampson | unknown | WF (child) |

| Date | Name | Race | Age | Crime | County | Occupation | Victim |
|---|---|---|---|---|---|---|---|
| September 14 | Will Adams | B | 30 | murder | Wake | unknown | BF/BM+ (child) |
| October 2 | Peter Smith | W | 63 | rape | Madison | unknown | WF (child) |
| December 16 | Preston Daniels | B | 23 | murder | Martin | unknown | BM |
| December 20 | Will Carter | B | 17 | rape | Duplin | unknown | WF (child) |
| **1906** | | | | | | | |
| March 1 | Bob Mitchell | B | 56 | murder | Bertie | unknown | BF (wife) |
| July 6 | Henry Scott | B | 25 | murder | (off the coast) | sailor | WM/BM+ |
| August 31 | Henry Bailey | B | | murder | Craven | unknown | WM |
| December 20 | Ben Williams | B | | murder | Wake | unknown | BM |
| **1907** | | | | | | | |
| January 8 | Henry Walker | B | 30 | burglary | Alamance | coachman | W |
| January 15 | Sylvester Barrett | B | 29 | murder | Pitt | unknown | WM (law) |
| February 8 | Frank Bohannon | B | | murder | Guilford | unknown | WM |
| February 8 | John Hodge | W | 50 | murder | Durham | carpenter | WF (wife) |
| February 8 | Freeman Jones | B | 35 | burglary | Durham | unknown | W |
| April 15 | Tom Walker | B | 30 | murder | Cumberland | distiller | WM+ (law) |
| April 20 | Will Banks | B | | murder | Ashe | miner | BM (uncle) |
| August 20 | James Rucker | B | | rape | Buncombe | unknown | BF (child, daughter) |
| **1908** | | | | | | | |
| April 16 | Sam Murchison | B | 30 | murder | Cumberland | unknown | WM (law) |
| May 7 | David Bryant | B | 15 | rape | Jones | unknown | WF (child) |

(continued)

TABLE 1 Executions under county authority in North Carolina, 1865–1909 (continued)

| Date | Name | Race | Age | Sentenced for | County | Occupation | Victim(s) |
|------|------|------|-----|---------------|--------|------------|-----------|
| November 20 | Lewis Fletcher | B | 23 | murder | Mecklenburg | unknown | BM |
| December 17 | Henry Harvey | B | 22 | murder | Richmond | unknown | BM |
| December 18 | Will Graham | B | 39 | rape | Cabarrus | unknown | WF |
| **1909** | | | | | | | |
| March 3 | Jackson Palmer | B | | rape | Sampson | unknown | WF |
| June 12 | Robert Robeson | B | | murder | Martin | unknown | WM |
| **1910** | | | | | | | |
| March 11 | Henry Spivey | B | 29 | murder | Bladen | unknown | BM |

M. Watt Espy, and John Ortiz Smykla. Executions in the United States, 1608–2002: The ESPY File. ICPSR08451-v5. Ann Arbor, MI: Inter-university Consortium for Political and Social Research [distributor], July 20, 2016, accessed December 16, 2017, https://doi.org/10.3886/ICPSR08451.v5; Daniel Allen Hearn, *Legal Executions in North and South Carolina: A Comprehensive Registry, 1866–1962* (Jefferson, NC: McFarland, 2015).

Credit: Created by the author.

## Appendix B

Executions in North Carolina, 1910–1961

Please see appendix A for a note on sourcing.

TABLE 2 Executions under state authority in North Carolina, 1910–1961

| Date | Name | Race | Age | Sentenced for | County | Occupation | Victim(s) |
|---|---|---|---|---|---|---|---|
| **1910** | | | | | | | |
| February 10 | Phillip Mills | B | 23 | murder | Transylvania | laborer | B? (infant) |
| March 18 | Walter Morrison | B | 37 | rape | Robeson | laborer | NF |
| **1911** | | | | | | | |
| February 15 | Nathan Montague | B | 28 | murder | Granville | laborer | WM/F+ (child) |
| February 24 | James Allison | W | 51 | murder | Buncombe | hostler | WM |
| May 5 | Lewis West | B | 24 | murder | Wilson | none/laborer | WM (law) |
| May 12 | Norman Lewis | B | 22 | murder | Nash | whiskey dealer | WM (law) |
| October 27 | Norval Marshall | B | 28 | rape | Warren | laborer | WF |
| November 24 | Ross French | N | 21 | rape | Swain | farmer | WF (child) |
| December 1 | Taylor Love | B | 30 | murder | Haywood | laborer | BM |
| December 29 | Louis Sandlin | W | 42 | murder | New Hanover | unknown | WF (wife) |
| **1912** | | | | | | | |
| May 17 | Brad Bagley | B | 35 | murder | Martin | unknown | WM (law) |
| June 21 | Andrew Wilkins | B | 30 | murder | Nash | laborer | BF (wife) |
| **1914** | | | | | | | |
| March 6 | Reddon Cobb | W | 24 | murder | Halifax | unknown | WM |
| March 19 | Sidney Finger | B | 18 | murder | Rowan | laborer | WM |
| August 21 | Grady Lane | B | 20 | murder | Moore | farmer | BM |
| August 28 | Jim Cameron | B | 25 | murder | Moore | laborer | WM |
| October 16 | Harvey Gannaway | B | 30 | murder | Forsyth | unknown | BF (wife) |
| December 4 | Howard Craig | B | 22 | rape | Stanly | laborer | WF (child) |

| Date | Name | Race | Age | Crime | County | Occupation | Victim |
|---|---|---|---|---|---|---|---|
| **1915** | | | | | | | |
| July 8 | Willie Bell | B | 23 | murder | Durham | laborer | WM |
| September 3 | Charles Trull | W | 22 | murder | Mecklenburg | unemployed | WM |
| **1916** | | | | | | | |
| January 28 | Jeff Dorsett | B | 27 | murder | Guilford | laborer | WM |
| January 28 | Ed Walker | B | 26 | murder | Guilford | laborer | WM |
| February 11 | James Cooper | B | 26 | murder | Rowan | laborer | BF |
| February 25 | Ernest Lowry | B | 24 | murder | Gaston | unknown | BM |
| February 25 | George Poston | B | 23 | murder | Gaston | laborer | BM |
| July 7 | Lawrence Swinson | B | 23 | burglary | New Hanover | laborer | W |
| July 21 | Will Black | B | 18 | rape | Greene | laborer | WF (child) |
| August 1 | Arthur Smith | B | 26 | murder | Cumberland | laborer | BF (wife) |
| August 4 | John Savage | B | 51 | murder | Washington | laborer | WM |
| **1917** | | | | | | | |
| May 25 | Bunke Mask | B | 24 | murder | Union | laborer | WM (law) |
| September 25 | Charles Williams | B | 60 | murder | Iredell | farmer | WM (law) |
| October 10 | Lee Perkins | B | 23 | burglary | Craven | laborer | W |
| November 9 | J. A. Terry | W | 60 | murder | Guilford | farmer | WM |
| **1918** | | | | | | | |
| March 15 | Earl Neville | B | 22 | rape | Wake | coachman | WF |
| April 26 | Willie Williams | B | 19 | rape | Buncombe | laborer | WF |
| May 24 | Frank Moore | B | 20 | murder | Duplin | laborer | WM |
| May 25 | Herbert Perry | B | 33 | rape | Granville | laborer (sawmill) | F (child) |

(continued)

TABLE 2 Executions under state authority in North Carolina, 1910–1961 (continued)

| Date | Name | Race | Age | Sentenced for | County | Occupation | Victim(s) |
|------|------|------|-----|---------------|--------|------------|-----------|
| June 7 | Lonnie Council | B | 38 | murder | Durham | laborer | BM |
| September 13 | Baxter Cain | B | 32 | murder | Rowan | night watchman | BM |
| December 20 | Napoleon Spencer | B | 16 | murder | Forsyth | laborer | WM/F |
| **1919** | | | | | | | |
| April 26 | Jim Warren | B | 19 | murder | Greene | laborer | WM |
| June 27 | Tom Gwynn | B | 23 | rape | Catawba | laborer | WF |
| November 14 | Aaron Dupree | B | 34 | murder | Hoke | laborer | WM |
| **1920** | | | | | | | |
| January 16 | Churchill Godley | W | 34 | rape | Johnston | printer | WF (child) |
| March 5 | Joseph Cain | W | 39 | murder | Surry | laborer | WM |
| March 5 | Sanford Gardner Cain | W | 43 | murder | Surry | laborer | WM |
| September 20 | Ralph Connor | B | 21 | murder | Iredell | farmer | WM (law) |
| November 5 | Andrew Jackson | B | 30 | rape | Lincoln | laborer | WF |
| December 3 | Tom Johnson | B | 20 | rape | Guilford | laborer | WF |
| December 3 | Jim McDonald | B | 30 | rape | Davidson | unknown | WF |
| **1921** | | | | | | | |
| March 21 | William Hopkins | W | 21 | murder | Sampson | laborer | WM |
| May 27 | Luke Frazier | B | 33 | murder | Craven | laborer | BM |
| October 10 | Frank Henderson | W | 34 | murder | Madison | farmer | WF (wife) |
| October 20 | J. T. Harris | W | 52 | murder | Buncombe | merchant | WM |
| October 31 | Harry Caldwell | B | 33 | murder | Wayne | laborer | WM |
| November 21 | William Westmoreland | W | 38 | murder | Iredell | cotton mill operator | WM |

| Date | Name | | Age | Crime | County | Occupation | BF (wife) |
|---|---|---|---|---|---|---|---|
| November 30 | Claude Morehead | B | 23 | murder | Guilford | laborer | |
| **1922** | | | | | | | |
| September 15 | Angus Murphy | B | 36 | rape | Moore | laborer | WF |
| September 15 | Jasper Thomas | B | 20 | rape | Moore | laborer | WF |
| October 12 | McIver Burnett | B | 16 | rape | Wake | laborer | WF |
| **1923** | | | | | | | |
| March 1 | Robert Williams | B | 21 | murder | Columbus | laborer | W |
| April 27 | William Hardison | B | 16 | murder | Onslow | unknown | WM |
| May 9 | Wiley Perry | B | 31 | murder | Granville | laborer | WM (law) |
| June 26 | Daniel Nobles | W | 37 | murder | Columbus | farmer | WM |
| June 28 | Ed Dill | B | 42 | rape | Beaufort | laborer | WF |
| October 5 | James Miller | B | 39 | murder | Lenoir | laborer | WM |
| November 28 | Vance Morgan | B | 23 | murder | Union | laborer | WM |
| December 7 | John Goss | B | 44 | rape | Mitchell | chain ganger | WF |
| December 28 | Lee Washington | B | 20 | rape | Nash | laborer | WF |
| **1925** | | | | | | | |
| January 5 | Kenneth Hale | B | 18 | murder | Davidson | laborer | WM |
| January 5 | John Leak | B | 24 | murder | Davidson | shoemaker | WM |
| February 18 | David Jones | B | 21 | murder | Chowan | unknown | WM |
| April 17 | Charles Stewart | W | 55 | murder | Brunswick | carpenter | WM+ (law) |
| April 17 | William Elmer Stewart | W | 23 | murder | Brunswick | laborer | WM+ (law) |
| April 21 | Leonard Walton | B | 29 | murder | Hoke | farmer | WM |
| May 8 | William Singleton | B | 17 | murder | Craven | farmer | WM |
| June 5 | James Collins | B | 19 | murder | Anson | laborer | WM |

(continued)

TABLE 2 Executions under state authority in North Carolina, 1910–1961 (continued)

| Date | Name | Race | Age | Sentenced for | County | Occupation | Victim(s) |
|---|---|---|---|---|---|---|---|
| June 12 | Will Williams | B | 25 | murder | Scotland | laborer | BM |
| June 19 | George Love | B | 33 | murder | Haywood | laborer | W |
| October 2 | John McMillan | B | 18 | rape | Moore | unknown | WF |
| October 2 | Thomas Robinson | B | 26 | rape | New Hanover | laborer | WF |
| 1926 | | | | | | | |
| January 8 | William Dawkins | B | 20 | murder | Forsyth | laborer | WM |
| January 22 | Arthur Montague | B | 22 | rape | Burke | cook | WF |
| June 11 | Fred Jones | B | 25 | murder | Forsyth | laborer | WM |
| September 21 | John Williams | B | 30 | murder | Halifax | farmer | BM |
| 1927 | | | | | | | |
| March 11 | Robert Lumpkin | B | 27 | murder | Robeson | laborer | WM (law) |
| April 22 | Ernest Walker | B | 39 | murder | Durham | janitor | BM |
| June 10 | Pearl Mitchell | B | 29 | murder | Chatham | farmer | WM |
| September 23 | George Bazemore | B | 25 | murder | Greene | unknown | WM |
| December 9 | James Hector Graham | B | 41 | murder | Hoke | unknown | WM |
| 1928 | | | | | | | |
| February 17 | David Devlin | B | 22 | murder | Rowan | unknown | WM (law) |
| April 27 | Clarence Thomas | B | 25 | murder | Forsyth | construction labor | WM (law) |
| May 25 | John Clyburn | B | 22 | murder | Mecklenburg | unknown | WM |
| September 28 | Larry Newsome | B | 24 | rape | Wayne | farmer | WF (child) |

| | | | | | | | |
|---|---|---|---|---|---|---|---|
| **1929** | | | | | | | |
| April 26 | Leo McCurrie | B | 28 | murder | Gaston | farmer | WM |
| June 28 | Freddie Wiley | B | 16 | rape | Randolph | unknown | WF |
| September 12 | Willis Buckner | W | 32 | rape | Craven | unknown | WF (child) |
| November 22 | Ernest Fox | B | 19 | murder | Edgecombe | unknown | WM |
| **1930** | | | | | | | |
| March 14 | Ray Evans | B | 21 | murder | Richmond | mechanic | WM (law) |
| April 4 | John Macon | B | 34 | murder | Randolph | laborer | WM (law) |
| April 17 | Robert Mangum | B | 22 | rape | Franklin | farmer | WF |
| May 9 | James Broomfield | B | 19 | burglary | Union | unknown | W |
| May 23 | James Spivey | W | 25 | murder | Lee | farmer | WF |
| September 26 | Berry Richardson | B | 20 | murder | Wilson | farmer | WM |
| September 26 | Aaron Sharp | B | 22 | murder | Wilson | farmer | WM |
| October 10 | Harvey Lawrence | B | 17 | burglary | Hertford | unknown | W |
| November 7 | Willie Massey | B | 25 | murder | Durham | farmer | BF (sister) |
| November 7 | Will Sloan | B | 28 | murder | Person | laborer | BF |
| **1931** | | | | | | | |
| January 23 | Sidney Gattis | B | 49 | murder | Durham | laborer | BF |
| February 13 | Henry Barden | B | 29 | burglary | Scotland | laborer | WM |
| February 13 | Dave McRae | B | 25 | murder | Vance | laborer | W |
| August 10 | Woodrow Wilson Autry | B | 19 | rape | Union | farmer | WF |

(continued)

TABLE 2 Executions under state authority in North Carolina, 1910–1961 (continued)

| Date | Name | Race | Age | Sentenced for | County | Occupation | Victim(s) |
|---|---|---|---|---|---|---|---|
| August 21 | Ben Goldston | B | 36 | murder | Chatham | farmer | BM |
| December 11 | J. W. Ballard | B | 17 | murder | Rowan | unknown | WM |
| December 11 | Bernice Matthews | B | 18 | murder | Rowan | unknown | WM |
| December 18 | Chevis Herring | B | 23 | murder | Sampson | unknown | WM |
| **1932** | | | | | | | |
| January 8 | Asbury Respus | B | 56 | rape | Guilford | unknown | WF (child) |
| March 25 | John Myers | B | 30 | murder | Pitt | truck driver | WM |
| April 29 | Dudley Moore | B | 19 | rape | Davidson | farmer | WF (foster mother) |
| July 15 | Plato Edney | W | 33 | murder | Henderson | brick layer | WF (wife) |
| August 26 | Nard Donnell | B | 24 | murder | Guilford | laborer | WM |
| October 14 | Leroy Lee | B | 24 | murder | Guilford | unknown | WM |
| December 16 | Alec Grier | B | 21 | murder | Lee | unknown | WM+ |
| December 16 | Harvey Wallace | B | 28 | murder | Gaston | unknown | WM |
| **1933** | | | | | | | |
| January 27 | Hezzie Avant | W | 30 | murder | Scotland | textile worker | WF |
| May 19 | David McNair | B | 23 | murder | Guilford | railroad worker | WF |
| August 4 | Olin Clay Fogleman | W | 30 | murder | Rockingham | unknown (bootlegger) | WM (law) |
| September 8 | Bryant Stone | W | 45 | murder | Wilkes | farmer | WM (son-in-law) |
| September 15 | Johnnie Lee | B | 21 | murder | Harnett | laborer | BM |

**1934**

| Date | Name | | Age | Crime | County | Occupation | |
|---|---|---|---|---|---|---|---|
| March 16 | Jesse Brooks | B | 46 | murder | Durham | railroad worker | WM |
| March 16 | James Johnson | B | 24 | murder | Hoke | unknown | BF |
| March 23 | Walter Thaxton | B | 30 | murder | Person | mechanic | WM |
| April 27 | Theodore Cooper | B | 29 | murder | Durham | cook | WM |
| May 18 | James Sheffield | W | 47 | murder | Haywood | salesman | WM |
| May 18 | Mike Stefanoff | W | 45 | murder | Alexander | laborer | WM |
| June 15 | Ossie Smith | B | 20 | murder | Northampton | farmer | WM |
| June 22 | Joe Dalton | W | 31 | murder | Henderson | mechanic | WF (wife) |
| July 6 | John Edwards | B | 17 | murder | Mecklenburg | truck driver | WM |
| July 6 | Clyde Ferrell | W | 25 | murder | Durham | mechanic | WM |
| September 21 | George Keaton | B | 28 | murder | Forsyth | butler | BF |
| September 28 | Emanuel Bittings | B | 42 | murder | Person | farmer | WM |
| September 28 | Willie Crockett | B | 22 | murder | Forsyth | laborer | BF (wife) |
| November 11 | Johnnie Hart | B | 22 | murder | Sampson | farmer | WM |
| November 11 | Preston Howard | B | 18 | murder | Sampson | none | WM |
| November 11 | Tom Johnson | B | 28 | murder | Sampson | truck driver | WM |
| December 7 | Robert Black | W | 25 | murder | Alexander | engineer | WM |
| December 7 | Bascom Green | W | 44 | murder | Alexander | textile worker | WM |
| December 7 | James Lester Green | W | 22 | murder | Alexander | textile worker | WM |
| December 13 | Rufus Satterfield | W | 44 | murder | Wayne | farmer | WM |

**1935**

| Date | Name | | Age | Crime | County | Occupation | |
|---|---|---|---|---|---|---|---|
| March 15 | Sidney Etheridge | W | 44 | murder | Onslow | electrician | WF |
| July 12 | Louis Sentelle | W | 39 | murder | Cleveland | textile worker | WF |

(continued)

TABLE 2 Executions under state authority in North Carolina, 1910–1961 (continued)

| Date | Name | Race | Age | Sentenced for | County | Occupation | Victim(s) |
|------|------|------|-----|---------------|--------|------------|-----------|
| July 12 | George Whitfield | B | 23 | murder | Guilford | unknown | WF |
| August 2 | Dortch Waller | B | 43 | murder | Granville | farmer | WM |
| August 2 | Taft Williams | B | 25 | murder | Columbus | farmer | BF (wife) |
| August 9 | Vander Glover | B | 39 | murder | Cumberland | truck driver | BM |
| August 9 | Houston McMillan | B | 19 | murder | Cumberland | truck driver | BM |
| September 6 | Caesar Miller | B | 18 | murder | Craven | dairyman | WM |
| October 4 | Arthur Gosnell | W | 20 | murder | Madison | farmer | WM |
| October 4 | Oris Gunter | W | 20 | murder | Madison | farmer | WM |
| October 4 | Robert Thomas | W | 23 | murder | Madison | farmer | WM |
| **1936** | | | | | | | |
| January 17 | Robert Dunlap | B | 27 | murder | Buncombe | farmer | BF |
| January 24 | Jimmy Lee (Allen) Foster | B | 18 | rape | Hoke | mechanic | WF |
| January 31 | Edward Jenkins | W | 48 | murder | Gaston | painter | WM |
| February 7 | William Long | B | 19 | murder | Alamance | laborer | BM |
| February 7 | James Sanford | B | 25 | murder | Durham | farmer | BM |
| February 7 | Thomas Watson | B | 30 | murder | Durham | truck driver | BM |
| March 19 | Jake Johnson | B | 35 | rape | Rockingham | laborer | WF |
| March 20 | Ed Hester | W | 19 | murder | Wake | textile worker | WM |
| March 27 | Bright Buffkin | W | 43 | murder | Columbus | farmer | WM |

| Date | Name | Race | Age | Crime | County | Occupation | Victim |
| --- | --- | --- | --- | --- | --- | --- | --- |
| May 8 | Lawrence Dingle | B | 32 | murder | Forsyth | laborer | BM |
| May 8 | Germay Williams | B | 25 | murder | Forsyth | farmer | BM |
| May 29 | Marvin Batten | W | 29 | murder | Johnston | farmer | WF |
| June 19 | John Horne | W | 38 | murder | Chowan | loomer (cotton mill) | WF (wife) |
| July 10 | Henry Grier | B | 43 | murder | Forsyth | laborer | BF |
| July 17 | William Hodgin | B | 36 | murder | Forsyth | carpenter | BM |
| August 21 | Willie Gallman | B | 21 | murder | Forsyth | tobacco factory | BM |
| August 21 | John Kinyon | B | 73 | rape | Granville | farmer | WF (child) |
| September 4 | George Alston | B | 24 | murder | Orange | butler | BF |
| September 4 | James Carden | W | 42 | murder | Durham | carpenter | WF (wife) |
| November 13 | John Pressley | B | 43 | murder | Gaston | farmer | BM |
| November 20 | Evans Macklin | B | 20 | murder | Halifax | farmer | WM (law) |
| November 20 | Willie Tate | B | 28 | murder | Pitt | janitor | WM |
| December 11 | Martin Moore | B | 22 | murder | Buncombe | hotel employee | WF |
| **1937** | | | | | | | |
| July 9 | Robert Brown | B | 19 | murder | Craven | farmer | WM |
| July 16 | Sam Jones | B | 21 | murder | Mecklenburg | laborer | W |
| July 16 | Fred Steele | B | 24 | murder | Mecklenburg | cook | W |
| July 23 | Fred Gray | B | 26 | murder | Onslow | farmer | BM |
| July 23 | Hunter Winchester | B | 24 | murder | Guilford | garage helper | BF (wife) |
| July 30 | Thomas Perry | B | 23 | rape | Wake | laborer | BF (wife) |
| July 30 | A. W. Watson | W | 21 | murder | Martin | mechanic | WM |
| August 6 | George Exum | B | 23 | murder | Wayne | farmer | BF (aunt) |

TABLE 2 Executions under state authority in North Carolina, 1910–1961 (continued)

| Date | Name | Race | Age | Sentenced for | County | Occupation | Victim(s) |
|---|---|---|---|---|---|---|---|
| August 13 | James McNeil | B | 23 | murder | Harnett | laborer | BF |
| August 13 | Leroy McNeil | B | 18 | murder | Robeson | farmer | WF |
| December 10 | Walter Caldwell | B | 37 | rape | Iredell | laborer | WF |
| December 10 | William Perry | B | 17 | rape | Chatham | farm worker | WF |
| **1938** | | | | | | | |
| January 21 | James Sermons | B | 30 | murder | Forsyth | factory worker | WM |
| February 4 | James Marshall | B | 30 | burglary | Wayne | laborer | W |
| February 18 | Milford Exum | W | 40 | murder | Wayne | storekeeper | BM |
| February 18 | Edgar Smoak | W | 40 | murder | New Hanover | carpenter | WF (child, daughter) |
| April 29 | Waddell Hadley | B | 22 | rape | Sampson | farmer | WF |
| April 29 | Sylvester Outlaw | B | 35 | rape | Duplin | farmer | WF |
| June 10 | Empie Baldwin | B | 25 | rape | Columbus | farmer | WF |
| June 17 | Lonnie Gardner | B | 27 | rape | Duplin | farmer | WF |
| June 17 | Apsom Outlaw | B | 29 | rape | Duplin | farmer | WF |
| July 1 | Wiley Brice | B | 37 | murder | Alamance | laborer | BM |
| July 1 | Bill Payne | W | 41 | murder | Buncombe | plumber | WM (law) |
| July 1 | John Washington Turner | W | 36 | murder | Buncombe | unknown | WM (law) |
| September 23 | George Ford | B | 20 | murder | Scotland | unknown | WM |
| September 23 | Thomas Jefferson | B | 18 | murder | Forsyth | laborer | WM |
| September 23 | Tom Linney | B | 32 | murder | Forsyth | laborer | WM |

| Date | Name | | Age | Crime | County | Occupation | |
|---|---|---|---|---|---|---|---|
| October 28 | Claude Bowser Jr. | B | 22 | murder | Halifax | laborer | BF |
| November 18 | Ed Robinson | B | 33 | rape | Iredell | truck driver | WF |
| December 2 | John Howie | B | 30 | rape | Forsyth | laborer | WF |
| December 9 | Baxter Parnell | W | 32 | murder | Cabarrus | farmer | WF (sister-in-law) |
| **1939** | | | | | | | |
| January 20 | King Solomon Stovall | B | 33 | murder | Granville | farmer | WM |
| April 7 | Clarence Bracey | B | 33 | murder | Vance | laborer | WM |
| April 7 | Batt Dejournette | B | 38 | murder | Guilford | sawmill worker | WM |
| May 5 | James Dixon | B | 30 | murder | Cabarrus | laborer | BF (wife) |
| May 26 | Edward Mattocks | B | 21 | murder | Onslow | laborer | WM |
| June 9 | Dave Burney | B | 47 | murder | Jones | farmer | BF |
| June 16 | Ed Alston | B | 29 | murder | Durham | tobacco factory worker | BF (elder) |
| July 7 | Alfred Capers | B | 24 | murder | Robeson | farmer | BM |
| July 7 | Bricey Hammond | N | 24 | murder | Robeson | farmer | WM |
| July 7 | James Henderson | B | 19 | rape | New Hanover | laborer | WF |
| September 1 | Arthur Morris | B | 25 | burglary | Wake | laborer | W |
| September 22 | James Godwin | W | 21 | murder | Guilford | student | WM |
| October 6 | Charles Fain | B | 26 | rape | Cherokee | mechanic | WF |
| October 27 | Willie Richardson | B | 19 | burglary | Nash | gardener | W |

(continued)

TABLE 2 Executions under state authority in North Carolina, 1910–1961 (continued)

| Date | Name | Race | Age | Sentenced for | County | Occupation | Victim(s) |
|------|------|------|-----|---------------|--------|------------|-----------|
| November 24 | Raymond Williams | B | 20 | murder | Sampson | domestic servant | WM |
| **1940** | | | | | | | |
| January 19 | Glenn Maxwell | B | 49 | murder | Alleghany | farmer | WM |
| January 19 | Clarence Rogers | B | 27 | murder | Durham | factory worker | WM |
| February 16 | Nathaniel Bryant | B | 18 | murder | Hoke | laborer | WM |
| February 16 | William Young | B | 23 | murder | Hoke | upholsterer | WM |
| March 15 | Robert Williams | B | 19 | rape | Cumberland | farmer | WF |
| April 5 | Zebulon Page | B | 28 | rape | Johnston | railroad worker | WF |
| May 24 | Simon Gibson | B | 23 | rape | New Hanover | laborer | WF |
| June 14 | Charlie Hopkins | B | 63 | murder | Rutherford | farmer | WM (law) |
| June 28 | Lee Flynn | W | 44 | murder | McDowell | farmer | WF (wife) |
| December 6 | Zedekiel Smith | B | 30 | murder | Sampson | farmer | WM |
| **1941** | | | | | | | |
| April 18 | Dollie Hudson | B | 27 | murder | Northampton | farmer | WM |
| May 2 | Sylvester Woodard | B | 34 | murder | Wayne | butcher | BF |
| May 23 | James Shaw | B | 21 | murder | Columbus | unknown | BM |
| June 6 | Fleet Wall | B | 35 | murder | Anson | farmer | BF (wife) |
| June 13 | Noah Cureton | B | 60 | murder | Mecklenburg | farmer | BM |
| August 22 | Hubert Cash | W | 41 | murder | Durham | metal worker | WF (wife) |
| September 5 | Tom Melvin | B | 42 | murder | Wayne | florist | WM |
| October 10 | George Peele | B | 20 | murder | Bertie | painter | WM |

| Date | Name | Race | Age | Crime | County | Occupation | Victim |
|---|---|---|---|---|---|---|---|
| December 12 | Luther Morrow | B | 26 | murder | Union | laborer | BF (wife) |
| **1942** | | | | | | | |
| January 9 | Roland Wescott | W | 21 | murder | New Hanover | electrician | WF (fiancee) |
| February 13 | Robert Sturdivant | B | 29 | murder | Bladen | laborer | BF (wife) |
| August 7 | Arthur Gibson | B | 32 | rape | Buncombe | hospital orderly | BF (child) |
| August 21 | Walter Smith | W | 64 | murder | Wayne | farmer | WM |
| October 30 | Herman Allen | W | 35 | murder | Johnston | painter | WM/F+ |
| October 30 | Otis Harris | B | 17 | rape | Bertie | farmer | WF |
| November 13 | William Long | B | 31 | murder | Pitt | farmer | BF+ (wife and aunt) |
| **1943** | | | | | | | |
| January 1 | Daniel Phillips | B | 29 | murder | Durham | laborer | WM |
| January 1 | Rosanna Phillips† | B | 25 | murder | Durham | maid | WM |
| January 29 | Sam Hairston | B | 22 | rape | Forsyth | farmer | WF |
| February 19 | Palmer Mears | W | 35 | murder | Robeson | farmer | WM |
| April 16 | John Henry Lee | B | 20 | rape | Camden | truck driver | WF |
| May 21 | Lewis Moody | B | 26 | murder | Northampton | laborer | BM |
| June 4 | Bill Bryant | W | 40 | murder | McDowell | laborer | WM |
| June 4 | Harvey Hunt | N | 21 | rape | Robeson | farmer | WF |
| June 4 | Purcell Smith | N | 22 | rape | Robeson | farmer | WF |
| June 18 | James Utley | B | 25 | murder | Montgomery | cook | BF (wife) |
| October 8 | William Poole | B | 30 | murder | Pasquotank | laborer | WM |

(continued)

TABLE 2 Executions under state authority in North Carolina, 1910–1961 (continued)

| Date | Name | Race | Age | Sentenced for | County | Occupation | Victim(s) |
|---|---|---|---|---|---|---|---|
| October 29 | Willie Smith | B | 38 | murder | Warren | cement finisher | WM |
| November 26 | John Redfern | B | 39 | murder | Wake | laborer | BM |
| December 10 | Clyde Grass | W | 32 | murder | Cabarrus | textile worker | WM/F+ |
| **1944** | | | | | | | |
| January 28 | Alec Harris | W | 48 | murder | Hoke | farmer | WM/F+ |
| February 18 | Andrew Farrell | W | 25 | rape | Durham | taxi drive | WF (child, stepdaughter) |
| February 25 | Waymon Grainger | B | 32 | murder | Columbus | laborer | WM |
| November 3 | James Taylor | B | 48 | murder | Wake | railroad worker | WM (law) |
| November 17 | Charles Alexander | B | 24 | rape | Halifax | farmer | BF (child) |
| November 24 | George Brooks | B | 20 | rape | Mecklenburg | railroad worker | WF |
| November 24 | James Buchanan | B | 19 | rape | Mecklenburg | truck driver | WF |
| December 29 | Ralph Thompson | B | 18 | murder | Mecklenburg | machinist | WM |
| December 29 | Melvin Wade | B | 23 | rape | Scotland | laborer | BF (child) |
| December 29 | Bessie Mae Williams† | B | 20 | murder | Mecklenburg | maid | WM |
| **1945** | | | | | | | |
| March 9 | Elmer Biggs | W | 22 | murder | Guilford | machinist | WM |
| March 9 | William Biggs | W | 20 | murder | Guilford | truck driver | WM |
| March 9 | John Messer | W | 20 | murder | Guilford | café worker | WM |
| May 25 | Horis Hill | B | 22 | murder | Jones | laborer | BF+ |

| Date | Name | Race | Crime | County | Occupation | Victim |
|---|---|---|---|---|---|---|
| June 6 | Lacy McDaniel | B | rape | Guilford | golf course worker | WF |
| June 22 | Henry French | B | murder | Montgomery | truck driver | BM/F+ |
| June 22 | William Jones | B | murder | Wake | porter | BF (wife) |
| October 26 | Burnett Williams | B | rape | Lee | laborer | WF |
| November 2 | Edward Mays | B | rape | Lee | farmer | WF |
| **1946** | | | | | | |
| February 15 | Walter Hightower | B | murder | Wilkes | tailor | BM |
| April 26 | Alligood King | B | rape | Lenoir | farmer | WF |
| May 4 | Thomas Hart | B | murder | Halifax | farmer | BM |
| May 24 | Gurney Herring | B | rape | Wayne | laborer | BF |
| June 21 | George Walker | B | rape | Harnett | farmer | WF (child) |
| June 28 | Fred Deaton | B | murder | Gaston | unknown | WM |
| June 28 | Fab Stewart | B | murder | Wake | laborer | BM |
| October 25 | Edward Floyd | W | murder | Northampton | farmer | WM/F+ (in-laws) |
| November 1 | Robert Nash | W | murder | Wake | projectionist | WF |
| November 22 | Charles Primus | B | rape | Wake | laborer | WF |
| December 13 | Herman Matthews | B | murder | Sampson | farmer | BM |
| December 13 | Calvin Williams | B | murder | Sampson | farmer | BM |
| **1947** | | | | | | |
| March 14 | Otis Ragland | B | rape | Martin | escapee | WF |
| March 28 | Benny Montgomery | B | murder | Union | farmer | WM |

(continued)

TABLE 2 Executions under state authority in North Carolina, 1910–1961 (continued)

| Date | Name | Race | Age | Sentenced for | County | Occupation | Victim(s) |
|---|---|---|---|---|---|---|---|
| April 4 | Richard Horton | B | 24 | murder | Wilkes | laborer | WM |
| April 11 | Eunice Martin | B | 30 | murder | Forsyth | dry cleaner | BF (wife) |
| May 23 | Ben McLeod | B | 27 | murder | Scotland | farmer | NM/F/WM+ (infant) |
| June 6 | James Farmer | B | 20 | murder | Johnston | farmer | WM |
| June 6 | Albert Sanders | B | 21 | murder | Johnston | farmer | WM |
| June 27 | Moses Artis | B | 42 | murder | Duplin | farmer | WM |
| June 27 | Woodrow Brown | B | 26 | rape | Wake | farmer | WF |
| June 27 | Roy Kirksey | B | 26 | murder | Columbus | farmer | BF (wife) |
| October 3 | Willie Cherry | B | 27 | rape | Northampton | laborer | WF |
| October 3 | Jethro Lampkin | B | 20 | murder | Mecklenburg | laborer | WM |
| October 3 | Richard McCain | B | 22 | murder | Mecklenburg | laborer | WM |
| October 3 | Robert Messer | W | 20 | murder | Jackson | laborer | WM/F |
| October 3 | Earl O'Dear | W | 23 | murder | Jackson | stone mason | WM/F |
| October 10 | Oscar Douglas | B | 40 | rape | Davie | sawmill worker | WF |
| October 31 | James Brooks | B | 30 | murder | Henderson | laborer | WM (law) |
| October 31 | Grady Brown | B | 27 | murder | Henderson | brick mason | WM (law) |
| October 31 | Thurman Munn | B | 25 | murder | Henderson | cook | WM (law) |
| October 31 | Lester Stanley | B | 28 | murder | Edgecombe | truck driver | BF (wife) |
| November 14 | Marvin Bell | W | 33 | rape | Wilkes | unknown | WF (child) |

| Date | Name | | Age | Crime | County | Occupation | Victim |
|------|------|---|-----|-------|--------|-----------|--------|
| November 14 | Ralph Letteral | W | 35 | rape | Wilkes | unknown | WF (child) |
| November 14 | Willie Little | B | 43 | rape | Wake | laborer | WF |
| **1948** | | | | | | | |
| January 2 | Frank Black | B | 20 | murder | Lenoir | laborer | WM |
| January 16 | John Breeze | B | 33 | murder | Orange | farmer | WF |
| April 23 | Booker Anderson | B | 29 | murder/arson | Pitt | truck driver | BF+ (children) |
| April 23 | Buster Hooks | B | 28 | rape | Randolph | laborer | WF |
| May 7 | James Jackson | B | 42 | murder | Burke | cook | WM |
| June 4 | George Hammonds | B | 47 | murder | Davidson | laborer | WM |
| June 4 | Henderson Wilson | B | 27 | murder | Davidson | farmer | WM |
| November 19 | James West | B | 21 | murder | Duplin | laborer | WM |
| **1949** | | | | | | | |
| January 28 | James Creech | W | 37 | murder | Johnston | tobacconist | WF (wife) |
| March 18 | Emmett Garner | W | 37 | murder | Harnett | farmer | WF (wife) |
| March 25 | Roy Cockrell | W | 42 | murder | Nash | farmer | WF (wife) |
| June 17 | James Lewis | B | 27 | murder | Robeson | farmer | BF (wife) |
| December 9 | Audie Brown | B | 26 | murder | Randolph | laborer | WM |
| December 9 | Monroe Medlin | B | 23 | murder | Mecklenburg | butler | WF |
| December 9 | Allen T. Reid | B | 30 | burglary | Wilson | farmer | W |
| December 16 | Uzelle Jones | B | 36 | murder | Hoke | farmer | BF |

(continued)

TABLE 2  Executions under state authority in North Carolina, 1910–1961 (continued)

| Date | Name | Race | Age | Sentenced for | County | Occupation | Victim(s) |
|------|------|------|-----|---------------|--------|------------|-----------|
| December 30 | Hector Chavis | N | 29 | murder | Robeson | laborer | WM |
| December 30 | Leander Jacobs | N | 28 | murder | Robeson | farmer | WM |
| **1950** | | | | | | | |
| January 6 | Lee Heller | B | 49 | murder | Catawba | laborer | BF (wife) |
| May 19 | Jack Bridges | W | 22 | murder | Wake | handyman | WM |
| July 21 | Claude Shackleford | W | 34 | rape | Guilford | textile worker | WF (child) |
| November 10 | Covey Lamb | W | 48 | murder | Wilson | fishmonger | WF (wife) |
| November 24 | Ernest Liles | W | 34 | rape | Franklin | laborer | WF |
| **1951** | | | | | | | |
| March 23 | Curtis Shedd | W | 30 | murder | Macon | farmer | WF+ (children) |
| March 29 | James Hall | W | 27 | murder | Jackson | laborer | WF (sister-in-law) |
| April 27 | John Rogers | B | 24 | murder | Sampson | farmer | WF |
| **1952** | | | | | | | |
| June 6 | John Roman | B | 30 | murder | Davidson | laborer | WF |
| **1953** | | | | | | | |
| May 1 | Lafayette Miller | B | 20 | murder | Beaufort | laborer | WM |

| Date | Name | Race | Age | Crime | County | Occupation | Victim |
|---|---|---|---|---|---|---|---|
| May 29 | Clyde Brown | B | 22 | rape | Forsyth | laborer | WF |
| May 29 | Raleigh Speller | B | 51 | rape | Bertie | laborer | WF |
| November 6 | Bennie Daniels | B | 21 | murder | Pitt | farmer | WM |
| November 6 | Lloyd Ray Daniels | B | 20 | murder | Pitt | farmer | WM |
| **1955** | | | | | | | |
| July 15 | Richard Scales | B | 29 | murder | Guilford | service station attndt | BF+ (child) |
| **1956** | | | | | | | |
| July 13 | Robert Conner | B | 31 | murder | Forsyth | laborer | BM |
| **1957** | | | | | | | |
| November 22 | Ross McAfee | B | 42 | burglary | Alexander | farmer | W |
| **1958** | | | | | | | |
| February 28 | Julius Bunton | B | 22 | rape | Guilford | laborer | WM |
| December 5 | Matthew Bass | B | 44 | rape | Wake | janitor | WF |
| **1961** | | | | | | | |
| October 27 | Theodore Boykin | B | 32 | murder | Duplin | saw mill worker | WF |

M. Watt Espy, and John Ortiz Smykla. Executions in the United States, 1608–2002: The ESPY File. ICPSR08451-v5. Ann Arbor, MI: Inter-university Consortium for Political and Social Research [distributor], July 20, 2016, accessed December 16, 2017, https://doi.org/10.3886/ICPSR08451.v5; Daniel Allen Hearn, *Legal Executions in North and South Carolina: A Comprehensive Registry, 1866–1962* (Jefferson, NC: McFarland, 2015).

Credit: Created by the author.

# Appendix C

## Lynchings and Possible Lynchings in North Carolina, 1865–1946

A note on sources: this appendix draws from Vann R. Newkirk's *Lynching in North Carolina*, data provided by E. M. Beck and Stuart Tolnay, and original research conducted in the newspaper database newspapers.com. Newkirk provides a list of 168 lynchings between 1865 and 1941, but it is not possible to substantiate all of those events, particularly during the Reconstruction period between 1865 and 1877. This absence of adequate documentation explains why Beck and Tolnay chose to produce a data set beginning in 1878. They document 116 lynching events, including 2 probable lynchings and 2 possible lynchings as well as one lynching of a person taken from North Carolina to South Carolina to be killed. By means of comparison, the recent report by the Equal Justice Initiative (EJI) lists 124 lynchings between 1877 and 1950. The EJI report includes 22 lynchings in New Hanover County, many of which are likely (EJI sourcing is unavailable) to have taken place during the Wilmington Coup of 1898. Other scholars, including Newkirk, Beck, and Tolnay, have not included those killings in their reckoning. This new accounting documents at least 175 lynchings in North Carolina.

The count here seeks to reconcile these two data sets with additional material gathered by students working with me and Elijah Gaddis. It includes a number of under- or undocumented lynchings during Reconstruction. By including such lynchings, this list presents a high but reasonable accounting that nonetheless likely underrepresents lynching in North Carolina. In this table, BT indicates that the event was documented by Beck and Tolnay, GK Gaddis and Kotch, and N indicates Newkirk.

This list does not include the victims of violence in Wilmington, because while we know the names of many people killed, we also believe that many more died than have been named, and that it might be better to treat Wilmington separately and thus avoid underrepresenting the extent of its lethal violence in list form here. It also removed some lynchings documented by Newkirk when it was determined that the victims lived. Other differences between this record and the others reflect a considered update to existing information; notation that more than one source documented an event does not mean these sources agreed on the details of that event.

Given the absence of documentation about many lynchings, there may be some unrecognized overlap between these three data sets. Due to space constraints this appendix includes a bare minimum of relevant information and leaves out important context. More information and documentation for lynchings identified and described by Gaddis and Kotch can be found at lynching.web.unc.edu. It is important not to take the word of the mob or newspaper reports as to the reason for a lynching, but it is documented here because it is helpful to understand how the event was understood at the time. These designations do not imply actual guilt, let alone legal guilt. When there is a more credible explanation, it has been provided. Victims of lynchings have been assigned simple racial designations that do not reflect the presence of biracial and triracial persons in the state, or of other complex questions of race and identity.

There are shortcomings to counting lynchings, not only in the absence of adequate documentation during Reconstruction (making accuracy an issue) but also in relation to attempted but failed attacks; killings that for one reason or another do not make the cut; lynchings foiled by law enforcement officers; and, perhaps most significantly, the countless acts of physical and psychological violence that took place alongside lynchings. Furthermore, to suggest that a lynching affected just one person, the victim, overlooks the resultant widespread, generational trauma.

The following list is an attempt to document what has been documented—to produce in one place a list of lynchings and possible lynchings, largely relying on work by other scholars, to provide one possible picture of lynching attempts in North Carolina that resulted in death. This list is likely incomplete and many of these incidents merit further investigation.

TABLE 3 Lynchings and possible lynchings in North Carolina, 1865–1946

| | Name | Date | Race | Sex | Explanation Offered | County | Source |
|---|---|---|---|---|---|---|---|
| 1. | unreported | February 1865 | B | M | unknown | Robeson | N |
| 2. | unreported | February 1865 | B | M | unknown | Robeson | N |
| 3. | unreported | February 1865 | B | M | unknown | Robeson | N |
| 4. | Thomas Bradley | August 1, 1865 | B | M | land dispute | Duplin | GK, N |
| 5. | John Hirst | August 1, 1865 | B | M | land dispute | Duplin | GK, N |
| 6. | John Middleton | August 1, 1865 | B | M | land dispute | Duplin | GK, N |
| 7. | Charles Winters | August 1, 1865 | B | M | land dispute | Duplin | GK, N |
| 8. | unreported | August 1, 1865 | B | U | land dispute | Duplin | GK, N |
| 9. | Richard Cotton | September 1865 | B | M | resisting punishment | Chatham | N |
| 10. | unreported | January 1866 | B | M | race prejudice | Beaufort | N |
| 11. | unreported | February 1866 | B | M | race prejudice | Duplin | N |
| 12. | unreported | February 1866 | B | U | unknown | Lenoir | N |
| 13. | unreported | February 1866 | B | U | unknown | Lenoir | N |
| 14. | unreported | February 1866 | B | U | unknown | Lenoir | N |
| 15. | unreported | February 1866 | B | U | unknown | Lenoir | N |
| 16. | unreported | February 14, 1866 | B | M | race prejudice | Lenoir | N |
| 17. | unreported | 1866 | B | M | race prejudice | Pitt | N |
| 18. | Jesse Hart | October 1866 | W | M | economic competition | Greene | GK, N |
| 19. | Mac Walker | October 23, 1866 | B | M | unknown | New Hanover | GK, N |
| 20. | unreported | January 1867 | B | M | rape | Greene | GK, N |
| 21. | unreported | January 1867 | B | M | rape | Greene | GK, N |
| 22. | unreported | January 1867 | B | M | rape | Greene | GK, N |
| 23. | unreported | January 1867 | B | M | rape | Greene | GK, N |
| 24. | unreported | January 1867 | B | M | rape | Greene | GK, N |

| # | Name | Date | Race | Sex | Reason | County | Source |
|---|---|---|---|---|---|---|---|
| 25. | unreported | January 1867 | W | M | rape | Greene | GK, N |
| 26. | unreported | January 1867 | W | M | rape | Greene | GK, N |
| 27. | Archie Beebe | February 11, 1867 | B | M | attempted rape | Cumberland | GK, N |
| 28. | James Norcum | November 1867 | B | M | land dispute | Washington | GK, N |
| 29. | Blue (child) | January 1869 | B | U | anti-Klan testimony | Moore | GK, N |
| 30. | Blue (child) | January 1869 | B | U | anti-Klan testimony | Moore | GK, N |
| 31. | Blue (child) | January 1869 | B | U | anti-Klan testimony | Moore | GK, N |
| 32. | Blue (child) | January 1869 | B | U | anti-Klan testimony | Moore | GK, N |
| 33. | Blue (wife) | January 1869 | B | F | anti-Klan testimony | Moore | GK, N |
| 34. | Bob Grady | January 24, 1869 | B | M | accused of various crimes | Lenoir | GK |
| 35. | Cater Grady | January 24, 1869 | B | M | accused of various crimes | Lenoir | GK |
| 36. | Richard Nobles | January 24, 1869 | W | M | accused of various crimes | Lenoir | GK |
| 37. | Daniel Smith | January 24, 1869 | B | M | accused of various crimes | Lenoir | GK |
| 38. | Lewis Cogden | March 14, 1869 | B | M | burglary | Greene | GK, N |
| 39. | Daniel Morrow | August 7, 1869 | B | M | murdered by the Klan | Orange | GK |
| 40. | Jefferson Morrow | August 7, 1869 | B | M | murdered by the Klan | Orange | GK |
| 41. | M. L. Shepard | August 16, 1869 | W | M | murdered by the Klan | Jones | GK, N |
| 42. | Cyrus Guy | December 1869 | B | M | arson | Orange | GK, N |
| 43. | Wright Woods | December 1869 | B | M | arson | Orange | GK, N |
| 44. | Wyatt Outlaw | February 26, 1870 | B | M | political influence | Alamance | GK, N |
| 45. | William Puryear | March 1870 | B | M | fallout from Outlaw lynching | Alamance | GK, N |
| 46. | John Stephens | March 21, 1870 | W | M | murdered by the Klan | Caswell | GK |
| 47. | Robin Jacobs | May 13, 1870 | B | M | murdered by the Klan | Caswell | GK |
| 48. | William Steadman | April 26, 1871 | W | U | retaliation for testimony | Rutherford | GK, N |
| 49. | Silas Weston | April 26, 1871 | B | M | retaliation for testimony | Rutherford | GK, N |

(continued)

TABLE 3 Lynchings and possible lynchings in North Carolina, 1865–1946 (continued)

| | Name | Date | Race | Sex | Explanation Offered | County | Source |
|---|---|---|---|---|---|---|---|
| 50. | Theodosia Weston | April 26, 1871 | B | F | retaliation for testimony | Rutherford | GK, N |
| 51. | David Weston | April 26, 1871 | B | M | retaliation for testimony | Rutherford | GK, N |
| 52. | Jule Davidson | December 21, 1878 | B | M | murder and robbery | Iredell | BT |
| 53. | Doyle Bryant | January 21, 1881 | B | M | murder | Sampson | BT |
| 54. | John Taylor | June 12, 1881 | B | M | rape | Rockingham | BT, GK, N |
| 55. | Estes Hairston | June 20, 1881 | B | M | rape | Stokes | BT |
| 56. | John Lindsay | June 20, 1881 | B | M | rape | Stokes | BT |
| 57. | Elijah Church | October 6, 1881 | W | M | murder | Alexander | BT, GK, N |
| 58. | Edmund Davis | October 17, 1881 | B | M | attempted rape | Union | BT, GK, N |
| 59. | John Brodie | December 1, 1881 | B | M | murder | Granville | BT |
| 60. | Shadrack Hester | December 1, 1881 | B | M | murder | Granville | BT |
| 61. | Isaiah Council | April 12, 1883 | B | M | attempted rape | Bertie | BT, GK, N |
| 62. | Archie Johnson | September 20, 1883 | B | M | rape | Richmond | BT, GK |
| 63. | Charles Campbell | October 16, 1883 | B | M | murder | Iredell | BT, GK, N |
| 64. | Lawrence White | November 8, 1883 | B | M | murder | Rowan | BT, GK, N |
| 65. | Erwin McCullough | April 1, 1884 | B | M | murder | Gaston | BT, GK, N |
| 66. | Henry Swain | May 15, 1884 | B | M | murder | Forsyth | BT |
| 67. | George Johnson | September 6, 1884 | B | M | rape | Rowan | BT, GK, N |
| 68. | Thomas Davis | December 24, 1884 | B | M | burglary | Johnston | GK, N |
| 69. | Charles Smith | December 24, 1884 | B | M | burglary | Johnston | BT, GK, N |
| 70. | Lee Staten | March 4, 1885 | B | M | murder, rape | Union | BT, GK, N |
| 71. | John Boggan | July 7, 1885 | B | M | rape | Anson | BT, GK, N |
| 72. | Jerry Finch | September 29, 1885 | B | M | murder | Chatham | BT, GK, N |

| | | | | | | | |
|---|---|---|---|---|---|---|---|
| 73. | Harriet Finch | September 29, 1885 | B | F | wife of accused murderer | Chatham | BT, GK, N |
| 74. | John Pattishall | September 29, 1885 | B | M | murder | Chatham | BT, GK, N |
| 75. | Lee Tyson | September 29, 1885 | B | M | murder | Chatham | BT, GK, N |
| 76. | Bud Mebane | October 3, 1885 | B | M | murder and rape | Caswell | BT, GK, N |
| 77. | John Lee | December 18, 1885 | W | M | murder | Richmond | BT, GK |
| 78. | Alfred Long | June 6, 1886 | B | M | murder | Davidson | BT |
| 79. | T. C. Powell | November 20, 1886 | W | M | murder | Edgecombe | N |
| 80. | Ben Hart | May 8, 1887 | B | M | rape | Edgecombe | BT, GK, N |
| 81. | unknown | August 20, 1887 | B | M | attempted rape | Wilson | BT |
| 82. | Eugene Hairston | August 25, 1887 | B | M | rape | Guilford | BT, GK, N |
| 83. | Jim Greene | December 25, 1887 | B | M | unknown | Richmond | BT |
| 84. | Jack Blount | January 26, 1888 | B | M | murder | Washington | BT, GK, N |
| 85. | Matthew Blount | January 26, 1888 | B | M | murder | Washington | BT, GK, N |
| 86. | Patterson Spruill | January 26, 1888 | B | M | murder | Washington | BT, GK, N |
| 87. | William Parker | March 13, 1888 | W | M | murder | Washington | BT, GK, N |
| 88. | Thomas Frazier | May 5, 1888 | W | M | murder | Beaufort | BT, GK, N |
| 89. | John Humphreys | July 15, 1888 | B | M | rape | Buncombe | BT, GK, N |
| 90. | Alonzo Smith | September 2, 1888 | B | M | arson, burglary | Granville | BT, GK, N |
| 91. | Henry Tanner | September 2, 1888 | B | M | murder | Granville | BT, GK, N |
| 92. | John Tanner | September 2, 1888 | B | M | murder | Granville | BT, GK, N |
| 93. | John Carson | December 2, 1888 | B | M | murder, burglary | Cleveland | BT, GK, N |
| 94. | John Sigmond | September 7, 1889 | B | M | rape | Gaston | BT, GK, N |
| 95. | David Boone | September 11, 1889 | B | M | murder | Burke | BT, GK, N |
| 96. | Franklin Stack | September 11, 1889 | W | M | murder | Burke | BT, GK, N |
| 97. | Robert Berrier | October 14, 1889 | W | M | murder, kidnapping | Davidson | BT, GK, N |

(continued)

TABLE 3 Lynchings and possible lynchings in North Carolina, 1865–1946 (continued)

| | Name | Date | Race | Sex | Explanation Offered | County | Source |
|---|---|---|---|---|---|---|---|
| 98. | John Starling | May 24, 1890 | W | M | murder | Johnston | BT, GK, N |
| 99. | Hezekiah Rankin | September 24, 1890 | B | M | attempted murder | Buncombe | BT, GK, N |
| 100. | Kinch Freeman | December 24, 1890 | B | M | murder | Hertford | BT, GK, N |
| 101. | Mack Best | September 8, 1891 | B | M | rape | Sampson | BT, GK, N |
| 102. | Lyman Purdie | May 1, 1892 | B | M | murder | Bladen | BT, GK, N |
| 103. | Alexander Whitley | June 9, 1892 | W | M | murder | Stanly | BT, GK, N |
| 104. | Thomas Allison | September 12, 1892 | W | M | murder | Surry | BT, GK, N |
| 105. | Joe Barco | October 1, 1892 | B | M | murder | Camden | BT |
| 106. | Carter Burnett | November 14, 1892 | B | M | rape | Granville | BT, GK, N |
| 107. | Duncan McPhatter | November 24, 1892 | B | M | murder | Scotland | BT, GK, N |
| 108. | Bob Ray | January 6, 1893 | B | M | murder/killed by posse | Moore | N |
| 109. | Daniel Slaughter | February 23, 1894 | W | M | murder | Alleghany | BT, GK, N |
| 110. | Holland English | April 2, 1894 | W | M | murder | Mitchell | BT, GK, N |
| 111. | James Bergeron | December 26, 1894 | W | M | murder | Beaufort | BT, GK, N |
| 112. | Robert Chambers | March 21, 1896 | B | M | attempted rape | Mitchell | BT, GK, N |
| 113. | Bob Brackett | August 11, 1897 | B | M | rape | Buncombe | BT |
| 114. | James Lafayette | March 2, 1898 | N | M | accused of spying | Burke | BT |
| 115. | Lafayette (child) | March 2, 1898 | N | F | daughter of above | Burke | BT |
| 116. | Tom Johnson | May 29, 1898 | B | M | murder and rape | Cabarrus | BT, GK, N |
| 117. | Joe Kiser | May 29, 1898 | B | M | murder and rape | Cabarrus | BT, GK, N |
| 118. | Joe Williams | July 23, 1898 | B | M | dispute with white family | Halifax | GK |
| 119. | Manly McCauley | October 28, 1898 | B | M | interracial relationship | Orange | GK |
| 120. | Mitch Mozeley | November 7, 1898 | B | M | rape | Macon | GK |
| 121. | George Maney | January 9, 1899 | W | M | murder | Cherokee | BT, GK, N |

| | | | | | | |
|---|---|---|---|---|---|---|
| 122. | Henry Jones | January 12, 1899 | B | M | murder | Chatham | BT, GK, N |
| 123. | Lewis Patrick | June 15, 1899 | B | M | murder | Carteret | BT, GK, N |
| 124. | George Ratcliffe | March 4, 1900 | B | M | rape | Haywood | BT, GK, N |
| 125. | George Ritter | March 22, 1900 | B | M | retaliation for testimony | Moore | BT, GK, N |
| 126. | Avery Mills | August 28, 1900 | B | M | murder | Rutherford | BT, GK, N |
| 127. | James Martindale | March 8, 1901 | W | M | attempted murder | Moore | BT, GK, N |
| 128. | D. B. Jones | June 18, 1901 | B | M | rape | Lenoir | GK, N |
| 129. | Jim Bailey | July 2, 1901 | B | M | rape | Johnston | BT |
| 130. | Luke Hough | August 21, 1901 | B | M | rape, attempted murder | Anson | BT, GK, N |
| 131. | Peter Mitchell | December 27, 1901 | B | M | rape | Northampton | BT |
| 132. | James Walker | March 25, 1902 | B | M | attempted murder | Martin | BT, GK, N |
| 133. | Harrison Gillespie | June 11, 1902 | B | M | murder | Rowan | BT, GK, N |
| 134. | James Gillespie | June 11, 1902 | B | M | murder | Rowan | BT, GK, N |
| 135. | Thomas Jones | August 25, 1902 | B | M | rape, attempted murder | Wayne | BT, GK, N |
| 136. | John Osborne | July 3, 1903 | B | M | rape | Union | BT, GK, N |
| 137. | Mama Ponton | August 21, 1903 | B | M | murder | Halifax | BT, GK, N |
| 138. | Dick Whitehead | June 18, 1904 | B | M | rape | Northampton | BT, GK, N |
| 139. | John Moore | August 27, 1905 | B | M | rape | Craven | BT, GK, N |
| 140. | J. V. Johnson | May 28, 1906 | W | M | murder | Anson | BT, GK, N |
| 141. | Jack Dillingham | August 6, 1906 | B | M | murder | Rowan | BT, GK, N |
| 142. | John Gillespie | August 6, 1906 | B | M | murder | Rowan | BT, GK, N |
| 143. | Nease Gillespie | August 6, 1906 | B | M | murder | Rowan | BT, GK, N |
| 144. | unreported | January 8, 1908 | B | M | swindling | Johnston | BT, GK, N |
| 145. | unreported | October 10, 1910 | B | M | burglary | Rockingham | BT, GK, N |
| 146. | Joseph McNeely | August 26, 1913 | B | M | murder | Mecklenburg | BT, GK, N |

(continued)

TABLE 3 Lynchings and possible lynchings in North Carolina, 1865–1946 (continued)

| | Name | Date | Race | Sex | Explanation Offered | County | Source |
|---|---|---|---|---|---|---|---|
| 147. | James Wilson | January 7, 1914 | B | M | murder | Johnston | BT, GK, N |
| 148. | Bessie Perry | March 12, 1915 | B | F | unknown | Vance | BT, GK, N |
| 149. | Josephine Perry | March 12, 1915 | B | F | unknown | Vance | BT, GK, N |
| 150. | John Richards | January 12, 1916 | B | M | murder | Wayne | BT, GK, N |
| 151. | Joseph Black | April 5, 1916 | B | M | father of accused rapist | Greene | BT, GK, N |
| 152. | Lazarus Rouse | August 1, 1916 | B | M | insulting white girls | Lenoir | BT, N |
| 153. | Peter Bazemore | March 23, 1918 | B | M | rape | Bertie | BT, GK, N |
| 154. | George Taylor | November 5, 1918 | B | M | rape | Wake | BT, GK, N |
| 155. | John Daniels | February 6, 1919 | B | M | murder | Onslow | BT, GK, N |
| 156. | Walter Tyler | August 20, 1919 | B | M | rape | Franklin | BT, GK, N |
| 157. | Powell Green | December 27, 1919 | B | M | murder | Franklin | BT, GK, N |
| 158. | Edward Roach | July 8, 1920 | B | M | attempted rape | Person | BT, GK, N |
| 159. | John Jeffress | August 20, 1920 | B | M | attempted rape | Alamance | BT |
| 160. | Plummer Bullock | January 24, 1921 | B | M | part of sprawling racial conflict | Warren | BT, GK, N |
| 161. | Alfred Williams | January 24, 1921 | B | M | part of sprawling racial conflict | Warren | BT, GK, N |
| 162. | Jerome Whitfield | August 14, 1921 | B | M | rape | Jones | BT, GK, N |
| 163. | Eugene Daniel | September 18, 1921 | B | M | trespassing | Chatham | BT, GK, N |
| 164. | Baynor Blackwell | August 6, 1922 | B | M | murder | Onslow | GK, N |
| 165. | Doc Bryant | May 25, 1926 | B | M | economic competition | Duplin | GK, N |
| 166. | Eliza Bryant | May 25, 1926 | B | F | economic competition | Duplin | GK, N |
| 167. | Broadus Miller | July 3, 1927 | B | M | murder | Burke | GK, N |
| 168. | Tom Bradshaw | August 2, 1927 | B | M | rape | Nash | GK, N |
| 169. | Willie McDaniel | June 29, 1929 | B | M | labor conflict | Mecklenburg | BT, GK, N |

| | Name | Date | | | Reason | County | Sources |
|---|---|---|---|---|---|---|---|
| 170. | Ella Mae Wiggins | September 14, 1929 | W | F | strike leader | Gaston | BT, GK, N |
| 171. | Laura Wood | February 11, 1930 | B | F | unknown | Cleveland | GK |
| 172. | Oliver Moore | August 20, 1930 | B | M | rape | Edgecombe | BT, GK, N |
| 173. | Percy Berry | April 19, 1932 | B | M | resisting white harassment | Craven | BT |
| 174. | Doc Rogers | August 27, 1933 | B | M | rape | Pender | BT, GK, N |
| 175. | Govan Ward | August 23, 1935 | B | M | murder | Franklin | BT, GK, N |
| 176. | Robert Melker | April 13, 1941 | B | M | resisting white harassment | Gaston | BT, G K, N |
| 177. | J. C. Farmer | Aug. 3, 1946 | B | M | altercation with police officer | Wilson | BT |

Credit: Created by the author.

# Notes

## Abbreviations Used in Notes

### Archives

NCC    North Carolina Collection, University of North Carolina, Chapel Hill, NC

NCSA    North Carolina Division of Archives and History, Raleigh, NC

PBL    Perkins and Bostock Library, Duke University, Durham, NC

SHC    Southern Historical Collection, University of North Carolina, Chapel Hill, NC

### Publications

Attorney General Report
    Report of the Attorney General of the State of North Carolina

Prison Report
    Biennial Report of the State's Prison

Public Laws [Date]
    Public Laws of the State of North Carolina Passed at the Session of [Date]

### Databases

Espy File
    M. Watt Espy, and John Ortiz Smykla. Executions in the United States, 1608–2002: The ESPY File. ICPSR08451-v5. Ann Arbor, MI: Inter-university Consortium for Political and Social Research [distributor].

Ancestry.com
    Provo, UT, USA: Ancestry.com Operations Inc., 2007.

### Organization

SBCPW    State Board of Charities and Public Welfare

## Introduction

1. "A Lesson of Surpassing Beauty," *News and Observer* (Raleigh, NC), November 12, 1922, Editorial Section, 8.

2. "Gray and Khaki on Parade Again," *News and Observer* (Raleigh, NC), November 12, 1922, 13.

3. S. A. Ashe, "Morris Schaff's Life of Jefferson Davis," and "Thomas Nelson Page's Chief Contribution," *News and Observer* (Raleigh, NC), November 12, 1922, 19 and Editorial Section, 13.

4. Capt. J. J. Laughinghouse, "Pitt County's Ku Klux Klan of Reconstruction Days," *News and Observer* (Raleigh, NC), November 12, 1922, Editorial Section, 1.

5. Laughinghouse, "Pitt County's Ku Klux Klan."

6. Carded Records Showing Military Service of Soldiers Who Fought in Confederate Organizations, 1903–1927. Record Group 109: War Department Collection of Confederate Records, 1825–1927. National Archives Identifier: 5886957; Henry T. King, Sketches of Pitt County: A Brief History of the County, 1704–1910 (Raleigh, NC: Edwards, 1911), 260.

7. Leonard Lanier, "Killing the Klansman, Remembering the General: The Opposing Memories of Bryan Grimes," unpublished paper given as part of the Filson Historical Society's Hard Hand of War Symposium, October 23–25, 2014, accessed June 13, 2018, http://filsonhistorical.org/wp-content/uploads/Lanier-Leonard-Killing-the-Klansman-Remembering-the-General-The-Opposing-Memories-of-Bryan-Grimes.pdf.

8. "Pitt County's Ku Klux Klan."

9. Myers, *Rebels against the Confederacy*, 184.

10. "General Bryan Grimes," *Observer* (Raleigh, NC), August 19, 1880, 2.

11. J. J. Laughinghouse, "Why Lynchings Continue," *News and Observer* (Raleigh, NC), June 29, 1902, 4.

12. "The Grimes Murder," *Goldsboro Messenger*, December 16, 1880, 3.

13. "Trial of William Parker for the Murder of General Grimes," *Evening Visitor* (Raleigh, NC), June 20, 1881, 2; Ashe, Weeks, and Van Noppen, *Biographical History of North Carolina*, 261.

14. "Not Guilty," *News and Observer* (Raleigh, NC), June 24, 1881, 2.

15. Laughinghouse, "Why Lynchings Continue," 4.

16. "Why Lynchings Continue," 4.

17. "Judge Lynch," *Fisherman and Farmer* (Edenton, NC), March 16, 1888, 4.

18. Campbell, "The Lynching of William Parker," 99–109.

19. "Lynching in Washington," *Southern Progress* (Washington, NC), March 13, 1888, 5.

20. Connor, *A Manual of North Carolina*, 339.

21. See, for instance, "Agricultural Work for Convicts," in American Prison Association Congress, *Proceedings of the Annual Congress of the American Prison Association, August 14–19* (Indianapolis: Wm. B. Burford, 1909), 48–49; Joseph Hyde Pratt, comp., *Proceedings of the Annual Convention of the North Carolina Good Roads Association, Held at Charlotte, NC, August 1 and 2, 1912* (Raleigh: Edwards and Broughton, 1912), 29–31.

22. Leonard Lanier, "The WWI Draft Bred Anti-War Feelings, Discontent," *Daily Advance* (Elizabeth City, NC), May 14, 2017. Published online at http://www.dailyadvance.com/Lifestyles-Columnists/2017/05/14/The-Draft-and-Its-Discontents.html.

23. Saunders, *Colonial Records of North Carolina*, 639.

24. Saunders, *Colonial Records of North Carolina*, 640.

25. Espy File, accessed December 28, 2017, https://doi.org/10.3886/ICPSR08451 .v5. For information on this resource, see the note on methods later in this introduction.

26. *Furman v. Georgia*, 408 U.S. 238 (1972); *Gregg v. Georgia*, 428 U.S. 153 (1976); *Callins v. Collins*, 510 U.S. 1141 (1994). The idea of evolving standards of decency was introduced in *Weems v. United States*, 217 U.S. 349 (1910) and so named in *Trop v. Dulles*, 356 U.S. 86 (1958). For more, see Matusiak, Vaughan, and del Carmen, "Progression," 253–71.

27. "The Death Penalty," *Wilmington Journal*, May 8, 1868, 2.

28. Untitled article, *Rutherford Star* (Rutherfordton, NC), June 9, 1868, 2.

29. Ed Book and Evie Staunton, "Last Hanging," *Gastonia Gazette*, July 26, 1972, B1.

30. "Fell into Eternity," *Durham Daily Globe*, February 8, 1894, 1.

31. Salmond, *Gastonia 1929*, 105–37.

32. Arnold, *Symbols of Government*.

33. Bohm, *DeathQuest*, 14.

34. Coates, "Punishment for Crime in North Carolina," 205; Spindel, *Crime and Society in North Carolina*, 45.

35. Banner, *Death Penalty*, 8–9; Spindel, *Crime and Society in North Carolina*, 134. The Espy File confirms only fifty-eight slave executions out of a total of ninety-two executions between 1726 and 1775. But the database available online is incomplete. See the end of this introduction and appendixes.

36. Kay and Cary, *Slavery*, 49–52.

37. Flanigan, "Criminal Procedure in Slave Trials," 538–39.

38. Kay and Cary, *Slavery*, 71.

39. *State v. Keath*, 83 N.C. 626, 627 (1880).

40. Radelet, "Execution of Whites for Crimes against Blacks," 539.

41. Johnson, *Ante-bellum North Carolina*, 498. Available via Documenting the American South, accessed June 23, 2018, https://docsouth.unc.edu/nc/johnson /johnson.html.

42. Friedman, *Crime and Punishment in American History*, 43. Psalm 51, the traditional text, came to be known as the neck verse; *An Act Concerning Slaves and Free Persons of Color*, North Carolina Revised Code of 1805, c. 6 s. 2 (1830), accessed on June 27, 2018, http://docsouth.unc.edu/nc/slavesfree/slavesfree.html.

43. For more on slavery, the courts, and North Carolina, see Greene, "*State v. Mann* Exhumed," 701–56.

44. Kay and Cary, *Slavery*, 88.

45. Kay and Cary, *Slavery*, 87–89; Fischer, *Suspect Relations*, 180–86; Kay and Cary, "'The Planters Suffer Little or Nothing'," 306.

46. Banner, *Death Penalty*, 6–7.

47. de Tocqueville, *Democracy in America*, 42.

48. Banner, *Death Penalty*, 98–99.

49. Johnson, *Ante-bellum North Carolina*, 646.

50. Espy File.

51. Quoted in Johnson, *Ante-bellum North Carolina*, 645. The quotation comes from Thomas Belsham's "The Importance of Truth and the Duty of Making an Open Profession of It," (1790).

52. Banner, *Death Penalty*, 134.

53. Davis, "Movement to Abolish Capital Punishment in America," 23–46; Banner, *Death Penalty*, 131.

54. *Hillsboro Recorder*, March 21, 1844. Quoted in Johnson, *Ante-bellum North Carolina*, 652.

55. Espy File.

56. Johnson, *Ante-bellum North Carolina*, 650.

57. Johnson, *Ante-bellum North Carolina*, 651.

58. There are some seminal works on the development of penal systems in North and South. On the roots of the prison in the Northeast, see Rothman, *Discovery of the Asylum*. On contrasting developments in the North and South, see Hindus, *Prison and Plantation*. And on the influences on the development of southern criminal justice systems, see Ayers, *Vengeance and Justice*.

59. Prison Report (1930–1932), 7, NCC; Zimmerman, "Penal Systems and Penal Reforms," 30.

60. *Greensboro Patriot*, February 21, 1846, as quoted and discussed in Ayers, *Vengeance and Justice*, 48–49.

61. Ols, "A History of the State's Prison," 6.

62. Prison Report (1930–1932), 7, NCC.

63. Ols, "History," 4–7; Zimmerman, "Penal Reforms," 81–83; Craven, "North Carolina's Prison System," 14–42.

64. The Constitution of the State of North Carolina, Article XI: Punishments, Penal Institutions, and Public Charities (Section 1, Punishments), accessed December 28, 2017, http://quod.lib.umich.edu/cgi/t/text/text-idx?c=moa;cc=moa;rgn=main;view=text;idno=AEY0617.0001.001; "Report of the Committee on Punishments, Penal Institutions, and Public Charities," *Journal of the Constitutional Convention of the State of North Carolina at Its Session 1868*, 292–93, accessed December 28, 2017, http://docsouth.unc.edu/nc/conv1868/conv1868.html.

65. SBCPW Report (Raleigh: The Board, 1911), 10, NCC.

66. SBCPW Report (1914), 7.

67. Penitentiary Commission, "Rules and By-Laws for the Government and Discipline of the North Carolina Penitentiary During Its Management by the Commission" (Raleigh: M. S. Littlefield, 1869), 17. Documenting the American South, UNC-CH, accessed on June 27, 2018, http://docsouth.unc.edu/nc/penitent/menu.html.

68. The inmates broadcast on WPTF, or "We Protect the Family," so named by the Durham Life Insurance Company that owned the Raleigh-based station.

69. SBCPW Report, 1911, 23.

70. For a look at the brutality of northeastern prisons, see Thompson, "Blinded by a 'Barbaric' South," 74–98.

71. *Citizens' Commission on Alternatives to Incarceration* (Raleigh, NC: The Commission, 1982), 35.

72. "Amputate Convicts' Feet; Rotted in Torture Cell," *News and Observer* (Raleigh, NC), March 7, 1935, 1.

73. "A Study of Prison Conditions in North Carolina," *Bulletin of the North Carolina State Board of Charities and Public Welfare* 6 (January–March 1923), 7–14, NCC.

74. SBCPW Report, 1912, 21.

75. Watson, "County Fiscal Policy," 286.

76. SBCPW Report, 1914, 1.

77. Prison Report (1903–1904), 9.

78. "Biennial Message of W. W. Kitchin to the General Assembly," *Public Documents of the State of North Carolina Session 1913* (Raleigh: Edwards and Broughton, 1915), 5.

79. Prison Report (1907–1908), 12; "Study of Prison Conditions," 8.

80. Prison Report (1907–1908), 12.

81. Prison Report (1927–1928), 32; Table 1: Movement of Prisoners; Report of the Director of Prisons, Biennial Report of the State Highway and Public Works Commission for 1938–1939 and 1939–1940, 393.

82. Prison Report (1924–1925), 7.

83. "Osborne Association Survey Reports on North Carolina Prison System" (March 14, 1950), W. Kerr Scott Papers, Box 68. North Carolina State Archives, Raleigh, NC.

84. Prison Report (1929–1930), 20.

85. Nell Battle Lewis, "Incidentally," *News and Observer* (Raleigh, NC), February 3, 1935, M3.

86. *Gregg v. Georgia*, 428 U.S. 153 (1976).

87. Public Policy Polling, Miami-Dade County, FL Survey Results, January 22–23, 2018, accessed March 9, 2018, https://www.scribd.com/document/372710919/Miami-PPP-Poll-on-the-Death-Penalty-2018.

88. Liam Stack, "Execution of Inmate Is Stopped," *New York Times*, November 15, 2017.

89. Blackman and McLaughlin, "The Espy File on American Executions," 209–27.

90. Snyder, "Criminal Law," 98–104.

## Chapter 1

1. Cutler, "Capital Punishment and Lynching," 183.

2. Tolnay and Beck, *Festival of Violence*; Vandiver, *Lethal Punishment*, 14–17. Amy Louise Wood also argues for "no consistent correlation." Wood, *Lynching and Spectacle*, 26.

3. Other studies of the relationship include Charles David Phillips, "Exploring Relations among Forms of Social Control," 361–74; Beck, Massey, and Tolnay, "The Gallows, the Mob, and the Vote," 317–31; Patrick Huber, "Caught Up in the Violent Whirlwind of Lynching," 135–60.

4. Cutler, "Capital Punishment and Lynching," 185.

5. Cox, *Caste, Class, and Race*, 571.

6. Waldrep, *The Many Faces of Judge Lynch*, 2.

7. Goldsby, *A Spectacular Secret*, 11.

8. Williams, *They Left Great Marks on Me*.

9. Garland, "Modes of Capital Punishment," 30.

10. The phrase "monopoly of force" is taken from Elias, *The Civilizing Process*.

11. See, for instance, Holloway, *Living in Infamy*.

12. For a broad look at the role of southern politicians in the federal anti-lynching drama, see Rable, "The South and the Politics of Anti-Lynching Legislation," 201–20.

13. The story of Johnson's life and death is told in rich detail in Bruce E. Baker, *The Mob Will Surely Take My Life*.

14. "An Act to Protect Prisoners Confined in Jail under the Charge of Crime until They Can Be Fairly Tried by a Jury of Good and Lawful Men in Open Court," *Public Laws and Resolutions of the General Assembly of the State of North Carolina, 1893*, Ch. 461, Sec. 1.

15. "Governor Aids in Investigation," *Charlotte News*, May 30, 1906, 1; "Lynchers Present Their Testimony," *Harrisburg Daily Independent* (Harrisburg, PA), July 17, 1907, 1.

16. "Lynch Law Arraigned," *Lincoln County News*, July 23, 1907, 1.

17. "Lynch Law Arraigned"; "John Jones Not Guilty," *Charlotte Observer*, July 20, 1907, 1.

18. "John Jones Not Guilty."

19. "Sheriff Warned to Seal His Lips," *News and Observer* (Raleigh, NC), July 26, 1907, 2.

20. "15 Years for Lyncher"; Baker, *Mob*, 118–19.

21. "15 Years for Lyncher," *Washington Post*, August 11, 1906, 4.

22. Baker, *Mob*, 112–17; "The Two Conspiracies," *North Carolinian* (Raleigh, NC), August 8, 1907, 5.

23. Baker, *Mob*, 117–18.

24. "Poor Old George Hall," *Union Republican* (Winston-Salem, NC), July 15, 1909, 8.

25. "The Lone Rowan Lyncher Caught," *Davie Record* (Mocksville, NC), July 27, 1909, 1; "George Hall Pardoned," *Concord Daily Tribune*, December 22, 1911, 1.

26. *State v. Columbus Adair*, 66 N.C. 298 (1872); "Execution of Two Murderers at Hendersonville, NC," *Charlotte Democrat*, July 30, 1872, 1.

27. See appendix C for more on sourcing and standards.

28. James A. Shepard to Governor T. W. Bickett, July 4, 1917, in Sanford Martin, ed., *Public Letters and Papers of Thomas Walter Bickett, Governor of North Carolina, 1917–1921* (Raleigh: Edwards and Broughton, 1923), 330.

29. John Dollard, *Caste and Class in a Southern Town*, 316.

30. Phillips, "Relations Among Forms of Social Control," 363.

31. Goldsby, *Spectacular Secret*, 8.

32. Rushdy, *The End of American Lynching*, 59.

33. These data were first published in Seth Kotch and Robert P. Mosteller, "Racial Justice Act," 2031–131.

34. Kotch and Mosteller, "Racial Justice Act," 2109, 2114.

35. Radelet, "Execution of Whites for Crimes against Blacks," 539; "Hanging in Rutherford," *News and Observer*, December 19, 1880, 2.

36. The term "brutal logic" is borrowed from Brundage, *Lynching in the New South*, 49.

37. Wells-Barnett, *Southern Horrors* (1892); *A Red Record* (1895); *Mob Rule in New Orleans* (1900). Wells-Barnett published *Southern Horrors* as Ida B. Wells but is referred to as Wells-Barnett here to recognize the name she later took and to avoid confusion.

38. White, *Rope and Faggot*.

39. Howard Washington Odum Papers, 1908–1982, Series 3: Organizational Material, circa 1920–1954, Folders 748–755, SHC.

40. Southern Commission on the Study of Lynching, "Lynchings and What They Mean: General Findings of the Southern Commission on the Study of Lynching" (Atlanta: The Commission, 1931).

41. Raper, *Tragedy of Lynching*, 1.

42. Raper, *Tragedy of Lynching*, 2.

43. Gist, "Negro in the Daily Press," 406.

44. Gist, "Negro in the Daily Press," 411.

45. S. C. Baker, "Negro Criminality," 27. Failing to capitalize the word "Negro" was an effort to denigrate African Americans and became a point of contention for some early twentieth-century activists, such as Lester A. Walton. See, for instance, Mencken, "Designations for Colored Folk," 161–74; Allen, "Sly Slurs: Mispronunciation and Decapitalization of Group Names," 217–24; Susan Curtis, *Colored Memories*. Capitalization or lack thereof has been retained in this book to place the cited work in this history.

46. Shay, *Judge Lynch*.

47. Brundage, "Conclusion: Reflections on Lynching Scholarship," 401–3.

48. Sarat, *From Lynch Mobs to the Killing State*; Messner, Baumer, and Rosenfeld, "Distrust of Government," 559–90; Garland, "Capital Punishment and American Culture," 347–76; Garland, "Death, Denial, Discourse," 136; Steiker and Steiker, "The American Death Penalty," 243–94; Jacobs, Carmichael, and Kent, "Vigilantism, Current Racial Threat, and Death Sentences," 656–77; Wright, "By the Books," 250–70.

49. Phillips, "Relations among Forms of Social Control"; Beck, Massey, and Tolnay, "Gallows."

50. Tolnay and Beck, *Festival of Violence*, 111.

51. Published in Mark Twain, *Europe and Elsewhere*.

52. Clarke, "Without Fear or Shame," 276.

53. Wright, "Between the World and Me," 18–19.

54. Data are available free with registration at http://lynching.csde.washington .edu/#/home. They were published in conjunction with Bailey and Tolnay, *Lynched*. This recent data refinement is described in Cook, "Converging to a National Lynching Database," 45–63; Newkirk, *Lynching in North Carolina*.

55. Trotti, "What Counts," 392.

56. Data are available at http://lynching.csde.washington.edu/#/home.

57. Trotti, "What Counts," 375–400.

58. Elaine Scarry, *The Body in Pain*, 60.

59. Claude A. Clegg III, *Troubled Ground*, xvi.

60. "Attacker Tells of Murdering Georgia Women," *Statesville Record and Landmark*, February 8, 1957, 1.

61. See lynchings in North Carolina mapped at redrecord.net.

62. Data gathered by and in the hands of the author. Available upon request.

63. Attorney General Report, 1893–1894 (Raleigh, NC: Josephus Daniels, 1895), 4. Quoted as written.

64. "Nash Negro Who Assaulted Girl Dies of Wounds," *News and Observer*, August 3, 1927, 1.

65. Ben Dixon MacNeill, "Wounds, Fatigue Cause of Death," *News and Observer*, August 6, 1927, 1.

66. Data drawn from Kotch and Mosteller, "Racial Justice Act."

67. "Negro Goes on Trial Today for Attacking White Woman of City," *Asheville Citizen*, November 2, 1925, 1; "Asheville Mob Enters Jail in Quest of Negro Prisoner," *News and Observer*, September 20, 1925, 1.

68. "Negro Leaders Advise Race of Present Duties," *Asheville Citizen*, November 2, 1925, 1.

69. "Preston Neely to Go on Trial Today," *Asheville Citizen*, November 6, 1925, 1.

70. Brief for the Defendant, *State v. Mansel*, 192 N.C. 20 (1925), 7.

71. "Supreme Court Decides Alvin Mansel Must Die," *Asheville Citizen*, May 28, 1926, 1.

72. Application for the Pardon of Alvin Mansel, in *Public Papers and Letters of Angus Wilton McLean, Governor or North Carolina, 1925–1929*, ed., David Leroy Corbitt (Raleigh: Edwards and Broughton, 1931), 756.

73. Bedau and Radelet, "Miscarriages of Justice," 145–46.

74. Alvin Mansel in the U.S. Social Security Death Index, Number: *247-12-8508*; Issue State: *South Carolina*; Issue Date: *Before 1951*. Ancestry.com.

75. Judge Grady, "Pistol in Hand, Foils Attempt to Lynch Negro Murderer," *News and Observer*, December 12, 1927, 1.

76. "Governor Lauds Action of Grady in Foiling Mob," *News and Observer*, December 13, 1927, 1.

77. *North Carolina, Death Certificates, 1909–1976*. Ancestry.com; Bertha Dobson in *North Carolina, Marriage Index, 1741–2004*. Ancestry.com.

78. See, for example, the following advertisements of the capture of an escaped slave: "Runaway," *Wilmington Gazette*, August 25, 1812, 3; "Twenty-Five Dolls [*sic*] Reward," *Newbern Sentinel*, June 17, 1836, 4.

79. "Guards Keep Order at Negro's Trial," *Greenville News*, April 23, 1930, 7.

80. "Death Sentence Is Given Negro," *Asheville Citizen-Times*, April 26, 1930, 8.

81. "Brief for the Appellant, Defendant," *State v. Harvey Lawrence* (No. 90), Fall Term, 1930, 2.

82. "Supreme Court Denies New Trial for Negro," *Burlington Daily News*, September 24, 1930, 1.

83. Jacquelyn Dowd Hall observed that the amount of discretion given to local law officers amounted to vigilantism. Hall, *Revolt Against Chivalry*, 140–41.

84. Woodrow Price, "Negro Facing Life Term Confesses Role in Crime," *News and Observer*, June 28, 1947, 1.

85. Editorial without headline, *Sampson Democrat* (Clinton, NC), 2.

86. Data culled from the so-called Espy File and amended are with the author and available upon request. M. Watt Espy and John Ortiz Smykla, Executions in the United States, 1608–2002: The Espy File. ICPSR08451-v5 (Ann Arbor, MI: Interuniversity Consortium for Political and Social Research [distributor]), July 20, 2016, accessed November 1, 2017, https://doi.org/10.3886/ICPSR08451.v5. The Espy File is not without errors, but for a single-state focus in which Espy data are supplemented by additional primary source research, errors such as misspelled names or imprecise notation of executed persons' convictions have little if any effect on its utility. See appendixes for an amended list of executions in North Carolina. For a rundown of concerns about Espy's accuracy, see note in appendix A and Blackman and McLaughlin, "The Espy File on American Executions," 209–27.

87. *Constitution of North Carolina of 1868*, accessed April 9, 2017, http://www .ncleg.net/library/Documents/Constitution_1868.pdf.

88. "Uphold the Law," *Union Republican* (Winston-Salem, NC), August 9, 1906, 2.

89. As described in *State v. McDaniel*, 60 N.C. 245 (1864).

90. Reasons for Pardons, Commutations, and Reprieves, 1912–1917, Locke Craig Papers, G.O. 55, 371, NCSA.

91. Savitz, "Capital Crimes," 359.

92. Rex Gore, "Facing Controversy: Struggling with Capital Punishment in North Carolina," a panel sponsored by the Southern Historical Collection and Wilson Library Special Collections, February 5, 2008.

93. James S. Manning, Attorney General Report (1923–1924), 316–18, NCC.

94. James Whitfield, "Five Die in Gas Chamber to Set Record at Prison," *News and Observer*, October 4, 1947, 4.

95. "Pays Penalty for Burglary Crime," *News and Observer*, July 8, 1916, 8.

96. "Lee Perkins Pays Death Penalty" *News and Observer*, October 11, 1917, 3.

97. *Coker v. State of Georgia*, 433 U.S. 584 (1977).

98. North Carolina Council on Human Relations, "Rape: Selective Execution Based on Race," 1, NCC.

99. Brundage, *Lynching in the New South*, 58–60.

100. "Ed. Dill Groans Between Shocks," *News and Observer*, June 29, 1929, 5.

101. "Toward Straight Thinking," Editorial, *Raleigh Carolinian*, January 4, 1947, 4.

102. "The Gallows," *Weekly Star* (Wilmington, NC), January 17, 1890, 1.

103. "All Over the State," *Goldsboro Headlight*, February 7, 1901, 1.

104. State Board of Charities and Public Welfare, "Capital Punishment in North Carolina" (Raleigh: North Carolina State Board of Charities and Public Welfare, 1929), 21, NCC.

105. "Wayne Man Dies for Rape Charge," *News and Observer*, May 25, 1946, 1.

106. "Negro Going to Death for Attack upon Negress," *News and Observer*, July 30, 1937, 18.

107. "Negro Going to Death for Attack upon Negress."

108. Dollard, *Caste and Class*, 145.

109. "Attackers of Negro Women and the Law," Editorial, *Carolina Times* (Durham, NC), April 15, 1938, 4.

110. "Churchill Godley Must Die Friday," *News and Observer*, January 13, 1920, 16.

111. "Churchill Godley Must Die Friday."

112. "Godley Resentful Against Everyone," *News and Observer*, January 20, 1920, 9.

113. Public Laws (1949), G.S. 1470, Sec. 1, Ch. 299, NCC.

114. Charles Craven, "State Finally Claims Life of Guilford County Rapist," *News and Observer*, July 22, 1950, 1.

115. "Orange County Sheriff Refuses to Release or Indict Man for Rape," *Carolina Times* (Durham, NC), January 31, 1938, 1.

116. "A White Woman's Word," Editorial, *Carolina Times* (Durham, NC), December 10, 1938, 4.

117. Clegg, *Troubled Ground*, 186.

118. "Lynched," *News and Observer*, May 10, 1887, 1.

119. Pfeifer, *Rough Justice*, 67.

120. Garland, *A Peculiar Institution*, 31.

121. "John Lee Lynched," *Rocket* (Rockingham, NC), December 24, 1885, 2.

122. "The Tarboro Lynching," *Greensboro North State*, October 8, 1885, 1.

123. "Tarboro Lynching," 1.

124. *State v. Exum*, 213 N.C. 16 (1938).

125. Wood, *Lynching and Spectacle*.

126. Clegg, *Troubled Ground*, 164.

127. "Nash Negro Who Assaulted Girl Dies of Wounds," *News and Observer*, August 3, 1927, 1.

128. Ben Dixon MacNeill, "Wounds, Fatigue Cause of Death," *News and Observer*, August 6, 1927, 1.

129. "Legal Lynchings," Editorial, *Carolina Times* (Durham, NC), March 12, 1938, 4.

130. "His Life Forfeit for a Foul Crime," *News and Observer*, October 28, 1911, 5.

131. "George Hall Pardoned," *Concord Daily Tribune*, December 22, 1911, 1.

132. Newkirk, *Lynching in North Carolina*, 80.

133. "Pastor Reveals Lynch Threat," *Amsterdam News*, June 8, 1946, 15.

134. Callahan, "The North Carolina Slave Patrol," 16.

135. "Hangings in North Carolina," *Sun* (Rutherfordton, NC), January 6, 1894, 6.

136. "Negro Thought Girl Would Not Tell," *Hickory Daily Record*, May 1, 1919, 1.

137. "Gwin [sic] Is Sentenced to Die on June 27," *Hickory Daily Record*, May 26, 1919, 1; "Large Crowd at Newton for Trial," *Hickory Daily Record*, May 26, 1919, 1.

138. Data are in the hands of the author and available upon request.

139. Public Laws (1865–1855), Ch. 40, Sec. 15, NCC.

140. Dick Barkley, "Hanging Tree Still Draws Visitors," *Daily Times-News* (Burlington, NC), November 26, 1959, 12; George Pennell, "Traipsin' in Historic West Asheville," *Asheville Citizen-Times*, October 27, 1960, 21.

141. Hill, *Beyond the Rope*, 104–5.

142. Corbitt, *Public Addresses*, 45–46.

143. Corbitt, *Public Addresses*, 1075.

144. See, for instance, Campney, *This Is Not Dixie*; Carrigan and Webb, *Forgotten Dead*; Pfeifer, *Lynching beyond Dixie*; and Ken Gonzales-Day, *Lynching in the West*.

145. Garland, *Peculiar Institution*, 33.

146. "Punish or Prevent," Editorial, reprinted in *News and Observer*, December 18, 1936, 4.

147. Rushdy, *American Lynching*, 64.

148. Garland, *Peculiar Institution*, 34.

## Chapter 2

1. "Out of Date Practice," *Morning Post* (Raleigh, NC), June 8, 1898, 2.

2. As quoted in Hartnett, *Executing Democracy*, 156.

3. Hartnett, *Executing Democracy*, 158–59.

4. For instance, the chief justice of the Supreme Court of North Carolina complained in 1914 of the "slow and cumbersome" pace of the death penalty process. *State v. Jim Cameron*, 166 N.C. 379 (1914).

5. Hale, *Making Whiteness*, 203.

6. "In the Line of Progress," *Morning Post* (Raleigh, NC), November 8, 1904, 1.

7. O'Brien, *The Idea of the American South*, 16, 41.

8. Quoted in Tindall, *The Emergence of the New South*, 227.

9. Tindall, *Emergence of the New South*, 224; O'Brien, *Idea of the American South*, 17.

10. *Goldsboro Messenger*, May 19, 1879, 3.

11. Homer Keever, "Witness Describes Dula Hanging," *Statesville Record and Landmark*, January 15, 1959 (orig. May 1, 1868), 3. For a sampling of newspaper reportage excoriating "morbid" crowds at hangings, see "Our State Contemporaries," *Wilmington Morning Star*, August 18, 1885, 3; "Awful Relic of Barbarism," *Semi-Weekly Messenger* (Wilmington, NC), April 18, 1905, 5; "Parrish Hang [*sic*]," *Wilmington Messenger*, January 11, 1890, 1; "Morbid Sentiment," *Wilson Mirror*, June 21, 1893, 2.

12. "Governor Asks for Indictment," *Asheville Citizen-Times*, February 21, 1902, 1.

13. "Trying to Learn," *Daily Review* (Wilmington, NC), July 9, 1879. See also "A Double Execution," *Western Sentinel* (Winston-Salem, NC), August 1, 1885, 1.

14. "Two Men Died by the Law's Strong Hand," *News and Observer*, July 9, 1902, 1.

15. "Dr. Hubert Royster Speaks of the Medical College," *Morning Post* (Raleigh, NC), March 2, 1902, 1.

16. "The Wages of Sin Death by the Rope," *News and Observer*, November 17, 1901, 1.

17. "Two Brothers Hanged," *News-Observer-Chronicle* (Raleigh, NC), July 14, 1894, 1.

18. "To Hang George Washington," *News and Observer*, November 14, 1895, 5.

19. "Our Gallows Is to Go to Salisbury," *Asheville Register*, June 7, 1902, 3.

20. "The Rope Broke and Louis Council Fell," *News and Observer*, November 2, 1901, 1.

21. "Partridge Paid the Death Penalty," *Greensboro Patriot*, April 12, 1905, 6.

22. "An Act to Proscribe the Mode of Capital Punishment in North Carolina," *Public Laws of the State of North Carolina Passed at Its Session of 1909* (Raleigh: E. M. Uzzell, 1909), Ch. 443, 758–61.

23. Between five thousand and seven thousand attended a hanging in Pitt County in 1899. John G. Duncan, "Dongola Murder Led to Last Public Hanging in Pitt County," *News and Observer*, June 11, 1967. Clipping File through 1975 (Capital Punishment), 207–9, NCC. For other evidence of public executions in the late 1890s, see Trina N. Seitz, "The Killing Chair: North Carolina's Experiment in Civility and the Execution of Allen Foster," *North Carolina Historical Review* 81, no. 1 (January 2004): 39–40; Bill East, "Man Recalls Hanging," *Winston-Salem Journal*, April 20, 1975. Clipping File through 1975 (Capital Punishment), 196, NCC.

24. "Nothing to Say on the Scaffold," *News and Observer*, December 21, 1906, 5.

25. R. L. Gray, "Durham Agog over First Hangings," *News and Observer*, February 8, 1907, 1.

26. "Two Hanged on Same Gallows," *News and Observer*, February 9, 1907, 1.

27. *Biennial Report of the Attorney General of the State of North Carolina* (1907–1908), 11, NCC.

28. Linders, "Execution Spectacle," 614–21. One instance of a majority-black execution crowd: "Two Suffer the Death Penalty," *News and Observer*, August 21, 1907, 1.

29. "Died on Gallows," *News and Observer*, September 1, 1906, 1.

30. Sims, *The Power of Femininity in the New South*, 107–8; Higginbotham, "African-American Women's History," 262–64.

31. Feimster, *Southern Horrors*, 40–41; Bardaglio, *Reconstructing the Household*, 66–68.

32. Feimster, *Southern Horrors*, 115.

33. Feimster, *Southern Horrors*, 115; Higginbotham, *Righteous Discontent*, 96–97, 184–94.

34. Gilmore, *Gender and Jim Crow*, 75–76; Sims, *Power of Femininity*, 83.

35. Hale, *Making Whiteness*, 32–33; Bay, "From the 'Ladies Car'," 150–75.

36. Kelley, "'We Are Not What We Seem'," 75–112.

37. Gilmore, *Gender and Jim Crow*, 44–45; Jones, *Labor of Love, Labor of Sorrow*, 112.

38. "Mills Hanged," *Henderson Gold Leaf*, May 3, 1895, 1.

39. "Evils of Public Executions," *Henderson Gold Leaf*, September 9, 1897, 2.

40. *Wilmington Messenger*, September 4, 1897, 2.

41. Jones, *Labor of Love*, 149–50.

42. Brown, "Negotiating and Transforming the Public Sphere, 76.

43. Haley, "'Like I Was a Man,'" 73; "Col. Carr on the Race Problem," *Farmer and Mechanic* (Raleigh, NC), May 30, 1889, 6; "Attackers of Negro Women and the Law," *Carolina Times* (Durham, NC), April 15, 1938, 4. Despite the fact that a rape conviction carried a mandatory capital sentence, no white man was ever executed for committing this crime against a black woman. Kotch and Mosteller, "The Racial Justice Act," 2109.

44. The idea that lynching protected white women was behind Jessie Daniel Ames's crusade against it. Hall, *Revolt against Chivalry*.

45. Brandon, *The Electric Chair*, 10–20, 51–63; Reynolds and Bernstein, "Edison and 'the Chair,'" 12–20.

46. Kearns, "The Chair, the Needle, and the Damage Done," 202. Quoting Brandon, who is quoting *People ex rel. Kemmler v. Durston*, 7 N.Y.S. 813, 818 (N.Y. Su Ct. 1889).

47. Moran, *Executioner's Current*, xx–xxi.

48. Kasson, *Civilizing the Machine*, 211–14.

49. Nye, *Electrifying America*, 144–46.

50. Brandon, *Electric Chair*, 177.

51. Brandon, *Electric Chair*, 177.

52. Driggs, "A Current of Electricity," 1178.

53. Nathans, "Quest for Progress," 387.

54. Nathans, "Quest for Progress," 387.

55. Dressner and Altschuler, "Sentiment and Statistics," 191–209, reprinted in Hall, *Police, Prison, and Punishment*, 249–67.

56. "Electricity as an Executioner," *Scientific American* 34, no. 2 (January 8, 1876): 16.

57. Bowers, Pierce, and McDevitt, *Legal Homicide*, 38.

58. S.B. 37, *Journal of the Senate of the State of North Carolina at Its Session of 1909* (Raleigh: E. M. Uzzell, 1909), 18.

59. *Public Laws* (1909), 758–61.

60. "Morrison Shocked to Death at Penitentiary," *News and Observer*, March 18, 1910, 1.

61. Prison Report (1909–10), 7–15, NCC.

62. "Today He Pays Penalty," *News and Observer*, March 18, 1910, 5.

63. Seitz, "Killing Chair," 43–44.

64. "Walter Morrison Pays Penalty for Crime," *Charlotte Daily Observer*, March 19, 1910, 8.

65. "Morrison Shocked to Death at Penitentiary."

66. Seitz, "Killing Chair," 43–44.

67. "Morrison Shocked to Death at Penitentiary."

68. "Morrison Shocked to Death at Penitentiary."

69. "First Electrocution Ends Walter Morrison's Life," *News and Observer*, March 19, 1910, 3.

70. "First Electrocution Ends Walter Morrison's Life."

71. Prison Report (1909–10), 15, NCC.

72. Prison Report (1909–10), 15, NCC.

73. "Shrieks of Negro Drown Death Roar," *News and Observer*, May 28, 1921, 3.

74. "Negroes Who Assaulted White Woman Pay Penalty of Death," *News and Observer*, September 16, 1922, 1.

75. "Two More Pay Penalty of Death," *News and Observer*, December 4, 1920, 2.

76. "Woman Looks on as Negro Dies," *News and Observer*, November 22, 1921, 10.

77. "Families Barred from Executions," *News and Observer*, October 6, 1925, 2.

78. Frank Smethurst, "Death Row Myth Holds Men Are Not Executed," *News and Observer*, November 23, 1924, 5.

79. "Negro Electrocuted for Killing Officer," *News and Observer*, November 15, 1918, 8; "Connor Goes to Death Weeping," *News and Observer*, September 21, 1920, 16; "John Goss Dies, Admitting Crime," *News and Observer*, December 8, 1923, 9.

80. Smethurst, "Death Row Myth," 5.

81. "Former Executioner in Critical Condition," *Greensboro Daily News*, September 30, 1929, 4.

82. "Warden Sale Dies Suddenly at Desk in State Prison," *News and Observer*, January 1, 1916, 5.

83. "Says Third Degree Sent Him Unjustly to Chair," *News and Observer*, January 18, 1936, 1.

84. "Negroes Forfeit Lives for Labor Day Murder," *News and Observer*, December 12, 1931, 12.

85. C. A. Upchurch, "Condemned Man Spurns Prayer on Death's Eve," *News and Observer*, March 15, 1935, 1; "Asking Whiskey, Etheridge Dies without a Minister," *News and Observer*, March 16, 1935, 1.

86. "Modern," Editorial, *News and Observer*, March 13, 1935, 4.

87. William S. Boyle, "Lethal Gas," *Commercial Law League Journal* 30 (June 1925), 249. Witnesses could smell the gas but were not harmed.

88. "White Is Executed in Nevada by Gas," *New York Times*, June 3, 1930, 40.

89. "Executed in Lethal Chamber," *New York Times*, June 23, 1934, 30.

90. Quoted in Seitz, "Transition of Methods of Execution," 106.

91. "Lethal Gas Gets O. K.; Parole System Studied," *News and Observer*, March 27, 1935, 1.

92. Louisiana and Mississippi maintained this practice, using an electric chair, until the 1950s. Harries and Cheatwood, *Geography of Execution*, 17.

93. "House Votes for Lethal Gas, but Not Public Show," *News and Observer*, April 4, 1935, 1; H.B. 66, *Public Laws* (1935); "State Senators Refuse to Back House on Bonus," *News and Observer*, January 19, 1935, 1.

94. "Death Chair to Remain; Claims 2 Victims Today," *News and Observer*, July 12, 1935, 1; "Three Youths Die in Electric Chair," *News and Observer*, October 5, 1935, 1.

95. "Says Third Degree Sent Him Unjustly to Chair," *News and Observer*, January 18, 1936, 1.

96. "Says Third Degree Sent Him Unjustly to Chair."

97. "Will Use Electricity in Executions by Gas," *News and Observer*, August 1, 1935, 20.

98. H. H. Wilson to Lester Rose, May 20, 1946. Prison Department, Central (State) Prison, Box 45: Warden's Correspondence, 1946–48, I-S, NCSA.

99. "New Lethal Cell to Begin Career," *News and Observer*, January 21, 1936, 16.

100. "First Gas Death Set for Friday," *News and Observer*, January 22, 1936, 9. The reporter transcribed his interview with Foster in dialect.

101. John A. Parris Jr., "Death Row Upset on Execution Eve," *News and Observer*, January 21, 1936, 1.

102. "Under the Dome," *News and Observer*, January 21, 1936, 1.

103. "First Lethal Gas Victim Dies in Torture as Witnesses Quail," *News and Observer*, January 25, 1936, 1. For much more on Foster, see Seitz, "Killing Chair."

104. Virginius Dabney, "Use of Death Gas Stirs Carolinians," *New York Times*, February 2, 1936, E11.

105. C. A. Upchurch Jr., "Death by Statute," *News and Observer*, February 2, 1936, O2.

106. "Gas Death Time Here Was Normal," *News and Observer*, January 30, 1936, 1.

107. "Slow Death Quite Usual in Gas Killings," *News and Observer*, January 31, 1936, 1.

108. "Under the Dome," *News and Observer*, January 27, 1936, 1.

109. Roy M. Brown to J. C. B. Ehringhaus, January 30, 1935. Ehringhaus Papers, General Assembly, 1933–37, Box 65: Capital Punishment, 1933–36, NCSA.

110. Clifton F. West, MD, to J. C. B. Ehringhaus, January 27, 1936, Ehringhaus Papers, General Correspondence, 1933–37, Box 155: Capital Punishment, 1934–36, NCSA.

111. J. C. B. Ehringhaus to Clifton F. West, January 31, 1936, Ehringhaus Papers, General Correspondence, 1933–37, Box 155: Capital Punishment, 1934–36, NCSA.

112. Ehringhaus to West, January 31, 1936. Officials attending to Foster's death used fifteen one-ounce pellets of potassium cyanide, dropped into a mixture of one quart of sulfuric acid and one quart of water. For Jenkins, they used three pints of acid and three quarts of water.

113. Numbers taken from *News and Observer* front pages, February 12, 1911, March 16, 1935, and May 2, 1953.

114. "Under the Dome," *News and Observer*, January 18, 1939, in Clippings File (Capital Punishment), 59, NCC.

115. Trotti, *Body in the Reservoir*, 167–80.

116. "Howard Craig Pays Penalty," *News and Observer*, December 5, 1914, 2. See also "Two More Pay Penalty of Death," *News and Observer*, December 4, 1920, 2.

117. Roy G. Brantley, "Lexington Killer-Rapist Dies in Gas Chamber for His Crime," *News and Observer*, June 7, 1952, 16.

118. "Jesse Brooks Dies in Electric Chair," *Durham Morning Herald*, March 17, 1934, 1.

119. "Two Negroes Die in Gas Chamber," *News and Observer*, July 17, 1937, 12.

120. "How Robeson Negro Poison Murderer Met Death by Gas," *Lumberton Robesonian*, August 16, 1937, 4.

121. "Chair Claims Two Victims; Deny Guilt to the End," *News and Observer*, August 3, 1935, 1.

122. "Widow of Negro's Victim Waits Near Death Chamber," *News and Observer*, December 10, 1927, 1.

123. "Long Battle with Law Brings Death," *News and Observer*, November 6, 1920, 10.

124. "Granville Negro Executed Here," *News and Observer*, January 21, 1939, 12. The paper made mention of a mask being used at a 1921 execution, too. See "J. T. Harris Goes to His Death in Electric Chair without a Word," *News and Observer*, October 21, 1921, 1.

125. "Witnesses Are Scarce for Negro's Execution," *News and Observer*, June 10, 1939, 1.

126. "Gas Chamber Takes Life of Johnston Tobacconist," *News and Observer*, January 29, 1949, 1; "James Creech Executed for Wife's Murder," *Asheville Citizen*, January 29, 1949, 2. Newspapers reported that Creech was the first man with more than a high school education to be executed in the state, but George Keaton attended two terms at Tuskegee Institute before his 1934 execution: "Death Row Poet Goes Mutely to His Doom," *News and Observer*, September 22, 1934, 12. Creech was the first such white man.

127. Foucault, *Discipline and Punish*.

128. Smethurst, "Death Row Myth," 5.

129. "Death Row Poet Goes Mutely to His Doom."

130. "Sampson Killers Pay Penalty in Triple Execution," *News and Observer*, November 17, 1934, 1.

131. Potter, "On Understanding the South," 460.

132. Brundage, *Lynching in the New South*, 27–28.

133. "State Takes Life of Ross McAfee," *Statesville Record and Landmark*, November 22, 1957, 1.


Chapter 3

1. *State v. Brooks*, 225 N.C. 662 (1945).

2. United States Census Bureau, Sixteenth Census of the United States: 1940, accessed May 15, 2017, https://www.ancestry.com/interactive/2442/m-t0627-02951 -00299?pid=152605614.

3. "Sentence of Young Slayer Commuted to Life Term," *Asheville Citizen*, April 24, 1945, 3.

4. "Governor Saves Boy from Death," *News and Observer*, December 21, 1945, 20.

5. "Two Governors," *Time*, January 7, 1946, 16.

6. Harvie Branscombe to R. Gregg Cherry, undated; Anne Wunderman to R. Gregg Cherry, undated telegram; Hugh Hunter to R. Gregg Cherry, January 9, 1946, in R. Gregg Cherry Papers—Agencies, Commissions, Departments, and Institutions, 1945–1948—Paroles Commission, May 1945–December 1949: Paroles Commission, NCSA.

7. Attorney General Report (1907–1908), 11, NCC.

8. In 1942, the Supreme Court ruled in *Betts v. Brody* that the constitution required legal representation only if a defendant could prove that he was a victim of

"special circumstances." *Gideon v. Wainwright* (1963) closed this loophole by guaranteeing the indigent access to counsel in state capital trials. Both rulings required state resources and energy that were not always forthcoming.

9. Edwin Gill, "Report of the Office of the Commissioner of Paroles, January 1, 1933–January 1, 1935" (Raleigh: The Commissioner, [1935?]), 8–13. Katherine R. Everett Law Library, UNC-CH.

10. "Board of Pardons," Editorial, *News and Observer*, January 19, 1913, 4.

11. Abramowitz and Paget, "Executive Clemency in Capital Cases," 141–42.

12. "Form and Content of Applications for Pardon," North Carolina General Statutes 147–21 (1869–1870, c.171; 1870–1871, c.61; Code, s. 3336; Rev., s. 5334; C.S., s. 7642).

13. "Indian Murderer Pays the Penalty," *News and Observer*, November 25, 1911, 5.

14. *State v. Floyd Stanley*, 198 N.C. 308; 151 S.E. 621 (1930).

15. Gordon M. Sears, "State Executes Johnston Youths," *News and Observer*, June 7, 1947, 10.

16. Adams, "Evolution of Law in North Carolina," 144–45.

17. Decision of C. J. Stacy, *State v. Herman Casey*, 210 N.C. 620 (1931).

18. Berman and Fastman, "Newly Discovered Evidence," 31.

19. Edwin B. Bridges to O. Max Gardner, February 21, 1929. O. Max Gardner Papers, General Correspondence, 1929–33, Box 95, Parole Commission re: Outline of Work, 1929, NCSA.

20. "Statutory Changes in N.C. in 1941," *North Carolina Law Review* 19 (June 1941): 476. Cases mentioned are *State v. Fleming*, 107 N.C. 905, 909, 12 S.E. 131, 132 (1890), *State v. Alston*, 113 N.C. 666, 18 S.E. 692 (1893), and *State v. Johnson*, 218 N.C. 604, 12 S.E. 2nd 278 (1940).

21. *State v. Huzy Jackson, alias Jimmy Cadoger, Alias Jimmy Cadozier*, 199 N.C. 321 (1930).

22. "Claim Five Are Now in Russia," *Asheville Citizen-Times*, August 21, 1930, 2. (Reporting on the ruling was bundled with an unrelated story.)

23. "Huzzy Jackson" [*sic*], *Paroles for Capital Criminals* (bound volume), vol. 7. State Agencies: Paroles Department, NCSA.

24. Affidavit for the Defense, *State v. Casey*, 210 N.C. 620 (1931).

25. *State v. Casey*.

26. J. Clarkson, dissenting, *State v. Casey*.

27. J. Brogden, dissenting. *State v. Casey*.

28. "New Trial Asked on Rape Charges," *News and Observer*, May 6, 1947, 17.

29. *State v. Willie Little, Alias James Harrington, Alias Chicken*, 227 N.C. 701 (1947).

30. "Three Rapists Meet Death in Prison's Gas Chamber," *News and Observer*, November 15, 1946, 2.

31. "This is Justice Checked," Editorial, *Concord Daily Tribune*, reprinted in *News and Observer*, November 24, 1924, 7.

32. Calculated from data in Prison Reports, 1910–25.

33. "A Survey of Statutory Changes in North Carolina," *North Carolina Law Review* 7 (June 1929): 382.

34. Coates, "Punishment for Crime in North Carolina," 211; Knepper, *North Carolina's Criminal Justice System*, 161–65.

35. Prison Records Group, Paroles, William W. Kitchin to Thomas W. Bickett, Commutations, 1910–1919, 189, NCSA.

36. "Governor Paroles Guptons; Grants Respites to Three," *News and Observer*, June 28, 1923, 1.

37. Edwin Gill, "Executive Clemency in Relation to Capital Punishment: A Report," 8. Nell Battle Lewis Papers: Social Welfare, LSHC.

38. Commutation data for North Carolina's capital criminals is scattered, incomplete, and restricted by law. Governors issued formal statements with each commutation; sociologist Elmer Johnson used these statements in his 1957 study of commutation in the state, a detailed study and the only one of its kind. These statements, while sometimes published in part in newspapers, are scattered throughout governors' papers, those of the Parole Board, the Prison, or those of the two organizations that administered it, the State Highway and Public Works Commission and the State Board of Charities and Public Welfare. Prison records include heavy, moldering ledgers recording and rerecording commutations for capital and noncapital sentences; governors' papers include some reports the chief executives requested, or collections of scattered data. The "Death Cases" files from the Parole Board, which presumably include commutation investigators' reports and other information on capital prisoners whose sentences were under consideration, are inexplicably restricted by state law. Employees at the Department of Corrections and the Office of Research and Planning, while helpful, were unable to explain why these files were restricted and unable to grant access. This lack of information means that this discussion relies on Elmer Johnson's data, relatively small samples of years for which reliable numbers appear in attorneys general and prison reports, and newspaper coverage.

39. Johnson, "Selective Factors in Capital Punishment," 167 (Table 4).

40. "McLean Spares Life of Negro," *News and Observer*, February 3, 1926, 8.

41. State Board of Charities and Public Welfare, *Capital Punishment in North Carolina* (Raleigh, NC: The Board, 1929). Page 8: Lewis also "rewrote and rearranged most of the material" in the publication; accessed March 14, 2018, https://archive .org/details/capitalpunishmenoonort.

42. Koren, *Summaries of State Laws*, 184.

43. Biennial Report of the State Hospital at Goldsboro, July 1, 1924 to June 30, 1925 (Raleigh: Bynum, 1926), 6, accessed March 14, 2018, http://docsouth.unc.edu /nc/goldsboro24/goldsboro24.html.

44. Koren, *Summaries of State Laws*, 181.

45. Biennial Report of the State Hospital at Raleigh, 8.

46. Biennial Report of the State Board of Charities and Public Welfare, December 1, 1920 to June 30, 1922 (Raleigh: The Board, 1922), 40a, NCC.

47. Castles, "Quiet Eugenics," 849–78.

48. "Commutation Announced for William J. Dunheen," *News and Observer*, May 10, 1945, 5.

49. "William Joseph Dunheen," Paroles (bound volume), vol. 10. State Agencies: Paroles Department, NCSA.

50. "Two Sides of Humanity," Editorial, *News and Observer*, January 12, 1926, 4.

51. *Roper v. Simmons*, 543 U.S. 551 (2005).

52. Streib, "Death Penalty for Children," 613–17.

53. Streib, *Death Penalty for Juveniles*, 202.

54. Prison Report, 1915–1916 (12), 1924–26 (39), and 1938–40 (393), NCC.

55. Neil Morgan, "Woman and Husband Die in Gas Chamber at Prison," *News and Observer*, January 2, 1943, 11.

56. "To the Electric Chair!," *Union Republican* (Winston-Salem, NC), August 15, 1912, 7.

57. Wellman, *Dead and Gone*, 73.

58. Wellman, *Dead and Gone*, 81.

59. Prison Department, Central (State) Prison, William W. Kitchin to Thomas W. Bickett, Bound Volume GO 55: Reasons for Pardons and Commutations, Reprieves, 1912–1917, 457, NCSA.

60. Prison Department, Central (State) Prison, Box 38: Death Sentences, 1910–1920, NCSA; "Ida Ball Warren," Editorial, *News and Observer*, November 10, 1926, 4.

61. "Ida Ball Warren to Keep Her Job," *Statesville Record and Landmark*, February 23, 1931, 7.

62. Neil Morgan, "Woman and Husband Die in Gas Chamber at Prison," *News and Observer*, January 2, 1943, 11.

63. "Three Executed in Gas Chamber," *News and Observer*, December 30, 1944, 10.

64. Zipf, *Bad Girls at Samarcand*, 4.

65. Cahn, "Spirited Youth or Fiends Incarnate," 152–81.

66. Bickford, "Imperial Modernity," 440.

67. "Man Who Once Faced Death Wins Parole," *News and Observer*, January 23, 1948, 11.

68. "Sentence Lifted on Negro Killer," *News and Observer*, July 8, 1938, 2.

69. "Grant Clemency to Doomed Negro," *News and Observer*, August 10, 1935, 2.

70. "Mace Wellman Is Given Death Sentence," *Statesville Daily Record*, August 13, 1942, 1.

71. "Supreme Court Upholds Iredell County Rape Case," *Statesville Daily Record*, November 5, 1942, 1.

72. "Attorney Land Tells Governor Rape Was an Act of Vengeance," *Statesville Daily Record*, November 18, 1942, 1.

73. C. C. Spaulding to J. Melville Broughton, November 6, 1942, in J. Melville Broughton Papers, Agencies, Commissions, Departments, and Institutions, 1941–44. Box 61: Folder: Paroles Commission, NCSA.

74. "Negro, Sentenced to Die, Now Is 'Free Man' Again," *News and Observer*, April 17, 1943, 1.

75. "Payment Is Ordered," *Statesville Record and Landmark*, May 13, 1971, 1.

76. William Mason Wellman, Social Security Death Lists, Ancestry.com. U.S., Social Security Death Index, 1935–2014.

77. Case summary re: Liles, Ernest; Case Summary re: Lamm, Covey C. and Case Summary re: Lewis, James Edward, in Board of Paroles, Box 46: Death Case Summaries, 1948–51, NCSA. See also "Churchill Godley Must Die Friday," *News and Observer*, January 13, 1920, 16, and "Governor Signs Death Warrant for First Time," *News and Observer*, November 3, 1927, 5.

78. Johnson, "Selective Factors in Capital Punishment," 167. See "Negro Gets Commutation on Eve of Execution Day," *News and Observer*, October 8, 1943, 5.

79. "Capital Punishment in North Carolina," 101.

80. Bitsy Clem to W. Kerr Scott, March 30, 1951, W. Kerr Scott Papers, Subject Files, 1951, Box 98: Paroles and Commutations, Paroles: General and A-C, NCSA.

81. Gerry Dickinson to W. Kerr Scott, March 20, 1951, W. Kerr Scott Papers, Subject Files, 1951, Box 98: Paroles and Commutations, Paroles: General and A-C, NCSA.

82. L. H. Stephenson to W. Kerr Scott, January 12, 1949, W. Kerr Scott Papers, Subject File, 1949: Creech Case, NCSA. Letter transcribed as written.

83. "Hoke Man Dies in Gas Chamber," *News and Observer*, January 29, 1944, 9.

84. *State v. Jim Cameron*, 166 N.C. 379 (1914).

85. *State v. Earl Neville*, 174 N.C. 731 (1918).

86. Prison Report (1911–1912), 12, NCC.

87. Gill, "Executive Clemency."

88. C. J. Parker Jr., "The State's Death Lottery," *News and Observer*, January 15, 1928, 4. This phrase is a version of *Dum Spiro Spero* ("While I breathe, I hope"), which is the state motto of South Carolina. Likening death row to South Carolina may have carried particular meaning to readers at the time.

89. "Why?," Cartoon, *News and Observer*, January 22, 1928, 4.

90. Gill, "Executive Clemency."

91. Johnson, "Selective Factors in Capital Punishment," 169.

92. Culled from Prison Reports, NCC.

93. "Passing the Buck on Death," Editorial, *News and Observer*, February 10, 1941, 2.

94. Sullivan, "Criminal Slang," 274.

95. Frank Smethurst, "Has Capital Punishment Been a Failure in North Carolina?," *News and Observer*, November 16, 1924, X1.

96. Compiled from Attorneys General Reports (1909–1924), NCC.

97. "Capital Punishment," Editorial, *News and Observer*, September 28, 1925, 4. See also Maynard Shipley, "Does Capital Punishment Prevent Convictions?," *American Law Review* 43 (May–June 1909): 321–34.

98. Edwin B. Bridges to O. Max Gardner, February 21, 1929. O. Max Gardner Papers, General Correspondence, 1929–1933, Box 95, Parole Commission re: Outline of Work, 1929, NCSA.

99. "Plyler Escapes Electric Chair," *News and Observer*, February 17, 1911, 3.

100. Thomas L. Johnson to Edwin Gill, January 31, 1942, in J. Melville Broughton Papers, Agencies, Commissions, Departments, and Institutions, 1941–1944, Box 61: Folder: Paroles Commission, NCSA.

101. "Walter Blue," *Paroles for Capital Criminals*, vol. 10 (bound volume), State Agency Records: Paroles, NCSA.

102. "Governor Paroles Guptons; Grants Reprieves to Three," *News and Observer*, June 28, 1923, 1. Other examples include "Governor Spares Life of Carter," *News and Observer*, December 2, 1934, 1.

103. April 27, 1923 entry, *Paroles for Capital Criminals*, vol. 1 (bound volume), State Agency Records: Paroles, NCSA. Article on confession: "Willie Hardison Exonerates Others as He Goes to Chair," *News and Observer*, April 28, 1923, 12.

104. "Commutations Go to Onslow Trio," *News and Observer*, June 29, 1923, 1. Other examples of post-conviction recommendations for commutations from trial participants appear in Cora Stegall, "Two Negroes Die in Gas Chamber," *News and Observer*, June 23, 1945, 2; "Governor Saves Bladen, Hertford Slayers," *News and Observer*, December 27, 1946, 22.

105. "Governor Denies Plea for Mercy," *News and Observer*, May 16, 1937, 1. See also "Governor Spares Guilford Slayer," *News and Observer*, January 3, 1946, 12.

106. "How the Courts Are Hurt," Editorial, *Charlotte Observer*, November 20, 1924, 3.

107. "This Is Justice Checked," *News and Observer*, November 24, 1924, 7.

108. "Common Sense," Editorial, *News and Observer*, January 7, 1939, 4.

109. "Under the Dome," *News and Observer*, February 7, 1941, 8.

110. C.S. 4233 (burglary) and C.S. 4238 (arson), c. 215, from "Statutory Changes in North Carolina Law in 1941," *North Carolina Law Review* 19 (June 1941): 444.

111. "Report of the Special Commission for the Improvement of the Administration of Justice," *Popular Government* 13 (January 1948): 13.

112. G.S. 14-17 (murder), G.S. 14-52 (burglary), G.S. 14-58 (arson), G.S. 14-21 (rape).

113. "Governor Paroles Guptons," 1.

114. Joseph Millings to W. Kerr Scott, undated, W. Kerr Scott Papers, Subject File, 1949, NCSA.

115. "Survey of the Decisions of the North Carolina Supreme Court," 439.

116. *State v. Conner*, 241 N.C. 468, 85 S.E.2d 584 (1955), as described in Graham, "Criminal Law," 665.

117. "An Act to Permit the State to Accept," 461–62.

118. Patrick, "Capital Punishment and Life Imprisonment," 421–26.

119. Charles Craven, "A Flower Vase, a Fan, and Death," *News and Observer*, July 14, 1956, 16.

120. *State v. Clyde Little*, 228 N.C. 417, Fall Term 1947, in Charles M. Shaffer Papers, Box 5, Volume 227: Fall 1947, 139, SHC. See also the case of Howard Hawley in "Granville Negro Saved from Gas Chamber in Second Trial," *News and Observer*, November 20, 1948, 14.

121. On the increasing use of life without parole, including as an alternative to a death sentence, see Ogletree and Sarat, *Life without Parole*.


## Chapter 4

1. "Five Die in N.C. Mass Execution," *Statesville Daily Record*, October 3, 1947, 1.

2. "Five Die in N.C. Mass Execution."

3. "Doubt," *Asheville Citizen-Times*, October 5, 1947, 4. See also "Quintuple Execution in North Carolina," *Capitol Journal* (Salem, OR), October 3, 1947, 1; "Quintuple Execution Held in North Carolina," *St. Louis Star and Times*, October 3, 1947, 27.

4. "Example," *Asheville Citizen-Times*, October 4, 1947, 4; "Local Execution Option," *Daily Times-News* (Burlington, NC), October 8, 1947, 4; "N.C. Warden Declares He Is Opposed to Executions," *Gastonia Gazette*, October 7, 1947, 6.

5. Numbers from the North Carolina Department of Public Safety, accessed October 11, 2017, https://www.ncdps.gov/Adult-Corrections/Prisons/Death-Penalty /List-of-persons-executed.

6. For instances of African American men sitting on juries in capital trials, see Hearn, *Legal Executions in North Carolina and South Carolina*.

7. de Tocqueville, *Democracy in America*, 363, 367.

8. "An Act Prescribing the Method of Drawing Jurors in New Hanover County and the Qualifications of Said Jurors," Public Laws (1909), Ch. 342, Sec. 1–4.

9. Altschuler and Deiss, "A Brief History of the Criminal Jury in the United States," 892–93.

10. *State v. Speller*, 229 N.C. 67, 70–71, 47 S.E.2d 537, 538–39 (1948). The clerk of court testified that African Americans composed between 35 and 40 percent of the eligible voters. During a retrial awarded to Speller on a procedural matter, jurors were summoned from nearby Warren County. Witnesses testified that in the year 1940, 1,077 white people and just 28 African Americans entered jury pools in a county with 15,109 African Americans and just 8,036 white people. *State v. Speller*, 230 N.C. 345; 53 S.E.2d 294 (1949).

11. *State v. Speller*.

12. *Brown v. Allen*, 344 U.S. 443 (1953).

13. Freedman, "Brown v. Allen," 1558–63.

14. Freedman, "Brown v. Allen," 1543.

15. Charles Craven, "Young Pastor Protests Executions," *News and Observer*, May 29, 1953, 1.

16. Craven, "Young Pastor Protests Executions."

17. Paul Green, "Work in Progress," November 2, 1953, no page number. In Paul Green Papers, Series 5.3: Capital Punishment, Capital Punishment: Notes, SHC.

18. Harold Garfinkel, "Research Note on Inter- and Intra-Racial Homicides," *Social Forces* 27 (May 1949): 376–77.

19. Garfinkel, "Research Note," 371.

20. Dollard, *Caste and Class in a Southern Town*, 105.

21. Garfinkel, "Research Note," 377.

22. "Taylor Love Pays Death Penalty," *News and Observer*, December 2, 1911, 5.

23. "Negro Executed in Gas Chamber," *News and Observer*, May 22, 1943, 5.

24. "State Executes Anson Murderer," *News and Observer*, June 7, 1941, 5. See also "Negro Electrocuted for Killing Another Negro," *News and Observer*, May 28, 1921, 3.

25. Race of condemned, race of victim, and crime gathered from newspaper reports and reconciled with the Espy File.

26. Garfinkel, "Research Note," 378.

27. For more information on the race-of-offender/race-of-victim relationship, see the appendixes.

28. "First White Man Is Electrocuted," *News and Observer*, February 25, 1911, 7; "Death Today in the Electric Chair," *News and Observer*, February 24, 1914, 2.

29. Haines, *Against Capital Punishment*, 8.

30. Davis, "Movement to Abolish Capital Punishment in America," 26–27.

31. See, broadly, Link, *Paradox of Southern Progressivism*.

32. For discussions of nineteenth and early twentieth-century arguments, see Dressner and Altschuler, "Sentiment and Statistics in the Progressive Era," 191–209, as appearing in Hall, *Police, Prison, and Punishment*.

33. Mackey, "Edward Livingston and the Origins of the Movement to Abolish Capital Punishment in America," 146–57, as appearing in Hall, *Police, Prison, and Punishment*, 435–56.

34. Davis, "Movement to Abolish Capital Punishment," 31–43; Galliher, Ray, and Cook, "Abolition and Reinstatement," 541–43.

35. Bedau, *Death Penalty in America*, 12; Galliher, Ray, and Cook, "Abolition and Reinstatement," 541–42.

36. Nice, "States and the Death Penalty," 1038; Galliher, Ray, and Cook, "Abolition and Reinstatement," 541.

37. Galliher, Ray, and Cook, "Abolition and Reinstatement," 556–57.

38. Grantham, *Southern Progressivism*, 173–77.

39. Zimmerman, "Penal Reform Movements," 462–92.

40. "Capital Punishment Due for Legislative Overhaul," *News and Observer*, July 5, 1938, 14.

41. "Saunders Bill to Get Floor Hearing," *News and Observer*, January 22, 1919, 1.

42. "Capital Punishment Argued in Lower House," *News and Observer*, January 24, 1919, 1.

43. "Capital Punishment," Editorial, *News and Observer*, January 25, 1919, 1.

44. "Capital Offenses Remain the Same," *News and Observer*, February 5, 1919, 1.

45. W. A. Stanbury to H. L. Canfield, April 24, 1925, in Henry Lee Canfield Papers, Box 1, Folder 2: 1925, SHC.

46. "League to End Executions," *Greensboro Record*, undated clipping, February 1923. Clipping File through 1975 (Capital Punishment), 4, NCC.

47. "Plan Abolition of Death Chair," *News and Observer*, July 1, 1925, 13.

48. Constitution and Bylaws, The Greensboro Society for the Abolition of Capital Punishment. Canfield Papers, Box 1, Folder 8: Miscellaneous and Undated, SHC.

49. Constitution and Bylaws, Canfield Papers.

50. "Capital Punishment Medieval, Says Dr. Taylor in Speech Here," *News and Observer*, May 16, 1928, 5.

51. H. L. Canfield to the Editor of the *Greensboro Daily News*, undated. In Canfield Papers, Box 1, Folder 11: Undated Sermons, Articles, SHC.

52. Untitled clipping from the *Wall Street Journal*, January 6, 1926. Canfield Papers, Box 1, Folder 11: Undated Sermons, Articles, SHC.

53. *Greensboro Daily News*, January 15, 1927. Clipping from Canfield Papers, Box 1, Folder 4: 1927–1928, SHC.

54. C. F. Hunt to H. L. Canfield, December 20, 1928. In Canfield Papers, Box 1, Folder 4: 1927–1928, SHC.

55. Nomira Waller to J. C. B. Ehringhaus, August 9, 1933, Ehringhaus Papers, Box 161: General Correspondence, NCSA. Text transcribed as written.

56. Exodus 21:22, *The Holy Bible*, New Revised Standard Version.

57. Leviticus 24:18–20.

58. Deuteronomy 21:20–21.

59. Matthew 5:38–39.

60. John 8:1–7.

61. Luke 23:39–43.

62. Romans 13:1–4.

63. "Describes Murder as Heinous Sin," Letter, *News and Observer*, April 15, 1935, 4.

64. A. B. Crumpler, "Favors Capital Punishment," Letter, *News and Observer*, May 15, 1925, 2.

65. Gilbreth L. Kerr to J. C. B. Ehringhaus, in Ehringhaus Papers, Box 161: General Correspondence, 1935, NCSA.

66. Mrs. G. E. Weeks, "Capital Punishment," Letter, *News and Observer*, 22 January 1928, M8.

67. J. C. B. Ehringhaus to Alice Haughton James, May 20, 1933, in Ehringhaus Papers, Box 161: General Correspondence, NCSA. Quoted as written in original.

68. Leidholdt, *Battling Nell*, 62–64.

69. "County Has First Woman Candidate," *News and Observer*, February 12, 1928, 1.

70. Quoted in Pyron, "Nell Battle Lewis," 66.

71. Cobb and Wilson, *Perspectives on the American South*, 63.

72. Lewis, "Incidentally," *News and Observer*, February 3, 1935, M3.

73. Lewis, "Incidentally," *News and Observer*, February 2, 1936, O2.

74. Pyron, "Nell Battle Lewis," 66.

75. Lewis, "Incidentally," *News and Observer*, September 7, 1924, M2.

76. Lewis, "Incidentally," *News and Observer*, February 3, 1935, M3.

77. Lewis, "Incidentally."

78. Lewis, "Incidentally," *News and Observer*, September 17, 1922, 6.

79. Lewis, "Incidentally," *News and Observer*, November 22, 1936, M2.

80. Lewis, "Incidentally," *News and Observer*, May 5, 1935, O6.

81. Lewis, "Incidentally," *News and Observer*, February 3, 1935, M3.

82. Nell Battle Lewis, "The North Carolina Conference for Social Service," *Social Forces* 1 (1922–1923): 265.

83. "Capital Punishment in North Carolina," 68, 116, 133, 143, respectively.

84. "Capital Punishment in North Carolina," 108–12.

85. "Capital Punishment in North Carolina," 75–79.

86. Charlotte Story Perkinson, "Why I Do Not Believe in Capital Punishment," *News and Observer*, February 26, 1928, O3.

87. Lewis, "Incidentally," *News and Observer*, February 3, 1935, M3.

88. Lewis, "Incidentally," *News and Observer*, January 29, 1933, 8.

89. Lewis, "Incidentally," *News and Observer*, August 4, 1935, M6.

90. Lewis, "Incidentally," *News and Observer*, February 9, 1936, M2.

91. Lewis, "Incidentally," *News and Observer*, February 9, 1936.

92. Lewis, "Incidentally."

93. Lewis, "Incidentally," *News and Observer*, January 31, 1937, M2.

94. Lewis, "Incidentally," *News and Observer*, February 2, 1936, O2.

95. Lewis, "Incidentally," *News and Observer*, January 24, 1926, M2.

96. "Torture Chamber," Editorial, *News and Observer*, June 20, 1941, 4.

97. "Murders and Maniacs," Editorial, *News and Observer*, September 9, 1935, 4.

98. "Preserving a Monster," Editorial, *News and Observer*, June 30, 1941, 4.

99. "Are you in favor of the death penalty for murder?," Gallup Organization. Gallup Poll (AIPO), December 1936 [survey question]. USGALLUP.36-59.Q03A.

100. "Do you favor or oppose capital punishment for murder?" and "Do you favor or oppose capital punishment for women convicted of murder?" Survey by Gallup Organization, December 1–December 6, 1937. iPOLL Databank.

101. "Some states have abolished capital punishment—executing persons who commit a murder—and have substituted life imprisonment instead. Do you favor or oppose capital punishment?" Louis Harris & Associates. Harris Survey, June 1966 [survey question]. USHARRIS.070366.R5.

102. Harris, "Oversimplification and Error," 429–55.

103. Frank Smethurst, "In My Opinion," *News and Observer*, April 7, 1934, 4.

104. "To Abolish Capital Punishment," Letter, *News and Observer*, January 24, 1939, 4.

105. "Under the Dome," *News and Observer*, February 9, 1939, 1.

106. Mrs. S. F. Thompson, "Abolish Capital Punishment," Letter, *News and Observer*, January 22, 1939, 4.

107. The case and its revelations about sexuality, adolescence, and deviance are described in Cahn, "Spirited Youth or Fiends Incarnate," 152–81.

108. Pyron, "Nell Battle Lewis," 76–77; Pearson, "Samarcand, Nell Battle Lewis, and the 1931 Arson Trial," 44–45.

109. Lewis, "Incidentally," *News and Observer*, August 28, 1932, 11.

110. For evidence of Cole's prominence in the social and business scene in Rockingham, see "Social," *Rockingham Post-Dispatch*, January 1, 1920, 12; "School Buildings," *Rockingham Post-Dispatch*, January 8, 1920, 1.

111. "Cotton Man Held for Shooting in Rockingham, NC," *Asheville Citizen-Times*, August 16, 1925, 2.

112. "W. W. Ormond Assassinated in Car in Rockingham," *Nashville Graphic* (Nashville, NC), August 20, 1925, 1.

113. "Rockingham Honors Ormond," *Statesville Record and Landmark*, August 20, 1925, 2.

114. "An Important Trial," *Asheville Citizen-Times*, September 27, 1925, 4.

115. Isaac London, "Stage Is All Set for Trial of W. B. Cole at Rockingham," *News and Observer*, September 28, 1925, 1.

116. Jonathan Daniels, "Bitterness Is Feature [on] First Day's Arguments to Jury in Cole Case," *News and Observer*, October 8, 1925, 1.

117. Jonathan Daniels, "Death Penalty Sought by State in Trial of Cole This Week in Rockingham Superior Court," *News and Observer*, September 27, 1925, M3.

118. "The Rockingham Case," *Albemarle Press*, September 17, 1925, 1.

119. Jonathan Daniels, "Cole Claims Vision in Prayer Stirred Him to Shoot Ormond; Thought He Had Right to Kill," *News and Observer*, October 3, 1925, 1.

120. "W. B. Cole Declared Sane and Is Set Free," *Rockingham Post-Dispatch*, October 15, 1925, 1.

121. "Cole is De-Glared [sic] Sane," *North Wilkesboro Hustler*, October 14, 1925, 1. Typographical error retained for ease of future discovery. "Cole-Ormond Case Again in Limelight," *Nashville Graphic* (Nashville, NC), January 7, 1926, 1. The $150,000 suit was settled for $15,000. "Cole-Ormond Suit Settled," *Statesville Record and Landmark*, June 17, 1926, 6.

122. "W. B. Cole Declared Sane and Is Set Free."

123. D. M. Castelloe, "Solemn Protest," Letter, *News and Observer*, October 15, 1925, 4.

124. E. Millard Qualls, "What Price Justice," Letter, *News and Observer*, October 16, 1925, 4.

125. G. W. Paschal, "The Cole Verdict," Letter, *News and Observer*, October 16, 1925, 4.

126. "Why the Verdict?," Letter, *News and Observer*, October 16, 1925, 4.

127. "Not Guilty (?)," Editorial, *New Bern Sun-Journal*, as appearing in *News and Observer*, October 15, 1925, 4.

128. Jonathan Daniels, "Union County Jury Finds Cole Not Guilty," *News and Observer*, October 12, 1925, 1.

129. C. H. Hamlin to J. C. B. Ehringhaus, February 21, 1934, Ehringhaus Papers, Box 161: General Correspondence, 1933–37; J. C. B. Ehringhaus to C. H. Hamlin, February 24, 1934, January 1949, 4, NCSA. Hamlin to Ehringhaus, February 21, 1934.

130. *State v. James Creech*, No. 218, Supreme Court of North Carolina, 229 N.C. 662; 51 S.E.2d 348.

131. Jay Jenkins, "Gas Chamber Takes Life of Johnston Tobacconist," *News and Observer*, January 29, 1949, 1.

132. Henry A. Grady to W. Kerr Scott, January 28, 1949, W. Kerr Scott Papers, Subject Files, 1949, Correspondence, NCSA.

133. J. Graham Spurrier to W. Kerr Scott, February 15, 1949. W. Kerr Scott Papers, Subject Files, 1949, Correspondence, NCSA.

134. "Death Row Poet Goes Mutely to His Doom," *News and Observer*, March 16, 1934, 12.

135. "Murder in the Minority," Editorial, *Asheville Citizen*, January 31, 1949, 4.

136. "Of Life and Death," Editorial, *Greensboro Daily News*, October 8, 1947, 6.

137. Mrs. W. H. to W. Kerr Scott, W. Kerr Scott Papers, Subject Files, 1949, Paroles: General, A-K, NCSA. Transcribed as written.

138. Mims, *The Advancing South*, 247.

139. "Dramatic Arts," in Powell, *Encyclopedia*, 352–53.

140. Powell, *Encyclopedia*, 352–53.

141. Paul Green to Theodore Dreiser (open letter), April 11, 1932, Laurence G. Avery, ed., *A Southern Life: Letters of Paul Green* (Chapel Hill: University of North Carolina Press, 2013), 202.

142. Ancestry.com. U.S., *Lists of Men Ordered to Report to Local Board for Military Duty, 1917–1918* [database online]. Provo, UT, USA: Ancestry.com Operations, Inc., 2013.

143. Avery, *A Southern Life*, 238.

144. "Author Retains Negro Attorneys," Miami News, April 15, 1934, 2.

145. Paul Green to J. C. B. Ehringhaus, Avery, *A Southern Life*, 235.

146. "Negro Who Tried Suicide Collapses in Death Chair," *News and Observer*, September 29, 1934, 1; *State v. Emanuel Bittings, Alias Spice Bittings*, 206 N.C. 798 (1934).

147. Monroe Medlin to Mom, no date, in Paul Green Papers, Series 5.3: Capital Punishment, Capital Punishment: Notes, SHC. Transcribed as written.

148. Gurney Herring to Children, May 24, 1946, in Paul Green Papers, Series 5.3: Capital Punishment, Capital Punishment: Notes, SHC.

149. Emmet Garner to Friends, undated, in Paul Green Papers, Series 5.3: Capital Punishment, Capital Punishment: Notes, SHC. Transcribed as written.

150. "For Capital Punishment," Letter, *Greensboro Daily News*, January 31, 1926, B5.

151. Crumpler, "Favors Capital Punishment," 2.

152. W. A. Wasdon, "Think of the Victims," Letter, *News and Observer*, January 2, 1939, 4.

153. "Murdering Ignorant Negroes," Editorial, *News and Observer*, April 5, 1934, 4.

154. Paul Green to E. M. Land, November 18, 1942, in Avery, *Southern Life*, 371–77.

155. Bedau and Radelet, "Miscarriages of Justice," 72; "William Mason Wellmon," *National Registry of Exonerations*. Accessed June 23, 2018, https://www.law.umich.edu/special/exoneration/Pages/casedetailpre1989.aspx?caseid=357.

156. "Negro, Sentenced to Die, Now Is 'Free Man' Again," *News and Observer*, April 17, 1943, 1.

157. Anonymous to J. M. Broughton, March 31, 1942, in Paul Green Papers, Series 5.3: Capital Punishment, Folder: Capital Punishment Notes, SHC.

158. "Innocent Man Paid for Time in N. C. Jail," *Asheville Citizen-Times*, May 13, 1971, 40.

159. "Dove, Frank, Fred Dove, and George Williams," in Bedau and Radelet, "Miscarriages," 111; "Confession Brings Freedom for Three," *Statesville Record and Landmark* (March 5, 1928), 2.

160. "Langley, Gus Colin," in Bedau and Radelet, "Miscarriages," 137–38; "Parole Granted to Gus Langley by Ehringhaus," *Asheville Citizen-Times*, October 31, 1934, 1.

161. Diary entry, April 15, 1967, in Marion A. Wright Papers, Series 3: Death Penalty, Box 17, Folder 309: Death Penalty, February 21–April 20, 1967, SHC.

162. Marion A. Wright to Harry Golden, August 27, 1967, Marion A. Wright Papers, Series 3: Death Penalty, Box 17, Folder 325: Death Penalty, August 18–April 31, 1967, SHC.

163. Whites achieved near-total disfranchisement of African Americans by 1900. Beck, Massey, and Tolnay, "The Gallows, the Mob, and the Vote," 322–23.

164. Summey, "Gender, Justice, and Jim Crow," iii.

165. Oral History Interview with Harvey E. Beech, September 25, 1996. Interview J-0075. Southern Oral History Program Collection (#4007), Southern Historical Collection, University of North Carolina at Chapel Hill, accessed October 9, 2017, http://docsouth.unc.edu/sohp/J-0075/excerpts/excerpt_5858.html.

166. "Fate of Daniels Cousins Hangs in Balance," *Carolina Times* (Durham, NC), February 25, 1950, 3.

167. See, for instance, Gershenhorn, *Louis Austin*; and "A Courageous Voice for Black Freedom," 57–92.

168. Gershenhorn, *Louis Austin*, 278–81.

169. "Toward Straight Thinking," Editorial, *Carolinian* (Raleigh, NC), January 4, 1947, 4.

170. For instance, see "Asks Governor to Commute Sentence to Life," *Carolinian* (Raleigh, NC), February 22, 1947, 1; "Governor to Rescue Again," Editorial, *Carolinian* (Raleigh, NC), May 17, 1947, 4; "Avoid Hysteria," Editorial, *Carolinian* (Raleigh, NC), June 14, 1947, 4; "'Miscarriage' Not Unexpected," Editorial, *Carolinian* (Raleigh, NC), August 16, 1947, 4; "Inviting More Trouble," Editorial, *Carolinian* (Raleigh, NC), August 23, 1947, 4.

171. Standing Committee on Legal Reserve of the Raleigh Branch of the NAACP to James W. Johnson, February 4, 1918, in Papers of the NAACP, Part 12, 1913–39, Series A: The South, Reel 18, PBL.

172. William Jay Walker Jr. to Prentice Thomas, January 27, 1943, in Papers of the NAACP, Part 12: Selected Branch Files, 1913–39, Series A, Reel 18, PBL.

173. W. R. Saxon to NAACP, November 3, 1938, in Papers of the NAACP, Part 8: Discrimination in the Criminal Justice System, Series B, Reel 16, PBL.

174. Walter White to W.R. Saxon, November 6, 1938, in Papers of the NAACP, Part 8: Discrimination in the Criminal Justice System, Series B, Reel 16, PBL.

175. Charles H. Houston to Mattie B. Tate, March 25, 1936, in Papers of the NAACP, Part 12: Selected Branch Files, 1913–39, Series A, Reel 18, PBL.

176. James Weldon Johnson to E. R. Merrick, September 24, 1925, in Papers of the NAACP, Part 8: Discrimination in the Criminal Justice System, Series B, Reel 8, PBL.

177. Frank R. Steward to Walter White, December 31, 1923, in Papers of the NAACP, Part 8: Discrimination in the Criminal Justice System, Series B, Reel 8, PBL; "Dock McCoy Submits Second Degree Murder," *Nashville Graphic* (Nashville, NC), November 29, 1923, 1.

178. "Hoey Snatches Condemned Man from Gas Chamber," *Carolina Times* (Durham, NC), 1; "Six Paroled by Broughton," *Statesville Daily Record*, July 21, 1944.

179. Walter White to Robert W. Bagnall, January 22, 1932, Papers of the NAACP, Part 8: Discrimination in the Criminal Justice System, Series B, Reel 8, PBL.

180. Algernon L. Butler to Walter White, February 1, 1932; Walter White to Will Alexander, February 2, 1932, in Papers of the NAACP, Part 8: Discrimination in the Criminal Justice System, Series B, Reel 8, PBL. Butler's fellow attorney on the case was Henry A. Grady Jr., whose father, a Superior Court judge, pulled a pistol in court to prevent a lynching attempt. See chapter 1.

181. Roy Wilkins to Algernon L. Butler, February 8, 1932. Papers of the NAACP, Part 8: Discrimination in the Criminal Justice System, Series B, Reel 8, PBL.

182. Algernon L. Butler to Roy Wilkins, February 17, 1932. Papers of the NAACP, Part 8: Discrimination in the Criminal Justice System, Series B, Reel 8, PBL; *State v. Herring* 201 N.C. 543, 544 (1931).

183. Clipping from the *Herald* (Columbia, TN), February 26, 1932, in Papers of the NAACP, Part 8: Discrimination in the Criminal Justice System, Series B, Reel 8, PBL.

184. Muller, "Legal Defense Fund's Capital Punishment Campaign," 160–61. NAACP records indicate a degree of investment in at least nine potentially capital cases in the first four decades of the twentieth century.

185. Hughes, *Fight for Freedom*, 128.

186. William Young and Nathaniel Bryant to Walter White, May 6, 1939; Nora Bryant to Walter White, May 7, 1939, in Papers of the NAACP, Part 8: Discrimination in the Criminal Justice System, Series B, Reel 15, PBL. Letter transcribed as written.

187. Thurgood Marshall to Nora Bryant, August 31, 1939, in Papers of the NAACP, Part 8: Discrimination in the Criminal Justice System, Series B, Reel 15, PBL.

188. Caswell J. Gates to Roy Wilkins, September 4, 1933 and Roy Wilkins to Caswell J. Gates, September 12, 1933, in Papers of the NAACP, Part 8: Discrimination in the Criminal Justice System, Series B, Reel 9, PBL.

189. Roy Wilkins to Arthur Spingarn, September 13, 1933, in Papers of the NAACP, Part 8: Discrimination in the Criminal Justice System, Series B, Reel 9, PBL.

190. *State v. Kelly*, 175 S.E. 294 (1934).

191. Perkinson, "Why I Do Not Believe in Capital Punishment."

192. "Gives Jury Say in Capital Cases as to Death or Life," *News and Observer*, January 26, 1917, 1.

193. "Capital Punishment," *King's Mountain Herald*, January 24, 1935, 4.

194. "Variety of Minor Bills Tossed into Assembly Hopper," *Daily Times-News* (Burlington, NC), January 29, 1935, 1.

195. "Death Penalties," *Daily Times-News* (Burlington, NC), October 7, 1937, 4 (reprinted editorial from *News and Observer*). See also "The Death Penalty," *Robesonian* (Lumberton, NC), October 6, 1937, 4; "Death Sentences," *Statesville Record and Landmark*, October 11, 1937, 4.

196. "Needed Reforms," *Daily Times-News* (Burlington, NC), December 29, 1938, 4.

197. "State Budget Big Problem in Assembly," *Asheville Citizen-Times*, February 18, 1939, 3; "Solons Boost Tax on Liquor and Incomes," *Asheville Citizen-Times*, February 28, 1939, 3.

198. S.B. 41, sec. 1, *Public Laws and Resolutions Passed by the General Assembly at the Session of 1941* (Charlotte: Observer Printing House, 1941), 304–5.

199. S.B. 41, sec. 1, *Public Laws and Resolutions Passed by the General Assembly at the Session of 1941* (Charlotte: Observer Printing House, 1941), 305; C.S. 4233 (burglary) and C.S. 4238 (arson), c. 215, from "Survey of Statutory Changes in North Carolina Law in 1941," *North Carolina Law Review* 19 (June 1941): 444.

200. Unsigned Editorial, *Robesonian* (Lumberton, NC), February 17, 1941, 4.

201. H.B. 150, sec. 2, *Session Laws and Resolutions Passed by the General Assembly of the State of North Carolina* (Raleigh: North Carolina General Assembly, 1949), 262–63.

202. "Life Imprisonment," *Robesonian* (Lumberton, NC), March 9, 1949, 1.

203. "Clemency Law Used First Time," *Statesville Daily Record*, March 26, 1949, 3.

204. "Abolish Capital Punishment—Sink," *Statesville Daily Record*, May 3, 1950, 2.

205. "Judge Raps Mercy Provision in Law," *Gastonia Gazette*, May 3, 1950, 8.

206. See, for instance, "The Rosenbergs," *High Point Enterprise*, April 7, 1951, 2; "Justice in America Follows Its Own Course," *Statesville Daily Record*, February 24, 1953, 4; "Jury Box Is Filled for Sheppard Trial," *Asheville Citizen-Times*, October 23, 1954.

207. "Jury Almost Completed for Washington Trial," *High Point Enterprise*, January 17, 1952, 12; "Complete Jury Is Sought for Trial of Sawyer," *High Point Enterprise*, March 19, 1952, 16; "Tarboro Chief Heard at Trial," *Evening Telegram* (Rocky Mount, NC), June 9, 1955, 1; "Four Chosen for Murder Trial Jury," *Robesonian* (Lumberton, NC), February 2, 1955, 1.

208. H.B. 326, Chapter 616, *Session Laws and Resolutions Passed by the General Assembly at the Regular Session, 1953*, 461–62.

209. "House Bill Would Allow Guilty Plea to Capital Crimes," *Asheville Citizen-Times*, March 21, 1953, 1.

210. "Scales to Face Trial," *Robesonian* (Lumberton, NC), March 7, 1955, 5.

211. Wasdon, "Think of the Victims," 4.

212. Roy Parker Jr., "Duplin Man Dies in Gas Chamber," *News and Observer*, October 28, 1961, 1.

213. "Capital Punishment," Editorial, *News and Observer*, September 28, 1925, 4.

214. "Murder and Mercy," *High Point Enterprise*, May 19, 1952, 2.

215. Walter A. Cotton, "Poison Gas against Electricity," *News and Observer*, July 17, 1938, M2.

216. Gallup Organization. Gallup Poll (AIPO), November 1953 [survey question]. USGALLUP.53-522.Q07A.

217. Gallup Organization. Gallup Poll (AIPO), March 1960 [survey question]. USGALLUP.60-625.Q003A.

218. Guy Munger, "Grim History of N.C. Executions," *News and Observer*, March 4, 1984, D1.

219. "Relic of Barbarism," Editorial, *News and Observer*, July 14, 1956, 4.

## Chapter 5

1. Interview with Velma Barfield, WBTV-Raleigh, undated, accessed July 5, 2017, https://www.youtube.com/watch?v=QsLZDcPun7k.

2. Eric Levin, "Cunning Poisoner—or Redeemed Christian—Velma Barfield Draws Nearer to Her Day of Execution," *People*, October 29, 1984.

3. "Around the Nation: Executed for Murder," *New York Times*, December 8, 1984.

4. Debbie Schupack, "Tenacious North Carolina Prosecutor Builds His Life on Death," *Los Angeles Times*, June 29, 1986, 39.

5. Fair Punishment Project, "America's Top Five Deadliest Prosecutors," June 2016, accessed July 5, 2017, http://fairpunishment.org/wp-content/uploads/2016/06/FPP-Top5Report_FINAL.pdf.

6. "Small N.C. District Is Giant on the Death Penalty," *News and Observer*, December 22, 1975, 1.

7. Richard A. Oppel Jr., "As Two Men Go Free, a Dogged Ex-Prosecutor Digs In," *New York Times*, September 7, 2014.

8. "N.C. Woman Is Convicted in Poisoning of Fiancé," *Asheville Citizen-Times*, December 3, 1978, 2; "N.C. Woman May Get Death Penalty," *Greenville News*, December 4, 1978, 30.

9. Ingle, "Final Hours," 224.

10. "Execution Decision Problem for Hunt," *Asheville Citizen-Times*, August 23, 1984, 2.

11. "Barfield Won't Appeal Death Penalty Decision," *Lansing State Journal*, September 28, 1984, 3.

12. Espy File.

13. Ingle, "Final Hours," 230.

14. Ingle, "Final Hours," 230.

15. "Hunt: Execution Presented Hard Choice," *Asheville Citizen-Times*, November 3, 1984, 10.

16. "She's Glad for Early Clemency Decision," *Asheville Citizen-Times*, September 9, 1984, 18.

17. Ingle, "Final Hours," 236.

18. "Prayers, Jeers Greet Execution," *Detroit Free Press*, November 3, 1984, 1.

19. Kathy Sawyer, "Woman Executed for Murder," *Washington Post*, November 2, 1984.

20. Coramae Richey Mann, "The Barfield Execution and the Irony of 'Equality,'" *Fort Lauderdale News*, November 11, 1984, 113.

21. Bella Stumbo, "Cold Killer or Loving Grandma?," *Los Angeles Times*, September 19, 1984, 22.

22. Garland, "Modes of Capital Punishment," 59.

23. Campbell, *Senator Sam Ervin*, 106.

24. For a history of voter suppression in North Carolina, see Redding, *Making Race, Making Power.*

25. Cunningham, *Klansville*, 111–13.

26. Cunningham, *Klansville*, 117–19.

27. Cunningham, *Klansville*, 5.

28. Chafe, *Civilities and Civil Rights*, 138–39.

29. Advertisement, *Statesville Record and Landmark*, March 24, 1964, 9.

30. Quoted in Garland, *A Peculiar Institution*, 236.

31. Elizabeth Pearsall, interviewed by Walter Campbell, May 15, 1988. Interview C-0056. Southern Oral History Program Collection (#4007), SHC, accessed June 6, 2017, http://dc.lib.unc.edu/cdm/compoundobject/collection/sohp/id/10505/rec/1.

32. Cecelski, *Along Freedom Road*, 26–27.

33. Flamm, *Law and Order*, 178.

34. *Mapp v. Ohio*, 367 U.S. 643 (1961), protects against unreasonable searches and seizures. *Miranda v. Arizona*, 384 U.S. 436 (1966), led to the creation of procedural safeguards for suspects now known as the Miranda warning. The warning lays out safeguards against self-incrimination. *Gideon v. Wainwright*, 372 U.S. 335 (1963), guarantees counsel as a condition of due process and requires states to appoint counsel as necessary.

35. "Opposition Is Testifying in Desegregation Hearing," *Daily Times* (Burlington, NC), August 6, 1969, 2.

36. "Forced Busing Is an Inane Program," Letter to the Editor, *Asheville Citizen-Times*, August 19, 1971, 4.

37. John Kilgo, "Booe Eyes Busing Issue," *Statesville Record and Landmark*, November 24, 1971, 33.

38. Jesse Helms for Senate Advertisement, *Robesonian* (Lumberton, NC), November 3, 1972, 3.

39. Mandery, *A Wild Justice*, 247–51.

40. Gottschalk, *Prison and the Gallows*, 104–5.

41. "Are you in favor of the death penalty for a person convicted of murder?" Survey by Gallup Organization, 1936–2016, accessed July 12, 2017, http://www.gallup.com/poll/1606/Death-Penalty.aspx.

42. Bae, *When the State No Longer Kills*, 2.

43. "Sanford Not in Favor Capital Punishment," *Daily Times-News* (Burlington, NC), February 27, 1961, 9; Banner, *The Death Penalty*, 220.

44. Lyn Nisbet, "Round the Capitol," *High Point Enterprise*, June 2, 1961, 2.

45. See, for instance, "Bill Would Abolish Death Penalty," *Asheville Citizen-Times*, March 1, 1961, 3; Robert Marks, "Good Morning," *High Point Enterprise*, March 5, 1961, 2.

46. "Church Group Urges N.C. Abolish Death Penalty," *High Point Enterprise*, May 30, 1961, 9.

47. "Stage Set for Full Debate on N.C. Capital Punishment," *High Point Enterprise*, June 6, 1961, 9.

48. "Capital Punishment to Continue in N.C.," *Asheville Citizen-Times*, June 9, 1961, 17.

49. "Death Penalty Sound," *Asheville Citizen-Times*, June 14, 1961, 4.

50. Bill East, "State Executions Nil for Decade as Death Penalty Awaits Rulings," *Robesonian* (Lumberton, NC), January 3, 1972, 6.

51. Reese Hart, "Death Penalty Carried Out for Last Time, Say Officials," *Robesonian* (Lumberton, NC), February 28, 1972, 2.

52. "Decade without Executions Gives Us Time to Reflect," *Asheville Citizen-Times*, January 9, 1971, 40.

53. *Lockett v. Ohio*, 438 U.S. 586, 599-600, 98 S. Ct. 2954, 2962-2963, 57 L. Ed. 2d 973 (1978).

54. *Furman v. Georgia*, 408 U.S. 238 (1972).

55. *Furman v. Georgia*.

56. *Furman v. Georgia*.

57. Paul Green, "Murdering Innocent Negroes," *News and Observer*, April 5, 1934, 4.

58. C. J. Parker Jr., "The State's Death Lottery," *News and Observer*, January 15, 1928, 4.

59. Johnson, "The Negro and Crime," 96.

60. Garland, *Peculiar Institution*, 232–33.

61. Smith, "The Supreme Court," 289.

62. Associated Press, "Officials Insist on Capital Punishment," *Asheville Citizen-Times* (July 1, 1972), 3.

63. Mandery, *Wild Justice*, 247–51.

64. Louis Harris, "Death Penalty Is Favored by Majority," *Daily Times-News* (Burlington, NC), June 11, 1973, 1.

65. Mandery, *Wild Justice*, 256.

66. Banner, *Death Penalty*, 268.

67. Uniform Crime Reports, accessed April 26, 2017, https://www.ucrdatatool.gov.

68. Steiker, "Capital Punishment and American Exceptionalism," 110–11.

69. Jerry Marshall, "Spiraling Crime Rate Forecast by Iredell Authorities," *Statesville Record and Landmark*, July 12, 1972, 4.

70. "N.C. Inmates Are to Be Resentenced," *Daily Times-News* (Burlington, NC), 1-A.

71. "Death Penalty Ban," *Asheville Citizen-Times*, July 4, 1972, 4.

72. "Backtalk: Death Penalty Ruling Questioned," *Asheville Citizen-Times*, July 8, 1972, 4.

73. "Down in Iredell," *Statesville Record and Landmark*, July 5, 1972, 1.

74. "Backtalk: Stern Measures," *Asheville Citizen-Times*, September 3, 1972, 4.

75. "Removing Death Penalty a Mistake," Letter to the Editor, *Daily Times-News* (Burlington, NC), October 4, 1972, 2.

76. Gene Wang, "Coed Opens Drive to Combat Crime," *Statesville Record and Landmark*, September 20, 1972, 6.

77. Devane, "The Origins of North Carolina's Post-*Furman* Death Penalty," 26.

78. "Nat'l Urban League Calls for Abolition Capital Punishment," *Carolina Times* (Durham, NC), March 8, 1969, 1.

79. "Legal Lynchings," Editorial, *Carolina Times* (Durham, NC), March 12, 1938, 4.

80. "NAACP Council Hails End of Death Penalty," *Carolina Times* (Durham, NC), July 8, 1972, 1.

81. Vernon Jordan, "Ban the Death Penalty," *Carolina Times* (Durham, NC), December 18, 1976, 4.

82. Annie B. Herbin, "Frye and Capital Punishment," *Future Outlook* (Greensboro, NC), July 7, 1972, 2.

83. Oshinsky, *Capital Punishment on Trial*, 60–61.

84. Associated Press, "Death Penalty May Be N. C. Issue in '73," *Asheville Citizen-Times*, July 1, 1972, 3.

85. *State v. Waddell*, 282 N.C. 431 (1973).

86. North Carolina Department of Public Safety, History of Capital Punishment in North Carolina, accessed December 28, 2017, http://www.doc.state.nc.us/dop /deathpenalty/DPhistory.htm.

87. Devane, "Origins," 12–13

88. Devane, "Origins," 22–23.

89. "Three Get Death Sentence in Tarboro in Rape Case," *Daily Times-News* (Burlington, NC), December 10, 1973, 23.

90. "Fights Execution," *Florence Morning News* (Florence, SC), January 14, 1974, 2.

91. Southern Poverty Law Center, "Jesse Lee Walston, Vernon Leroy Brown, and Bobby Hines," accessed July 21, 2017, https://www.splcenter.org/seeking-justice /case-docket/jesse-lee-walston-vernon-leroy-brown-and-bobby-hines.

92. Lampkin, "The Tarboro Three."

93. Law of April 8, 1974, Ch. 1201, 1974 Sess. Laws, 2d Sess. 323 (rewriting N.C. Gen. Stat. §§ 14-17 (murder), 14-21 (rape), 14-52 (burglary), 14-58 (arson)).

94. Devane, "Origins," 13.

95. "No Holshouser Meeting; Abernathy Hits Death Law," *News and Observer*, April 10, 1974, 24.

96. Mike Hannigan and Tony Platt, "Interview with Angela Davis," *Crime and Social Justice*, [no vol. number], no. 3 (Summer 1975): 30.

97. Ginny Carroll, "4,000 March Here in Peaceful Protest," *News and Observer*, July 5, 1974, 1.

98. Joan Little's first name is pronounced like the name Joanne.

99. McNeil, "Body, Sexuality, and Self-Defense," 235–61.

100. Reston, *The Innocence of Joan Little*, 6.

101. Little, "I Am Joan," 46.

102. McNeil, "Body, Sexuality, and Self-Defense," 251–52.

103. Farmer, "Free Joan Little."

104. McGuire, "Joan Little," 204–6.

105. McGuire, "Joan Little," 212.

106. John Kilgo, "Death Penalty Bill Seen as Best Effort Yet," *Robesonian* (Lumberton, NC), April 11, 1974, 30.

107. Oshinsky, *Capital Punishment on Trial*, 62–63.

108. "Revised Death Penalty Bill Is Enacted," *Robesonian* (Lumberton, NC), April 5, 1974, 1.

109. James A. Kidney, "High Court to View N.C. Execution Law," *Daily Tar Heel* (Chapel Hill, NC), October 30, 1974, 1.

110. "Death Penalty Case Set," *Chapel Hill Newspaper*, October 29, 1974, 1.

111. Paul Clancy, "Court Hears N.C. Death Case," *News and Observer*, April 22, 1975, 1. Elreta Melton Alexander became the first African American to be elected to a district court judgeship in 1968.

112. Paul Clancy, "Fowler Case May Clarify Status of Death Penalty," *News and Observer*, April 20, 1975, 1.

113. "From the North Carolina Death House, Jesse Fowler Launches a Historic Appeal," *People*, May 5, 1975.

114. "Angela Raps Repression in State," *Gastonia Gazette*, February 17, 1974, 54; *State v. Poole*, 203 S.E.2d 786 (1974).

115. Oshinsky, *Capital Punishment on Trial*, 62.

116. *Woodson v. North Carolina*, 96 S. Ct. 2978 (1976).

117. *Gregg v. Georgia*, 96 S. Ct. 2909 (1976), *Profitt v. Florida*, 96 S. Ct. 2960 (1976), *Jurek v. Texas*, 96 S. Ct. 2950 (1976), and *Roberts v. Louisiana*, 96 S. Ct. 3001 (1976).

118. Rhoads, "Resurrection of Capital Punishment," 546–47.

119. Rehnquist, Dissenting Opinion, *Woodson v. North Carolina*, 428 U.S. 280 (1976), 313.

120. *McGautha v. California*, 402 U.S. 183 (1971); Rehnquist, Dissenting Opinion, *Woodson v. North Carolina*, 313; Stack, *Dead Wrong*, 6–7.

121. Stack, *Dead Wrong*, 7.

122. Haines, *Against Capital Punishment*, 45–46.

123. Zimring, "The Unexamined Death Penalty," 1401.

124. Robinson and Dubber, "American Model Penal Code," 325.

125. Zimring and Hawkins, *Capital Punishment*, 84–85; Banner, *Death Penalty*, 269–70.

126. Zimring and Hawkins, *Capital Punishment*, 101–2.

127. "High Tribunal Holds Death Penalty Legal," *High Point Enterprise*, July 2, 1976, 1.

128. "New Death Law for N.C. Seen," *High Point Enterprise*, July 3, 1976, 3.

129. "Wood Opposes Death Penalty Despite Supreme Court Ruling," *High Point Enterprise*, July 3, 1976, 7.

130. Privette for Governor Advertisement, *Daily Times-News* (Burlington, NC), August 16, 1975, 7.

131. "Wood Has Earned Respect," *Asheville Citizen-Times*, August 12, 1976, 4.

132. "Quick Approval Expected for Demo Platform," *Daily Times-News* (Burlington, NC), July 13, 1976, 10.

133. "Voters Favor ERA, Option," *Daily Times-News* (Burlington, NC), October 26, 1976.

134. "Court Grants Inmate's Request for Execution," *Statesville Record and Landmark*, November 11, 1976, 1.

135. "The Law: After Gilmore, Who's Next?" *Time*, January 31, 1977.

136. "Squad Executes Gilmore," *Daily Times-News*, January 17, 1977, 1; Lily Rothman, "The Strange Story of the Man Who Chose Execution by Firing Squad," *Time*, March 12, 2015.

137. Paul Clancy, "Court Hears N.C. Death Case," *News and Observer*, April 22, 1975, 1.

138. "N.C. News: 2-Part Capital Case Trials Eyed," *Asheville Citizen-Times*, August 26, 1976, 37.

139. "Lawmakers Hear Death Penalty Arguments," *Daily Times-News* (Burlington, NC), February 3, 1977, 3.

140. "Death Penalty Is Argued," *Statesville Record and Landmark*, February 17, 1977, 1.

141. "Death Penalty Chosen," *Daily Times-News* (Burlington, NC), May 5, 1977, 1.

142. "State Passes Death Penalty," *Daily Times-News* (Burlington, NC), May 18, 1977.

143. "N.C. Death Penalty Nears Enactment," *News and Observer*, May 18, 1977, 1.

144. "Death Penalty: Attention Turns to First Degree Rape," *Daily Times-News*, May 19, 1977, 1.

145. Craig, "Capital Punishment in North Carolina," 913–14.

146. N.C. Gen. Stat. 15A-2000(e) (1978).

147. N.C. Gen. Stat. 15A-2000(f) (1978).

148. N.C. Gen. Stat. 15A-2000(b) (1978).

149. Stan Swofford, "Death Penalty," Editorial, *News and Observer*, November 13, 1983, B1.

150. "Students Express Views on Death Penalty," *Burlington Times-News*, June 2, 1977, 4A.

151. Gottschalk, *Prison and the Gallows*, 115.

152. Death Penalty Information Center, accessed May 18, 2018, https://deathpenaltyinfo.org/state_by_state.

153. "Death Penalty: Attention Turns to First Degree Rape," *Daily Times-News*, May 19, 1977, 1.

154. "Rape Bill Delayed," *Statesville Record and Landmark*, June 9, 1977, 6-A.

155. *Coker v. Georgia*, 433 U.S. 584 (1977).

156. "Allsbrook Surprised by Ruling," *Statesville Record and Landmark*, June 29, 1977.

157. "Execution Is Ordered under New State Law," *Statesville Record and Landmark*, October 22, 1977, 1. Jones was awarded a new trial by the North Carolina Supreme Court. *State of North Carolina v. James Calvin Jones*, 251 S.E.2d 425 (1979). He was retried and sentenced to life imprisonment. He was paroled in 2002. "People Removed from Death Row," North Carolina Department of

Public Safety, accessed July 21, 2017, https://www2.ncdps.gov/Index2.cfm?a =000003,002240,002327,002338.

158. "Executions Are Studied," *Statesville Record and Landmark*, December 14, 1977, 65.

159. "AMA Proposal Would Ban Death Injections," *Asheville Citizen-Times*, July 20, 1980, 9.

160. "Murderer Executed in Texas," *Asheville Citizen-Times*, December 7, 1982, 1.

161. Ed Martin, "Drugs Would Quietly End Life of Condemned Prisoner," *News and Observer*, January 12, 1984, A17.

162. "Foes Say Injections 'More Palatable,'" *Asheville Citizen-Times*, April 20, 1983, 23.

163. "Hanging Suggested for Death Penalty," *Asheville Citizen-Times*, June 17, 1983, 17.

164. "Injection Death Is Quick," *Asheville-Citizen Times*, January 9, 1984, 1.

165. Doug Clark, "Holliman's Death Penalty View Matters," *News and Record* (Greensboro, NC), January 31, 2007, A9.

166. "After Velma Barfield: Are Executions Gaining Acceptance?," *Albuquerque Journal*, November 7, 1984, A-7. Republished from *Newsday*.

167. Johnson and Martin, "Public's Conditional Response to Supreme Court Decisions," 304–5.

168. Simon, *Governing through Crime*, 34.

169. Marshall Frady, "Death in Arkansas," *New Yorker*, February 22, 1993, 105.

170. Emma Craigie, "Short Circuit the Killing States," *Observer* (London), May 31, 1992, 52.

171. "Holshouser Addresses Students," *High Point Enterprise*, January 27, 1974, 12.

172. "Gubernatorial Candidate Jim Hunt Urged Community Involvement," *Robesonian* (Lumberton, NC), April 13, 1976, 10.

173. Ed Brackett, "Hunt, Gardner Kick Off Race," *Asheville Citizen-Times*, May 12, 1992, 7A.

174. "Gov. Easley Denies Clemency in Landmark Execution," WRAL.com, December 1, 2005, accessed July 9, 2017, http://www.wral.com/news/local/story /1091304/.

175. Bob Geary, "Gov. Purdue 'Thinking Hard' about Capital Punishment and the Racial Justice Act?," *Indy Week* (Raleigh, NC), December 11, 2011.

176. Matthew Burns, "McCrory Signs Repeal of Racial Justice Act," WRAL.com (Raleigh, NC), June 19, 2013, accessed March 9, 2018, http://www.wral.com /mccrory-signs-repeal-of-racial-justice-act/12570643.

177. Radelet and Zsembik, "Executive Clemency," 280.

178. Nakell and Hardy, *Arbitrariness of the Death Penalty*, 80–82. See also Grosso, O'Brien, and Woodworth, "A Stubborn Legacy," 1531–59.

179. Radelet and Pierce, "Race and Death Sentencing in North Carolina," 2127–28.

180. Unah, "Choosing Those Who Will Die," 168.

181. "Sampson Negro Squares Account," *News and Observer*, March 22, 1921, 16.

182. "Negroes Forfeit Lives for Labor Day Murder," *News and Observer*, December 12, 1931, 12.

183. "Woman Watches Assailant Executed at State Prison," *News and Observer*, October 13, 1922, 1.

184. "Families Barred from Executions," *News and Observer*, October 6, 1925, 2.

185. Jay Hensley, "Night Vigil," *Asheville Citizen-Times*, January 13, 1984, 1.

186. Dan Ward, "Legal Maneuvers," *Asheville Citizen-Times*, March 16, 1984, 8.

187. See, for instance, Jim Nesbitt, "Hunt Refuses to Halt Woman's Execution," *Orlando Sentinel*, September 28, 1984, A-1; "Victims' Relatives Ask Death for Murderer," *Santa Fe New Mexican*, September 20, 1984, A-10; "Families Group to Seek Justice," *Asheville Citizen-Times*, November 2, 1984, 14.

188. Mastrocinque, "Overview of the Victims' Rights Movement," 95–110.

189. Jill Lepore, "The Rise of the Victims'-Rights Movement," *New Yorker*, May 21, 2018. Published online, accessed June 23, 2018. https://www.newyorker .com/magazine/2018/05/21/the-rise-of-the-victims-rights-movement.

190. Ginsberg, "Mighty Crime Victims," 911–46.

191. Ginsberg, "Mighty Crime Victims," 919.

## Conclusion

1. See, broadly, Ogletree and Sarat, *Life without Parole*.

2. Lynda Holmes, "The Case of Marie Hill: Will She Be a Martyr?," *Nashville Graphic* (Nashville, NC), January 8, 1970, 9.

3. "Marie Hill Death Sentence Is Condemned by Local NAACP," *Rocky Mount Telegram*, May 28, 1969, 13.

4. "Abernathy Says Death Penalty Meant to Kill Blacks," *Jet*, January 29, 1970, 24.

5. See, for instance, William A. Shires, "A Prediction: Marie Will Live," *Gastonia Gazette*, January 10, 1970.

6. *State v. Hill*, 183 S.E.2d 97 (1971), 279 N.C. 371.

7. Studies include O'Brien and Grosso, "Confronting Race," 463–504; Grosso, O'Brien, Woodworth, "A Stubborn Legacy," 1531–59; O'Brien and Grosso, "Beyond Batson's Scrutiny," 1623–54.

8. Jessica Jones, "Controversy Surrounds N.C. 'Racial Justice Act,'" *NPR*, December 1, 2011.

9. Campbell Robinson, "Bias Law Used to Move Man off Death Row," *New York Times*, April 21, 2012, A1.

10. Jessica Jones, "House Lawmakers Definitively Pass Racial Justice Act Repeal," *WUNC*, June 6, 2013, accessed December 12, 2017, http://wunc.org/post /house-lawmakers-definitively-pass-racial-justice-act-repeal.

11. Paul Woolverton, "N.C. Supreme Court to Hear Racial Justice Act Death Row Cases," *Fayetteville Observer*, March 2, 2018.

12. S.B. 306 Session 2013, Section 1(a)-(b), accessed December 11, 2017, https:// www.ncleg.net/Sessions/2013/Bills/Senate/PDF/S306v4.pdf.

13. Accessed December 11, 2017, https://www.ncleg.net/Sessions/2015/Bills /House/PDF/H774v3.pdf.

14. *North Carolina Department of Correction v. North Carolina Medical Board*, 675 S.E.2d 641 (2009); North Carolina Medical Board, "Position Statement: Capital Punishment," January 2007, amended June 2009, accessed December 11, 2017, https://www.ncmedboard.org/resources-information/professional-resources /laws-rules-position-statements/position-statements/capital_punishment.

15. Matthew Burns and Laura Leslie, "NC Changes Its Execution Method," *WRAL*, November 5, 2013, accessed December 11, 2017, http://www.wral.com/nc -changes-its-execution-method/13077523/.

16. *Weems v. United States*, 217 U.S. 349 (1910), 217.

17. Ellsworth and Gross, "Hardening of the Attitudes," 22.

18. Barkan and Cohn, "Racial Prejudice," 202–9. Cochran and Chamlin, "Enduring Racial Divide," 85–99.

19. *Callin v. Collins*, 510 U.S. 1141 (1994).

20. Concurring Opinion, *Callins v. Collins*, 510 U.S. 1141 (1994).

21. Garland, "Modes of Capital Punishment," 61.

22. Berry, "American Procedural Exceptionalism," 481–514.

23. Cook, "Potential Savings," 489–529.

24. Matthew Burns, "Top Lawmakers Demand NC Resume Carrying out Executions," *WRAL*, December 9, 2017, accessed March 16, 2018, http://www.wral.com /top-lawmakers-demand-nc-resume-carrying-out-executions/17171192/.

25. See, broadly, Bandes, "Victims, Closure, and the Sociology of Emotion," 1–26; Madeira, *Killing McVeigh*.

26. Ellsworth and Gross, "Hardening of the Attitudes," 19.

27. "Stay of Execution Granted to Mo. Inmate with Rare Medical Condition," *KCTV* News, March 19, 2018, accessed March 21, 2018, http://www.kctv5.com/story /37756655/lawyers-execution-could-be-gruesome-due-to-rare-condition; Merit Kennedy, "Oklahoma Plans to Use Nitrogen for Executions," *NPR*, March 15, 2018, accessed March 21, 2018, https://www.npr.org/sections/thetwo-way/2018/03/15 /593870687/oklahoma-plans-to-use-nitrogen-for-executions; Sandee LaMotte, "Death Row Inmate Sues after 'Botched' Execution," *CNN*, March 7, 2018, accessed March 21, 2018, https://www.cnn.com/2018/03/07/health/alabama-execution-lawsuit/index .html.

28. North Carolina Department of Public Safety, "List—Removed from Death Row," accessed March 21, 2018, https://www.ncdps.gov/our-organization/adult-correction /prisons/death-penalty/list-removed-death-row.

# Bibliography

## Manuscript Collections

Chapel Hill, NC
  North Carolina Collection, University of North Carolina at Chapel Hill
    Annual Report of the State Board of Charities and Public Welfare
    Annual Report of Attorneys General
    Biennial Report of the State Prison Department
    Biennial Report of the State Hospital at Goldsboro, July 1, 1924, to June 30,
      1925. Raleigh: Bynum Printing Company, 1926. http://docsouth.unc.edu
      /nc/goldsboro24/goldsboro24.html.
    *Citizens' Commission on Alternatives to Incarceration.* Raleigh, NC: The
      Commission, 1982.
    Gill, Edwin. "Report of the Office of the Commissioner of Paroles, January 1,
      1933–January 1, 1935." Raleigh: The Commissioner, undated, ca. 1935.
    North Carolina Council on Human Relations, "Rape: Selective Execution
      Based on Race."
    Public and Private Laws Passed by the General Assembly of the State of
      North Carolina.
    "Report of the Committee on Punishments, Penal Institutions, and Public
      Charities." *Journal of the Constitutional Convention of the State of North
      Carolina at Its Session 1868.*
    State Board of Charities and Public Welfare. *Capital Punishment in North
      Carolina* (Raleigh: State Board of Charities and Public Welfare, 1929).
  Southern Historical Collection, University of North Carolina at Chapel Hill
    Henry Canfield Papers
    Paul Green Papers
    Howard W. Odum Papers
    Charles M. Shaffer Papers
    Marion Wright Papers
Durham, NC
  William R. Perkins Library, Bostock Library, and Rubenstein Rare Book
      and Manuscript Library
    National Association for the Advancement of Colored People Papers
Raleigh, NC
  North Carolina Division of Archives and History
    Board of Paroles Papers
    Nell Battle Lewis Papers

Governors' Papers
    J. Melville Broughton Papers
    R. Gregg Cherry Papers
    Locke Craig Papers
    J. C. B. Ehringhaus Papers
    O. Max Gardner Papers
    W. W. Kitchin Papers
    W. Kerr Scott Papers
Prison Department, Central (State) Prison Papers

## Newspapers and Periodicals

*Albemarle Press*
*Albuquerque Journal*
*Amsterdam News*
*Asheville Citizen*
*Asheville Citizen-Times*
*Asheville Register*
*Baltimore Post*
*Burlington Daily News*
*Capitol Journal* (Salem, OR)
*Carolina Times* (Durham, NC)
*Carolinian* (Raleigh, NC)
*Chapel Hill Newspaper*
*Charlotte Daily Observer*
*Charlotte Democrat*
*Charlotte News*
*Chicago Tribune*
*Concord Daily Tribune*
*Daily Advance* (Elizabeth City, NC)
*Daily Review* (Wilmington, NC)
*Daily Tar Heel* (Chapel Hill, NC)
*Daily Times-News* (Burlington, NC)
*Davie Record* (Mocksville, NC)
*Detroit Free Press*
*Durham Daily Globe*
*Durham Morning Herald*
*Evening Telegram* (Rocky Mount, NC)
*Evening Visitor* (Raleigh, NC)
*Farmer and Mechanic* (Raleigh, NC)
*Fayetteville Observer*
*Fisherman and Farmer* (Edenton, NC)
*Florence Morning News* (Florence, SC)
*Fort Lauderdale News*
*Future Outlook* (Greensboro, NC)

*Gastonia Gazette*
*Goldsboro Headlight*
*Goldsboro Messenger*
*Greensboro Daily News*
*Greensboro North State*
*Greensboro Patriot*
*Greenville News*
*Harrisburg Daily Independent*
    (Harrisburg, PA)
*Henderson Gold Leaf*
*Herald* (Columbia, TN)
*Hickory Daily Record*
*High Point Enterprise*
*Hillsboro Recorder*
*Indy Week* (Raleigh, NC)
*King's Mountain Herald*
*Lansing State Journal*
*Lincoln County News*
*Los Angeles Times*
*Lumberton Robesonian*
*Miami News*
*Morning Post* (Raleigh, NC)
*Nashville Graphic* (Nashville, NC)
*Newbern Sentinel*
*New Bern Sun-Journal*
*News and Observer* (Raleigh, NC)
*News and Record* (Greensboro, NC)
*News-Observer-Chronicle* (Raleigh, NC)
*New Yorker*
*New York Herald*
*New York Times*
*North Wilkesboro Hustler*
*Observer* (London)
*Orlando Sentinel*

*People*
*Prison News*
*Raleigh Carolinian*
*Raleigh Sentinel*
*Richmond Times-Dispatch*
*Robesonian* (Lumberton, NC)
*Rocket* (Rockingham, NC)
*Rockingham Post-Dispatch*
*Rocky Mount Telegram*
*Rutherford Star* (Rutherfordton, NC)
*Sampson Democrat* (Clinton, NC)
*Santa Fe New Mexican*
*Semi-Weekly Messenger*
   (Wilmington, NC)
*Southern Progress* (Washington, NC)
*Statesville Daily Record*
*Statesville Record and Landmark*

*St. Louis Star and Times*
*Sun* (Rutherfordton, NC)
*Time*
*Times-Picayune*
*Union Republican* (Winston-Salem, NC)
*Wall Street Journal*
*Washington Post*
*Washington Star*
*Weekly Star* (Wilmington, NC)
*Western Sentinel* (Winston-Salem, NC)
*Wilmington Gazette*
*Wilmington Messenger*
*Wilmington Morning Star*
*Wilson Mirror*
*Winston-Salem Journal*

## Databases

Ancestry.com. http://ancestry.com.

The ESPY File. ICPSR08451-v5. Ann Arbor, MI: Inter-university Consortium for Political and Social Research [distributor], July 20, 2016. https://doi.org/10.3886/ICPSR08451.v5.

National Registry of Exonerations. https://www.law.umich.edu/special/exoneration/.

Newspapers.com. http://newspapers.com.

Uniform Crime Reports. https://www.ucrdatatool.gov.

## Theses and Dissertations

Callahan, B. F. "The North Carolina Slave Patrol." MA thesis, University of North Carolina at Chapel Hill, 1983.

Craven, Charles K. "North Carolina's Prison System: A Chronological History through 1950." MA thesis, University of North Carolina at Chapel Hill, 1987.

Devane, Mary M. "The Origins of North Carolina's Post-*Furman* Death Penalty: The General Assembly Arbitrates between the United States Supreme Court and the Public, 1972–1977." MA thesis, University of North Carolina at Chapel Hill, 1995.

Lampkin, Brian. "The Tarboro Three: Rape, Race, and Secrecy in a Small Town." MA thesis, East Carolina University, 2011.

Pearson, Susan. "Samarcand, Nell Battle Lewis, and the 1931 Arson Trial." Senior Honors Essay, History. University of North Carolina at Chapel Hill, 1989.

Seitz, Katrina Nanette. "The Transition of Methods of Execution in North Carolina: A Descriptive Social History of Two Time Periods, 1935 & 1983." PhD diss., Sociology. Virginia Polytechnic Institute and State University, 2001.

Summey, Virginia Lyndsay. "Gender, Justice, and Jim Crow: North Carolina Elreta Alexander and the Long Civil Rights Era." MA thesis, University of Montana, 2012.

Zimmerman, Hilda Jane. "Penal Systems and Penal Reforms in the South since the Civil War." PhD diss., University of North Carolina at Chapel Hill, 1947.


## Oral History

Elizabeth Pearsall, interviewed by Walter Campbell, May 15, 1988. Interview C-0056. Southern Oral History Program Collection (#4007), Southern Historical Collection, The Louis Round Wilson Special Collections Library, University of North Carolina at Chapel Hill. Accessed June 6, 2017. http://dc.lib .unc.edu/cdm/compoundobject/collection/sohp/id/10505/rec/1.


## Books and Articles

Abramowitz, Elkan, and David Paget. "Executive Clemency in Capital Cases." *New York University Law Review* 39 (1964): 141–42.

"An Act to Permit the State to Accept, with the Approval of the Court, a Plea of Guilty for First Degree Murder, First Degree Burglary, Arson, or Rape," *Session Laws and Resolutions Passed by the General Assembly of the State of North Carolina, 1983* (Winston-Salem, NC: Winston Printing, 1953), 461–62.

Adams, William J. "Evolution of Law in North Carolina." *North Carolina Law Review* 2, no. 3 (April 1924): 133–45.

Allen, Irving Lewis. "Sly Slurs: Mispronunciation and Decapitalization of Group Names." *Journal of Omnastics* 36, nos. 3 & 4 (September–December 1988): 217–24.

Altschuler, Albert W., and Andrew G. Deiss. "A Brief History of the Criminal Jury in the United States." *University of Chicago Law Review* 61, no. 3 (Summer 1994): 867–928.

American Prison Association Congress. "Proceedings of the Annual Congress of the American Prison Association, August 14–19." Indianapolis: Wm. B. Burford, Printer, 1909.

Arnold, Thurman. *Symbols of Government*. New Haven, CT: Yale University Press, 1935.

Ashe, Samuel A., Stephen V. Weeks, and Charles L. Van Noppen, eds. *Biographical History of North Carolina, from Colonial Times to the Present*. Greensboro, NC: Charles L. Van Noppen, 1907.

Avery, Laurence G., ed. *A Southern Life: Letters of Paul Green*. Chapel Hill: University of North Carolina Press, 2013.

Ayers, Edward L. *Vengeance and Justice: Crime and Punishment in the 19th-Century American South*. New York: Oxford University Press, 1984.

Bae, Sangmin. *When the State No Longer Kills: International Human Rights Norms and the Abolition of Capital Punishment*. Albany: State University of New York Press, 2005.

Bailey, Amy Kate, and Stuart E. Tolnay. *Lynched: The Victims of Southern Mob Violence*. Chapel Hill: University of North Carolina Press, 2015.

Baker, Bruce E. *The Mob Will Surely Take My Life: Lynchings in the Carolinas, 1871–1947*. London: Continuum, 2008.

Baker, S. C. "Negro Criminality." *North Carolina Law Journal* 1, no. 1 (March 1900): 27–33.

Bandes, Susan A. "Victims, Closure, and the Sociology of Emotion." *Law and Contemporary Problems* 72, no. 2 (2009): 1–26.

Banner, Stuart. *The Death Penalty: An American History*. Cambridge, MA: Harvard University Press, 2002.

Bardaglio, Peter W. *Reconstructing the Household: Families, Sex, and the Law in the Nineteenth-Century South*. Chapel Hill: University of North Carolina Press, 1995.

Barkan, Steven E., and Steven F. Cohn. "Racial Prejudice and Support for the Death Penalty among Whites." *Journal of Research in Crime and Delinquency* 31, no. 2 (May 1994): 202–9.

Barkley Brown, Elsa. "Negotiating and Transforming the Public Sphere: African American Political Life from Slavery to Freedom." In *Time Longer than Rope: A Century of African American Activism, 1850–1950*, edited by Charles M. Payne and Adam Green, 68–110. New York: New York University Press, 2003.

Baumgartner, Frank R., Marty Davidson, Kaneesha R. Johnson, et al. *Deadly Justice: A Statistical Portrait of the Death Penalty*. New York: Oxford University Press, 2018.

Baumgartner, Frank R., Suzanna De Boef, and Amber Boydston. *The Decline of the Death Penalty and the Discovery of Innocence*. New York: Cambridge University Press, 2008.

Bay, Mia. "From the 'Ladies Car' to the 'Colored Car': Black Female Travelers in the Segregated South." In *The Folly of Jim Crow: Rethinking the Segregated South*, edited by Stephanie Cole and Natalie J. Ring, 150–75. Arlington: The University of Texas at Arlington, 2012.

Beck, E. M., James L. Massey, and Stewart E. Tolnay. "The Gallows, the Mob, and the Vote: Lethal Sanctioning of Blacks in North Carolina and Georgia, 1882–1930." *Law & Society Review* 23, no. 2 (1989): 317–31.

Bedau, Hugo Adam. *The Death Penalty in America: Current Controversies*. New York: Oxford University Press, 1998.

Bedau, Hugo Adam, and Michael L. Radelet. "Miscarriages of Justice in Potentially Capital Cases." *Stanford Law Review* 40, no. 1 (November 1987): 21–180.

Berman, Frederick S., and Lainie R. Fastman. "Newly Discovered Evidence: A Defendant's Chance for a New Trial." *New York Law School Law Review* 28, no. 1 (1983–1984): 31–50.

Berry, William W. "American Procedural Exceptionalism: A Deterrent or Catalyst for Death Penalty Abolition?" *Cornell Journal of Law and Public Policy* 17, no. 3 (2008): 481–514.

Bickford, Annette Louise. "Imperial Modernity, National Identity, and Capital Punishment in the Samarcand Arson Case, 1931." *Nations and Nationalism* 13, no. 3 (2007): 437–60.

Blackman, Paul H., and Vance McLaughlin. "The Espy File on American Executions: User Beware." *Homicide Studies* 15, no. 3 (2011): 209–27.

Bohm, Robert M. *DeathQuest: An Introduction to the Theory and Practice of Capital Punishment in the United States.* 5th ed. New York: Routledge, 2017.

Bowers, William J., Glenn L. Pierce, and John F. McDevitt. *Legal Homicide: Death as Punishment in America, 1864–1982.* Boston: Northeastern University Press, 1984.

Boyle, William S. "Lethal Gas." *Commercial Law League Journal* 30, no. 6 (June 1925): 248–49.

Brandon, Craig. *The Electric Chair: An Unnatural American History.* Jefferson, NC: McFarland, 1999.

Brown, Elsa Barkley. "Negotiating and Transforming the Public Sphere: African American Political Life from Slavery to Freedom." In *Time Longer than Rope: A Century of African American Activism, 1850–1950,* ed. Charles M. Payne and Adam Green, 76. New York: New York University Press, 2003.

Brundage, W. Fitzhugh. "Conclusion: Reflections on Lynching Scholarship." *American Nineteenth Century History* 6, no. 3 (September 2005): 401–3.

——. *Lynching in the New South: Georgia and Virginia, 1880–1930.* Urbana: University of Illinois Press, 1993.

Cahn, Susan. "Spirited Youth or Fiends Incarnate: The Samarcand Arson Case and Female Adolescence in the American South." *Journal of Women's History* 9, no. 4 (Winter 1998): 152–81.

Campbell, James A. "The Lynching of William Parker: The Criminal Justice System at Work in 19th Century North Carolina." *American Journal of Criminal Justice* 7, no. 2 (September 1982): 99–109.

Campbell, Karl E. *Senator Sam Ervin, Last of the Founding Fathers.* Chapel Hill: University of North Carolina Press, 2007.

Campney, Brent M. S. *This Is Not Dixie: Racist Violence in Kansas 1861–1927.* Urbana: University of Illinois Press, 2017.

Carrigan, William D., and Clive Webb. *Forgotten Dead: Mob Violence against Mexicans in the United States, 1848–1928.* New York: Oxford University Press, 2013.

Castles, Katherine. "Quiet Eugenics: Sterilization in North Carolina's Institutions for the Mentally Retarded, 1945–1965." *Journal of Southern History* 68, no. 4 (November 2002): 849–78.

Cecelski, David S. *Along Freedom Road: North Carolina and the Fate of Black Schools in the South.* Chapel Hill: University of North Carolina Press, 1994.

Chafe, William H. *Civilities and Civil Rights: Greensboro, North Carolina, and the Black Struggle for Freedom.* New York: Oxford University Press, 1980.

Clarke, James W. "Without Fear or Shame: Lynching, Capital Punishment, and the Subculture of Violence in the American South." *British Journal of Political Science* 28, no. 2 (April 1998): 269–89.

Clegg, Claude A., III. *Troubled Ground: A Tale of Murder, Lynching, and Reckoning in the New South.* Urbana: University of Illinois Press, 2010.

Coates, Albert. "Punishment for Crime in North Carolina." *North Carolina Law Review* 17, no. 3 (April 1939): 205–32.

Cobb, James C., and Charles R. Wilson, eds. *Perspectives on the American South.* New York: Gordon and Breach Science, 1985.

Cochran, John K., and Mitchell B. Chamlin. "The Enduring Racial Divide in Death Penalty Support." *Journal of Criminal Justice* 34, no. 1 (January–February 2006): 85–99.

Connor, R. D. W., ed. *A Manual of North Carolina.* Raleigh, NC: Edwards and Broughton, 1915.

Cook, Lisa D. "Converging to a National Lynching Database: Recent Developments and a Way Forward." *Historical Methods* 45, no. 2 (2012): 45–63.

Cook, Philip J. "Potential Savings from Abolition of the Death Penalty in North Carolina," *American Law and Economics Review* 11, no. 2 (Fall 2009): 489–529.

Corbitt, David Leroy, ed. *Public Addresses and Papers of Governor Robert Gregg Cherry, 1945–1949.* Raleigh, NC: Council of State, 1951.

———, ed. *Public Papers and Letters of Angus Wilton McLean, Governor of North Carolina, 1925–1929.* Raleigh, NC: Edwards and Broughton, 1931.

Cox, Oliver C. *Caste, Class, and Race: A Study in Social Dynamics.* New York: Monthly Review, 1959.

Craig, Joel M. "Capital Punishment in North Carolina: The 1977 Death Penalty Statute and the North Carolina Supreme Court." *North Carolina Law Review* 59, no. 5 (June 1981): 911–42.

Cunningham, David. *Klansville, U.S.A.* New York: Oxford University Press, 2013.

Curtis, Susan. *Colored Memories: A Biographer's Quest for the Elusive Lester A. Walton.* Columbia: University of Missouri Press, 2008.

Cutler, J. E. "Capital Punishment and Lynching." *Annals of the American Academy of Political and Social Science* 29, no. 1 (May 1907): 182–85.

Davis, David Brion. "The Movement to Abolish Capital Punishment in America, 1787–1861." *American Historical Review* 63, no. 1 (October 1957): 23–46.

Dollard, John. *Caste and Class in a Southern Town.* New Haven: Yale University Press, 1937.

Dressner, Richard B., and Glenn C. Altschuler. "Sentiment and Statistics in the Progressive Era: The Debate on Capital Punishment in New York." *New York History* 56, no. 2 (April 1975): 191–209.

Driggs, Ken. "A Current of Electricity Sufficient in Intensity to Cause Immediate Death: A Pre-Furman History of the Electric Chair." *Stetson Law Review* 22, no. 3 (Summer 1993): 1169–1210.

"Electricity as an Executioner." *Scientific American* 34, no. 2. (January 8, 1876): 16.

Elias, Norbert. *The Civilizing Process: Sociogenetic and Phylogenic Observations.* Translated by Edmund Jephcott. Oxford: Blackwell, [1936], 2000.

Ellsworth, Phoebe C., and Samuel R. Gross. "Hardening of the Attitudes: Americans' Views on the Death Penalty." *Journal of Social Forces* 50, no. 2 (Summer 1994): 19–52.

Farmer, Ashley. "Free Joan Little: Anti-Rape Activism, Black Power, and the Black Freedom Movement." *Black Perspectives* (February 4, 2016).

Feimster, Crystal N. *Southern Horrors: Women and the Politics of Rape and Lynching.* Cambridge, MA: Harvard University Press, 2011.

Fischer, Kirsten. *Suspect Relations: Sex, Race, and Resistance in Colonial North Carolina.* Ithaca, NY: Cornell University Press, 2002.

Flamm, Michael W. *Law and Order: Street Crime, Civil Unrest, and the Crisis of Liberalism in the 1960s.* New York: Columbia University Press, 2005.

Flanigan, Daniel J. "Criminal Procedure in Slave Trials in the Antebellum South." *Journal of Southern History* 40, no. 4 (November 1974): 537–64.

"Form and Content of Applications for Pardon," North Carolina General Statutes 147–21 (1869–1870, c. 171; 1870–1871, c. 61; Code, s. 3336; Rev., s. 5334; C.S., s. 7642).

Foucault, Michel. *Discipline and Punish: The Birth of the Prison.* Translated by Alan Sheridan. New York: Vintage Books, 1995.

Freedman, Eric M. "Brown v. Allen: The Habeas Corpus Revolution That Wasn't." *Alabama Law Review* 51, no. 4 (2000): 1541–624.

Friedman, Lawrence M. *Crime and Punishment in American History.* New York: Basic Books, 1993.

Galliher, John F., Gregory Ray, and Brent Cook. "Abolition and Reinstatement of Capital Punishment during the Progressive Era and Early 20th Century." *Journal of Criminal Law and Criminology* 83, no. 3 (Autumn 1992): 538–76.

Garfinkel, Harold. "Research Note on Inter- and Intra-Racial Homicides." *Social Forces* 27, no. 4 (May 1949): 369–81.

Garland, David. "Capital Punishment and American Culture." *Punishment and Society* 7, no. 4 (2005): 347–76.

———. "Death, Denial, Discourse: On the Forms and Functions of American Capital Punishment." In *Crime, Social Control, and Human Rights: From Moral Panics to States of Denial, Essays in Honour of Stanley Cohen*, edited by David Downes, Paul Rock, Conor Gearty, and Christine Chinkin, 136–56. New York: Routledge, 2013.

———. "Modes of Capital Punishment: The Death Penalty in Historic Perspective." In *America's Death Penalty: Between Past and Present*, edited by David Garland, Randall McGowan, and Michael Meranze, 30–71. New York: New York University Press, 2011.

———. *A Peculiar Institution: Capital Punishment in the Age of Abolition.* Cambridge, MA: Harvard University Press, 2010.

Gershenhorn, Jerry. "A Courageous Voice for Black Freedom: Louis Austin and the Carolina Times in Depression-Era North Carolina." *North Carolina Law Review* 87, no. 1 (January 2010): 57–92.

——. *Louis Austin and the* Carolina Times: *A Life in the Long Black Freedom Struggle*. Chapel Hill: University of North Carolina Press, 2018.

Gilmore, Glenda Elizabeth. *Gender and Jim Crow: Women and the Politics of White Supremacy in North Carolina, 1896–1920*. Chapel Hill: University of North Carolina Press, 1996.

Ginsberg, Raphael. "Mighty Crime Victims: Victims' Rights and Neoliberalism in the American Conjuncture." *Cultural Studies* 28, nos. 5–6 (2014): 911–46.

Gist, Noel P. "The Negro in the Daily Press." *Social Forces* 10, no. 3 (1931–32): 405–11.

Goldsby, Jacqueline. *A Spectacular Secret: Lynching in American Life and Literature*. Chicago: University of Chicago Press, 2006.

Gonzales-Day, Ken. *Lynching in the West, 1850–1935*. Durham, NC: Duke University Press, 2006.

Gottschalk, Marie. *The Prison and the Gallows: The Politics of Mass Incarceration in America*. New York: Cambridge University Press, 2006.

Graham, William E., Jr. "Criminal Law: Improper Court Response to Spontaneous Jury Inquiry as to Pardon and Parole Possibilities." *North Carolina Law Review* 33, no. 4 (June 1955): 665–69.

Grantham, Dewey. *Southern Progressivism: The Reconciliation of Progress and Tradition*. Knoxville: University of Tennessee Press, 1983.

Greene, Sally. "*State v. Mann* Exhumed." *North Carolina Law Review* 87, no. 3 (2009): 701–56.

Grosso, Catherine M., Barbara O'Brien, and George G. Woodworth. "A Stubborn Legacy: Race in Jury Selection in 173 Post-Batson Capital Trials." *Iowa Law Review* 97, no. 5 (July 2012): 1531–60.

Haines, Herbert H. *Against Capital Punishment: The Anti-Death Penalty Movement in America 1972–1994*. New York: Oxford University Press, 1996.

Hale, Grace Elizabeth. *Making Whiteness: The Culture of Segregation in the South, 1890–1940*. New York: Vintage Books, 1998.

Haley, Sarah. "'Like I Was a Man': Chain Gangs, Gender, and the Domestic Carceral Sphere in Jim Crow Georgia." *Signs* 39, no. 1 (Autumn 2013): 53–77.

Hall, Jacquelyn Dowd. *Revolt against Chivalry: Jessie Daniel Ames and the Women's Campaign Against Lynching*. Rev. ed. New York: Columbia University Press, 1993.

Hall, Kermit L., ed. *Police, Prison, and Punishment: Major Historical Interpretations*. New York: Garland, 1987.

Hannigan, Mike, and Tony Platt. "Interview with Angela Davis." *Crime and Social Justice*, no. 3 (Summer 1975): 30–35.

Harries, Keith, and Derral Cheatwood. *The Geography of Execution: The Capital Punishment Quagmire in America*. Lanham, MD: Rowan and Littlefield, 1997.

Harris, Philip W. "Oversimplification and Error in Public Opinion Surveys on Capital Punishment." *Justice Quarterly* 3, no. 4 (1986): 429–55.

Hartnett, John. *Executing Democracy: Capital Punishment and the Making of America 1835–1843*. East Lansing: Michigan State University Press, 2012.

Hearn, Daniel Allen. *Legal Executions in North Carolina and South Carolina, 1866–1962*. Jefferson, NC: McFarland, 2015.

Higginbotham, Evelyn Brooks. "African-American Women's History and the Metalanguage of Race." *Signs* 17, no. 2 (Winter 1992): 251–74.

———. *Righteous Discontent: The Women's Movement in the Black Baptist Church, 1880–1920*. Cambridge, MA: Harvard University Press, 1993.

Hill, Karlos K. *Beyond the Rope: The Impact of Lynching on Black Culture and Memory*. New York: Cambridge University Press, 2016.

Hindus, Michael Stephen. *Prison and Plantation: Crime, Justice, and Authority in Massachusetts and South Carolina, 1767–1878*. Chapel Hill: University of North Carolina Press, 1980.

Holloway, Pippa. *Living in Infamy: Felon Disfranchisement and the History of American Citizenship*. New York: Oxford University Press, 2014.

Huber, Patrick. "Caught Up in the Violent Whirlwind of Lynching: The 1885 Quadruple Lynching in Chatham County, North Carolina." *North Carolina Historical Review* 75, no. 2 (1998): 135–60.

Hughes, Langston. *Fight for Freedom*. In *The Collected Works of Langston Hughes*, vol. 10. Edited by Christopher C. De Santis. Columbia: University of Missouri Press, 2001.

Ingle, Joseph B. "Final Hours: The Execution of Velma Barfield." *Loyola of Los Angeles Law Review* 23, no. 1 (1989): 221–36.

Jacobs, David, Jason T. Carmichael, and Stephanie L. Kent. "Vigilantism, Current Racial Threat, and Death Sentences." *American Sociological Review* 70, no. 4 (August 2005): 656–77.

Johnson, Elmer H. "Selective Factors in Capital Punishment." *Social Forces* 36, no. 2 (December 1957): 165–69.

Johnson, Guion Griffis. *Ante-bellum North Carolina: A Social History*. Chapel Hill: University of North Carolina Press, 1937.

Johnson, Guy B. "The Negro and Crime." *Annals of the American Academy of Political and Social Science* 217, no. 1 (September 1941): 93–104.

Johnson, Timothy R., and Andrew D. Martin. "The Public's Conditional Response to Supreme Court Decisions." *American Political Science Review* 92, no. 2 (June 1998): 299–309.

Jones, Jacqueline. *Labor of Love, Labor of Sorrow: Black Women, Work, and Family from Slavery to the Present*. New York: Vintage Books, [1985], 1995.

Kasson, John F. *Civilizing the Machine: Technology and Republican Values in America*. New York: Hill and Wang, 1999.

Kay, Marvin L. Michael, and Lorin Lee Cary. "'The Planters Suffer Little or Nothing': North Carolina Compensation for Executed Slaves, 1748–1772." *Science and Society* 40, no. 3 (Fall 1976): 288–306.

———. *Slavery in North Carolina, 1748–1775*. Chapel Hill: University of North Carolina Press, 1995.

Kearns, Timothy S. "The Chair, the Needle, and the Damage Done: What the Electric Chair and the Rebirth of the Method-of-Execution Challenge Could

Mean for the Future of the Eighth Amendment." *Cornell Journal of Law and Public Policy* 15, no. 1 (2005–6): 197–229.

Kelley, Robin D. G. "'We Are Not What We Seem': Rethinking Black Working-Class Opposition in the Jim Crow South." *Journal of American History* 80, no. 1 (June 1993): 75–112.

King, Henry T. *Sketches of Pitt County: A Brief History of the County, 1704–1910.* Raleigh, NC: Edwards, 1911.

Knepper, Paul. *North Carolina's Criminal Justice System.* Durham, NC: Carolina Academic Press, 1999.

Koren, John. *Summaries of State Laws Relating to the Insane.* New York: National Committee for Mental Hygiene, 1917.

Kotch, Seth, and Robert P. Mosteller. "The Racial Justice Act and the Long Struggle with Race and the Death Penalty in North Carolina." *North Carolina Law Review* 88, no. 6 (2010): 2031–131.

Leidholdt, Alexander S. *Battling Nell: The Life of Southern Journalist Cornelia Battle Lewis, 1893–1956.* Baton Rouge: Louisiana State University Press, 2009.

Lepore, Jill. "The Rise of the Victims'-Rights Movement." *New Yorker.* May 21, 2018. Published online, accessed June 23, 2018. https://www.newyorker.com /magazine/2018/05/21/the-rise-of-the-victims-rights-movement.

Lewis, Nell Battle. "The North Carolina Conference for Social Service." *Social Forces* 1, no. 1 (1922–23): 265–68.

Linders, Annulla. "The Execution Spectacle and State Legitimacy: The Changing Nature of the American Execution Audience, 1833–1937." *Law & Society Review* 36, no. 3 (2002): 607–56.

Link, William A. *The Paradox of Southern Progressivism.* Chapel Hill: University of North Carolina Press, 1993.

Little, Joan. "I Am Joan." *Southern Exposure* 6, no. 1 (undated, ca. 1977): 42–47.

Mackey, Philip English. "Edward Livingston and the Origins of the Movement to Abolish Capital Punishment in America." *Louisiana History* 16, no. 2 (Spring 1975): 146–57.

Madeira, Jody Lyneé. *Killing McVeigh: The Death Penalty and the Myth of Closure.* New York: New York University Press, 2012.

Mandery, Evan J. *A Wild Justice: The Death and Resurrection of Capital Punishment in America.* New York: Norton, 2013.

Martin, Sanford, ed. *Public Letters and Papers of Thomas Walter Bickett, Governor of North Carolina, 1917–1921.* Raleigh: Edwards and Broughton, 1923.

Mastrocinque, Jeanna M. "An Overview of the Victims' Rights Movement: Historical, Legislative, and Research Developments." *Sociology Compass* 4, no. 2 (2010): 95–110.

Matusiak, Matthew C., Michael S. Vaughan, and Rolando V. del Carmen. "The Progression of 'Evolving Standards of Decency' in U.S. Supreme Court Decisions." *Criminal Justice Review* 39, no. 3 (2014): 253–71.

McGuire, Danielle L. "Joan Little and the Triumph of Testimony." In *Freedom Rights: New Perspectives on the Civil Rights Movement*, edited by Danielle L.

McGuire and John Dittmer, 191–221. Lexington: University Press of Kentucky, 2011.

McNeil, Genna Rae. "The Body, Sexuality, and Self-Defense in *State vs. Joan Little, 1974–1975*." *Journal of African American History* 93, no. 2 (Spring 2008): 235–61.

Mencken, H. L. "Designations for Colored Folk." *American Speech* 19, no. 3 (1944): 161–74.

Messner, Steven F., Eric P. Baumer, and Richard Rosenfeld. "Distrust of Government, the Vigilante Tradition, and Support for Capital Punishment." *Law & Society Review* 40, no. 3 (2006): 559–90.

Mims, Edwin. *The Advancing South: Stories of Progress and Reaction*. Garden City, NY: Doubleday, Page, and Company, 1926.

Moran, Richard. *Executioner's Current: Thomas Edison, George Westinghouse, and the Invention of the Electric Chair*. New York: Knopf Doubleday, 2007.

Muller, Eric L. "The Legal Defense Fund's Capital Punishment Campaign: The Distorting Influence of Death." *Yale Law and Policy Review* 4, no. 1 (1985): 158–87.

Myers, Barton A. *Rebels against the Confederacy: North Carolina's Unionists*. New York: Cambridge University Press, 2014.

Nakell, Barry, and Kenneth A. Hardy. *The Arbitrariness of the Death Penalty*. Philadelphia: Temple University Press, 1987.

Nathans, Sydney. "The Quest for Progress: North Carolina, 1870–1920." In *The Way We Lived in North Carolina*, edited by Joe A. Mobley, 1–112. Chapel Hill: University of North Carolina Press, 2003.

Newkirk, Vann R. *Lynching in North Carolina, 1865–1941*. Jefferson, NC: McFarland, 2009.

Nice, David C. "The States and the Death Penalty." *Western Political Quarterly* 45, no. 4 (December 1992): 1037–48.

Nye, David. *Electrifying America: Social Meanings of a New Technology, 1880–1940*. Cambridge, MA: MIT Press, 1992.

O'Brien, Barbara, and Catherine M. Grosso. "Beyond Batson's Scrutiny: A Preliminary Look at Racial Disparities in Prosecutorial Preemptory Strikes following the Passage of the North Carolina Racial Justice Act." *University of California, Davis Law Review* 46, no. 5 (2013): 1623–54.

——. "Confronting Race: How a Confluence of Social Movements Convinced North Carolina to Go Where the *McClesky* Court Wouldn't." *Michigan State Law Review* 2011, no. 3 (2011): 463–504.

O'Brien, Michael. *The Idea of the American South, 1920–1941*. Baltimore: Johns Hopkins University Press, 1979.

Ogletree, Charles, and Austin Sarat. *Life without Parole, America's Other Death Penalty?* New York: New York University Press, 2012.

Ols, Fred. "A History of the State's Prison," *Prison News* 1, no. 2 (November 15, 1926).

Oshinsky, David M. *Capital Punishment on Trial: Furman v. Georgia and the Death Penalty in Modern America*. Lawrence: University Press of Kansas, 2010.

Patrick, Clarence H. "Capital Punishment and Life Imprisonment in North Carolina, 1946 to 1968: Implications for Abolition of the Death Penalty." *Wake Forest Intramural Law Review* 6, no. 3 (1970): 417–30.

Pfeifer, Michael J. *Lynching Beyond Dixie: American Mob Violence Beyond the South.* Urbana: University of Illinois Press, 2013.

———. *Rough Justice: Lynching and Society, 1874–1947.* Urbana: University of Illinois Press, 2006.

Phillips, Charles David. "Exploring Relations among Forms of Social Control: The Lynching and Execution of Blacks in North Carolina, 1889–1918." *Law & Society Review* 21, no. 3 (1987): 361–74.

Potter, David M. "On Understanding the South: A Review Article." *Journal of Southern History* 30, no. 4 (November 1964): 451–62.

Powell, William S. *The Encyclopedia of North Carolina.* Chapel Hill: University of North Carolina Press, 2006.

Pratt, Joseph Hyde, comp. *Proceedings of the Annual Convention of the North Carolina Good Roads Association, Held at Charlotte, NC, August 1 and 2, 1912.* Raleigh, NC: Edwards and Broughton, 1912.

*Public Documents of the State of North Carolina Session 1913.* Raleigh, NC: Edwards and Broughton, 1915.

*Public Laws and Resolutions of the General Assembly of the State of North Carolina.* (Years and publishers vary.) NCC and online: http://ncgovdocs.org/guides /sessionlawslist.htm.

Pyron, Darden Asbury. "Nell Battle Lewis (1893–1956) and the New Southern Woman." In *Perspectives on the American South,* edited by James Cobb and Charles Wilson, 63–76. New York: Gordon and Breach, 1985.

Rable, George C. "The South and the Politics of Anti-Lynching Legislation, 1920–1940." *Journal of Southern History* 51, no. 1 (May 1985): 201–20.

Radelet, Michael L. "Execution of Whites for Crimes against Blacks: Exception to the Rule?" *Sociological Quarterly* 30, no. 4 (December 1989): 529–44.

Radelet, Michael L., and Glenn L. Pierce. "Race and Death Sentencing in North Carolina, 1980–2007." *University of North Carolina Law Review* 89, no. 6 (September 1, 2011): 2119–60.

Radelet, Michael L., and Barbara A. Zsembik. "Executive Clemency in Post-Furman Capital Cases." *University of Richmond Law Review* 27, no. 3 (1993): 289–314.

Raper, Arthur F. *The Tragedy of Lynching.* Chapel Hill: University of North Carolina Press, 1933.

Redding, Kent. *Making Race, Making Power: North Carolina's Road to Disfranchisement.* Urbana: University of Illinois Press, 2003.

"Report of the Special Commission for the Improvement of the Administration of Justice." *Popular Government* 15, no. 1 (Chapel Hill: University of North Carolina Institute of Government, January 1949).

Reston, James. *The Innocence of Joan Little: A Southern Mystery.* New York: Times Books, 1977.

Reynolds, Terry S., and Theodore Bernstein. "Edison and 'the Chair.'" *Technology and Society Magazine* 8, no. 1 (March 1989): 19–28.

Rhoads, Michael D. "Resurrection of Capital Punishment: The 1976 Death Penalty Cases." *Dickinson Law Review* 81, no. 3 (1976–77): 543–73.

Robinson, Paul H., and Marcus D. Dubber. "The American Model Penal Code: A Brief Overview." *New Criminal Law Review* 10, no. 3 (Summer 2007): 319–41.

Rothman, David J. *The Discovery of the Asylum*. New York: Routledge, [1971], 2002.

Rushdy, Ashraf H. A. *American Lynching*. New Haven, CT: Yale University Press, 2012.

———. *The End of American Lynching*. New Brunswick, NJ: Rutgers University Press, 2012.

Salmond, John A. *Gastonia 1929: The Story of the Loray Mill Strike*. Chapel Hill: University of North Carolina Press, 2015.

Sarat, Austin J. *From Lynch Mobs to the Killing State: Race and the Death Penalty in America*. New York: New York University Press, 2006.

Saunders, William L., ed. *The Colonial Records of North Carolina*. Vol. 2, 1713 to 1728. Raleigh, NC: P. M. Hale, 1886.

Savitz, Leonard D. "Capital Crimes as Defined in American Statutory Law." *Journal of Criminal Law, Criminology and Police Science* 46, no. 3 (1955–56): 365–63.

Scarry, Elaine. *The Body in Pain: The Making and Unmaking of the World*. New York: Oxford University Press, 1985.

Seitz, Trina N. "The Killing Chair: North Carolina's Experiment in Civility and the Execution of Allen Foster." *North Carolina Historical Review* 81, no. 1 (January 2004): 38–72.

Shay, Frank. *Judge Lynch: His First Hundred Years*. New York: Ives Washburn, 1938.

Shipley, Maynard. "Does Capital Punishment Prevent Convictions?" *American Law Review* 43, no. 3 (May–June 1909): 321–34.

Simon, Jonathan. *Governing through Crime: How the War on Crime Transformed American Democracy and Created a Culture of Fear*. New York: Oxford University Press, 2007.

Sims, Anastasia. *The Power of Femininity in the New South: Women's Organizations and Politics in North Carolina, 1880–1930*. Columbia: University of South Carolina Press, 1997.

Smith, Stephen F. "The Supreme Court and the Politics of Death." *Virginia Law Review* 94, no. 2 (April 2008): 283–384.

Snyder, Franklin A. "Criminal Law: Burglary in North Carolina." *Carolina Law Review* 35, no. 1 (December 1956): 98–104.

Southern Commission on the Study of Lynching. "Lynchings and What They Mean: General Findings of the Southern Commission on the Study of Lynching." Atlanta: The Commission, 1931.

Spindel, Donna J. *Crime and Society in North Carolina, 1663–1776*. Baton Rouge: Louisiana State University Press, 1989.

Stack, Richard A. *Dead Wrong: Violence, Vengeance, and the Victims of Capital Punishment*. Westport, CT: Praeger, 2006.

Steiker, Carol S. "Capital Punishment and American Exceptionalism." *Oregon Law Review* 81, no. 1 (2002): 97–130.

Steiker, Carol S., and Jordan M. Steiker, "The American Death Penalty and the (In)Visibility of Race." *University of Chicago Law Review* 82, no. 1 (Winter 2015): 243–94.

Streib, Victor L. "Death Penalty for Children: The American Experiences with Capital Punishment for Crimes Committed When under Age Eighteen." *Oklahoma Law Review* 36, no. 3 (Summer 1983): 613–42.

———. *Death Penalty for Juveniles.* Bloomington: Indiana University Press, 1987.

Sullivan, Joseph L. "Criminal Slang." *Law Student's Helper* 19, no. 9 (September 1911): 273–75.

"A Survey of Statutory Changes in North Carolina." *North Carolina Law Review* 7, no. 4 (June 1929): 363–412.

"Survey of Statutory Changes in North Carolina Law in 1941." *North Carolina Law Review* 19, no. 4 (June 1941): 435–550.

"A Survey of the Decisions of the North Carolina Supreme Court for the Spring and Fall Terms of 1953." *North Carolina Law Review* 32, no. 4 (June 1954): 379–518.

Thompson, Heather Ann. "Blinded by a 'Barbaric' South: Prison Horrors, Inmate Abuse, and the Ironic History of Penal Reform in the Postwar United States." In *The Myth of Southern Exceptionalism*, edited by Joseph Crespino and Matthew Lassiter, 74–98. New York: Oxford University Press, 2009.

Tindall, George. *The Emergence of the New South, 1913–1945.* Baton Rouge: Louisiana State University Press, 1967.

Tocqueville, Alexis de. *Democracy in America.* Translated by Arthur Goldhammer. New York: Library of America, 2004 (original New York: Century Company, 1898).

Tolnay, Stewart E., and E. M. Beck. *Festival of Violence: An Analysis of Southern Lynchings, 1882–1930.* Urbana: University of Illinois Press, 1995.

Trotti, Michael. *The Body in the Reservoir: Murder and Sensationalism in the South.* Chapel Hill: University of North Carolina Press, 2008.

———. "What Counts: Trends in Racial Violence in the Postbellum South." *Journal of American History* 100, no. 2 (September 2013): 375–400.

Twain, Mark. *Europe and Elsewhere.* New York: Harper Brothers, 1929.

Unah, Isaac. "Choosing Those Who Will Die: The Effect of Race, Gender, and Law in Prosecutorial Decision to Seek the Death Penalty in Durham, North Carolina." *Michigan State Journal of Race and Law* 15, no. 1 (2009): 135–80.

Vandiver, Margaret. *Lethal Punishment: Lynchings and Legal Executions in the South.* New Brunswick, NJ: Rutgers University Press, 2006.

Waldrep, Christopher. *The Many Faces of Judge Lynch: Extralegal Violence and Punishment in America.* New York: Palgrave Macmillan, 2002.

Watson, Alan D. "County Fiscal Policy in Colonial North Carolina." *North Carolina Historical Review* 55, no. 3 (July 1978): 284–305.

Wellman, Manly Wade. *Dead and Gone: Classic Crimes of North Carolina.* Chapel Hill: University of North Carolina Press, 1980.

Wells-Barnett, Ida B. *Mob Rule in New Orleans: Robert Charles and His Fight to the Death.* Chicago, IL: Alexander Street Press, 1900.

———. *A Red Record: Tabulated Statistics and Alleged Causes of Lynchings in the United States.* Chicago, IL: Donohue & Henneberry, 1895.

———. *Southern Horrors: Lynch Law in All Its Phases*. New York: New York Age Print, 1892.

White, Walter. *Rope and Faggot: A Biography of Judge Lynch*. New York: Knopf, 1929.

Williams, Kidada E. *They Left Great Marks on Me: African American Testimonies of Racial Violence from Emancipation to World War I*. New York: New York University Press, 2012.

Wood, Amy Louise. *Lynching and Spectacle: Witnessing Racial Violence in America, 1890–1940*. Chapel Hill: University of North Carolina Press, 2009.

Wright, George C. "By the Books: The Legal Execution of Kentucky Blacks." In *Under Sentence of Death*, edited by W. Fitzhugh Brundage, 250–70. Chapel Hill: University of North Carolina Press, 1997.

Wright, Richard. "Between the World and Me." *Partisan Review* 2, no. 88 (1935): 18–19.

Zimmerman, Jane. "The Penal Reform Movements in the South during the Progressive Era, 1890–1917." *Journal of Southern History* 17, no. 4 (November 1951): 462–92.

Zimring, Franklin E. "The Unexamined Death Penalty: Capital Punishment and the Reform of the Modern Penal Code." *Columbia Law Review* 105, no. 4 (May 2005): 1396–415.

Zimring, Franklin E., and Gordon Hawkins. *Capital Punishment and the American Agenda*. New York: Cambridge University Press, 1986.

Zipf, Karin L. *Bad Girls at Samarcand: Sexuality and Sterilization in a Southern Juvenile Reformatory*. Baton Rouge: Louisiana State University Press, 2016.

# Index

Abernathy, Ralph, 167, 180
Act to Regulate Capital Executions,
    An (1868), 61
Adair, Columbus, 28
Adair, Govan, 28
African American men, death penalty
    and, 12, 155–56, 191; burglary and,
    43–44, 47–48, 56, 98, 111, 143;
    execution numbers and, 30, 35, 45,
    56, 82, 103–4, 156, 177; executions
    and, 10, 60, 67–70, 74–79, 151;
    executive clemency and, 85, 87, 95,
    104; racial discrimination and, 21, 22,
    23, 162, 165, 169, 176, 177, 179, 183;
    racism and, 18, 19, 25–26, 36–37, 54,
    55, 78–79, 82–83, 99, 139, 142, 147,
    181–82; slave executions and, 8–9, 11,
    241nn35, 42; targeting of and, 5, 7, 24,
    29–30, 58, 80, 122, 141, 157, 180, 186;
    white supremacy and, 7, 59, 79, 129,
    166, 186. *See also* Lynching; Murders;
    Rape
African Americans, 15; anti-death
    penalty activism and, 122, 142–48,
    165, 267n184; dehumanization of
    and, 32, 81, 245n45; *Furman v.
    Georgia* and, 156, 161–62, 165, 179; as
    lawyers and judges and, 143, 144, 169,
    273n111; newspapers and, 143–44,
    165; voting rights and, 142, 157,
    260n10, 266n163; women executed
    and, 6, 11, 95, 96–97, 154; women in
    audiences at public executions and,
    62–64. *See also* African American
    men, death penalty and; Jim Crow;
    Juries; Lynching; Murders; Rape;
    Slavery; White supremacy

Alabama, 43, 139, 174, 188
Alexander, Will, 146
Alexander-Ralston, Elreta Melton, 143
Allison, James, 117–18
American Indians, 4, 30, 174, 177
American Law Institute, 170–71
American League to Abolish Capital
    Punishment, 119, 124
American Medical Association, 174
American Prison Association, 13
Americans for Effective Law Enforce-
    ment, 179
Ames, Jessie Daniel, 42, 251n44
Amsterdam, Anthony, 169, 172
Andrews, David, 114
Anson County, 26–27
Anti-death penalty activism, 19, 21,
    118–20, 180; African Americans and,
    122, 142–48, 165, 267n184; Canfield
    and, 121, 122–25, 150, 151; doctors
    and, 174, 182–83; General Assembly
    and, 120–21, 134–35, 148–49, 150,
    160–61, 166, 172–73; Green and, 100,
    112, 121, 135, 138–40, 141, 150, 151,
    162; Lewis and, 112, 121, 126–35, 151,
    162; protests and, 114, 155, 167
Anti-lynching activists, 35, 42, 50,
    251n44
Arizona, 21, 73, 119
Arkansas, 176
Arnold, Thurman, 7
Arson, 55, 120, 121, 134–35, 187; as
    capital crime and, 7, 13, 17, 42; not
    executing and, 97–98, 104
Asheville, 37, 60, 144–45
*Asheville Citizen-Times*, 111, 133, 135, 136,
    138, 161, 164, 178

Mandatory death penalty in North Carolina; Murders; Rape

*Capital Punishment in North Carolina* (SBCPW), 38, 41, 93–94, 99, 129–31, 140, 162

*Carolina Times*, 47–48, 51, 143, 144, 165

*Carolinian*, 45, 143, 144

Carter, Jimmy, 162

Casey, Herman, 90–91

Castrations, 9, 94

Central Prison, 39, 78, 79, 95, 104, 111, 161, 164, 168, 171, 181; death chamber and, 5, 67–69, 72, 73–74, 80, 81, 82; early conditions and, 14–15; first executions and, 62, 67; protests against death penalty and, 155, 167. *See also* Prison system

Chambers, Julius, 180

Chapman, Glen, 184

*Charlotte Observer*, 107

Cheever, George B., 57

Cherry, R. Gregg, 54, 85, 94, 102, 111

Cherry, Willie, 44, 111

Cherry Hospital, 94

*Chicago Tribune*, 33

Christy, Samuel P., 95–96, 98

Citizens' Committee of One Hundred, 15

Civil Rights Act of 1875, 113

Civil Rights Act of 1965, 157

Civil rights movement, 20, 32, 155, 156–59, 171, 179, 180, 183

Civil War, 1, 2, 11, 119

Clark, Walter C., 102–3

Clarkson, Heriot, 90–91

Clegg, Claude A., III, 35

Clem, Bitsy, 101

Clinton, Bill, 176

Coffey, Reed, 98

*Coker v. Georgia*, 174

Cole, W. B., 135–37, 264n121

Colonial times, 4–5, 7–9, 10

Colorado, 73, 76, 119

Commission for Interracial Cooperation, 146

Communism, 134

Commutations, 26, 86–110, 256n38; African American men and, 85, 87, 95, 104. *See also* Executive clemency; Exonerations

*Concord Tribune*, 92

Confederate Army, 2, 9

Congress of Racial Equality (CORE), 143

Connecticut, 10

*Connecticut Yankee in King Arthur's Court, A* (Twain), 65–66

Connor, Ralph, 71

Cooper, Roy, 176

Corporal punishment, 15, 97, 120

Cotton, Walter A., 151–52

Council, Louis, 60–61

Cox, Oliver C., 24

Craig, Howard, 78

Craig, Locke, 35, 43, 66, 96, 103

Creech, James, 101, 135, 137–38, 254n126

Criminology, 14

Cutler, James, 23

Dabney, Virginius, 76

Daniels, Bennie, 113–14

Daniels, Frank, 108–9

Daniels, Jonathan, 136, 137

Daniels, Josephus, 1, 126

Darrow, Clarence, 124

Davis, Angela, 167, 168, 169–70

Davis, Edwin, 67

Death penalty: abolition and, 10, 21, 118–20, 185; aggravating and mitigating factors and, 5, 171, 173; the Bible and, 21, 57, 118, 241n42; bifurcated sentencing and, 5, 171; decline of and, 20–21, 23, 80–81, 171; execution numbers and, 7, 174; history of failure and, 186–87; lynching relationship with and, 23, 24–25, 32, 186, 243n2; mental incapacity or insanity and, 176; modern period and, 166, 170–71, 179, 185; not executing and, 18, 21, 187–88; politics and, 19, 163, 175–76, 183, 184; popular support for and, 19,

Death penalty (cont.)
133–34, 152, 159–60, 163, 175, 183; reform, early twentieth century and, 66–67; state stability and, 24–25, 244n10; traveling death chamber and, 73, 252n92; victims and, 184, 185, 187; violent crime and, 57, 163, 164–65, 183–84, 185–86. *See also* Electrocutions; Gas executions; Lethal injection

Death Penalty Information Center, 22

Death penalty in North Carolina: abolition and, 11, 12, 19, 120–25, 160–61; African American women and, 6, 11, 95, 96–97, 154, 177, 180–81; the Bible and, 120, 124–25, 128; bifurcated sentencing and, 153–54, 172–73, 184; burning and, 5, 11, 12; colonial times and, 4–5, 7–9, 10; data and, 22, 30, 191–206, 208–27, 241n35, 247n86; education and, 138, 254n126; failures of and, 19, 184, 187; legal representation and, 21, 86–87, 88–89, 91, 92, 100, 102–3, 105–6, 113, 135, 139, 254–55n8; limited audiences and, 6, 29, 58, 61–62, 67, 69–71, 79, 80, 82, 178; lynching relationship with and, 18, 25–26, 29–30, 32, 35, 36, 37, 40–41, 43, 50, 51, 56, 58, 82; mental incapacity or insanity and, 5, 6, 7, 21, 41, 93–95, 129, 130, 132, 133, 184–85; modern period and, 5, 21, 153, 155, 156, 158, 171–74, 176, 177, 179, 184, 185, 186, 187; nineteenth century and, 10, 11, 12, 192–206; not executing and, 18, 21, 110, 188; politics and, 20, 155, 159, 171–72, 174, 176; popular support for and, 152, 172, 173, 176, 183; poverty and, 7, 21, 41, 129, 180, 184, 254–55n8; reform, early twentieth century and, 57–58, 59, 66; sheriffs and, 19, 30, 59–62, 67; standards of decency and, 5, 241n26; state executions and, 4, 19, 29–30, 36, 58, 64, 67, 85–86, 88, 92, 95, 103, 208–27; underclass and, 97,
129, 130, 135, 137, 138; vengeance and, 86, 178, 179, 187; victims and, 140–41, 173, 177–79, 185, 191; "whitening" of audience and, 58, 71, 82, 83; white people and, 46–47, 93, 103–4, 135–38, 154, 156, 177, 251n43, 254n126, 264n121; white victims and, 37, 56, 62, 82–83, 114–15, 157, 162, 177–78, 179, 181; women and, 6, 11, 95–98, 134, 153–55, 167–68, 171, 175, 177, 180–81. *See also* African American men, death penalty and; Capital crimes; Electrocutions; Execution numbers in North Carolina; Executive clemency; Gas executions; Hangings; Juries; Mandatory death penalty in North Carolina; *News and Observer* (Raleigh); Public executions; Technologies of death penalty; Teenagers and youths, death penalty and

Death row in North Carolina, 17, 258n88; death penalty appeals and, 80, 181–82, 183; before executions and, 74–75; not executed and, 94, 98, 164, 184–85, 188; population of and, 95, 104–5, 109, 129, 150, 164, 166, 169, 171, 174; sympathy for inmates of and, 103–7, 137, 138, 140–41; white men and, 46, 93; women and, 98, 153–55, 167–68

Decline of death penalty in North Carolina, 111–12, 134, 138, 143, 152, 159–60; execution concealment and, 6–7, 80; executive clemency and, 87, 183; life imprisonment and, 19, 20, 55, 109–10, 150, 151, 180, 187; lynching and, 54

DeGraff, Peter, 6

Delaware, 43

*Democracy in America* (de Tocqueville), 10, 112

Democratic Party, 172, 173, 175, 176

Desegregation, 158

De Tocqueville, Alexis, 10, 112

Deuteronomy, 124

Marshall, Thurgood, 143, 146, 147, 161, 169
Massachusetts, 11, 119
Matthews, Bernice, 72, 178
McAfee, Ross, 82–83
McCain, Richard, 111
McCollum, Henry, 184–85
McCoy, C. A., 139
McCoy, Dock, 145–46
McCrory, Pat, 176, 182
McDuffie, James, 173
McKenna, Joseph, 183
McKissick, Floyd, 143
McLean, Angus, 38, 93, 101, 142, 178
McMullen, Harry, 148
McNeill, Leroy, 79
Mechanics and Farmers Bank, 146
Mecklenburg County, 15
Medical Association of the Carolinas and Virginia, 32
Medlin, Monroe, 140
Messer, Robert, 111
Michigan, 11
Miller, William, 11
Minnesota, 119
Mississippi, 115, 157, 252 (n. 92)
Missouri, 188
Modern Penal Code (MPC), 170–71, 173
Moody, Lewis, 116
Moore County, 36, 60, 97
Morrison, Cameron, 35, 93, 103, 106–7, 108–9
Morrison, Walter, 67–69, 151
Mosaic law, 124, 128, 134
Murders, 22, 52, 105–6, 172; African Americans on African Americans and, 115–17, 162; African Americans on whites and, 117, 139, 145–46, 156, 162, 169, 174, 177–78; African American women as murderers and, 6, 95–97; as capital crime and, 10, 13–14, 17, 18, 39, 90, 104, 152, 167, 169; executive clemency and, 93, 94, 96–97, 102, 104, 106, 107, 142; first executions for and, 4–6, 8–9;

mandatory death penalty relaxed and, 17, 55, 170, 187; whites on African Americans and, 8–9, 117–18, 156; women as murderers and, 6, 95–97, 133, 153–55, 167–68. See also Lynching
Murphy, Angus, 70

Nash, Frederick, 12
National Alliance against Racist and Political Repression, 167
National Association for the Advancement of Colored People (NAACP), 157; anti-death penalty activism and, 143, 144–45, 146–47, 180, 267n184; lynching and, 24, 31, 33
National Guard, 37, 39, 52
Native Americans. See American Indians
Nevada, 73, 171
Neville, Earl, 102–3, 144
New Bern Sun-Journal, 137
New Hampshire, 11, 162
New Hanover County, 60, 84, 112, 228
New Jersey, 10
Newkirk, Vann, 30, 33, 228
News and Observer (Raleigh), 1–2, 3, 35, 44, 46, 62, 134, 136, 150, 162, 164; anti-death penalty activism and, 114, 126, 127, 133, 148; commutations and, 87, 94, 96–97, 103, 104–5; death penalty abolition and, 120–21, 125; death penalty defense and, 140–41, 151, 152, 172; electrocutions and, 78–79, 82, 116, 178; gas executions and, 73, 74–75, 76–77, 78–79, 96–97; juries and, 105, 107–8, 151
Newsday, 175
Newsome, Larry, 39, 40
New Testament, 125, 128
New York, 7, 10, 11, 13, 65, 66, 67, 89, 119, 146
New York Times, 76
Nixon, Richard M., 158, 163, 170

## H. EUGENE AND LILLIAN YOUNGS LEHMAN SERIES

Lamar Cecil, *Wilhelm II: Prince and Emperor, 1859–1900* (1989).

Carolyn Merchant, *Ecological Revolutions: Nature, Gender, and Science in New England* (1989).

Gladys Engel Lang and Kurt Lang, *Etched in Memory: The Building and Survival of Artistic Reputation* (1990).

Howard Jones, *Union in Peril: The Crisis over British Intervention in the Civil War* (1992).

Robert L. Dorman, *Revolt of the Provinces: The Regionalist Movement in America* (1993).

Peter N. Stearns, *Meaning Over Memory: Recasting the Teaching of Culture and History* (1993).

Thomas Wolfe, *The Good Child's River*, edited with an introduction by Suzanne Stutman (1994).

Warren A. Nord, *Religion and American Education: Rethinking a National Dilemma* (1995).

David E. Whisnant, *Rascally Signs in Sacred Places: The Politics of Culture in Nicaragua* (1995).

Lamar Cecil, *Wilhelm II: Emperor and Exile, 1900–1941* (1996).

Jonathan Hartlyn, *The Struggle for Democratic Politics in the Dominican Republic* (1998).

Louis A. Pérez Jr., *On Becoming Cuban: Identity, Nationality, and Culture* (1999).

Yaakov Ariel, *Evangelizing the Chosen People: Missions to the Jews in America, 1880–2000* (2000).

Philip F. Gura, *C. F. Martin and His Guitars, 1796–1873* (2003).

Louis A. Pérez Jr., *To Die in Cuba: Suicide and Society* (2005).

Peter Filene, *The Joy of Teaching: A Practical Guide for New College Instructors* (2005).

John Charles Boger and Gary Orfield, eds., *School Resegregation: Must the South Turn Back?* (2005).

Jock Lauterer, *Community Journalism: Relentlessly Local* (2006).

Michael H. Hunt, *The American Ascendancy: How the United States Gained and Wielded Global Dominance* (2007).

Michael Lienesch, *In the Beginning: Fundamentalism, the Scopes Trial, and the Making of the Antievolution Movement* (2007).

Eric L. Muller, *American Inquisition: The Hunt for Japanese American Disloyalty in World War II* (2007).

John McGowan, *American Liberalism: An Interpretation for Our Time* (2007).

Nortin M. Hadler, M.D., *Worried Sick: A Prescription for Health in an Overtreated America* (2008).

William Ferris, *Give My Poor Heart Ease: Voices of the Mississippi Blues* (2009).

Colin A. Palmer, *Cheddi Jagan and the Politics of Power: British Guiana's Struggle for Independence* (2010).

W. Fitzhugh Brundage, *Beyond Blackface: African Americans and the Creation of American Mass Culture, 1890–1930* (2011).

Michael H. Hunt and Steven I. Levine, *Arc of Empire: America's Wars in Asia from the Philippines to Vietnam* (2012).

Nortin M. Hadler, M.D., *The Citizen Patient: Reforming Health Care for the Sake of the Patient, Not the System* (2013).

Louis A. Pérez Jr., *The Structure of Cuban History: Meanings and Purpose of the Past* (2013).

Jennifer Thigpen, *Island Queens and Mission Wives: How Gender and Empire Remade Hawai'i's Pacific World* (2014).

George W. Houston, *Inside Roman Libraries: Book Collections and Their Management in Antiquity* (2014).

Philip F. Gura, *The Life of William Apess, Pequot* (2015).

Daniel M. Cobb, ed., *Say We Are Nations: Documents of Politics and Protest in Indigenous America since 1887* (2015).

Daniel Maudlin and Bernard L. Herman, eds., *Building the British Atlantic World: Spaces, Places, and Material Culture, 1600–1850* (2016).

William Ferris, *The South in Color: A Visual Journal* (2016).

Lisa A. Lindsay, *Atlantic Bonds: A Nineteenth-Century Odyssey from America to Africa* (2017).

Mary Elizabeth Basile Chopas, *Searching for Subversives: The Story of Italian Internment in Wartime America* (2017).

John M. Coggeshall, *Liberia, South Carolina: An African American Appalachian Community* (2018).

Malinda Maynor Lowery, *The Lumbee Indians: An American Struggle* (2018).

Seth Kotch, *Lethal State: A History of the Death Penalty in North Carolina* (2019).